Approaches to Peace

A READER IN PEACE STUDIES

Second Edition

Edited by

David P. Barash
University of Washington

New York   Oxford
OXFORD UNIVERSITY PRESS
2010

Oxford University Press, Inc., publishes works that further Oxford University's
objective of excellence in research, scholarship, and education.

Oxford   New York
Auckland   Cape Town   Dar es Salaam   Hong Kong   Karachi
Kuala Lumpur   Madrid   Melbourne   Mexico City   Nairobi
New Delhi   Shanghai   Taipei   Toronto

With offices in
Argentina   Austria   Brazil   Chile   Czech Republic   France   Greece
Guatemala   Hungary   Italy   Japan   Poland   Portugal   Singapore
South Korea   Switzerland   Thailand   Turkey   Ukraine   Vietnam

Published by Oxford University Press, Inc.
198 Madison Avenue, New York, New York 10016
http://www.oup.com

Oxford is a registered trademark of Oxford University Press

Library of Congress Cataloging-in-Publication Data
Approaches to peace : a reader in peace studies / edited by David P. Barash. — 2nd ed.
    p.   cm.
  Includes bibliographical references and index.
  ISBN 978-0-19-538286-0 (pbk. : alk. paper)   1. Peace.   2. International relations.   I. Barash, David P.
JZ5538.A67 2010
327.1'72—dc22

                                                                        2009016615

Printing Number: 9 8 7 6 5 4 3 2

Printed in the United States of America
on acid-free paper

Brief Contents

Contents

Preface

I t is often with a sense of quiet celebration that an author begins work on succeeding editions of a previously published book. After all, the very fact that a second—or twenty-second—edition is warranted speaks to the success of the project itself. In this case, although the book *Approaches to Peace* has been successful, as measured by the enthusiasm of instructors and students, or the number of course adoptions, it simply cannot be concluded that we have been especially successful in approaching peace. There is regrettably little in the ten years that intervene between the first and second editions that warrants patting ourselves on our collective backs for a job well done.

Indeed, it is difficult in the year 2009 to maintain the same cautious optimism that many of us felt in 1999, when memories of democratic successes (lowercase "d") were fresh and the prospect beckoned of building a worldwide consensus in favor of negative peace (the prevention of war) as well as positive peace, in its diverse and alluring manifestations. Since then, the possibility of a "peace dividend" following the end of the Cold War has been squandered, the specter of terrorism has been horribly enhanced, the United States has engaged in an ill-conceived and disastrous war that has not only cost tens of thousands of lives but has also diminished its status as well as the ability of cooperative international institutions to solve our shared, planetary problems. Among these are economic inequity, continued denial of human rights, the ever-increasing pressure of population, and the largely unaddressed emergence of worldwide environmental threats including (but not limited to) drastic and potentially irreversible climate change.

If this weren't bad enough, the world in general and the United States in particular failed to grasp what may have been a unique opportunity to dispense with nuclear weapons altogether or at least to move vigorously toward a nonnuclear future. Instead, although worldwide thermonuclear war seems blessedly unlikely, the threat of nuclear proliferation has if anything accelerated, such that it now constitutes a greater danger to planetary survival than in the immediate aftermath of the U.S.–Soviet arms race.

But this is no time for despair, and not only because "hope springs eternal." More than ever before, the world has become a "global village," with nearly instantaneous, real-time information sharing that makes it increasingly difficult for wrongdoing to go unnoticed. Even though human rights are still not universally enjoyed, they are universally aspired to (although they may be defined differently by different people), and even the most egregious governments have been unable to keep their citizens isolated in their aspirations. If our problems are great—and they are—the human potential for solving problems has never been greater. Major new actors have entered the scene . . . actually, old actors, notably India and China, which brings both new threats and new opportunities in an increasingly multipolar world. The field of peace studies has itself expanded, and not simply because the need for it has grown; so too has awareness of human potential, deriving at least in part from enthusiasm over past successes as well as frustration over how close we have come to getting things right.

Moreover, and at the risk of "outing" my own political predisposition and that of nearly all practitioners of peace studies, we cannot but rejoice at the opportunities available to the United States and to the world because of the termination of the presidency of George W. Bush and its replacement by Barack Obama. Only time will tell, of course, whether these opportunities will be grasped—but it is hard to imagine that things will be worse!

For those endeavoring to approach peace, there is no shortage of challenges, practical as well as intellectual. Fortunately, there is also no shortage of inspiration and of insight. I hope this revised volume will help its readers appreciate those challenges while profiting from the inspiration and insight of others, even as they develop their own.

Toward that end, this second edition of *Approaches to Peace* contains some notable changes, beyond an updating of the "study questions" and "suggestions for further reading" that conclude each chapter. For example, there is an entirely new chapter on "responding to terrorism," whose appropriateness is, tragically, too obvious to require explanation. It includes selections from the RAND Corporation, Samuel P. Huntington, Eqbal Ahmad, Richard Falk, Robert Pape, and Charles P. Webel. It has been a pleasure to add a number of pieces to the existing chapters, all of them published in the last ten years and—in my opinion at least—all of them likely to become, if not classics, at least representative of important thinking and perhaps highly influential in themselves.

I am delighted to have incorporated the following into this second edition (in some cases these are articles in their entirety; in others, representative selections from longer, often book-length works): "War Is a Force That Gives Us Meaning," by Chris Hedges; "Ten Nuclear Myths," by David Krieger and Angela McCrackien; "A World Free of Nuclear Weapons," by George P. Shultz, William J. Perry, Henry A. Kissinger, and Sam Nunn; "A Powerful Peace," by Jonathan Schell; "An Insider's Guide to the UN," by Linda Fasulo; Al Gore's "Nobel Prize Acceptance Speech"; Jeffrey Sachs on "Global Economic Solidarity"; a clarification of the Islamic concept of "jihad," by Ali Gomaa, grand mufti of Egypt; "A Human Approach to World Peace," by the Dalai Lama; Chalmers Johnson on "Empire v. Democracy: Why Nemesis Is at Our Door"; Bishop Desmond Tutu's view of reconciliation, "No Future Without Forgiveness"; and Victoria Bonney's thoughtful yet urgent call to action, "Antiwar Activists, Where Are You?"

At the same time, I had to make the painful, difficult decision to delete some material that appeared in the first edition. This was necessitated by the need to keep the final product manageable in size and—no less important—in purchase cost for financially challenged students. It does not reflect on my respect for the pieces thus eliminated, and indeed, I urge interested students to pursue and read them: a selection from Barbara Tuchman's *The Guns of August,* from Jonathan Schell's "The Gift of Time," and from Immanuel Kant's *Perpetual Peace*; William V. O'Brien's *The Conduct of Just and Limited War* and Marrack Goulding's "The Evolution of United Nations Peacekeeping"; Oxfam's excellent "An Agenda for Change" (although such an agenda—necessarily updated—is still urgently needed); George F. Kennan's "A Christian's View of the Arms Race"; Nigel Young's "Peace Movements in History"; and Vaclav Havel's "The Politics of Responsibility."

Please don't misunderstand: it remains everyone's responsibility to approach peace and to help his or her country and world to do so! I truly do not know if time is short, but there can be no doubt that the situation is not only urgent with danger but also pregnant with great hope.

ACKNOWLEDGMENTS

I thank my students at the University of Washington, particularly those from my class, Psychology 207, "Psychology of Peace," for serving as guinea pigs as I tried out various inclusions and exclusions and—even more so—for making useful suggestions. In this regard, special thanks are owed to Aditya Ganapathiraju, a remarkable young man, as dedicated as he is brilliant. Also, deep gratitude to Jennifer Carpenter for encouraging me to undertake the revised second edition of this project and to Thomas Pold, who worked hard and wonderfully well to make it a reality. Finally, I thank James H. Radford, Bradford University; Joshua B. Spero, Fitchburg State College; Joseph B. Underhill, Augsburg College; and Rossen V. Vassilev, The Ohio State University, for their suggestions.

David P. Barash
Redmond, Washington

Approaches to *Approaches to Peace*

"There is no way to peace," wrote theologian and antiwar activist A. J. Muste. "Peace is the way." Maybe so, but there are, at least, ways of *approaching* peace, and this book investigates some of them.

Rephrasing Muste, we might say that peace is never fully achieved; it can only be approached. Mathematicians call something "asymptotic" if it can be infinitely (or rather, infinitesimally) approached but never quite reached. Peace, then, may be an asymptote. Unfortunately, we do not yet have the luxury of bemoaning a "near miss," regretting that although we approach peace very closely, it continues to elude us, remaining just beyond our grasp. The hard reality is that peace can barely be glimpsed, never mind grasped; what is frustrating, therefore, is not that peace is so close but that it remains so far away.

Yet there is cause for hope. The Cold War is over. From Berlin to Johannesburg, seemingly intractable systems of oppression have collapsed, with remarkably little overt violence, and, in at least some cases, with the beginning of genuine reconciliation. More people—especially in Latin America—live under democracy than ever before. Environmental consciousness is widespread and increasingly acknowledged, along with the importance of human rights. Nonetheless, human beings are faced with many problems: a polluted and otherwise threatened planet composed of resources that are finite and whose limits may soon be reached (or may in many cases have already been exceeded); gross maldistribution of wealth, as a result of which the great majority of human beings are unable to realize their potential and vast numbers die prematurely; persistent patterns of social and political injustice, in which racism, sexism, and other forms of unfairness abound and in which representative government is relatively rare, and torture and other forms of oppression are distressingly common. And this is only a partial list.

Despite all of these difficulties, daunting enough even if the world were to cooperate actively in their solution, the remarkable fact is that enormous sums of money and vast reserves of material, time, and energy are expended, not in solving what we might call the "problems of peace" but rather in threatening and actually making war on one another. If it wasn't so tragic, the situation would be so absurd as to be high comedy. It seems unlikely that human beings will ever achieve anything approaching heaven on earth; however, it also seems reasonable to hope—and perhaps even to demand—that we will someday behave far more responsibly and establish a society based on the needs of the entire planet and the beings that inhabit it, a society that is just and sustainable and one that is not characterized by major outbreaks of self-defeating violence.

In this book, we'll explore some of the prospects of, and the obstacles to, achieving such a world. We shall do so by sampling an array of classic, near-classic, and potentially "future classic" readings. My hope is that *Approaches to Peace* will serve as a kind of core curriculum around which courses in peace studies can cohere. This book, then, will have been successful if it proves to be a convenient source of certain essential and provocative writings, a useful touchstone from which students and instructors can voyage out into the important and exciting field of peace studies, defining it for themselves as they go.

A quick explanation and apology is therefore called for: assembling a collection of such readings is unavoidably arbitrary. Different editors would doubtless come up with different selections, particularly as the field of peace studies is itself a "work in progress." There is no shortage of suitable readings, however, and it has been painful to omit so many excellent candidates. Similarly, it has been difficult—and a bit arrogant—to abridge many of them. But to some extent, *Approaches to Peace* may be useful insofar as it doesn't go too far in indulging anyone's preference, even its editor's! So if this book whets the appetite but doesn't entirely satisfy, if it leaves the reader wanting more, then so much the better.

Students of peace are, ironically, a feisty and even occasionally combative lot...perhaps because their enterprise is especially likely to attract its share of dissidents. Different instructors may therefore want to branch out from this book and devote special attention to those topics of special concern to them: feminism and women's rights, for example, or specific regions of current violence and war; the history of recent conflicts; detailed proposals for a peaceful future; ideas of environmental and economic amelioration; exposé of egregious human rights abuses; additional sources of religious and/or ethical inspiration; case studies of particular crusaders for peace, human rights, nonviolence, and so forth.

Approaches to Peace reflects the assumption—characteristic of peace studies—that peace can and must include not only the absence of war ("negative peace") but also the establishment of life-affirming and life-enhancing values and structures ("positive peace"). Thus, an important concept in peace studies is that, as logicians might put it, negative peace is a necessary but not sufficient condition for positive peace. This book also assumes that there are no simple solutions to the problems of either peace or war; the war–peace dilemma is complex, interconnected, and often poorly understood. On the other hand, there is much to be gained by exploring the various dimensions of war and peace, including the prospects of achieving a just, sustainable world: in short, a way of living that will nurture life itself and of which its citizens can be proud. A degree of optimism seems warranted, not simply as an article of faith but based on the realistic premise that once human beings understand the situation and their own best interests, they can behave rationally, creatively, and with compassion. As we shall see, there are positive steps to be taken that will diminish humanity's reliance on organized violence to settle conflicts and that will begin the construction of a better, more truly peaceful world.

To some scholars, peace studies may appear redundant because most of its subject matter can legitimately be covered in various other academic disciplines, nearly all of which are better established: history, psychology, anthropology, sociology, literature, political science, economics, and so forth. But the reality is that students are unable to take courses in all of these fields, and if they wanted to cover the peace-related material, they would have to pick and choose, like a gourmet eating just a couple of shrimp from one casserole, picking out a few candied raisins from the dessert, and so on. Peace studies offers, instead, a unique focus on peace, just as women's studies selects material from traditional disciplines that relate specifically to women, or environmental studies focuses on the environment.

There is another way in which peace studies is special. Unlike the usual social science approach, which prides itself on being "value free," peace studies unblushingly acknowledges biases and preferences. It is scholarly but not disinterested. It does not simply encourage the study of peace but is in *favor* of peace: peace, we proclaim, is better than war, just as social justice is better than injustice, environmental integrity is better than destruction, and so forth. Peace studies is thus similar to medical science, which freely admits to a preference for health over disease. (Think of it as offering a kind of "planetary medicine.")

Despite the enormous ills of our planet, there is reason to believe that our most pressing problem is not hunger, disease, poverty, social inequity, overpopulation, or environmental degradation but rather the violence that human beings commit and threaten to commit against others. This is especially true in modern times, with the invention of nuclear weapons, but is valid, too, in a world of "merely" conventional arms. Consider the deep irony of a planet, beset with desperate crises, whose inhabitants nonetheless spend their time and energies fighting with each other, thereby making things even worse: imagine a small, overcrowded lifeboat facing severe shortages of food and water, springing leaks, tossed about in stormy seas, and facing a long trip to safe harbor. Imagine further that within this lifeboat there are sufficient resources to patch the leaks,[1] keep everyone nourished, build adequate oars and makeshift sails so as to complete the voyage safely (maybe even enjoyably) . . . but squabbling breaks out among the occupants. Precious supplies, including the compass, get thrown overboard, and the boat itself is in danger of capsizing.

Perhaps try a different image. Imagine that a space probe headed for Mars has run into serious technical difficulties: the air supply is endangered, the energy source has begun to fail, and the craft has entered an unexpected meteor shower . . . whereupon the astronauts, instead of dealing with their problems, begin a fistfight among themselves!

It is indeed paradoxical that in a time of unique danger and difficulty, the inhabitants of planet Earth waste their time, resources, and energy—as well as their lives—fighting

---

[1] Or for an even more disquieting scenario, imagine that resources are *not* sufficient.

among themselves and/or preparing to do so. Sadly, there is nothing new in the human experience about recourse to war. What is new, however, is its profound inappropriateness: with the wolf at the door, we leap to our feet, grab a gun . . . and begin shooting each other!

It is also noteworthy that after decades on the brink of nuclear annihilation, the world situation has changed dramatically, notably with the dissolution of the former Soviet Union and the widespread disavowal of communism. This has deprived many of the most war-prone individuals of a feared (or favorite) enemy. And yet, such extraordinary reworking of the global map has not resulted in a comparable reworking of military expenditures, at least on the part of the United States. This may be because there has not been a comparable restructuring of the intellectual and emotional map or of social relationships based on power, violence, or the threat of violence.

Any attempt to approach peace, if it is to be meaningful, must also approach this problem of redrawing the "conceptual cartography" through which most people structure their view of the world and their place in it. *Approaches to Peace* is perhaps best approached this way: as an offering to help its readers make some progress in approaching peace in as many ways as possible and regardless of whether—or even, where—they eventually arrive.

CHAPTER 1

Approaches to War

It may seem perverse to begin our survey of "approaches to peace" by looking at the causes of war. But it can't be helped. War is humanity's most inhumane and destructive endeavor. Destroying not only lives, property, the environment, hopes, and dreams, it also wreaks havoc with any prospects for "positive peace," the goal for which most workers in peace studies strive. Accordingly, we must understand some of the causes of war. And this, alas, is easier said than done.

Mark Twain is reputed to have said that it was easy to stop smoking; he had done it hundreds of times! Similarly, it is easy to identify the causes of war: it seems there are hundreds of them.

"War" does not exist as a generality. There are, instead, individual wars, just as there are individual human beings. And just as every person is unique (not only genetically but also in the private trajectory of his or her experience), it can be argued that the causes of *each* war require detailed study. The danger thus exists that in attempting to unravel the causes of war, or even of a particular war, we will fall into the error portrayed by poet John Saxe, when he depicted the blind men and the elephant:

> It was six men from Industan, to learning much inclined,
> Who went to see the elephant (though all of them were blind),
> that each by observation might satisfy his mind...

Each felt a different part of the elephant, and so the one touching the legs thought it was a tree, the one touching the tail thought it was a snake, and so forth. As it turned out, the blind men

> disputed loud and long, each in his opinion stiff and strong,
> though each was partly in the right, and all of them were wrong.

Trying to comprehend the cause(s) of war, each of the efforts presented in this chapter is similarly "wrong." But if we put them all together—and add a number of others, which considerations of space have prevented inclusion in this book—it is possible to get a comprehensive view of the peculiar, complex elephant that is war. Despite the fact that every person is unique, it is also true that useful generalizations can be made about *Homo sapiens*. Similar generalizations can be made about that "species" of human behavior known as war.

It goes almost without saying that—at least from the Western perspective—every effect must have a preexisting cause, and war should be no exception, even though there has been vigorous debate as to how best to categorize these causative factors. Not surprisingly, and not inappropriately, the search for war's causes has often become an effort to finger a limited number of identifiable culprits, or villains:

> In the eighteenth century, many philosophers thought that the ambitions of absolute monarchs were the main cause of war; pull down the mighty, and wars would become rare. Another theory contended that many wars came from the Anglo-French rivalry for colonies and commerce: restrain that quest, and peace would be more easily preserved. The wars following the French Revolution fostered an idea that popular revolutions were becoming the main cause of international war. In the nineteenth century, monarchs who sought to unite their troubled country by a glorious foreign war were widely seen as culprits. At the end of that century the capitalists' chase for markets or investment outlets became a popular villain. The First World War convinced many writers that armaments races and arms salesmen had become the villains, and both world wars fostered the idea that militarist regimes were the main disturbers of the peace.[1]

Circumstances thus do not only influence events but also the interpretation of events. During the United States–Soviet Cold War for example (not a direct shooting war but a period of heightened tensions, characterized by a vigorous nuclear arms race in addition to many "proxy wars," as in Korea, Vietnam, and Afghanistan), peace researchers tended to emphasize the clash of ideologies, the role of misunderstandings and misperceptions, as well as the potential danger of false alarms, while attributing roughly equal blame to expansionist tendencies on the part of the United States and the Soviet Union. Much attention was also given to the dynamics of arms races and the dangers of crisis decision making. With the Cold War gone—but with war and warlike situations continuing—emphasis has shifted to nationalist passions as well as to religious and ethnic conflicts.

Some researchers, attempting a more detached perspective, have looked to possible causes that are less situation linked, in the process coming up with theories connecting the onset of wars to factors as diverse as grand cycles of history and sunspots; population pressure; sexual competition and frustration; early childhood experiences; protein shortage; even the existence of pure, unmitigated evil.

Preferred explanations are also influenced by political orientation. Thus, capitalism is often blamed by leftists, communism by conservatives. Progressive and left-leaning thinkers are generally more likely to attribute war to misunderstandings and other psychological factors, whereas those of the political right are generally more comfortable identifying what they see as innate human depravity. Nor is professional orientation irrelevant:

---

[1] Geoffrey Blainey, *The Causes of War* (New York: Free Press, 1973).

biologists, for example, are prone to suggest that insight into the causes of war can be derived from consulting the human gene pool as well as by examining aggressive behavior in animals. Psychologists are likely to emphasize the importance of individual experience, whether early in life or as a result of learning and social conditioning, perceptions, and misperceptions. For many anthropologists, nontechnological war among "primitive" people can provide models for the more elaborate war of modern nation-states. Sociologists are inclined toward explanations that involve complex group processes, such as stability, national image, and the dynamics of industrialization or militarization. For political scientists, war-proneness cannot be meaningfully separated from the governmental systems involved or from reigning political ideologies. Economists, not surprisingly, are struck not only by the economic consequences of war and preparation for war but also by the role of markets, competition, and economic systems in predisposing a country toward war. Mathematically inclined analysts examine quantitative models, including the so-called Prisoner's Dilemma, whereas theologians, psychiatrists, lawyers, and military specialists all have their own favored interpretations of why and under what conditions people are likely to resort to war.

This diversity should be seen as a source of hope, not discouragement. After all, it would be absurd to think that anything as complex as war could be "explained" in a single, simple way. (If it could, then the problem of war would probably have been solved long ago, and this book would be concerned only with "positive peace!") When it comes to understanding the causes of war, diversity is not only a source of strength, it is also more likely to yield answers.

In attempting to assess the causes of any war, or of war in general, it is important to distinguish between the announced reason(s) for its outbreak, which are often excuses concocted as public justification, and the actual, underlying causes, which may not even be accessible to the participants. One must also identify not only immediate precipitating factors (often military, political, or economic) but also preexisting historical antecedents as well as any other causes that may lie deeper yet, within the specific individuals involved, and also, perhaps, within human beings generally.

Take a recent undeclared war, the so-called Gulf War of 1991, in which the United States mobilized and led a multinational, United Nations coalition that drove Iraqi forces out of Kuwait. What was its cause? Here are just a few possibilities.

1. The role of leaders: The Iraqi leader, Saddam Hussein, was a violent, aggressive dictator, who took an opportunity to invade his defenseless neighbor, hoping to enhance his political prestige; and/or, the United States president George Bush was largely responsible because he felt personally challenged and perceived a need to banish his "wimp" image before the next presidential election.

2. Economic factors: Iraq sought to gain the economic benefits that would come from capturing Kuwaiti oil fields; and/or United States economic dependence on Middle Eastern oil made it willing to "trade blood for oil."

3. Psychological decision-making factors: Saddam Hussein misunderstood the position of the United States when the U.S. ambassador indicated that Iraq's border dispute with Kuwait was an Iraqi–Kuwaiti matter and not one that the United States considered vital to its "national

interest"; and/or the American public's fears and hatreds were aroused by reports of Iraqi bru-
tality toward Kuwaitis; and/or the Iraqi public was envious of the ostentatious wealth of the
neighboring Kuwaitis; and/or Arab people, frustrated by their inability to defeat Israel, were
eager to vent their rage against other enemies.

4. Historical factors: British colonialism actually caused the war, for when the British withdrew
   from the area, they created an artificial border between Iraq and Kuwait because the British
   wanted to establish a pliant sheikdom that would permit Western oil companies to dominate
   the extraction of petroleum from the region; and/or the U.S. military and political leadership
   wanted to prove that it had outgrown the "Vietnam syndrome," a supposed hesitatancy in the
   aftermath of the U.S. military debacle in Vietnam.

5. The military-industrial complex: The U.S. military wanted to test an array of newly developed
   weapons and also to demonstrate its importance because, with the ending of the Cold War,
   people had begun to question the value of maintaining a huge military establishment; and/
   or the U.S. "military-industrial complex" was eager for a war so it could profit from greater
   demand for new weapons systems.

6. International politics: Iraq's invasion of Kuwait was a clear invasion of international law, such
   that the maintenance of long-term peace and stability required a clear and vigorous response;
   and/or with the end of the Cold War, the United States no longer felt constrained by the prospect that the Soviet Union (previously Iraq's ally) would support Iraq.

For better or worse, a different list—similar in its complexity, unique in its specifics—
can be constructed for every war. It would be a useful exercise, in fact, to select a few wars
and do just that. The fact that the causes of war are often complex, diffuse, and multidi-
mensional does not mean that searching for them is a waste of time. Out of that search
can come a deeper understanding of the dilemma that is war; moreover, our insights into
the causes of war will have great influence on methods of preventing specific ones as well
as on the prospects for eliminating war altogether.

Sigmund Freud

WHY WAR?

Psychiatric theories of war emphasize the role of individuals, both as leaders and as personal participants. Carl G. Jung, for example, attached special importance to the existence of a "dark side" within human nature. For Jungian analysts, this dark side, unacceptable to one's consciousness, is "projected" onto an Other, who becomes the Enemy, imbued with an array of hateful traits . . . which actually originate within one's self. Jung was impressed with what he considered the human "collective unconscious," including powerful images such as those of heroes and enemies. Alfred Adler attributed great importance to interpersonal struggles for social dominance and to the "inferiority complex."

The American psychiatrist Harry Stack Sullivan felt that human fears and anxieties derived from inhibited communication, which in turn gave rise to terror-ridden distortions, which in their turn produce a tendency to strike out at those one does not understand and who are different. For Erik Erikson, personal wholeness and healthy integration can be threatened by confusing social ambiguity, both at home and in the society; as a result, according to Erikson, the confused individual may seek refuge in "totalism," which leads to unquestioning identification of the Self with the State, along with equally total rejection of the selfhood of others. Another important psychiatric theorist of war was Erich Fromm, who examined the formation of various "malignant," pathological personalities, especially among despotic, violence-prone leaders such as Hitler and Stalin.

The towering figure among psychiatrists looking for the causes of war, however, was Sigmund Freud, founder of psychoanalysis. For Freud, there is a direct link between aggression—a behavior of individuals—and the social phenomenon that is war, in that both are manifestations of the same underlying drive system. He believed that much "inhumane" behavior was in fact all too human, deriving from the operation of "Thanatos," or the death instinct, which he saw as opposed to "Eros," the life instinct. Although many of Freud's notions appear quaint today, and some of them could be seen as downright crackpot, his identification of the unconscious remains central to nearly all efforts to explain war (and most other behavior) at the level of the individual.

In 1932 Albert Einstein was invited by the League of Nations to initiate an exchange of views with another renowned person on a subject of Einstein's choosing. Einstein selected the question, "Is there any way of delivering mankind from the menace of war?" and his chosen correspondent was Sigmund Freud. A selection from Freud's response is reprinted here.

———— ⬦ ————

"Why War" from *The Collected Papers*, Vol. 5, by Sigmund Freud. 1959. Edited by James Strachey. Published by Basic Books by arrangement with The Hogarth Press and the Institute of Psycho-Analysis, London. Reprinted by permission of Basic Books, a subsidiary of Perseus Books Group.

Conflicts of interest between man and man are resolved, in principle, by the recourse to violence. It is the same in the animal kingdom, from which man cannot claim exclusion; nevertheless, men are also prone to conflicts of opinion, touching, on occasion, the loftiest peaks of abstract thought, which seem to call for settlement by quite another method. This refinement is, however, a late development. To start with, brute force was the factor which, in small communities, decided points of ownership and the question which man's will was to prevail. Very soon physical force was implemented, then replaced, by the use of various adjuncts; he proved the victor whose weapon was the better or handled the more skillfully. Now, for the first time, with the coming of weapons, superior brains began to oust brute force, but the object of the conflict remained the same: one party was to be constrained, by the injury done him or impairment of his strength, to retract a claim or a refusal. This end is most effectively gained when the opponent is definitively put out of action—in other words, is killed. This procedure has two advantages; the enemy cannot renew hostilities, and, second, his fate deters others from following his example. Moreover, the slaughter of a foe gratifies an instinctive craving—a point to which we shall revert hereafter. However, another consideration may be set off against this will to kill: the possibility of using an enemy for servile tasks if his spirit be broken and his life spared. Here violence finds an outlet not in slaughter but in subjugation. Hence springs the practice of giving quarter; but the victor, having from now on to reckon with the craving for revenge that rankles in his victim, forfeits to some extent his personal security.

Thus, under primitive conditions, it is superior force—brute violence or violence backed by arms—that lords it everywhere. We know that in the course of evolution this state of things was modified, a path was traced that led away from violence to law. But what was this path? Surely it issued from a single verity: that the superiority of one strong man can be overborne by an alliance of many weaklings, that *l'union fait la force*. Brute force is overcome by union, the allied might of scattered units makes good its right against the isolated giant. Thus we may define

"right" (i.e., law) as the might of a community. Yet it, too, is nothing else than violence, quick to attack whatever individual stands in its path, and it employs the selfsame methods, follows like ends, with but one difference; it is the communal, not individual, violence that has its way. But, for the transition from crude violence to the reign of law, a certain psychological condition must first obtain. The union of the majority must be stable and enduring. If its sole *raison d'être* be the discomfiture of some overweening individual and, after his downfall, it be dissolved, it leads to nothing. Some other man, trusting to his superior power, will seek to reinstate the rule of violence, and the cycle will repeat itself unendingly. Thus the union of the people must be permanent and well organized; it must enact rules to meet the risk of possible revolts, must set up machinery ensuring that its rules—the laws—are observed and that such acts of violence as the laws demand are duly carried out. This recognition of a community of interests engenders among the members of the group a sentiment of unity and fraternal solidarity which constitutes its real strength.

So far I have set out what seems to me the kernel of the matter: the suppression of brute force by the transfer of power to a larger combination, founded on the community of sentiments linking up its members. All the rest is mere tautology and glosses. Now, the position is simple enough so long as the community consists of a number of equipollent individuals. The laws of such a group can determine to what extent the individual must forfeit his personal freedom, the right of using personal force as an instrument of violence, to ensure the safety of the group. But such a combination is only theoretically possible; in practice the situation is always complicated by the fact that, from the outset, the group includes elements of unequal power, men and women, elders and children, and, very soon, as a result of war and conquest, victors and the vanquished—that is, masters and slaves—as well. From this time on the common law takes notice of these inequalities of power, laws are made by and for the rulers, giving the servile classes fewer rights....

Thus we see that, even within the group itself, the exercise of violence cannot be avoided when conflicting interests are at stake. But the common needs and habits of men who live in fellowship under the same sky favor a speedy issue of such conflicts and, this being so, the possibilities of peaceful solutions make steady progress. Yet the most casual glance at world history will show an unending series of conflicts between one community and another or a group of others, between large and smaller units, between cities, countries, races, tribes, and kingdoms, almost all of which were settled by the ordeal of war. Such wars end either in pillage or in conquest and its fruits, the downfall of the loser. No single all-embracing judgment can be passed on these wars of aggrandizement. Some, like the war between the Mongols and the Turks, have led to unmitigated misery; others, however, have furthered the transition from violence to law, since they brought larger units into being, within whose limits a recourse to violence was banned and a new regime determined all disputes. Thus the Roman conquests brought that boon, the *Pax Romana*, to the Mediterranean lands. The French kings' lust for aggrandizement created a new France, flourishing in peace and unity. Paradoxical as it sounds, we must admit that warfare well might serve to pave the way to that unbroken peace we so desire, for it is war that brings vast empires into being, within whose frontiers all warfare is proscribed by a strong central power. In practice, however, this end is not attained, for as a rule the fruits of victory are but short-lived, the new-created unit falls asunder once again, generally because there can be no true cohesion between the parts that violence has welded. Hitherto, moreover, such conquests have only led to aggregations which, for all their magnitude, had limits, and disputes between these units could be resolved only by recourse to arms. For humanity at large the sole result of all these military enterprises was that, instead of frequent not to say incessant little wars, they had now to face great wars which, for all they came less often, were so much the more destructive....

I now can comment on another of your statements. You are amazed that it is so easy to infect men with the war fever, and you surmise that man has in him an active instinct for hatred and destruction, amenable to such stimulations. I entirely agree with you. I believe in the existence of this instinct and have been recently at pains to study its manifestations. In this connection may I set out a fragment of that knowledge of the instincts, which we psychoanalysts, after so many tentative essays and gropings in the dark, have compassed? We assume that human instincts are of two kinds: those that conserve and unify, which we call "erotic" (in the meaning Plato gives to *eros* in his *Symposium*) or else "sexual" (explicitly extending the popular connotation of "sex"); and, second, the instincts to destroy and kill, which we assimilate as the aggressive or destructive instincts. These are, as you perceive, the well-known opposites, love and hate, transformed into theoretical entities; they are, perhaps, another aspect of those eternal polarities, attraction and repulsion, which fall within your province. But we must be chary of passing overhastily to the notions of good and evil. Each of these instincts is every whit as indispensable as its opposite, and all the phenomena of life derive from their activity, whether they work in concert or in opposition. It seems that an instinct of either category can operate but rarely in isolation; it is always blended ("alloyed," as we say) with a certain dosage of its opposite, which modifies its aim or even, in certain circumstances, is a prime condition of its attainment. Thus the instinct of self-preservation is certainly of an erotic nature, but to gain its ends this very instinct necessitates aggressive action. In the same way the love instinct, when directed to a specific object, calls for an admixture of the acquisitive instinct if it is to enter into effective possession of that object. It is the difficulty of isolating the two kinds of instinct in their manifestations that has so long prevented us from recognizing them.

If you travel with me a little further on this road, you will find that human affairs are complicated in yet another way. Only exceptionally does an action follow on the stimulus of a single instinct, which is per se a blend of *eros* and destructiveness.... Thus, when a nation is summoned to engage in war, a whole gamut of human motives may respond to this appeal; high and low motives, some openly avowed, others slurred over. The lust for aggression and destruction is certainly included; the innumerable cruelties of history and man's daily life confirm its prevalence and strength. The stimulation of these destructive impulses by appeals to idealism and the erotic instinct naturally facilitates their release. Musing on the atrocities recorded on history's page, we feel that the ideal motive has often served as a camouflage for the lust of destruction; sometimes, as with the cruelties of the Inquisition, it seems that, while the ideal motives occupied the foreground of consciousness, they drew their strength from the destructive instincts submerged in the unconscious. Both interpretations are feasible.

You are interested, I know, in the prevention of war, not in our theories, and I keep this fact in mind. Yet I would like to dwell a little longer on this destructive instinct which is seldom given the attention that its importance warrants. With the least of speculative efforts we are led to conclude that this instinct functions in every living being, striving to work its ruin and reduce life to its primal state of inert matter. Indeed it might well be called the "death instinct," whereas the erotic instincts vouch for the struggle to live on. The death instinct becomes an impulse to destruction when, with the aid of certain organs, it directs its action outward, against external objects. The living being, that is to say, defends its own existence by destroying foreign bodies. But, in one of its activities, the death instinct is operative *within* the living being, and we have sought to trace back a number of normal and pathological phenomena to this *introversion* of the destructive instinct. We have even committed the heresy of explaining the origin of human conscience by some such "turning inward" of the aggressive impulse. Obviously when this internal tendency operates on too large a scale, it is no trivial matter, rather a positively morbid state of things; whereas the diversion of the destructive impulse toward the external world must have beneficial effects. Here is then the biological justification for all those vile, pernicious propensities which we now are combating. We can but own that they are really more akin to nature than this our stand against them, which, in fact, remains to be accounted for....

The upshot of these observations, as bearing on the subject in hand, is that there is no likelihood of our being able to suppress humanity's aggressive tendencies. In some happy corners of the earth, they say, where nature brings forth abundantly whatever man desires, there flourish races whose lives go gently by, unknowing of aggression or constraint. This I can hardly credit; I would like further details about these happy folk. The Bolshevists, too, aspire to do away with human aggressiveness by ensuring the satisfaction of material needs and enforcing equality between man and man. To me this hope seems vain. Meanwhile they busily perfect their armaments, and their hatred of outsiders is not the least of the factors of cohesion amongst themselves. In any case, as you too have observed, complete suppression of man's aggressive tendencies is not in issue; what we may try is to divert it into a channel other than that of warfare.

From our "mythology" of the instincts, we may easily deduce a formula for an indirect method of eliminating war. If the propensity for war be due to the destructive instinct, we have always its counteragent, *eros*, to our hand. All that produces ties of sentiment between man and man must serve us as war's antidote. These ties are of two kinds. First, such relations as those toward a beloved object, void though they be of sexual intent. The psychoanalyst need feel no compunction in mentioning "love" in this connection; religion uses the same language: "Love thy neighbor as thyself." A pious injunction easy to enounce, but hard to carry out! The other bond of sentiment is by way of identification. All that brings out the significant resemblances between men calls into play this feeling of community, identification, whereon is founded, in large measure, the whole edifice of human society.

...The ideal conditions would obviously be found in a community where every man subordinated his instinctive life to the dictates of reason. Nothing less than this could bring about so thorough and so durable a union between men, even if this involved the severance of mutual ties of sentiment. But surely such a hope is utterly Utopian, as things are. The other indirect methods of preventing war are certainly more feasible, but entail no quick results. They conjure up an ugly picture of mills which grind so slowly that, before the flour is ready, men are dead of hunger.

As you see, little good comes of consulting a theoretician, aloof from worldly contacts, on practical and urgent problems! Better it were to tackle each successive crisis with means that we have ready to our hands. However, I would like to deal with a question which, though it is not mooted in your letter, interests me greatly. Why do we, you and I and many another, protest so vehemently against war, instead of just accepting it as another of life's odious importunities? For it seems a natural thing enough, biologically sound and practically unavoidable. I trust you will not be shocked by my raising such a question. For the better conduct of an inquiry it may be well to don a mask of feigned aloofness. The answer to my query may run as follows: because every man has a right over his own life, and war destroys lives that were full of promise; it forces the individual into situations that shame his manhood, obliging him to murder fellow men, against his will; it ravages material amenities, the fruits of human toil, and much besides. Moreover, wars, as now conducted, afford no scope for acts of heroism according to the old ideals, and, given the high perfection of modern arms, war today would mean the sheer extermination of one of the combatants, if not of both. This is so true, so obvious, that we can but wonder why the conduct of war is not banned by general consent. Doubtless either of the points I have just made is open to debate. It may be asked if the community, in its turn, cannot claim a right over the individual lives of its members. Moreover, all forms of war cannot be indiscriminately condemned; so long as there are nations and empires, each prepared callously to exterminate its rival, all alike must be equipped for war. But we will not dwell on any of these problems; they lie outside the debate to which you have invited me. I pass on to another point, the basis, as it strikes me, of our common hatred of war. It is this: we cannot do otherwise than hate it. Pacifists we are, since our organic nature wills us thus to be. Hence it comes easy to us to find arguments that justify our standpoint.

This point, however, calls for elucidation. Here is the way in which I see it. The cultural development of mankind (some, I know, prefer to call it civilization) has been in progress since immemorial antiquity. . . . It well may lead to the extinction of mankind, for it impairs the sexual function in more than one respect, and even today the uncivilized races and the backward classes of all nations are multiplying more rapidly than the cultured elements. This process may, perhaps, be likened to the effect of domestication on certain animals—it clearly involves physical changes of structure—but the view that cultural development is an organic process of this order has not yet become generally familiar. The psychic changes which accompany this process of cultural change are striking and not to be gainsaid. They consist in the progressive rejection of instinctive ends and a scaling down of instinctive reactions. Sensations which delighted our forefathers have become neutral or unbearable to us; and, if our ethical and aesthetic ideals have undergone a change, the causes of this are ultimately organic. On the psychological side two of the most important phenomena of culture are, first, a strengthening of the intellect, which tends to master our instinctive life, and, second, an introversion of the aggressive impulse, with all its consequent benefits and perils. Now war runs most emphatically counter to the psychic disposition imposed on us by the growth of culture; we are therefore bound to resent war, to find it utterly intolerable. With pacifists like us it is not merely an intellectual and affective repulsion, but a constitutional intolerance, an idiosyncrasy in its most drastic form. And it would seem that the aesthetic ignominies of warfare play almost as large a part in this repugnance as war's atrocities.

How long have we to wait before the rest of men turn pacifist? Impossible to say, and yet perhaps our hope that these two factors—man's cultural disposition and a well-founded dread of the form future wars will take—may serve to put an end to war in the future.

Konrad Z. Lorenz

ON AGGRESSION

Maybe human beings are "instinctively" aggressive. Not surprisingly, this approach has been especially prominent among biologists, themselves strongly influenced by a Darwinian approach to human nature. Of these, perhaps the most influential has been the Austrian ethologist Konrad Z. Lorenz, who shared a Nobel Prize in 1973 for his research on animal behavior. According to his thinking, there are a variety of positive, adaptive advantages to animal—and human—aggression. This is not to say that Lorenz extolled human aggressiveness; rather, he sought to understand its origin, pointing out that with the advent of modern technology, the human penchant for violence has become *Homo sapiens'* greatest danger, especially in conjunction with "militant enthusiasm" and, ironically, a *lack* of human instincts when it comes to restraints on violence.

In recent years, a more sophisticated version of instinctivism has gained currency. Known as "sociobiology," this approach is even more avowedly evolutionary, emphasizing that the capacity for aggressiveness is within the biological repertoire of human beings, just as it is for many living things. But so are cooperation and altruism. The key, then, is to identify circumstances in which people are predisposed to one behavior pattern or the other. Although biologists no longer accept "good of the species" arguments, we have chosen the following selection because the writings of Konrad Lorenz have been so influential.

What is the value of all this fighting? In nature, fighting is such an ever-present process, its behavior mechanisms and weapons are so highly developed and have so obviously arisen under the selection pressure of a species-preserving function, that it is our duty to ask this Darwinian question.

The layman, misguided by sensationalism in press and film, imagines the relationship between the various "wild beasts of the jungle" to be a bloodthirsty struggle, all against all. In a widely shown film, a Bengal tiger was seen fighting with a python, and immediately afterward the python with a crocodile. With a clear conscience I can assert that such things never occur under natural conditions. What advantage would one of these animals gain from exterminating the other? Neither of them interferes with the other's vital interests.

Darwin's expression, "the struggle for existence," is sometimes erroneously interpreted as the struggle between different species. In reality, the struggle Darwin was thinking of and which drives evolution forward is the competition between near relations. What causes a species to disappear or become transformed into a different species is the profitable "invention" that falls by chance to one or a few of its members in the everlasting gamble of hereditary change. The descendants of these lucky ones gradually outstrip all others until the particular species consists only of individuals who possess the new "invention."

There are, however, fightlike contests between members of different species: at night an owl kills and eats even well-armed birds of prey, in spite of their vigorous defense, and when these birds meet the owl by day they attack it ferociously. Almost every animal capable of self-defense, from the smallest rodent upward, fights furiously when it is cornered and has no means of escape. Besides these three particular types of inter-specific fighting, there are other, less typical cases; for instance, two cave-nesting birds of different species may fight for a nesting cavity. Something must be said here about these three types of inter-specific fighting in order to explain their peculiarity and to distinguish them from the *intra*-specific aggression which is really the subject of this book.

The survival value of inter-specific fights is much more evident than that of intra-specific contests. The way in which a predatory animal and its prey influence each other's evolution is a classical example of how the selection pressure of a certain function causes corresponding adaptations. The swiftness of the hunted ungulate forces its feline pursuers to evolve enormous leaping power and sharply armed toes. Paleontological discoveries have shown impressive examples of such evolutionary competition between weapons of attack and those of defense. The teeth of grazing animals have achieved better and better grinding power, while, in their parallel evolution, nutritional plants have devised means of protecting themselves against being eaten, as by the storage of silicates and the development of hard, wooden thorns. This kind of "fight" between the eater and the eaten never goes so far that the predator causes extinction of the prey: a state of equilibrium is always established between them, endurable by both species. The last lions would have died of hunger long before they had killed the last pair of antelopes or zebras; . . .

The opposite process, the "counteroffensive" of the prey against the predator, is more nearly related to genuine aggression. Social animals in particular take every possible chance to attack the "eating enemy" that threatens their safety. This process is called "mobbing." Crows or other birds "mob" a cat or any other nocturnal predator, if they catch sight of it by day. . . .

All the cases described above, in which animals of different species fight against each other, have one thing in common: every one of the fighters gains an obvious advantage by its behavior or, at least, in the interests of preserving the species it "ought to" gain one. But intra-specific aggression, aggression in the proper and narrower sense of the word, also fulfills a species-preserving function. Here, too, the Darwinian question "What for?" may and must be asked. Many people will not see the obvious justification for this question, and those accustomed to the classical psychoanalytical way of thinking will probably regard it as a frivolous attempt to vindicate the life-destroying principle or, purely and simply, evil. The average normal civilized human being witnesses aggression only when two of his fellow citizens or two of his domestic animals fight, and therefore sees only its evil effects. In addition there is the alarming progression of aggressive actions ranging from cocks fighting in the barnyard to dogs biting each other, boys thrashing each other, young men throwing beer mugs at each other's heads, and so on to barroom brawls about politics, and finally to wars and atom bombs.

With humanity in its present cultural and technological situation, we have good reason to consider intra-specific aggression the greatest of all dangers. We shall not improve our chances of counteracting it if we accept it as something metaphysical and inevitable, but on the other hand, we shall perhaps succeed in finding remedies if we investigate the chain of its natural causation. Wherever man has achieved the power of voluntarily guiding a natural phenomenon in a certain direction, he has owed it to his understanding of the chain of causes which formed it. Physiology, the science concerned with the normal life processes and how they fulfill their species-preserving function, forms the essential foundation for pathology, the science investigating their disturbances. Let us forget for a moment that the aggression drive has become derailed under conditions of civilization, and let us inquire impartially into its natural causes. For the reasons already given, as good Darwinians we must inquire into the species-preserving function which, under natural—or rather precultural—conditions, is fulfilled by fights within the species, and which by the process of selection has caused the advanced development of intra-specific fighting behavior in so many higher animals. It is not only fishes that fight their own species: the majority of vertebrates do so too, man included.

Darwin had already raised the question of the survival value of fighting, and he has given us an enlightening answer: It is always favorable to the future of a species if the stronger of two rivals takes possession either of the territory or of the desired female....

Unless the special interests of a social organization demand close aggregation of its members, it is obviously most expedient to spread the individuals of an animal species as evenly as possible over the available habitat. To use a human analogy: if, in a certain area, a larger number of doctors, builders, and mechanics want to exist, the representatives of these professions will do well to settle as far away from each other as possible.

The danger of too dense a population of an animal species settling in one part of the available biotope and exhausting all its sources of nutrition and so starving can be obviated by a mutual repulsion acting on the animals of the same species, effecting their regular spacing out, in much the same manner as electrical charges are regularly distributed all over the surface of a spherical conductor. This, in plain terms, is the most important survival value of intra-specific aggression....

I think it has been adequately shown that the aggression of so many animals toward members of their own species is in no way detrimental to the species but, on the contrary, is essential for its preservation. However, this must not raise false hopes about the present situation of mankind. Innate behavior mechanisms can be thrown completely out of balance by small, apparently insignificant changes of environmental conditions. Inability to adapt quickly to such changes may bring about the destruction of a

species, and the changes which man has wrought in his environment are by no means insignificant. An unprejudiced observer from another planet, looking upon man as he is today, in his hand the atom bomb, the product of his intelligence, in his heart the aggression drive inherited from his anthropoid ancestors, which this same intelligence cannot control, would not prophesy long life for the species. Looking at the situation as a human being whom it personally concerns, it seems like a bad dream, and it is hard to believe that aggression is anything but the pathological product of our disjointed cultural and social life.

And one could only wish it were no more than that! Knowledge of the fact that the aggression drive is a true, primarily species-preserving instinct enables us to recognize its full danger: it is the spontaneity of the instinct that makes it so dangerous. If it were merely a reaction to certain external factors, as many sociologists and psychologists maintain, the state of mankind would not be as perilous as it really is, for, in that case, the reaction-eliciting factors could be eliminated with some hope of success. It was Freud who first pointed out the essential spontaneity of instincts, though he recognized that of aggression only rather late. He also showed that lack of social contact, and above all deprivation of it (*Liebesverlust*), were among the factors strongly predisposing to facilitate aggression. However, the conclusions which many American psychologists drew from this correct surmise were erroneous. It was supposed that children would grow up less neurotic, better adapted to their social environment, and less aggressive if they were spared all disappointments and indulged in every way. An American method of education, based on these surmises, only showed that the aggressive drive, like many other instincts, springs "spontaneously" from the inner human being, and the results of this method of upbringing were countless unbearably rude children who were anything but nonaggressive....

It is a curious paradox that the greatest gifts of man, the unique faculties of conceptual thought and verbal speech which have raised him to a level high above all other creatures and given him mastery over the globe, are not altogether blessings, or at least are blessings that have to be paid for very dearly indeed. All the great dangers threatening humanity with extinction are direct consequences of conceptual thought and verbal speech. They drove man out of the paradise in which he could follow his instincts with impunity and do or not do whatever he pleased. There is much truth in the parable of the tree of knowledge and its fruit, though I want to make an addition to it to make it fit into my own picture of Adam: that apple was thoroughly unripe! Knowledge springing from conceptual thought robbed man of the security provided by his well-adapted instincts long, long before it was sufficient to provide him with an equally safe adaptation. Man is, as Arnold Gehlen has so truly said, by nature a jeopardized creature. . . .

I have spoken of the inhibitions controlling aggression in various social animals, preventing it from injuring or killing fellow members of the species. As I explained, these inhibitions are most important and consequently most highly differentiated in those animals which are capable of killing living creatures of about their own size. A raven can peck out the eye of another with one thrust of its beak, a wolf can rip the jugular vein of another with a single bite. There would be no more ravens and no more wolves if reliable inhibitions did not prevent such actions. Neither a dove nor a hare nor even a chimpanzee is able to kill its own kind with a single peck or bite; in addition, animals with relatively poor defense weapons have a correspondingly great ability to escape quickly, even from specially armed predators which are more efficient in chasing, catching, and killing than even the strongest of their own species. Since there rarely is, in nature, the possibility of such an animal's seriously injuring one of its own kind, there is no selection pressure at work here to breed in killing inhibitions. The absence of such inhibitions is apparent to the animal keeper, to his own and to his animals' disadvantage, if he does not take seriously the intra-specific fights of completely "harmless" animals. Under the unnatural conditions of captivity, where a defeated animal cannot escape from its victor, it may be killed slowly and cruelly. In my book

King Solomon's Ring, I have described in the chapter "Morals and Weapons" how the symbol of peace, the dove, can torture one of its own kind to death, without the arousal of any inhibition.

Anthropologists concerned with the habits of Australopithecus have repeatedly stressed that these hunting progenitors of man have left humanity with the dangerous heritage of what they term "carnivorous mentality." This statement confuses the concepts of the carnivore and the cannibal, which are to a large extent, mutually exclusive. One can only deplore the fact that man has definitely not got a carnivorous mentality! All his trouble arises from his being a basically harmless, omnivorous creature, lacking in natural weapons with which to kill big prey, and, therefore, also devoid of the built-in safety devices which prevent "professional" carnivores from abusing their killing power to destroy fellow members of their own species. A lion or a wolf may, on extremely rare occasions, kill another by one angry stroke, but, all heavily armed carnivores possess sufficiently reliable inhibitions which prevent the self-destruction of the species.

In human evolution, no inhibitory mechanisms preventing sudden manslaughter were necessary, because quick killing was impossible anyhow; the potential victim had plenty of opportunity to elicit the pity of the aggressor by submissive gestures and appeasing attitudes. No selection pressure arose in the prehistory of mankind to breed inhibitory mechanisms preventing the killing of conspecifics until, all of a sudden, the invention of artificial weapons upset the equilibrium of killing potential and social inhibitions. When it did, man's position was very nearly that of a dove which, by some unnatural trick of nature, has suddenly acquired the beak of a raven. One shudders at the thought of a creature as irascible as all prehuman primates are, swinging a well-sharpened handax. Humanity would indeed have destroyed itself by its first inventions, were it not for the very wonderful fact that inventions and responsibility are both the achievements of the same specifically human faculty of asking questions.

Not that our prehuman ancestor, even at a stage as yet devoid of moral responsibility, was a fiend incarnate; he was by no means poorer in social instincts and inhibitions than a chimpanzee, which, after all, is—his irascibility not withstanding—a social and friendly creature. But whatever his innate norms of social behavior may have been, they were bound to be thrown out of gear by the invention of weapons. If humanity survived, as, after all, it did, it never achieved security from the dan-ger of self-destruction. If moral responsibility and unwilling-ness to kill have indubitably increased, the ease and emotional impunity of killing have increased at the same rate. The distance at which all shooting weap-ons take effect screens the killer against the stimulus situation which would otherwise activate his kill-ing inhibitions. The deep, emotional layers of our personality simply do not register the fact that the crooking of the forefinger to release a shot tears the entrails of another man. No sane man would even go rabbit hunting for pleasure if the necessity of kill-ing his prey with his natural weapons brought home to him the full, emotional realization of what he is actually doing.

The same principle applies, to an even greater degree, to the use of modern remote-control weap-ons. The man who presses the releasing button is so completely screened against seeing, hearing, or oth-erwise emotionally realizing the consequences of his action, that he can commit it with impunity—even if he is burdened with the power of imagination. Only thus can it be explained that perfectly good-natured men, who would not even smack a naughty child, proved to be perfectly able to release rockets or to lay carpets of incendiary bombs on sleeping cities, thereby committing hundreds and thousands of children to a horrible death in the flames. The fact that it is good, normal men who did this, is as eerie as any fiendish atrocity of war! ...

Militant enthusiasm is particularly suited for the paradigmatic illustration of the manner in which a phylogenetically evolved pattern of behav-ior interacts with culturally ritualized social norms and rites, and in which, though absolutely indis-pensable to the function of the compound sys-tem, it is prone to miscarry most tragically if not strictly controlled by rational responsibility based on causal insight. The Greek word *enthousiasmos*

implies that a person is possessed by a god; the German *Begeisterung* means that he is controlled by a spirit, a *Geist*, more or less holy.

In reality, militant enthusiasm is a special-ized form of communal aggression, clearly dis-tinct from and yet functionally related to the more primitive forms of petty individual aggression. Every man of normally strong emotions knows, from his own experience, the subjective phenom-ena that go hand in hand with the response of militant enthusiasm. A shiver runs down the back and, as more exact observation shows, along the outside of both arms. One soars elated, above all the ties of everyday life, one is ready to abandon all for the call of what, in the moment of this specific emotion, seems to be a sacred duty. All obstacles in its path become unimportant; the instinctive inhibitions against hurting or killing one's fellows lose, unfortunately, much of their power. Rational considerations, criticisms, and all reasonable argu-ments against the behavior dictated by militant enthusiasm are silenced by an amazing reversal of all values, making them appear not only untenable but base and dishonorable. Men may enjoy the feeling of absolute righteousness even while they commit atrocities. Conceptual thought and moral responsibility are at their lowest ebb. As a Ukrai-nian proverb says: "When the banner is unfurled, all reason is in the trumpet." ...

Anybody who has ever seen the correspond-ing behavior of the male chimpanzee defending his band or family with self-sacrificing courage will doubt the purely spiritual character of human enthusiasm. The chimp, too, sticks out his chin, stiffens his body, and raises his elbows; his hair stands on end, producing a terrifying magnifica-tion of his body contours as seen from the front. The inward rotation of his arms obviously has the purpose of turning the longest-haired side outward to enhance the effect. The whole combination of body attitude and hair-raising constitutes a bluff. This is also seen when a cat humps its back, and is calculated to make the animal appear bigger and more dangerous than it really is. Our shiver, which in German poetry is called a *"heiliger Schauer,"* a "holy" shiver, turns out to be the vestige of a prehuman vegetative response of making a fur bristle which we no longer have.

To the humble seeker of biological truth there cannot be the slightest doubt that human militant enthusiasm evolved out of a communal defense response of our prehuman ancestors. The unthinking single-mindedness of the response must have been of high survival value even in a tribe of fully evolved human beings. It was necessary for the individual male to forget all his other allegiances in order to be able to dedicate himself, body and soul, to the cause of the communal battle....

The object which militant enthusiasm tends to defend has changed with cultural development. Originally it was certainly the community of concrete, individually known members of a group, held together by the bond of personal love and friendship. With the growth of the social unit, the social norms and rites held in common by all its members became the main factor holding it together as an entity, and therewith they became automatically the symbol of the unit....

Like the triumph ceremony of the greylag goose, militant enthusiasm in man is a true autonomous instinct: it has its own appetitive behavior, its own releasing mechanisms, and, like the sexual urge or any other strong instinct, it engenders a specific feeling of intense satisfaction. The strength of its seductive lure explains why intelligent men may behave as irrationally and immorally in their political as in their sexual lives. Like the triumph ceremony, it has an essential influence on the social structure of the species. Humanity is not enthusiastically combative because it is split into political parties, but it is divided into opposing camps because this is the adequate stimulus situation to arouse militant enthusiasm in a satisfying manner....

The first prerequisite for rational control of an instinctive behavior pattern is the knowledge of the stimulus situation which releases it. Militant enthusiasm can be elicited with the predictability of a reflex when the following environmental situations arise. First of all, a social unit with which the subject identifies himself must appear to be threatened by some danger from outside. That which is threatened may be a concrete group of people, the family or a little community of close friends, or else it may be a larger social unit held together and symbolized by its own specific social norms and rites....

A second key stimulus which contributes enormously to the releasing of intense militant enthusiasm is the presence of a hated enemy from whom the threat to the above "values" emanates. This enemy, too, can be of a concrete or of an abstract nature. It can be "the" Jews, Huns, Boches, tyrants, etc., or abstract concepts like world capitalism, Bolshevism, fascism, and any other kind of ism; it can be heresy, dogmatism, scientific fallacy, or whatnot. Just as in the case of the object to be defended, the enemy against whom to defend it is extremely variable, and demagogues are well versed in the dangerous art of producing supranormal dummies to release a very dangerous form of militant enthusiasm.

A third factor contributing to the environmental situation eliciting the response is an inspiring leader figure. Even the most emphatically antifascistic ideologies apparently cannot do without it, as the giant pictures of leaders displayed by all kinds of political parties prove clearly enough....

A fourth, and perhaps the most important, prerequisite for the full eliciting of militant enthusiasm is the presence of many other individuals, all agitated by the same emotion. Their absolute number has a certain influence on the quality of the response. Smaller numbers at issue with a large majority tend to obstinate defense with the emotional value of "making a last stand," while very large numbers inspired by the same enthusiasm feel the urge to conquer the whole world in the name of their sacred cause. Here...the excitation grows in proportion, perhaps even in geometrical progression, with the increasing number of individuals. This is exactly what makes militant mass enthusiasm so dangerous.

Margaret Mead

WARFARE IS ONLY AN INVENTION—NOT A
BIOLOGICAL NECESSITY

Instinctivist theories of human aggressiveness have been criticized, especially because such views seem to promote the notion that warfare is "in our genes" and, hence, cannot be prevented. There is, indeed, some evidence that people who are politically conservative and typically promilitary disproportionately tend to believe that human beings are "naturally" aggressive, untrustworthy, and incapable of changing. In any event, the prevailing view among social scientists is that there is no "war instinct," even though aggressiveness may sometimes be readily evoked.

Anthropologists concern themselves largely with the activities of non-Western, typically nontechnological societies. There is legitimate debate about whether such study casts valuable light on modern, technological war-making. Some emphasize that the two situations are quite different, whereas others argue that examination of "primitive" war might help illuminate the conditions under which group violence has evolved. Some anthropologists, for example, claim that the capacity for warfare developed along with adaptations for hunting large game; others have emphasized competition for mates, for social prestige, or between rival bands.

A cross-cultural perspective on war reveals, among other things, a widespread tendency to dehumanize members of other tribes, often using literally animalizing terms to describe strangers and enemies. War-making is also typically associated with an array of rituals, with the enhancement of group cohesion, as well as with ritual purification connected with the taking of human life. A schism of sorts also exists among anthropologists, with some convinced that "primitive war" is functional (although not necessarily good) in meeting various ecological and social needs, whereas others claim that it is essentially dysfunctional, a social pathology.

In general, however, anthropologists have contributed less heavily to the study of war than might be expected. An exception is Margaret Mead, whose brief essay, reprinted here, has become a classic statement of the anti-instinctivist school.

⎯⎯⎯⎯⎯⎯⎯⎯⎯ ⟨⊜⟩ ⎯⎯⎯⎯⎯⎯⎯⎯⎯

Is war a biological necessity, a sociological inevitability, or just a bad invention? Those who argue for the first view endow man with such pugnacious instincts that some outlet in aggressive behavior is necessary if man is to reach full human stature. . . . A basic, competitive, aggressive, warring human nature is assumed, and those who wish to outlaw war or outlaw competitiveness merely try

From "Warfare Is Only an Invention—Not a Biological Necessity" by Margaret Mead. 1940. *Asia*, XL:402–5.

to find new and less socially destructive ways in which these biologically given aspects of man's nature can find expression. Then there are those who take the second view: warfare is the inevitable concomitant of the development of the state, the struggle for land and natural resources of class societies springing not from the nature of man, but from the nature of history. War is nevertheless inevitable unless we change our social system and outlaw classes, the struggle for power, and possessions; and in the event of our success warfare would disappear, as a symptom vanishes when the disease is cured.

One may hold a sort of compromise position between these two extremes; one may claim that all aggression springs from the frustration of man's biologically determined drives and that, since all forms of culture are frustrating, it is certain each new generation will be aggressive and the aggression will find its natural and inevitable expression in race war, class war, nationalistic war, and so on. All three of these positions are very popular today among those who think seriously about the problems of war and its possible prevention, but I wish to urge another point of view, less defeatist, perhaps, than the first and third and more accurate than the second: that is, that warfare, by which I mean recognized conflict between two groups *as groups*, in which each group puts an army (even if the army is only fifteen pygmies) into the field to fight and kill, if possible, some of the members of the army of the other group—that warfare of this sort is an invention like any other of the inventions in terms of which we order our lives, such as writing, marriage, cooking our food instead of eating it raw, trial by jury, or burial of the dead, and so on. Some of this list anyone will grant are inventions: trial by jury is confined to very limited portions of the globe; we know that there are tribes that do not bury their dead but instead expose or cremate them; and we know that only part of the human race has had the knowledge of writing as its cultural inheritance. But, whenever a way of doing things is found universally, such as the use of fire or the practice of some form of marriage, we tend to think at once that it is not an invention at all but an attribute

of humanity itself. And yet even such universals as marriage and the use of fire are inventions like the rest, very basic ones, inventions which were, perhaps, necessary if human history was to take the turn that it has taken, but nevertheless inventions. At some point in his social development man was undoubtedly without the institution of marriage or the knowledge of the use of fire.

The case for warfare is much clearer because there are peoples even today who have no warfare. Of these the Eskimos are perhaps the most conspicuous examples, but the Lepchas of Sikkim described by Geoffrey Gorer in *Himalayan Village* are as good.[2] Neither of these peoples understands war, not even defensive warfare. The idea of warfare is lacking, and this idea is as essential to really carrying on war as an alphabet or a syllabary is to writing. But, whereas the Lepchas are a gentle, unquarrelsome people, and the advocates of other points of view might argue that they are not full human beings or that they had never been frustrated and so had no aggression to expand in warfare, the Eskimo case gives no such possibility of interpretation. The Eskimos are not a mild and meek people; many of them are turbulent and troublesome. Fights, theft of wives, murder, cannibalism, occur among them— all outbursts of passionate men goaded by desire or intolerable circumstance. Here are men faced with hunger, men faced with loss of their wives, men faced with the threat of extermination by other men, and here are orphan children, growing up miserably with no one to care for them, mocked and neglected by those about them. The personality necessary for war, the circumstances necessary to goad men to desperation are present, but there is no war. When a traveling Eskimo entered a settlement, he might have to fight the strongest man in the settlement to establish his position among them, but this was a test of strength and bravery, not war. The idea of warfare, of one *group* organizing against another *group* to maim and wound and kill them was absent. And, without that idea, passions might rage but there was no war.

---

[2] G. Gorer, *Himalayan Village* (London: M. Joseph, 1938).

But, it may be argued, is not this because the Eskimos have such a low and undeveloped form of social organization? They own no land, they move from place to place, camping, it is true, season after season on the same site, but this is not something to fight for as the modern nations of the world fight for land and raw materials. They have no permanent possessions that can be looted, no towns that can be burned. They have no social classes to produce stress and strains within the society which might force it to go to war outside. Does not the absence of war among the Eskimos, while disproving the biological necessity of war, just go to confirm the point that it is the state of development of the society which accounts for war and nothing else?

We find the answer among the pygmy peoples of the Andaman Islands in the Bay of Bengal. The Andamans also represent an exceedingly low level of society; they are a hunting and food-gathering people; they live in tiny hordes without any class stratification; their houses are simpler than the snow houses of the Eskimo. But they knew about warfare. The army might contain only fifteen determined pygmies marching in a straight line, but it was the real thing nonetheless. Tiny army met tiny army in open battle, blows were exchanged, casualties suffered, and the state of warfare could only be concluded by a peacemaking ceremony.

Similarly, among the Australian aborigines, who built no permanent dwellings but wandered from water hole to water hole over their almost desert country, warfare—and rules of "international law"—were highly developed. The student of social evolution will seek in vain for his obvious causes of war, struggle for lands, struggle for power of one group over another, expansion of population, need to divert the minds of a populace restive under tyranny, or even the ambition of a successful leader to enhance his own prestige. All are absent, but warfare as a practice remained, and men engaged in it and killed one another in the course of a war because killing is what is done in wars.

From instances like these it becomes apparent that an inquiry into the causes of war misses the fundamental point as completely as does an insistence upon the biological necessity of war. If a people have

an idea of going to war and the idea that war is the way in which certain situations, defined within their society, are to be handled, they will sometimes go to war. If they are a mild and unaggressive people, like the Pueblo Indians, they may limit themselves to defensive warfare, but they will be forced to think in terms of war because there are peoples near them who have warfare as a pattern, and offensive, raiding, pillaging warfare at that. When the pattern of warfare is known, people like the Pueblo Indians will defend themselves, taking advantage of their natural defenses, the mesa village site, and people like the Lepchas, having no natural defenses and no idea of warfare, will merely submit to the invader. But the essential point remains the same. There is a way of behaving which is known to a given people and labeled as an appropriate form of behavior; a bold and warlike people like the Sioux or the Maori may label warfare as desirable as well as possible, a mild people like the Pueblo Indians may label warfare as undesirable, but to the minds of both peoples the possibility of warfare is present. Their thoughts, their hopes, their plans are oriented about this idea—that warfare may be selected as the way to meet some situation.

So simple peoples and civilized peoples, mild peoples and violent, assertive peoples, will all go to war if they have the invention, just as those peoples who have the custom of dueling will have duels and peoples who have the pattern of vendetta will indulge in vendetta. And, conversely, peoples who do not know of dueling will not fight duels, even though their wives are seduced and their daughters ravished; they may on occasion commit murder but they will not fight duels. Cultures which lack the idea of the vendetta will not meet every quarrel in this way. A people can use only the forms it has. So the Balinese have their special way of dealing with a quarrel between two individuals: if the two feel that the causes of quarrel are heavy, they may go and register their quarrel in the temple before the gods, and, making offerings, they may swear never to have anything to do with each other again.... But in other societies, although individuals might feel as full of animosity and as unwilling to have any further contact as do the Balinese, they cannot register their quarrel with the gods and go on quietly about their business because registering quarrels with the gods is not an invention of which they know....

In many parts of the world, war is a game in which the individual can win counters—counters which bring him prestige in the eyes of his own sex or of the opposite sex; he plays for these counters as he might, in our society, strive for a tennis championship. Warfare is a frame for such prestige-seeking merely because it calls for the display of certain skills and certain virtues; all of these skills—riding straight, shooting straight, dodging the missiles of the enemy and sending one's own straight to the mark—can be equally well exercised in some other framework and, equally, the virtues—endurance, bravery, loyalty, steadfastness—can be displayed in other contexts. The tie-up between proving oneself a man and proving this by a success in organized killing is due to a definition which many societies have made of manliness. And often, even in those societies which counted success in warfare a proof of human worth, strange turns were given to the idea, as when the plains Indians gave their highest awards to the man who touched a live enemy rather than to the man who brought in a scalp—from a dead enemy—because the latter was less risky. Warfare is just an invention known to the majority of human societies by which they permit their young men either to accumulate prestige or avenge their honor or acquire loot or wives or slaves or sago lands or cattle or appease the bloodlust of their gods or the restless souls of the recently dead. It is just an invention, older and more widespread than the jury system, but nonetheless an invention.

... Grant that war is an invention, that it is not a biological necessity nor the outcome of certain special types of social forms, still, once the invention is made, what are we to do about it?...Warfare is here, as part of our thought; the deeds of warriors are immortalized in the words of our poets, the toys of our children are modeled upon the weapons of the soldier, the frame of reference within which our statesmen and our diplomats work always contains war. If we know that it is not inevitable, that it is due to historical accident that warfare is one of the ways in which we think of behaving, are we given any hope by that? What hope is there of persuading nations to abandon war, nations so thoroughly imbued with the idea that resort to war is, if not actually desirable and noble, at least inevitable whenever certain defined circumstances arise?

In answer to this question I think we might turn to the history of other social inventions, and inventions which must once have seemed as firmly entrenched as warfare. Take the methods of trial which preceded the jury system: ordeal and trial by combat. Unfair, capricious, alien as they are to our feeling today, they were once the only methods open to individuals accused of some offense. The invention of trial by jury gradually replaced these methods until only witches, and finally not even witches, had to resort to the ordeal....In each case the old method was replaced by a new social invention. The ordeal did not go out because people thought it unjust or wrong; it went out because a method more congruent with the institutions and feelings of the period was invented. And, if we despair over the way in which war seems such an ingrained habit of most of the human race, we can take comfort from the fact that a poor invention will usually give place to a better invention.

For this, two conditions, at least, are necessary. The people must recognize the defects of the old invention, and someone must make a new one. Propaganda against warfare, documentation of its terrible cost in human suffering and social waste, these prepare the ground by teaching people to feel that warfare is a defective social institution. There is further needed a belief that social invention is possible and the invention of new methods which will render warfare as out of date as the tractor is making the plow, or the motor car the horse and buggy. A form of behavior becomes out of date only when something else takes its place, and, in order to invent forms of behavior which will make war obsolete, it is a first requirement to believe that an invention is possible.

Chris Hedges

WAR IS A FORCE THAT GIVES US MEANING

There is an irony in the public's attention to war. On the one hand, most people detest it, considering war among the greatest misfortunes to befall human beings. But on the other, people eagerly listen to war stories, songs, and marches; avidly read accounts of battles; flock to parades and movies that celebrate armed conflict; and revere war heroes. Because war is almost universally reviled—as opposed to soldiers, who are typically admired— only rarely are the *attractions* of war faced honestly and openly; yet those attractions are undeniable, as indicated not only by the public's almost insatiable appetite for war-related material but—even more troublesome—by the persistence of war itself. Even those peace activists who agree with Margaret Mead's claim that "warfare is only an invention—not a biological necessity," believe that there is a need to confront its appeal.

There are many reasons for war's perverse attractiveness, ranging from sheer thrill seeking, with its physical and sexual opportunities, to its potential for expressing genuine altruism and, indeed, heroism. High on the list is a connection to other combatants, including even, on occasion, the opponents. A U.S. combat veteran of World War II wrote that

> we are liberated from our individual impotence and are drunk with the power that union with our fellows brings. In moments like these many have a vague awareness of how isolated and separate their lives have hitherto been.... With the boundaries of the self expanded, they sense a kinship never known before. Their "I" passes insensibly into a "we." ... At its height, this sense of comradeship is an ecstasy.[3]

Reflections of this sort may be discomfiting to those of us seeking to eliminate war, or at least, to reduce its frequency and intensity. But an honest approach to peace requires nothing less than an honest recognition of war's appeal, including the extent to which it offers many a sense of "meaning." In this regard, former war correspondent Chris Hedges offers an honest and troubling account.

War and conflict have marked most of my adult life. I have been in ambushes on desolate stretches of Central American roads, locked in unnerving firefights in the marshes in southern Iraq, imprisoned in the Sudan, beaten by Saudi military police, deported from Libya and Iran, captured and held for a week by Iraqi Republican Guards, strafed by Russian MiG-21s in central Bosnia, shot at by Serb snipers, and shelled with deafening rounds of artillery in Sarajevo that threw out thousands of deadly

---

[3] J. Glen Gray, *The Warriors: Reflections on Men in Battle* (New York: Harper & Row, 1967).

bits of iron fragments. I have seen too much of violent death. I have tasted too much of my own fear. I have painful memories that lie buried most of the time. It is never easy when they surface.

And yet there is a part of me that remains nostalgic for war's simplicity and high. The enduring attraction of war is this: even with its destruction and carnage, it gives us what we all long for in life. It gives us purpose, meaning, a reason for living. Only when we are in the midst of conflict does the shallowness and vapidness of our lives become apparent. Trivia dominates our conversations and increasingly our news. And war is an enticing elixir. It gives us resolve, a cause. It allows us to be noble. And those that have the least meaning in their lives—the impoverished refugees in Gaza, the disenfranchised North African immigrants in France, even the lost legions of youth that live in the splendid indolence and safety of the industrialized world—are all susceptible to war's appeal.

WAR AS CULTURE

I learned early on that war forms its own culture. The rush of battle is a potent and often lethal addiction, for war is a drug, one I ingested for many years. It is peddled by mythmakers—historians, war correspondents, filmmakers, novelists, and the state—all of whom endow it with qualities it often does possess: excitement, exoticism, power, chances to rise above our small stations in life, and a bizarre and fantastic universe that has a grotesque and dark beauty. It dominates culture, distorts memory, corrupts language, and infects everything around it, even humor, which becomes preoccupied with the grim perversities of smut and death. Fundamental questions about the meaning, or meaninglessness, of our place on the planet are laid bare when we watch those around us sink to the lowest depths. War exposes the capacity for evil that lurks just below the surface within all of us.

And so it takes little in wartime to turn ordinary men into killers. Most give themselves willingly to the seduction of unlimited power to destroy, and all feel the peer pressure. Few, once in bottle, can find the strength to resist.

The historian Christopher Browning noted the willingness to kill in *Ordinary Men,* his study of Reserve Police Battalion 101 in Poland during World War ll. On the morning of July 12, 1942, the battalion was ordered to shoot 1,800 Jews in the village of Jozefow in a daylong action. The men in the unit had to round up the Jews, march them into the forest, and one by one order them to lie down in a row. The victims, including women, infants, children, and the elderly, were shot dead at close range.

Battalion members were offered the option to refuse, an option only about a dozen men took, although more asked to be relieved once the killing began. Those who did not want to continue, Browning says, were disgusted rather than plagued by conscience. When the men returned to the barracks, they "were depressed, angered, embittered, and shaken." They drank heavily. They were told not to talk about the event, "but they needed no encouragement in that direction."

WAR AS MYTH

The most recent U.S. conflicts have insulated the public and U.S. troops from both the disgust and pangs of conscience. The Gulf War—waged from bombers high above the fray and reported by carefully controlled journalists—made war fashionable again. It was a cause the nation willingly embraced. It exorcised the ghosts of Vietnam. It gave us heroes and the heady belief in our own military superiority and technology. It almost made war fun. And the chief culprit was, as in many conflicts, not the military but the press. Television reporters happily disseminated the spoon-fed images that served the propaganda effort of the military and the state.

These images did little to convey the reality of war. Pool reporters, those guided around in groups by the military, wrote once again about "our boys" eating packaged army food, practicing for chemical weapons attacks, and bathing out of buckets in the desert. It was war as spectacle—war, if we are honest, as entertainment. The images and stories were designed to make us feel good about our nation, about ourselves. The families and soldiers being blown to bits by iron fragmentation bombs just over the border in Iraq were faceless and nameless phantoms.

The moment I stepped off an Army C-130 military transport in Dhahran, Saudi Arabia, to cover the

Persian Gulf War, I was escorted to a room with several dozen other reporters and photographers. I was told to sign a paper that said I would abide by the severe restrictions placed on the press. The restrictions authorized "pool reporters" to be escorted by the military on field trips. Most of the press sat in hotel rooms and rewrote the bland copy filed by the pool or used the pool video and photos. I violated this agreement the next morning when I went into the field without authorization. The rest of the war, most of which I spent dodging military police and trying to talk my way into units, was a forlorn and lonely struggle against the heavy press control.

The notion that the press was used in the war is incorrect. The press wanted to be used. It saw itself as part of the war effort. Most reporters sent to cover a war don't really want to go near the fighting. They do not tell this to their editors and indeed will moan and complain about restrictions. The handful who actually head out into the field have a bitter enmity with the hotel room warriors. But even those who do go out are guilty of distortion—maybe more so. For they not only believe the myth, feed off the drug, but also embrace the cause. They may do it with more skepticism. They certainly expose more lies and misconceptions. But they believe. We all believe. When you stop believing, you stop going to war.

I knew a Muslim soldier, a father, who fought on the front lines around Sarajevo. His unit, in one of the rare attempts to take back a few streets controlled by the Serbs, pushed across Serb lines. They did not get very far. The fighting was heavy. As he moved down the street, he heard a door swing open and fired a burst from his AK-47 assault rifle. A twelve-year-old girl dropped dead. He saw in the body of the unknown girl lying prostrate in front of him the image of his own twelve-year-old daughter. He broke down. He had to be helped back to the city. He was lost for the rest of the war, shuttered inside his apartment, nervous, morose, and broken. This experience is far more typical of warfare than the Rambo heroics we are fed by the state and the entertainment industry. The cost of killing is all the more bitter because of the deep disillusionment that war usually brings.

WAR AS CRUSADE

The disillusionment comes later. Each generation again responds to war as innocents. Each generation discovers its own disillusionment—often at a terrible price.

"We believed we were there for a high moral purpose," wrote Philip Caputo in his book on Vietnam, *Rumor of War*. "But somehow our idealism was lost, our morals corrupted, and the purpose forgotten."

Once again the United States stands poised on the threshold of war. "We go forward," President George W. Bush assures us, "to defend freedom and all that is good and just in the world." He is not shy about warning other states that they either stand with us in the war on terrorism or will be counted as aligned with those that defy us. This too is a crusade.

But the war on terrorism is different in that we Americans find ourselves in the dangerous position of going to war not against a state but a phantom. The crusade we have embarked upon in the war on terrorism is targeting an elusive and protean enemy. The battle we have begun is never-ending. But it may be too late to wind back the heady rhetoric. We have embarked on a campaign as quixotic as the one mounted to destroy us. As it continues, as terrorist attacks intrude on our lives, as we feel less and less secure, the acceptance of all methods to lash out at real and perceived enemies will distort and deform our democracy.

And yet, the campaign's attraction seems irresistible. War makes the world understandable, a black-and-white tableau of them and us. It suspends thought, especially self-critical thought. All bow before the supreme effort. We are one. Most of us willingly accept war as long as we can fold it into a belief system that paints the ensuing suffering as necessary for a higher good; for human beings seek not only happiness but also meaning. And tragically, war is sometimes the most powerful way in human society to achieve meaning.

William Graham Sumner

WAR AND OTHER ESSAYS

Sociological perspectives on war tend to fall into two camps. A German school, under the influence of the philosopher Georg Hegel, and later, sociologists such as von Bernhardi, Gumplowicz, and Ranzenhofer, developed a "sociology of conflict," which saw warfare as necessary and desirable for the evolution of society. "War," wrote Hegel, in *Philosophy of Right*, "has the higher meaning that through it...the ethical health of nations is maintained;...war prevents a corruption of nations which a perpetual peace would produce."

By contrast, an Anglo-French-American tradition, represented initially by John Stuart Mill, Auguste Comte, and Émile Durkheim, focused on the differentiation and integration of social groups, the role of group consensus, and what they saw as the problem of "in-group amity, out-group enmity." They were interested in the role of war in the development of the nation-state, and they treated national competition less as a desired outcome than as an objective fact of life to be analyzed and understood.

Others have sought to understand the relationship between industrialization and war as well as the powerful and complex phenomenon of nationalism. The following selection is by William Graham Sumner, one of the founders of American sociology.

We have heard our political leaders say from time to time that, "War is necessary," "War is a good thing." They were trying to establish a major premise which would suggest the conclusion, "Therefore let us have a little war now," or "It is wise, on general principles, to have a war once in a while." That argument may be taken as the text of the present essay. It has seemed to me worthwhile to show from the history of civilization just what war has done and has not done for the welfare of mankind.

In the eighteenth century it was assumed that the primitive state of mankind was one of Arcadian peace, joy, and contentment. In the nineteenth century the assumption went over to the other extreme—that the primitive state was one of universal warfare. This, like the former notion, is a great exaggeration. Man in the most primitive and uncivilized state known to us does not practice war all the time; he dreads it. He might rather be described as a peaceful animal. Real warfare comes with the collisions of more developed societies....

War arises from the competition of life, not from the struggle for existence. In the struggle for existence a man is wrestling with nature to extort from her the means of subsistence. It is when two men are striving side by side in the struggle for existence to extort from nature the supplies they need that they come into rivalry, and a collision of interest with each other takes place. This collision may be light and unimportant, if the supplies are large and the number of men small, or it may be harsh and violent, if there are many men striving for a small supply. This collision we call the competition of life. Of course, men are in the competition of life with beasts, reptiles, insects, and plants—in short, with all organic forms; we will, however, confine

From *War and Other Essays* by Graham Sumner. 1911. New Haven, CT: Yale University Press.

our attention to men. The greater or less intensity of the competition of life is a fundamental condition of human existence....The members of the unit group work together. The Australian or Bushman hunter goes abroad to seek meat food, while the woman stays by the fire at a trysting place with the children and collects plant food. They cooperate in the struggle for existence, and the size of the group is fixed by the number who can work together to the greatest advantage under their mode of life. Such a group, therefore, has a common interest. It must have control of a certain area of land; hence it comes into collision of interest with every other group. The competition of life, therefore, arises between groups not between individuals, and we see that the members of the ingroup are allies and joint partners in one interest while they are brought into antagonism of interest with all outsiders....

Each group must regard every other as a possible enemy on account of the antagonism of interests, and so it views every other group with suspicion and distrust, although actual hostilities occur only on specific occasion. Every member of another group is a stranger; he may be admitted as a guest, in which case rights and security are granted him, but, if not so admitted, he is an enemy. We can now see why the sentiments of peace and cooperation inside are complementary to sentiments of hostility outside. It is because any group, in order to be strong against an outside enemy, must be well disciplined, harmonious, and peaceful inside; in other words, because discord inside would cause defeat in battle with another group. Therefore the same conditions which made men warlike against outsiders made them yield to the control of chiefs, submit to discipline, obey law, cultivate peace, and create institutions inside. The notion of rights grows up in the ingroup from the usages established there securing peace. There was a double education, at the same time, out of the same facts and relations. It is no paradox at all to say that peace makes war and that war makes peace. There are two codes of morals and two sets of mores, one for comrades inside and the other for strangers outside, and they arise from the same interests. Against outsiders it was meritorious to kill, plunder, practice blood revenge, and to steal women

and slaves, but inside none of these things could be allowed because they would produce discord and weakness. Hence, in the ingroup, law (under the forms of custom and taboo) and institutions had to take the place of force. Every group was a peace group inside, and the peace was sanctioned by the ghosts of the ancestors who had handed down the customs and taboos. Against outsiders religion sanctioned and encouraged war, for the ghosts of the ancestors, or the gods, would rejoice to see their posterity and worshipers once more defeat, slay, plunder, and enslave the ancient enemy.

...A peaceful society must be industrial because it must produce instead of plundering; it is for this reason that the industrial type of society is the opposite of the militant type. In any state on the continent of Europe today these two types of societal organization may be seen interwoven with each other and fighting each other. Industrialism builds up; militancy wastes. If a railroad is built, trade and intercourse indicate a line on which it ought to run; military strategy, however, overrules this and requires that it run otherwise. Then all the interests of trade and intercourse must be subjected to constant delay and expense because the line does not conform to them. Not a discovery or invention is made but the war and navy bureaus of all the great nations seize it to see what use can be made of it in war. It is evident that men love war; when two hundred thousand men in the United States volunteer in a month for a war with Spain which appeals to no sense of wrong against their country and to no other strong sentiment of human nature, when their lives are by no means monotonous or destitute of interest, and where life offers chances of wealth and prosperity, the pure love of adventure and war must be strong in our population. Europeans who have to do military service have no such enthusiasm for war as war. The presence of such a sentiment in the midst of the most purely industrial state in the world is a wonderful phenomenon. At the same time the social philosophy of the modern civilized world is saturated with humanitarianism and flabby sentimentalism. The humanitarianism is in the literature; by it the reading public is led to suppose that the world is advancing along some line which they call "progress" toward peace and brotherly love. Nothing could be more mistaken. We read of fist law and constant war in the Middle Ages and think that life must have been full of conflicts and bloodshed then, but modern warfare bears down on the whole population with a frightful weight through all the years of peace. Never, from the day of barbarism down to our own time, has every man in a society been a soldier until now, and the armaments of today are immensely more costly than ever before. There is only one limit possible to the war preparations of a modern European state; that is, the last man and the last dollar it can control. What will come of the mixture of sentimental social philosophy and warlike policy? There is only one thing rationally to be expected, and that is a frightful effusion of blood in revolution and war during the century now opening.

It is said that there are important offsets to all the burden and harm of this exaggerated militancy. That is true. Institutions and customs in human society are never either all good or all bad. We cannot adopt either peacefulness or warlikeness as a sole true philosophy. Military discipline educates; military interest awakens all the powers of men, so that they are eager to win and their ingenuity is quickened to invent new and better weapons. In history the military inventions have led the way and have been afterward applied to industry. Chemical inventions were made in the attempt to produce combinations which would be destructive in war; we owe some of our most useful substances to discoveries which were made in this effort. The skill of artisans has been developed in making weapons, and then that skill has been available for industry. The only big machines which the ancients ever made were battering rams, catapults, and other engines of war. The construction of these things familiarized men with mechanical devices which were capable of universal application. Gunpowder was discovered in the attempt to rediscover Greek fire; it was a grand invention in military art, but we should never have had our canals, railroads, and other great works without such explosives. Again, we are indebted to the chemical experiments in search of military agents for our friction matches.... We find, then,

that in the past, war has played a great part in the irrational nature process by which things have come to pass. But the nature processes are frightful; they contain no allowance for the feelings and interests of individuals—for it is only individuals who have feelings and interests. The nature elements never suffer, and they never pity. If we are terrified at the nature processes, there is only one way to escape them; it is the way by which men have always evaded them to some extent; it is by knowledge, by rational methods, and by the arts. The facts which have been presented about the functions of war in the past are not flattering to the human reason or conscience. They seem to show that we are as much indebted for our welfare to base passion as to noble and intelligent endeavor. At the present moment things do not look much better. We talk of civilizing lower races, but we never have done it yet; we have exterminated them. Our devices for civilizing them have been as disastrous to them as our firearms. At the beginning of the twentieth century the great civilized nations are making haste, in the utmost jealousy of each other, to seize upon all the outlying parts of the globe; they are vying with each other in the construction of navies by which each may defend its share against the others. What will happen? As they are preparing for war, they certainly will have war, and their methods of colonization and exploitation will destroy the aborigines. In this way the human race will be civilized—but by the extermination of the uncivilized—unless the men of the twentieth century can devise plans for dealing with aborigines which are better than any which have yet been devised. No one has yet found any way in which two races, far apart in blood and culture, can be amalgamated into one society with satisfaction to both. Plainly, in this matter which lies in the immediate future, the only alternatives to force and bloodshed are more knowledge and more reason....

Can peace be universal? There is no reason to believe it. It is a fallacy to suppose that, by widening the peace group more and more, it can at last embrace all mankind. What happens is that, as it grows bigger, differences, discords, antagonisms, and war begin inside of it on account of the divergence of interests. Since evil passions are a part of human nature and are in all societies all the time, a part of the energy of the society is constantly spent in repressing them. If all nations should resolve to have no armed ships anymore, pirates would reappear upon the ocean; the police of the seas must be maintained. We could not dispense with our militia; we have too frequent need of it now. But police defense is not war in the sense in which I have been discussing it. War in the future will be the clash of policies of national vanity and selfishness when they cross each other's path.

If you want war, nourish a doctrine. Doctrines are the most frightful tyrants to which men ever are subject, because doctrines get inside of a man's own reason and betray him against himself. Civilized men have done their fiercest fighting for doctrines. The reconquest of the Holy Sepulcher, "the balance of power," "no universal dominion," "trade follows the flag," "he who holds the land will hold the sea," "the throne and the altar," the revolution, the faith—these are the things for which men have given their lives. What are they all? Nothing but rhetoric and phantasms. Doctrines are always vague; it would ruin a doctrine to define it, because then it could be analyzed, tested, criticized, and verified; but nothing ought to be tolerated which cannot be so tested. Somebody asks you with astonishment and horror whether you do not believe in the Monroe Doctrine. You do not know whether you do or not because you do not know what it is, but you do not dare to say that you do not because you understand that it is one of the things which every good American is bound to believe in. Now when any doctrine arrives at that degree of authority, the name of it is a club which any demagogue may swing over you at any time and apropos of anything. In order to describe a doctrine, we must have recourse to theological language. A doctrine is an article of faith. It is something which

you are bound to believe not because you have some rational grounds for believing it true, but because you belong to such and such a church or denomination. The nearest parallel to it in politics is the "reason of state." The most frightful injustice and cruelty which has ever been perpetrated on earth has been due to the reason of state....

What has just been said suggests a consideration of the popular saying, "In time of peace prepare for war." If you prepare a big army and navy and are all ready for war, it will be easy to go to war; the military and naval men will have a lot of new machines, and they will be eager to see what they can do with them. There is no such thing nowadays as a state of readiness for war. It is a chimera, and the nations which pursue it are falling into an abyss of wasted energy and wealth. When the army is supplied with the latest and best rifles, someone invents a new field gun; then the artillery must be provided with that before we are ready. By the time we get the new gun, somebody has invented a new rifle, and our rival nation is getting that; therefore we must have it—or one a little better. It takes two or three years and several millions to do that. In the meantime somebody proposes a more effective organization which must be introduced; signals, balloons, dogs, bicycles, and every other device and invention must be added, and men must be trained to use them all. There is no state of readiness for war; the notion calls for never-ending sacrifices. It is a fallacy. It is evident that to pursue such a notion with any idea of realizing it would absorb all the resources and activity of the state; this the great European states are now proving by experiment. A wiser rule would be to make up your mind soberly what you want, peace or war, and then to get ready for what you want; for what we prepare for is what we shall get.

Irving Janis

VICTIMS OF GROUPTHINK

The preamble to the UNESCO[4] constitution states that "since wars begin in the minds of men, it is in the minds of men that the defenses of peace must be constructed." This is generally interpreted to mean that all individuals (of both sexes!) are crucial to preventing war. However, some students of peace and war would amend this sentence to begin, "Since wars begin in the minds of the crucial, decisionmaking elite of each country..." It is widely acknowledged that the psychology of decision-making plays a key role in influencing the immediate outcome (although this is not to deny the importance of other factors—historical, economic, sociological, etc.—in setting the stage).

Psychologically minded researchers have identified a number of factors involved in going to war, decisions that have often proved ill-advised not only on moral grounds but also based on their immediate, practical outcomes. Here is but a sample: Robert Jervis has inquired into various patterns of misperception, by which decision-makers labor under inaccurate views of reality. Ole Holsti has investigated the costly consequences of stress during decision making under crisis conditions. Morton Deutsch analyzed the process of hostile interactions by which the mutually reinforcing impressions of adversaries can spiral out of control. Ralph White has pointed out the role of fear and of such "motivated misperceptions" as the "diabolical enemy image" combined with a self-righteous "moral self-image."

Irving Janis, a social psychologist, has provided a great service by identifying an important syndrome, which he calls "groupthink," whereby small groups tend to be vulnerable to a dangerous psychological process. In the following selection, from his book, *Victims of Groupthink*, Janis examines the ill-conceived and ill-fated Bay of Pigs invasion in 1961. More than 40 years after his path-breaking research, Janis's concept of groupthink was revisited to help explain the Bush Administration's invasion of Iraq in 2003.

⸺⸺⸺ ❧ ⸺⸺⸺

NOBODY IS PERFECT

Year after year newscasts and newspapers inform us of collective miscalculations—companies that have unexpectedly gone bankrupt because of misjudging their market, federal agencies that have mistakenly authorized the use of chemical insecticides that poison our environment, and White House executive committees that have made ill-conceived foreign policy decisions that inadvertently bring the major

---

[4] United Nations Educational, Scientific, and Cultural Organization.

powers to the brink of war. Most people, when they hear about such fiascoes, simply remind themselves that, after all, "organizations are run by human beings," "to err is human," and "nobody is perfect." But platitudinous thoughts about human nature do not help us to understand how and why avoidable miscalculations are made.

Fiasco watchers who are unwilling to set the problem aside in this easy fashion will find that contemporary psychology has something to say (unfortunately not very much) about distortions of thinking and other sources of human error. The deficiencies about which we know the most pertain to disturbances in the behavior of each individual in a decision-making group—temporary states of elation, fear, or anger that reduce a person's mental efficiency; chronic blind spots arising from a person's social prejudices; shortcomings in information processing that prevent a person from comprehending the complex consequences of a seemingly simple policy decision. One psychologist has suggested that because the information processing capabilities of every individual are limited, no responsible leader of a large organization ought to make a policy decision without using a computer that is programmed to spell out all the probable benefits and costs of each alternative under consideration. The usual way of trying to counteract the limitations of individuals' mental functioning, however, is to relegate important decisions to groups.

IMPERFECTIONS OF GROUP DECISIONS

Groups, like individuals, have shortcomings. Groups can bring out the worst as well as the best in man. Nietzsche went so far as to say that madness is the exception in individuals but the rule in groups. A considerable amount of social science literature shows that in circumstances of extreme crisis, group contagion occasionally gives rise to collective panic, violent acts of scapegoating, and other forms of what could be called group madness. Much more frequent, however, are instances of mindless conformity and collective misjudgment of serious risks, which are collectively laughed off in a clubby atmosphere of relaxed conviviality. . . .

Lack of vigilance and excessive risk taking are forms of temporary group derangement to which decision-making groups made up of responsible executives are not at all immune. Sometimes the main trouble is that the chief executive manipulates his advisers to rubber-stamp his own ill-conceived proposals. . . . I shall be dealing mainly with a different source of defective decision making, which often involves a much more subtle form of faulty leadership: During the group's deliberations, the leader does not deliberately try to get the group to tell him what he wants to hear but is quite sincere in asking for honest opinions. The group members are not transformed into sycophants. They are not afraid to speak their minds. Nevertheless, subtle constraints, which the leader may reinforce inadvertently, prevent a member from fully exercising his critical powers and from openly expressing doubts when most others in the group appear to have reached a consensus. . . .

I use the term "groupthink" as a quick and easy way to refer to a mode of thinking that people engage in when they are deeply involved in a cohesive in-group, when the members' strivings for unanimity override their motivation to realistically appraise alternative courses of action. "Groupthink" is a term of the same order as the words in the newspeak vocabulary George Orwell presents in his dismaying *1984*—a vocabulary with terms such as "doublethink" and "crimethink." By putting groupthink with those Orwellian words, I realize that groupthink takes on an invidious connotation. The invidiousness is intentional: groupthink refers to a deterioration of mental efficiency, reality testing, and moral judgment that results from in-group pressures. . . .

At least six major defects in decision making contribute to failures to solve problems adequately. First, the group's discussions are limited to a few alternative courses of action (often only two) without a survey of the full range of alternatives. Second, the group fails to reexamine the course of action initially preferred by the majority of members from the standpoint of nonobvious risks and drawbacks that had not been considered when it was originally evaluated. Third, the members neglect courses of action initially evaluated as unsatisfactory by the majority of the group: They spend little or no time discussing whether they have overlooked nonobvious gains or whether there are ways of reducing the seemingly prohibitive costs that had made the alternatives seem undesirable. Fourth, members make little or no attempt to obtain information from experts who can supply sound estimates of losses and gains to be expected from alternative courses of action. Fifth, selective bias is shown in the way the group reacts to factual information and relevant judgments from experts, the mass media, and outside critics. The members show interest in facts and opinions that support their initially preferred policy and take up time in their meetings to discuss them, but they tend to ignore facts and opinions that do not support their initially preferred policy. Sixth, the members spend little time deliberating about how the chosen policy might be hindered by bureaucratic inertia, sabotaged by political opponents, or temporarily derailed by the common accidents that happen to the best of well-laid plans. Consequently, they fail to work out contingency plans to cope with foreseeable setbacks that could endanger the overall success of the chosen course of action.

I assume that these six defects and some related features of inadequate decision-making result from groupthink. But, of course, each of the six can arise from other common causes of human stupidity as well—erroneous intelligence, information overload, fatigue, blinding prejudice, and ignorance. Whether produced by groupthink or by other causes, a decision suffering from most of these defects has relatively little chance of success....

At first I was surprised by the extent to which the groups in the fiascoes I have examined adhered to group norms and pressures toward uniformity. Just as in groups of ordinary citizens, a dominant characteristic appears to be remaining loyal to the group by sticking with the decisions to which the group has committed itself, even when the policy is working badly and has unintended consequences that disturb the conscience of the members. In a sense, members consider loyalty to the group the highest form of morality. That loyalty requires each member to avoid raising controversial issues, questioning weak arguments, or calling a halt to softheaded thinking.

Paradoxically, softheaded groups are likely to be extremely hard-hearted toward out-groups and enemies. In dealing with a rival nation, policy makers comprising an amiable group find it relatively easy to authorize dehumanizing solutions such as large-scale bombings. An affable group of government officials is unlikely to pursue the difficult and controversial issues that arise when alternatives to a harsh military solution come up for discussion. Nor are the members inclined to raise ethical issues that imply that this "fine group of ours, with its humanitarianism and its high-minded principles, might be capable of adopting a course of action that is inhumane and immoral."

Many other sources of human error can prevent government leaders from arriving at well worked out decisions, resulting in failures to achieve their practical objectives and violations of their own standards of ethical conduct. But, unlike groupthink, these other sources of error do not typically entail increases in hard-heartedness along with softheadedness. Some errors involve blind spots that stem from the personality of the decision-makers. Special circumstances produce unusual fatigue and emotional stresses that interfere with efficient decision making. Numerous institutional features of the social structure in which the group is located may also cause inefficiency and prevent adequate communication with experts. In addition, well-known interferences with sound thinking arise when the decision-makers comprise a noncohesive group. For example, when the members have no sense of loyalty to the group and regard themselves merely as representatives of different departments, with clashing interests, the meetings may become bitter power struggles, at the expense of effective decision making.

The concept of groupthink pinpoints an entirely different source of trouble, residing neither in the individual nor in the organizational setting. Over and beyond all the familiar sources of human error is a powerful source of defective judgment that arises in cohesive groups—the concurrence-seeking tendency, which fosters overoptimism, lack of vigilance, and sloganistic thinking about the weakness and immorality of out-groups. This tendency can take its toll even when the decision-makers are conscientious statesmen trying to make the best possible decisions for their country and for all mankind.

I do not mean to imply that all cohesive groups suffer from groupthink, though all may display its symptoms from time to time. Nor should we infer from the term "groupthink" that group decisions are typically inefficient or harmful. On the contrary, a group whose members have properly defined roles, with traditions and standard operating procedures that facilitate critical inquiry, is probably capable of making better decisions than any individual in the group who works on the problem alone. And yet the advantages of having decisions made by groups are often lost because of psychological pressures that arise when the members work closely together, share the same values, and above all face a crisis situation in which everyone is subjected to stresses that generate a strong need for affiliation. In these circumstances, as conformity pressures begin to dominate, groupthink and the attendant deterioration of decision-making set in.

The central theme of my analysis can be summarized in this generalization, which I offer in the spirit of Parkinson's laws: *The more amiability and esprit de corps among the members of a policymaking ingroup, the greater is the danger that independent critical thinking will be replaced by groupthink, which is likely to result in irrational and dehumanizing actions directed against out-groups. . . .*

The Kennedy administration's Bay of Pigs decision ranks among the worst fiascoes ever perpetrated by a responsible government. Planned by an overambitious, eager group of American intelligence officers who had little background or experience in military matters, the attempt to place a small brigade of Cuban exiles secretly on a beachhead in Cuba with the ultimate aim of overthrowing the government of Fidel Castro proved to be a "perfect failure." The group that made the basic decision to approve the invasion plan included some of the most intelligent men ever to participate in the councils of government. Yet all the major assumptions supporting the plan were so completely wrong that the venture

began to founder at the outset and failed in its earliest stages.

THE "ILL-STARRED ADVENTURE"

Ironically, the idea for the invasion was first suggested by John F. Kennedy's main political opponent, Richard M. Nixon. As vice president during the Eisenhower administration, Nixon had proposed that the United States government secretly send a trained group of Cuban exiles to Cuba to fight against Castro. In March 1960, acting on Nixon's suggestion, President Dwight D. Eisenhower directed the Central Intelligence Agency to organize Cuban exiles in the United States into a unified political movement against the Castro regime and to give military training to those who were willing to return to their homeland to engage in guerrilla warfare. The CIA put a large number of its agents to work on this clandestine operation, and they soon evolved an elaborate plan for a military invasion. Apparently without informing President Eisenhower, the CIA began to assume in late 1960 that they could land a brigade of Cuban exiles not as a band of guerrilla infiltrators but as an armed force to carry out a full-scale invasion.

Two days after the inauguration in January 1961, President John F. Kennedy and several leading members of his new administration were given a detailed briefing about the proposed invasion by Allen Dulles, head of the CIA, and General Lyman Lemnitzer, chairman of the Joint Chiefs of Staff. During the next eighty days, a core group of presidential advisers repeatedly discussed this inherited plan informally and in the meetings of an advisory committee that included three Joint Chiefs of Staff. In early April 1961, at one of the meetings with the president, all the key advisers gave their approval to the CIA's invasion plan. Their deliberations led to a few modifications of details, such as the choice of the invasion site.

On April 17, 1961, the brigade of about fourteen hundred Cuban exiles, aided by the United States Navy, Air Force, and the CIA, invaded the swampy coast of Cuba at the Bay of Pigs. Nothing went as planned. On the first day, not one of the four ships containing reserve ammunition and supplies arrived;

the first two were sunk by a few planes in Castro's air force, and the other two promptly fled. By the second day, the brigade was completely surrounded by twenty thousand troops of Castro's well-equipped army. By the third day, about twelve hundred members of the brigade, comprising almost all who had not been killed, were captured and ignominiously led off to prison camps....

An important symptom of groupthink is the illusion of being invulnerable to the main dangers that might arise from a risky action in which the group is strongly tempted to engage. Essentially, the notion is that "If our leader and everyone else in our group decides that it is okay, the plan is bound to succeed. Even if it is quite risky, luck will be on our side." A sense of "unlimited confidence" was widespread among the "New Frontiersmen" as soon as they took over their high government posts, according to a Justice Department confidant, with whom Robert Kennedy discussed the secret CIA plan on the day it was launched:

> It seemed that, with John Kennedy leading us and with all the talent he had assembled, *nothing could stop us*. We believed that if we faced up to the nation's problems and applied bold, new ideas with common sense and hard work, we would overcome whatever challenged us....

Once this euphoric phase takes hold, decision making for everyday activities, as well as long-range planning, is likely to be seriously impaired. The members of a cohesive group become very reluctant to carry out the unpleasant task of critically assessing the limits of their power and the real losses that could arise if their luck does not hold. They tend to examine each risk in black-and-white terms. If it does not seem overwhelmingly dangerous, they are inclined simply to forget about it, instead of developing contingency plans in case it materializes. The group members know that no one among them is a superman, but they feel that somehow the group is a supergroup, capable of surmounting all risks that stand in the way of carrying out any desired course of action: "Nothing can stop us!" Athletic teams and military combat units may often benefit from members' enthusiastic confidence in the power and luck

of their group. But policymaking committees usually do not.

We would not expect sober government officials to experience such exuberant esprit de corps, but a subdued form of the same tendency may have been operating—inclining the president's advisers to become reluctant about examining the drawbacks of the invasion plan. In group meetings, this groupthink tendency can operate like a low-level noise that prevents warning signals from being heeded. Everyone becomes somewhat biased in the direction of selectively attending to the messages that feed into the members' shared feelings of confidence and optimism, disregarding those that do not....

In a concurrence-seeking group, there is relatively little healthy skepticism of the glib ideological formulas on which rational policymakers, like many other people who share their nationalistic goals, generally rely in order to maintain self-confidence and cognitive mastery over the complexities of international politics. One of the symptoms of groupthink is the members' persistence in conveying to each other the cliché and oversimplified images of political enemies embodied in long-standing ideological stereotypes. Throughout their deliberations they use the same old stereotypes, instead of developing differentiated concepts derived from an openminded inquiry enabling them to discern which of their original ideological assumptions, if any, apply to the foreign policy issue at hand. Except in unusual circumstances of crisis, the members of a concurrence-seeking group tend to view any antagonistic out-group against whom they are plotting not only as immoral but also as weak and stupid. These wishful beliefs continue to dominate their thinking until an unequivocal defeat proves otherwise, whereupon—like Kennedy and his advisers—they are shocked at the discrepancy between their stereotyped conceptions and actuality....

The sense of group unity concerning the advisability of going ahead with the CIA's invasion plan appears to have been based on superficial appearances of complete concurrence, achieved at the cost of self-censorship of misgivings by several of the members. From post-mortem discussions with participants, Sorensen concluded that among the men in the State Department, as well as those on the White House staff, "doubts were entertained but never pressed, partly out of a fear of being labelled 'soft' or undaring in the eyes of their colleagues." Schlesinger was not at all hesitant about presenting his strong objections in a memorandum he gave to the president and the secretary of state. But he became keenly aware of his tendency to suppress objections when he attended the White House meetings of the Kennedy team, with their atmosphere of assumed consensus:

> In the months after the Bay of Pigs I bitterly reproached myself for having kept so silent during those crucial discussions in the Cabinet Room, though my feelings of guilt were tempered by the knowledge that a course of objection would have accomplished little save to *gain me a name as a nuisance.* . . .

Schlesinger says that when the Cuban invasion plan was being presented to the group, "virile poses" were conveyed in the rhetoric used by the representatives of the CIA and the Joint Chiefs of Staff. He thought the State Department representatives and others responded by becoming anxious to show that they were not softheaded idealists but really were just as tough as the military men. Schlesinger's references to the "virile" stance of the militant advocates of the invasion plan suggest that the members of Kennedy's in-group may have been concerned about protecting the leader from being embarrassed by their voicing "unvirile" concerns about the high risks of the venture. . . .

At a large birthday party for his wife, Robert Kennedy, who had been constantly informed about the Cuban invasion plan, took Schlesinger aside and asked him why he was opposed. The president's brother listened coldly and then said, "You may be right or you may be wrong, but the president has made his mind up. Don't push it any further. Now is the time for everyone to help him all they can." Here is another symptom of groupthink, displayed by a highly intelligent man whose ethical code committed him to freedom of dissent. What he was saying,

in effect, was, "You may well be right about the dangerous risks, but I don't give a damn about that; all of us should help our leader right now by not sounding any discordant notes that would interfere with the harmonious support he should have."

When Robert Kennedy told Schlesinger to lay off, he was functioning in a self-appointed role that I call being a "mindguard." Just as a bodyguard protects the president and other high officials from injurious physical assaults, a mindguard protects them from thoughts that might damage their confidence in the soundness of the policies to which they are committed or to which they are about to commit themselves. . . .

The group pressures that help to maintain a group's illusions are sometimes fostered by various leadership practices, some of which involve subtle ways of making it difficult for those who question the initial consensus to suggest alternatives and to raise critical issues. The group's agenda can readily be manipulated by a suave leader, often with the tacit approval of the members, so that there is simply no opportunity to discuss the drawbacks of a seemingly satisfactory plan of action. This is one of the conditions that fosters groupthink.

President Kennedy, as leader at the meetings in the White House, was probably more active than anyone else in raising skeptical questions; yet he seems to have encouraged the group's docility and uncritical acceptance of the defective arguments in favor of the CIA's plan. At each meeting, instead of opening up the agenda to permit a full airing of the opposing considerations, he allowed the CIA representatives to dominate the entire discussion. The president permitted them to refute immediately each tentative doubt that one of the others might express, instead of asking whether anyone else had the same doubt or wanted to pursue the implications of the new worrisome issue that had been raised. . . .

Although the available evidence consists of fragmentary and somewhat biased accounts of the deliberations of the White House group, it nevertheless reveals gross miscalculations and converges on the symptoms of groupthink. My tentative conclusion is that President Kennedy and the policy advisers who decided to accept the CIA's plan were victims of groupthink. If the facts I have culled from the accounts given by Schlesinger, Sorensen, and other observers are essentially accurate, the groupthink hypothesis makes more understandable the deficiencies in the government's decision making that led to the enormous gap between conception and actuality.

The failure of Kennedy's inner circle to detect any of the false assumptions behind the Bay of Pigs invasion plan can be at least partially accounted for by the group's tendency to seek concurrence at the expense of seeking information, critical appraisal, and debate. The concurrence-seeking tendency was manifested by shared illusions and other symptoms, which helped the members to maintain a sense of group solidarity. Most crucial were the symptoms that contributed to complacent overconfidence in the face of vague uncertainties and explicit warnings that should have alerted the members to the risks of the clandestine military operation—an operation so ill-conceived that among literate people all over the world the name of the invasion site has become the very symbol of perfect failure.

Michael Howard

THE CAUSES OF WAR

The defining quality of war is violence: organized, armed violence on the part of large groups of people. Yet, war does not always involve strong, out-of-control emotion. For soldiers, boredom (either repetitive drill or prolonged periods of inaction) is typically more prominent than "action," such that actual combat is sometimes seen as a relief. It has also been argued that for political and military elites as well, war-making is more likely to involve a reasoned decision than a spasm of aggressiveness.

Deterrence—whether nuclear or nonnuclear—is supposed to rely on such a careful, rational calculus, in which a would-be aggressor is expected to be "deterred" by recognizing that the cost of launching a war will be greater than any potential benefits that might accrue. The thinking is similar to the so-called "rational actor" model used by economists, in which consumers are expected to get the maximum value for their money, and businesses are predicted to behave in a way that (rationally) maximizes their profits. It is, of course, debatable whether human beings limit their motivations to such dry and reasoned decisions, especially when issues of pride, prestige, fear, hope, revenge, anger, and so on—not to mention life and death!—are involved. There is also the fact that whatever their "best judgment," people are prone to making mistakes. Among other things, because most wars do not end in a tie, roughly half the participants were incorrect if they assumed they would win. Further, wars may begin in the reasoned hope of generating greater political support and internal cohesiveness within a country, although as they drag on, they often become destabilizing instead.

In any event, historians and political scientists in particular have been partial to emphasizing the role of coolly reasoned, hardheaded "realpolitik," or "power politics," in the causation of war. In his book *On War*, Carl von Clausewitz, Prussian spokesperson for the military aspects of realpolitik, made the renowned observation that war is "the continuation of politics by other means." For Clausewitz, war, although often brutal, should not be senseless but rather "an act of violence to compel the enemy to fulfill our will."

In this view, war is merely one of many tools employed by politicians and strategists. This is essentially the perspective of most conservative students of war, including British military historian Michael Howard.

It is true, and it is important to bear in mind…that before 1914 war was almost universally considered an acceptable, perhaps an inevitable and for many people a desirable, way of settling international differences, and that the war generally foreseen was expected to be, if not exactly brisk and cheerful, then certainly brief; no longer, certainly, than the war of 1870 between France and Prussia that was consciously or unconsciously taken by that generation as a model. Had it not been so generally felt that war was an acceptable and tolerable way of solving international disputes, statesmen and soldiers would no doubt have approached the crisis of 1914 in a very different fashion.

But there was nothing new about this attitude to war. Statesmen had always been able to assume that war would be acceptable at least to those sections of their populations whose opinion mattered to them, and in this respect the decision to go to war in 1914—for continental statesmen at least—in no way differed from those taken by their predecessors of earlier generations. The causes of the Great War are thus in essence no more complex or profound than those of any previous European war, or indeed than those described by Thucydides as underlying the Peloponnesian War: "What made war inevitable was the growth of Athenian power and the fear this caused in Sparta." In Central Europe, there was the German fear that the disintegration of the Habsburg Empire would result in an enormous enhancement of Russian power—power already becoming formidable as French-financed industries and railways put Russian manpower at the service of her military machine. In Western

Europe, there was the traditional British fear that Germany might establish a hegemony over Europe which, even more than that of Napoleon, would place at risk the security of Britain and her own possessions, a fear fueled by the knowledge that there was within Germany a widespread determination to achieve a world status comparable with her latent power. Considerations of this kind had caused wars in Europe often enough before. Was there really anything different about 1914?

Ever since the eighteenth century, war had been blamed by intellectuals upon the stupidity or the self-interest of governing elites (as it is now blamed upon "military-industrial complexes"), with the implicit or explicit assumption that if the control of state affairs were in the hands of sensible men—businessmen, as Richard Cobden thought, the workers, as Jean Jaurès thought—then wars would be no more.

By the twentieth century, the growth of the social and biological sciences was producing alternative explanations. As Quincy Wright expressed it in his massive *A Study of War* (1942), "Scientific investigators…tended to attribute war to immaturities in social knowledge and control, as one might attribute epidemics to insufficient medical knowledge or to inadequate public health services." The Social Darwinian acceptance of the inevitability of struggle, indeed of its desirability if mankind was to progress, the view, expressed by the elder Moltke but very widely shared at the turn of the century, that perpetual peace was a dream and not even a beautiful dream, did not survive the Great War in those countries where the bourgeois-liberal culture was dominant, Britain and the United States. The failure of these nations to appreciate that such bellicist views, or variants of them, were still widespread in other areas of the world, those dominated by Fascism and by Marxism-Leninism, was to cause embarrassing misunderstandings, and possibly still does.

For liberal intellectuals, war was self-evidently a pathological aberration from the norm, at best a ghastly mistake, at worst a crime. Those who initiated wars must in their view have been criminal, or sick, or the victims of forces beyond their power to control. Those who were so accused disclaimed responsibility for the events of 1914, throwing it on others or saying the whole thing was a terrible mistake for which no one was to blame. None of them, with their societies in ruins around them and tens of millions dead, were prepared to say courageously: "We only acted as statesmen always have in the past. In the circumstances then prevailing, war seemed to us to be the best way of protecting or forwarding the national interests for which we were responsible. There was an element of risk, certainly, but the risk might have been greater had we postponed the issue. Our real guilt does not lie in the fact that we started the war. It lies in our mistaken belief that we could win it."

The trouble is that if we are to regard war as pathological and abnormal, then all conflict must be similarly regarded; for war is only a particular kind of conflict between a particular category of social groups: sovereign states. It is, as Clausewitz put it, "a clash between major interests that is resolved by bloodshed—that is the only way in which it differs from other conflicts." If one had no sovereign states, one would have no wars, as Rousseau rightly pointed out—but, as Hobbes equally rightly pointed out, we would probably have no peace either. As states acquire a monopoly of violence, war becomes the only remaining form of conflict that may legitimately be settled by physical force. The mechanism

of legitimization of authority and of social control that makes it possible for a state to moderate or eliminate conflicts within its borders or at very least to ensure that these are not conducted by competitive violence—the mechanism to the study of which historians have quite properly devoted so much attention—makes possible the conduct of armed conflict with other states, and on occasion—if the state is to survive—makes it necessary.

These conflicts arise from conflicting claims, or interests, or ideologies, or perceptions; and these perceptions may indeed be fueled by social or psychological drives that we do not fully understand and that one day we may learn rather better how to control. But the problem is the control of social conflict *as such*, not simply of war. However inchoate or disreputable the motives for war may be, its initiation is almost by definition a deliberate and carefully considered act and its conduct, at least at the more advanced levels of social development, a matter of very precise central control. If history shows any record of "accidental" wars, I have yet to find them. Certainly statesmen have sometimes been surprised by the nature of the war they have unleashed, and it is reasonable to assume that in at least 50 percent of the cases they got a result they did not expect. But that is not the same as a war begun by mistake and continued with no political purpose.

Statesmen in fact go to war to achieve very specific ends, and the reasons for which states have fought one another have been categorized and recategorized innumerable times. Vattel, the Swiss lawyer, divided them into the necessary, the customary, the rational, and the capricious. Jomini, the Swiss strategist, identified ideological, economic, and popular wars, wars to defend the balance of power, wars to assist allies, wars to assert or to defend rights. Quincy Wright, the American political scientist, divided them into the idealistic, the psychological, the political, and the juridical. Bernard Brodie in our own times has refused to discriminate: "Any theory of the causes of war in general or any war in particular that is not inherently eclectic and comprehensive," he stated, "...is bound for that very reason to be wrong." Another contemporary analyst, Geoffrey Blainey, is on the contrary unashamedly reductionist. All war aims, he wrote, "are simply varieties of power. The vanity of nationalism, the will to spread an ideology, the protection of kinsmen in an adjacent land, the desire for more territory...all these represent power in different wrappings. The conflicting aims of rival nations are always conflicts of power."

In principle, I am sure that Bernard Brodie was right: no single explanation for conflict between states, any more than for conflict between any other social groups, is likely to stand up to critical examination. But Blainey is right as well. Quincy Wright provided us with a useful indicator when he suggested that "while animal war is a function of instinct and primitive war of the mores, civilized war is primarily a function of state politics."

Medievalists will perhaps bridle at the application of the term "primitive" to the sophisticated and subtle societies of the Middle Ages, for whom war was also a "function of the mores," a way of life that often demanded only the most banal of justifications. As a way of life, it persisted in Europe well into the seventeenth century, if no later. For Louis XIV and his court war was, in the early years at least, little more than a seasonal variation on hunting. But by the eighteenth century, the mood had changed. For Frederick the Great, war was to be preeminently a function of *Staatspolitik,* and so it has remained ever since. And although statesmen can be as emotional or as prejudiced in their judgments as any other group of human beings, it is very seldom that their attitudes, their perceptions, and their decisions are not related, however remotely, to the fundamental issues of *power,* that capacity to control their environment on which the independent existence of their states and often the cultural values of their societies depend.

And here perhaps we do find a factor that sets interstate conflict somewhat apart from other forms of social rivalry. States may fight—indeed as often as not they do fight—not over any specific issue such as might otherwise have been resolved by peaceful means, but in order to acquire, to enhance, or to preserve their capacity to function as independent actors in the international system at all. "The stakes of war," as Raymond Aron has reminded us, "are the existence, the creation, or the elimination of States." It is a somber analysis, but one which the historical record very amply bears out.

It is here that those analysts who come to the study of war from the disciplines of the natural sciences, particularly the biological sciences, tend, it seems to me, to go astray. The conflicts between states which have usually led to war have normally arisen, not from any irrational and emotive drives, but from almost a superabundance of analytic rationality. Sophisticated communities (one hesitates to apply to them Quincy Wright's word, "civilized") do not react simply to immediate threats. Their intelligence (and I use the term in its double sense) enables them to assess the implications that any event taking place anywhere in the world, however remote, may have for their own capacity, immediately to exert influence, ultimately perhaps to survive. In the later Middle Ages and the early Modern period, every child born to every prince anywhere in Europe was registered on the delicate seismographs that monitored the shifts in dynastic power. Every marriage was a diplomatic triumph or disaster. Every stillbirth, as Henry VIII knew, could presage political catastrophe.

Today, the key events may be different. The pattern remains the same. A malfunction in the political mechanism of some remote African community, a coup d'état in a minuscule Caribbean republic, an insurrection deep in the hinterland of Southeast Asia, an assassination in some emirate in the Middle East—all these will be subjected to the kind of anxious examination and calculation that was devoted a hundred years ago to the news of comparable events in the Balkans: an insurrection in Philippopoli, a coup d'état in Constantinople, an assassination in Belgrade. To whose advantage will this ultimately redound, asked the worried diplomats, ours or *theirs?* Little enough in itself, perhaps, but will it not precipitate or strengthen a trend, set in motion a tide whose melancholy withdrawing roar will strip us of our friends and influence and leave us isolated in a world dominated by adversaries deeply hostile to us and all that we stand for?

There have certainly been occasions when states have gone to war in a mood of ideological fervor like the French republican armies in 1792; or of swaggering aggression like the Americans against Spain in 1898 or the British against the Boers a year later; or to make more money, as did the British in the War of Jenkins' Ear in 1739; or in a generous desire to help peoples of similar creed or race, as perhaps the Russians did in helping the Bulgarians fight the Turks in 1877 and the British dominions certainly did in 1914 and 1939. But, in general, men have fought during the past two hundred years neither because they are aggressive nor because they are acquisitive animals, but because they are reasoning ones: because they discern, or believe that they can discern, dangers before they become immediate, the possibility of threats before they are made.

But be this as it may, in 1914 many of the German people, and in 1939 nearly all of the British, felt justified in going to war, not over any specific issue that could have been settled by negotiation, but *to maintain their power;* and to do so while it was still possible, before they found themselves so isolated, so impotent, that they had no power left to maintain and had to accept a subordinate position within an international system dominated by their adversaries. "What made war inevitable was the growth of Athenian power and the fear this caused in Sparta." Or, to quote another grimly apt passage from Thucydides:

> The Athenians made their Empire more and more strong...[until] finally the point was reached when Athenian strength attained a peak plain for all to see and the Athenians began to encroach upon Sparta's allies. It was at this point that Sparta felt the position to be no longer tolerable and decided by starting the present war to employ all her energies in attacking and if possible destroying the power of Athens.

You can vary the names of the actors, but the model remains a valid one for the purposes of our analysis. I am rather afraid that it still does.

Something that has changed since the time of Thucydides, however, is the nature of the power that appears so threatening. From the time of Thucydides until that of Louis XIV, there was basically only one source of political and military power—control of territory, with all the resources in wealth and manpower that this provided. This control might come through conquest, or through alliance, or through marriage, or through purchase, but the power of princes could be very exactly computed in terms of the extent of their territories and the number of men they could put under arms.

In seventeenth-century Europe, this began to change. Extent of territory remained important, but no less important was the effectiveness with which the resources of that territory could be exploited. Initially there were the bureaucratic and fiscal mechanisms that transformed loose bonds of territorial authority into highly structured centralized states whose armed forces, though not necessarily large, were permanent, disciplined, and paid.

Then came the political transformations of the revolutionary era that made available to these state systems the entire manpower of their country, or at least as much of it as the administrators were able to handle. And finally came the revolution in transport, the railways of the nineteenth century that turned the revolutionary ideal of the "Nation in Arms" into a reality. By the early twentieth century, military power—on the continent of Europe, at least—was seen as a simple combination of military manpower and railways. The quality of armaments was of secondary importance, and political intentions were virtually excluded from account. The growth of power was measured in terms of the growth of populations and of communications; of the number of men who could be put under arms and transported to the battlefield to make their weight felt in the initial and presumably decisive battles. It was the mutual perception of threat in those terms that turned Europe before 1914 into an armed camp, and it was their calculations within this framework that reduced German staff officers increasingly to despair and launched their leaders on their catastrophic gamble in 1914, which started the First World War.

But already the development of weapons technology had introduced yet another element into the international power calculus, one that has in our own age become dominant. It was only in the course of the nineteenth century that technology began to produce weapons systems—initially in the form of naval vessels—that could be seen as likely in themselves to prove decisive, through their qualitative and quantitative superiority, in the event of conflict. But as war became increasingly a matter of competing technologies rather than competing armies, so there developed that escalatory process known as the "arms race." As a title, the phrase, like so many coined by journalists to catch the eye, is misleading.

"Arms races" are in fact continuing and open-ended attempts to match power for power. They are as much means of achieving stable or, if possible, favorable power balances as were the dynastic marriage policies of Valois and Habsburg. To suggest that they in themselves are causes of war implies a naive if not totally mistaken view of the relationship between the two phenomena. The causes of war remain rooted, as much as they were in the preindustrial age, in perceptions by statesmen of the growth of hostile power and the fears for the restriction, if not the extinction, of their own. The threat, or rather the fear, has not changed, whether it comes from aggregations of territory or from dreadnoughts, from the numbers of men under arms or from missile systems. The means that states employ to sustain or to extend their power may have been transformed, but their objectives and preoccupations remain the same.

"Arms races" can no more be isolated than wars themselves from the political circumstances that give rise to them, and like wars they will take as many different forms as political circumstances dictate. They may be no more than a process of competitive modernization, of maintaining a status quo that commands general support but in which no participant wishes, whether from reasons of pride or of prudence, to fall behind in keeping his armory up to date. If there are no political causes for fear or rivalry, this process need not in itself be a destabilizing factor in international relations. But arms races may, on the other hand, be the result of a quite deliberate assertion of an intention to *change* the status quo, as was, for example, the German naval challenge to Britain at the beginning of this century.

This challenge was an explicit attempt by Admiral Alfred von Tirpitz and his associates to destroy the hegemonic position at sea which Britain saw as essential to her security, and, not inconceivably, to replace it with one of their own. As British and indeed German diplomats repeatedly explained to the German government, it was not the German naval program in itself that gave rise to so much alarm in Britain. It was the intention that lay behind it. If the status quo was to be maintained, the German challenge had to be met.

The naval race could quite easily have been ended on one of two conditions. Either the Germans could have abandoned their challenge, as had the French in the previous century, and acquiesced in British naval supremacy; or the British could have yielded as gracefully as they did, a decade or so later, to the United States and abandoned a status they no longer had the capacity, or the will, to maintain. As it was, they saw the German challenge as one to which they could and should respond, and their power position as one which they were prepared, if necessary, to use force to preserve. The British naval program was thus, like that of the Germans, a signal of political intent; and that intent, that refusal to acquiesce in a fundamental transformation of the power balance, was indeed a major element among the causes of the war. The naval competition provided a very accurate indication and measurement of political rivalries and tensions, but it did not cause them; nor could it have been abated unless the rivalries themselves had been abandoned.

It was the general perception of the growth of German power that was awakened by the naval challenge, and the fear that a German hegemony on the Continent would be the first step to a challenge to her own hegemony on the oceans, that led Britain to involve herself in the continental conflict in 1914 on the side of France and Russia. "What made war inevitable was the growth of *Spartan* power," to reword Thucydides, "and the fear which this caused in *Athens.*" In the Great War that followed, Germany was defeated, but survived with none of her latent power destroyed. A "false hegemony" of Britain and France was established in Europe that could last only so long as Germany did not again mobilize her resources to challenge it. German rearmament in the 1930s did not of itself mean that Hitler wanted war (though one has to ignore his entire philosophy if one is to believe that he did not); but it did mean that he was determined, with a great deal of popular support, to obtain a free hand on the international scene.

With that free hand, he intended to establish German power on an irreversible basis; this was the message conveyed by his armament program. The armament program that the British reluctantly adopted in reply was intended to show that, rather than submit to the hegemonic aspirations they feared from such a revival of German power, they would fight to preserve their own freedom of action. Once again to recast Thucydides:

> Finally the point was reached when German strength attained a peak plain for all to see, and the Germans began to encroach upon Britain's allies. It was at this point that Britain felt the position to be no longer tolerable and decided by starting this present war to employ all her energies in attacking and if possible destroying the power of Germany.

What the Second World War established was not a new British hegemony, but a Soviet hegemony over the Euro-Asian landmass from the Elbe to Vladivostok; and that was seen, at least from Moscow, as an American hegemony over the rest of the world; one freely accepted in Western Europe as a preferable alternative to being absorbed by the rival hegemony. Rival armaments were developed to define and preserve the new territorial boundaries, and . . . arms competition began. . . .

The trouble is that what is seen by one party as the breaking of an alien hegemony and the establishment of equal status will be seen by the incumbent powers as a striving for the establishment of an alternate hegemony, and they are not necessarily wrong. In international politics, the appetite often comes with eating; and there really may be no way to check an aspiring rival except by the mobilization of stronger military power. An arms race then becomes almost a necessary surrogate for war, a test of national will and strength; and arms control becomes possible only when the underlying power balance has been mutually agreed.

We would be blind, therefore, if we did not recognize that the causes which have produced war in the past are operating in our own day as powerfully as at any time in history. . . .

But times *have* changed since Thucydides. They have changed even since 1914. These were, as we have seen, bellicist societies in which war was a normal, acceptable, even a desirable way of settling differences. The question that arises today is, how widely and evenly spread is that intense revulsion against war that at present characterizes our own society? For if war is indeed now *universally* seen as being unacceptable as an instrument of policy, then all analogies drawn from the past are misleading, and although power struggles may continue, they will be diverted into other channels. But if that revulsion is not evenly spread, societies which continue to see armed force as an acceptable means for attaining their political ends are likely to establish a dominance over those which do not. Indeed, they will not necessarily have to fight for it.

My second and concluding point is this: whatever may be the underlying causes of international conflict, even if we accept the role of atavistic militarism or of military-industrial complexes or of sociobiological drives or of domestic tensions in fueling it, wars begin with conscious and reasoned decisions based on the calculation, made by *both* parties, that they can achieve more by going to war than by remaining at peace.

Johan Galtung

A STRUCTURAL THEORY OF IMPERIALISM

What about social and economic factors? It seems likely that poverty, for example, can lead to anger, desperation, and willingness to go to war. However, poor countries are not especially likely to make war on richer countries, seeking their wealth; if anything, national poverty may be a restraint on war-making because military forces require expensive high-tech weaponry. The opposite is more likely: wealthy countries attacking poorer ones, not only because they feel that they can get away with it but also out of fear that nearby "hungry" states are ultimately threatening to their security.

At the same time, poverty, and being exploited and oppressed generally, appears to predispose to civil wars and revolutionary unrest. (This, in turn, poses an important question: What about wars of national liberation or those to end oppression and exploitation?) Traditional Marxist—especially Leninist—doctrine states that imperialism drives capitalist states to make war on each other when their extraterritorial ambitions collide. Another perspective emphasizes the role of a promilitary elite, later extended to include military-industrial complexes, in which professional soldiers, politicians, and industrialists promote antagonism among states to enhance their own careers and profits.

In the following excerpt, famed peace researcher Johan Galtung addresses traditional concerns about imperialism and colonialism. His analysis applies more broadly, however, to economic underdevelopment and inequality in general.

This theory takes as its point of departure two of the most glaring facts about this world: the tremendous inequality, within and between nations, in almost all aspects of human living conditions, including the power to decide over those living conditions; *and* the resistance of this inequality to change. The world consists of Center and Periphery nations; and each nation, in turn, has its centers and periphery. Hence, our concern is with the mechanism underlying this discrepancy, particularly between the center in the Center, and the periphery in the Periphery. In other words, how to conceive of, how to explain, and how to counteract inequality as one of the major forms of *structural violence*. Any theory of liberation from structural violence presupposes theoretically and practically adequate ideas of the dominance system against which the liberation is directed; and the special type of dominance system to be discussed here is *imperialism*.

Imperialism will be conceived of as a dominance relation between collectivities, particularly between nations. It is a sophisticated type of dominance relation which cuts across nations, basing itself on a bridgehead which the center in the Center nation establishes in the center of the Periphery nation, for the joint benefit of both. It should not be confused with other ways in which one collectivity can dominate another in the sense of exercising power over it. Thus, a military occupation of B by A may seriously curtail B's freedom of action, but is not for that reason an imperialist relationship unless it is set up in a special way. The same applies to the *threat* of conquest and possible occupation, as in a balance of power relationship. Moreover, *subversive* activities may also be brought to a stage where a nation is dominated by the pinpricks exercised against it from below, but this is clearly different from imperialism.

Thus, imperialism is a species in a genus of dominance and power relationships. It is a subtype of something and has itself subtypes to be explored later. Dominance relations between nations and other collectivities will not disappear with the disappearance of imperialism; nor will the end to one type of imperialism (e.g., political or economic) guarantee the end to another type of imperialism (e.g., economic or cultural). Our view is not reductionist in the traditional sense pursued in Marxist-Leninist theory, which conceives of imperialism as an economic relationship under private capitalism, motivated by the need for expanding markets, and which bases the theory of dominance on a theory of imperialism. According to this view, imperialism and dominance will fall like dominoes when the capitalistic conditions for economic imperialism no longer obtain. According to the view we develop here, imperialism is a more general structural relationship between two collectivities and has to be understood at a general level in order to be understood and counteracted in its more specific manifestations—just like smallpox is better understood in a context of a theory of epidemic diseases, and these diseases better understood in a context of general pathology.

Briefly stated, imperialism is a system that splits up collectivities and relates some of the parts to each other in relations of *harmony of interest*, and other parts in relations of *disharmony of interest*, or *conflict of interest*....

"Conflict of interest" is a special case of conflict in general, defined as a situation where parties are pursuing incompatible goals. In our special case,

these goals are stipulated by an outsider as the "true" interests of the parties, disregarding wholly or completely what the parties themselves say explicitly are the values they pursue....

Let us conclude this discussion by pointing out that a gap in living condition, or at least one important kind, is a necessary, if not sufficient, condition for conflict or disharmony of interest. If in addition the gap can be observed over time, a more satisfactory basis for a diagnosis in terms of imperialism may emerge.

...In our two-nation world, imperialism can be defined as one way in which the Center nation has power over the Periphery nation, so as to bring about a condition of disharmony of interest between them. Concretely, *Imperialism* is a relation between a Center and a Periphery nation so that

1. there is *harmony of interest* between the *center in the Center* nation and the *center in the Periphery* nation,
2. there is more *disharmony of interest* within the Periphery nation than within the Center nations,
3. there is *disharmony of interest* between the *periphery in the Center* nation and the *periphery in the Periphery* nation.

Diagrammatically it looks something like Figure 1. This complex definition, borrowing largely from Lenin, needs spelling out. The basic idea is, as mentioned, that the center in the Center nation has a bridgehead in the Periphery nation, and a well-chosen one: the center in the Periphery nation. This is established such that the Periphery center is tied to the

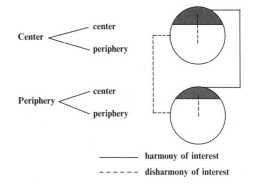

FIGURE I The Structure of Imperialism.

Center center with the best possible tie: the tie of harmony of interest. They are linked so that they go up together and down, even under, together. How this is done in concrete terms will be explored in the subsequent sections.

Inside the two nations there is disharmony of interest.... Moreover, the gap is not decreasing, but is at best constant. But the basic idea, absolutely fundamental for the whole theory to be developed, is that *there is more disharmony in the Periphery nation than in the Center nation*. At the simplest static level of description this means there is more inequality in the Periphery than in the Center. At the more complex level we might talk in terms of the gap opening more quickly in the Periphery than in the Center, where it might even remain constant. Through welfare state activities, redistribution takes place and disharmony is reduced for at least some dimensions, including income, but usually excluding power.

If we now would capture in a few sentences what imperialism is about, we might perhaps say something like this:

In the Periphery nation, the center grows more than the periphery, due partly to how interaction between center and periphery is organized. Without necessarily thinking of economic interaction, the center is more enriched than the periphery—in ways to be explored below. However, for part of this enrichment, the center in the Periphery only serves as a transmission belt (e.g., as commercial firms, trading companies) for value (e.g., raw materials) forwarded to the Center nation. This value enters the Center in the center, with some of it drizzling down to the periphery in the Center. Importantly, there is less disharmony of interest in the Center than in the Periphery, so that *the total arrangement is largely in the interest of the periphery in the Center*. Within the Center the two parties may be opposed to each other. But in the total game, the periphery see themselves more as the partners of the center in the Center than as the partners of the periphery in the Periphery—and this is the essential trick of that game. Alliance formation between the two peripheries is avoided, while the Center nation becomes more and the Periphery nation less cohesive—and hence less able to develop long-term strategies.

Actually, concerning the three criteria in the definition of imperialism as given above it is clear that no. 3 is implied by nos. 1 and 2. The two centers are tied together and the Center periphery is tied to its center: that is the whole essence of the situation. If we now presuppose that the center in the Periphery is a smaller proportion of that nation than the center in the Center, we can also draw one more implication: *there is disharmony of interest between the Center nation as a whole and the Periphery nation as a whole*. But that type of finding, frequently referred to, is highly misleading because it blurs the harmony of interest between the two centers and leads to the belief that imperialism is merely an international relationship, *not a combination of intra- and international relations.*

However, even if the definition given above purports to define the pure case of imperialism, we may nevertheless fruitfully think in terms of degenerate cases. Thus, the first point in the definition about harmony between the two centers is obviously the most important one. If the second point does not hold, and consequently not the third point either, it may still be fruitful to talk about imperialism. But in this degenerate case the two peripheries may more easily find each other, since they are now only kept apart by geographical distance (assuming that the two nations are nation-states, often even located far apart), not in addition by disharmony of interest. Thus, if the relationship between the two peripheries and their centers should become more similar, periphery alliance formation might easily be the result, and the two centers would have to resort to more direct means of violence rather than, or in addition to, the delicate type of structural violence that characterizes the pure type of imperialistic relationship.

But what if there is no distinction between center and periphery in the two nations; what if they are completely horizontal societies? In that case, we should not talk about the dominance relationship whereby the Center nation extracts something from the Periphery nation as an imperialistic one, but rather as something else—looting, stealing, etc. Where there is no bridgehead from the Center nation in the center of the Periphery nation, there cannot be any imperialism by this definition.

Kenneth Boulding

NATIONAL IMAGES AND INTERNATIONAL SYSTEMS

Nationalism is one of the most powerful forces of modern times. It can be beautiful, reflecting the yearning of people to associate themselves with others, evoking compassion, love, respect for one's past, one's culture, even the natural environment. In offering perhaps its most famous definition, French philosopher and historian J. Ernest Renan suggested that nationalism is

> a grand solidarity constituted by the sentiment of sacrifices which one has made and those that time is disposed to make again....The existence of a nation is an everyday plebiscite.[5]

At the same time, nationalism can become malevolent, fostering chauvinism, group intolerance, and violent divisions between people, which threaten to destroy the values it claims to venerate. "By nationalism," wrote George Orwell,

> I mean first of all the habit of assuming that human beings can be classified like insects and that whole blocks of millions or tens of millions of people can be confidently labeled "good" or "bad." But secondly—and this is much more important—I mean the habit of identifying oneself with a single nation or other unit, placing it beyond good or evil and recognizing no other duty than that of advancing its own interests.[6]

Here Kenneth Boulding—one of the founders of peace studies—discusses the phenomenon of national "images."

───────────────── ⊗ ─────────────────

We must recognize that the people whose decisions determine the policies and actions of nations do not respond to the "objective" facts of the situation, whatever that may mean, but to their "image" of the situation. It is what we think the world is like, not what it is really like, that determines our behavior. If our image of the world is in some sense "wrong," of course, we may be disappointed in our expectations, and we may therefore revise our image; if this revision is in the direction of the "truth" there is presumably a long-run tendency for the "image" and the "truth" to coincide. Whether this is so or not, it is always the image, not the truth, that immediately determines behavior. We act according to the way the world appears to us, not necessarily according to the way it "is." Thus...it is one

---

[5.] J. Ernest Renan, *What Is a Nation?* (Paris: Calmann-Levy, 1882).
[6] George Orwell, *Such, Such Were the Joys* (New York: Harcourt, Brace, 1953).

nation's image of the hostility of another, not the "real" hostility, which determines its reaction. The "image," then, must be thought of as the total cognitive, affective, and evaluative structure of the behavior unit, or its internal view of itself and its universe.

Generally speaking, the behavior of complex organizations can be regarded as determined by *decisions*, and a decision involves the selection of the most preferred position in a contemplated field of choice. Both the field of choice and the ordering of this field by which the preferred position is identified lie in the image of the decision-maker. Therefore, in a system in which decision-makers are an essential element, the study of the ways in which the image grows and changes, both of the field of choice and of the valuational ordering of this field, is of prime importance. The image is always in some sense a product of messages received in the past. It is not, however, a simple inventory or "pile" of such messages but a highly structured piece of information capital, developed partly by its inputs and outputs of information and partly by internal messages and its own laws of growth and stability.

The images which are important in international systems are those which a nation has of itself and of those other bodies in the system which constitute its international environment. At once a major complication suggests itself. A nation is some complex of the images of the persons who contemplate it, and as there are many different persons, so there are many different images. The complexity is increased by the necessity for inclusion, in the image of each person or at least of many persons, his image of the image of others. This complexity, however, is a property of the real world, not to be evaded or glossed over. It can be reduced to simpler terms if we distinguish between two types of persons in a nation—the powerful, on the one hand, and the ordinary, on the other. This is not, of course, a sharp distinction. The power of a decision-maker may be measured roughly by the number of people which his decisions potentially affect, weighted by some measure of the effect itself. Thus the head of a state is powerful, meaning that his decisions affect the lives of millions of people; the ordinary person is not powerful, for his decisions affect only himself and

the lives of a few people around him. There is usually a continuum of power among the persons of a society: thus in international relations there are usually a few very powerful individuals in a state—the chief executive, the prime minister, the secretary of state or minister of foreign affairs, the chiefs of staff of the armed forces. There will be some who are less powerful but still influential—members of the legislature, of the civil service, even journalists, newspaper owners, prominent businessmen, grading by imperceptible degrees down to the common soldier, who has no power of decision even over his own life. For purposes of the model, however, let us compress this continuum into two boxes, labeled the "powerful" and the "ordinary," and leave the refinements of power and influence for later studies.

We deal, therefore, with two representative images, (1) the image of the small group of powerful people who make the actual decisions which lead to war or peace, the making or breaking of treaties, the invasions or withdrawals, alliances, and enmities which make up the major events of international relations, and (2) the image of the mass of ordinary people who are deeply affected by these decisions but who take little or no direct part in making them. The tacit support of the mass, however, is of vital importance to the powerful. The powerful are always under some obligation to represent the mass, even under dictatorial regimes. In democratic societies the aggregate influence of the images of ordinary people is very great; the image of the powerful cannot diverge too greatly from the image of the mass without the powerful losing power. On the other hand, the powerful also have some ability to manipulate the images of the mass toward those of the powerful. This is an important object of instruments as diverse as the public education system, the public relations departments of the armed services, the Russian "agit-prop," and the Nazi propaganda ministry.

In the formation of the national images, however, it must be emphasized that impressions of nationality are formed mostly in childhood and usually in the family group. It would be quite fallacious to think of the images as being cleverly imposed on the mass by the powerful. If anything, the reverse is the case: the image is essentially a mass image, or what might be called a "folk image," transmitted through the family and the intimate face-to-face group, both in the case of the powerful and in the case of ordinary persons. Especially in the case of the old, long-established nations, the powerful share the mass image rather than impose it; it is passed on from the value systems of the parents to those of the children, and agencies of public instruction and propaganda merely reinforce the images which derived essentially from the family culture. This is much less true in new nations which are striving to achieve nationality, where the family culture frequently does not include strong elements of national allegiance but rather stresses allegiance to religious ideals or to the family as such. Here the powerful are frequently inspired by a national image derived not from family tradition but from a desire to imitate other nations, and here they frequently try to impose their images on the mass of people. Imposed images, however, are fragile by comparison with those which are deeply internalized and transmitted through family and other intimate sources.

Whether transmitted orally and informally through the family or more formally through schooling and the written word, the national image is essentially a *historical* image—that is, an image which extends through time, backward into a supposedly recorded or perhaps mythological past and forward into an imagined future. The more conscious a people is of its history, the stronger the national image is likely to be. To be an Englishman is to be conscious of "1066 and All That" rather than of "Constantine and All That," or "1776 and All That." A nation is the creation of its historians, formal and informal. The written word and public education contribute enormously to the stability and persistence of the national images. The Jews, for instance, are a creation of the Bible and the Talmud, but every nation has its bible, whether formed into a canon or not—noble words like the Declaration of Independence and the Gettysburg Address—which crystallize the national image in a form that can be transmitted almost unchanged from generation to generation. It is no exaggeration to say that the function of the historian is to pervert the truth

in directions favorable to the images of his readers or hearers. Both history and geography as taught in national schools are devised to give "perspective" rather than truth: that is to say, they present the world as seen from the vantage point of the nation. The national geography is learned in great detail, and the rest of the world is a fuzzy outline; the national history is emphasized and exalted; the history of the rest of the world is neglected or even falsified to the glory of the national image.

It is this fact that the national image is basically a lie, or at least a perspective distortion of the truth, which perhaps accounts for the ease with which it can be perverted to justify monstrous cruelties and wickednesses. There is much that is noble in the national image. It has lifted man out of the narrow cage of self-centeredness, or even family-centeredness, and has forced him to accept responsibility, in some sense, for people and events far beyond his face-to-face cognizance and immediate experience. It is a window of some sort on both space and time and extends a man's concern far beyond his own little lifetime and petty interests. Nevertheless, it achieves these virtues usually only at the cost of untruth, and this fatal flaw constantly betrays it. Love of country is perverted into hatred of the foreigner, and peace, order, and justice at home are paid for by war, cruelty, and injustice abroad.

In the formation of the national image the consciousness of great *shared* events and experiences is of the utmost importance. A nation is a body of people who are conscious of having "gone through something" together. Without the shared experience, the national image itself would not be shared, and it is of vital importance that the national image be highly similar. The sharing may be quite vicarious; it may be an experience shared long ago but constantly renewed by the ritual observances and historical memory of the people, like the Passover and the Captivity in the case of the Jews. Without the sharing, however, there is no nation. It is for this reason that war has been such a tragically important element in the creation and sustenance of the national image. There is hardly a nation that has not been cradled in violence and nourished by further violence. This is not, I think, a necessary property of war itself. It is rather that, especially in more primitive societies, war is the one experience which is dramatic, obviously important, and shared by everybody....

We now come to the central problem, which is that of the impact of national images on the relations among states, that is, on the course of events in international relations. The relations among states can be described in terms of a number of different dimensions. There is, first of all, the dimension of simple geographical space. It is perhaps the most striking single characteristic of the national state as an organization, by contrast with organizations such as firms or churches, that it thinks of itself as occupying, in a "dense" and exclusive fashion, a certain area of the globe. The schoolroom maps which divide the world into colored shapes which are identified as nations have a profound effect on the national image. Apart from the very occasional condominium, it is impossible for a given plot of land on the globe to be associated with two nations at the same time. The territories of nations are divided sharply by frontiers carefully surveyed and frequently delineated by a chain of customs houses, immigration stations, and military installations. We are so accustomed to this arrangement that we think of it as "natural" and take it completely for granted. It is by no means the only conceivable arrangement, however. In primitive societies the geographical image is not sharp enough to define clear frontiers; there may be a notion of the rough territory of a tribe, but, especially among nomadic peoples, there is no clear concept of a frontier and no notion of a nation as something that has a shape on a map. In our own society the shape on the map that symbolizes the nation is constantly drilled into the minds of both young and old, both through formal teaching in schools and through constant repetition in newspapers, advertisements, cartoons, and so on. A society is not inconceivable, however, and might even be desirable, in which nations governed people but not territories and claimed jurisdiction over a defined set of citizens, no matter where on the earth's surface they happened to live.

The territorial aspect of the national state is important in the dynamics of international relations

because of the *exclusiveness* of territorial occupation. This means that one nation can generally expand only at the expense of another; an increase in the territory of one is achieved only at the expense of a decrease in the territory of another. This makes for a potential conflict situation. This characteristic of the nation does not make conflict inevitable, but it does make it likely and is at least one of the reasons why the history of international relations is a history of perpetual conflict.

The territorial aspect of international relations is complicated by the fact that in many cases the territories of nations are not homogeneous but are composed of "empires," in which the populations do not identify themselves with the national image of the dominant group. Thus when one nation conquers another and absorbs the conquered territory into an empire, it does not thereby automatically change the culture and allegiances of the conquered nation. The Poles remained Polish for a hundred and twenty-five years of partition between Germany, Austria, and Russia. The Finns retained their nationality through eight hundred years of foreign rule and the Jews, through nearly two thousand years of dispersion. If a nation loses territory occupied by disaffected people, this is much less damaging than the loss of territory inhabited by a well-disposed and loyal population. Thus Turkey, which was the "sick man of Europe" as long as it retained its heterogeneous empire, enjoyed a substantial renewal of national health when stripped of its empire and pushed back to the relatively homogeneous heartland of Anatolia. In this case the loss of a disaffected empire actually strengthened the national unit.

The image of the map shape of the nations may be an important factor affecting the general frame of mind of the nation. There is a tendency for nations to be uneasy with strong irregularities, enclaves, detached portions, and protuberances or hollows. The ideal shape is at least a convex set, and there is some tendency for nations to be more satisfied if they have regularly round or rectangular outlines. Thus the detachment of East Prussia from the body of Germany by the Treaty of Versailles was an important factor in creating the fanatical discontent of the Nazis.

A second important dimension of the national image is that of hostility or friendliness. At any one time a particular national image includes a rough scale of the friendliness or hostility of, or toward, other nations. The relationship is not necessarily either consistent or reciprocal—in nation A the prevailing image may be that B is friendly, whereas in nation B itself the prevailing image may be one of hostility toward A; or again in both nations there may be an image of friendliness of A toward B but of hostility of B toward A. On the whole, however, there is a tendency toward both consistency and reciprocation—if a nation A pictures itself as hostile toward B, it usually also pictures B as hostile toward it, and the image is likely to be repeated in B. One exception to this rule seems to be observable: most nations seem to feel that their enemies are more hostile toward them than they are toward their enemies. This is a typical paranoid reaction; the nation visualizes itself as surrounded by hostile nations toward which it has only the nicest and friendliest of intentions.

An important subdimension of the hostility-friendliness image is that of the stability or security of the relationship. A friendly relationship is frequently formalized as an alli-ance. Alliances, however, are shifting; some friendly relations are fairly permanent, others change as the world kaleidoscope changes, as new enemies arise, or as governments change. Thus.... most people in the United States visualized Germany and Japan, even before the outbreak of the war, as enemies, and after Hitler's invasion of Russia, Russia was for a while regarded as a valuable friend and ally.... We can roughly classify the reciprocal relations of nations along some scale of friendliness-hostility. At one extreme we have stable friendliness, such as between Britain and Portugal or between Britain and the Commonwealth countries. At the other extreme we have stable hostility—the "traditional enemies" such as France and Germany. Between these extremes we have a great many pairs characterized by shifting alliances. On the whole, stable friendly relations seem to exist mainly between strong nations and weaker nations which they have an interest in preserving and stable hostile relations between adjacent nations each of which has played a large part in the formation of the other.

GLAMORIZED NATIONALISM: SOME EXAMPLES IN POETRY

In his essay "Christianity and Patriotism," Leo Tolstoy pitied "the good-natured foolish people, who, showing their healthy white teeth as they smile, gape like children, naively delighted at the dressed-up admirals and presidents, at the flags waving above them, and at the fireworks, and the playing bands." Most wars begin with similar bursts of nationalistic enthusiasm. Tolstoy warned, however, that such euphoria is typically short-lived, with the flags, bands, and glowing sense of being part of a glorious enterprise, greater than one's self being replaced by

> only the desolate wet plain, cold, hunger, misery—in front of them the slaughterous enemy, behind them the relentless government, blood, wounds, agonies, rotting corpses and a senseless, useless death.

In the aftermath of war, military exploits are often celebrated and dramatized, in the process generating a powerful blend of emotion and nationalism. Virtually no society is immune to this tendency to glamorize and thus legitimize acts of violent heroism, which are often taught to children, thereby becoming part of the national mythology. In turn, such images are available not only to support ongoing wars but also to fuel enthusiasm for future ones. Here are three examples.

───────────────────────── ⨎ ─────────────────────────

THE DEFENSE OF THE ALAMO:
JOAQUIN MILLER

Santa Anna came storming, as a storm might
    come;
There was rumble of cannon; there was rattle of
    blade;
There was cavalry, infantry, bugle and
    drum—
Full seven proud thousand in pomp and parade,
The chivalry, flower of all Mexico;
And a gaunt two hundred in the Alamo!

And thirty lay sick, and some were shot through;
For the siege had been bitter, and bloody and long.
"Surrender, or die"—"Men, what will you do?"
And Travis, great Travis, drew sword, quick and
    strong;
Drew a line at his feet… "Will you come? Will
    you go?
I die with my wounded, in the Alamo."

Then Bowie gasped, "Guide me over that line!"
Then Crockett, one hand to the sick, one hand to
    his gun,
Crossed with him; then never a word
    or a sign,
Till all, sick or well, all, all, save but one,
One man. Then a woman stopped praying
    and slow
Across, to die with the heroes of the Alamo.

Then that one coward fled, in the night, in that
    night
When all men silently prayed and thought
Of home; of tomorrow; of God and the right,
Till dawn; then Travis sent his single last cannon-
    shot,

In answer to insolent Mexico,
From the old bell-tower of the Alamo.

Then came Santa Anna; a crescent of flame!
Then the red escalade; then the fight hand to
    hand;
Such an unequal fight as never had name
Since the Persian hordes butchered that doomed
    Spartan band.
All day—all day and all night, and the morning,
    so slow,
Through the battle smoke mantling
    the Alamo.

Then silence! Such silence! Two thousand lay
    dead
In a crescent outside! And within? Not
    a breath
Save the gasp of a woman, with gory, gashed
    head,
All alone, with her dead there, waiting
    for death;
And she but a nurse. Yet when shall we know
Another like this of the Alamo?

Shout "Victory, victory, victory ho!"
I say, 'tis not always with the hosts that win:
I say that the victory, high or low,
Is given the hero who grapples with sin,
Or legion or single; just asking to know
When duty fronts death in his Alamo.

THE CHARGE OF THE LIGHT BRIGADE:
ALFRED, LORD TENNYSON

Half a league, half a league,
Half a league onward,
All in the valley of Death

Rode the six hundred.
"Forward, the Light Brigade!
Charge for the guns!" he said:
Into the valley of Death
Rode the six hundred.

"Forward, the Light Brigade!"
Was there a man dismay'd?
Not though the soldier knew
Some one had blunder'd:
Theirs not to make reply,
Theirs not to reason why,
Theirs but to do and die:
Into the valley of Death
Rode the six hundred.

Cannon to right of them,
Cannon to left of them,
Cannon in front of them
Volley'd and thunder'd;
Storm'd at with shot and shell,
Boldly they rode and well,
Into the jaws of Death,
Into the mouth of Hell
Rode the six hundred:

Flash'd all their sabres bare,
Flash'd as they turn'd in air,
Sabring the gunners there,
Charging an army, while
All the world wonder'd:
Plunged in the battery-smoke,
Right through the line they broke;
Cossack and Russian
Reel'd from the sabre-stroke
Shatter'd and sunder'd.
Then they rode back, but not—
Not the six hundred.

Cannon to right of them,
Cannon to left of them,
Cannon behind them
Volley'd and thunder'd;
Storm'd at with shot and shell,
While horse and hero fell,
They that had fought so well

Came through the jaws of Death
Back from the mouth of Hell,
All that was left of them,
Left of six hundred.

When can their glory fade?
Oh, the wild charge they made!
All the world wonder'd.
Honor the charge they made!
Honor the Light Brigade,
Noble six hundred!

BATTLE HYMN OF THE REPUBLIC: JULIA WARD HOWE

Mine eyes have seen the glory of the coming of
    the Lord:
He is trampling out the vintage where the grapes of
    wrath are stored;
He hath loosed the fateful lightning of his terrible
    swift sword:
His truth is marching on.

I have seen him in the watch-fires of a hundred
    circling camps;
They have builded him an altar in the evening dews
    and damps;
I can read his righteous sentence by the dim and
    flaring lamps:
His day is marching on.

I have read a fiery gospel, writ in burnished rows
    of steel:
"As ye deal with my contemners, so with you my
    grace shall deal;
Let the Hero, born of woman, crush the serpent
    with his heel,
Since God is marching on."

He has sounded forth the trumpet that shall never
    call retreat;
He is sifting out the hearts of men before his
    judgment-seat:
O, be swift, my soul, to answer him! be jubilant,
    my feet!
Our God is marching on.

In the beauty of the lilies Christ was born across
    the sea,
With a glory in his bosom that transfigures you
    and me;
As he died to make men holy, let us die to make
    men free,
While God is marching on.

He is coming like the glory of the morning on
    the wave,
He is wisdom to the mighty, he is honor to the
    brave,
So the world shall be his footstool, and the soul of
    wrong his slave,
Our God is marching on!

Michael T. Klare

REDEFINING SECURITY: THE NEW GLOBAL SCHISMS

It is sometimes said that generals are always prepared to refight the last war. Similarly, it is possible that in focusing on explanations for past wars, we give insufficient attention to the causes of future conflicts. (On the other hand, it seems likely that certain fundamental characteristics—of "human nature," social systems, etc.—are likely to be relatively unchanged from one time to the next.) In the last selection of this chapter, we present an effort by a noted peace researcher to look ahead and anticipate "new global schisms" that may characterize violent conflict in the twenty-first century. Note especially the suggestion that interstate wars have been and will be replaced by intrastate conflicts.

Geopolitical boundaries—notably those separating rival powers and major military blocs—have constituted the principal "fault lines" of international politics during much of the twentieth century. Throughout the Cold War, the world's greatest concentrations of military strength were to be found along such key dividing lines as the Iron Curtain between East and West in Europe and the demilitarized zone between North and South Korea.

When the Cold War ended, many of these boundaries quickly lost their geopolitical significance. With the reunification of Germany and the breakup of the Soviet Union, the divide between East and West in Europe ceased to have any meaning. Other key boundaries—for example, the demilitarized zone in Korea—retained their strategic importance, but elsewhere thousands of miles of previously fortified frontier became open borders with a minimal military presence. The strategic alliances associated with these divisions also lost much of their prominence: the Warsaw Treaty Organization was eliminated altogether, while NATO was given new roles and missions in order to forestall a similar fate.

BATTLE LINES OF THE FUTURE

The changes associated with the Cold War's end have been so dramatic and profound that it is reasonable to question whether traditional assumptions regarding the nature of global conflict will continue to prove reliable in the new, post–Cold War era. In particular, one could question whether conflicts between states (or groups of states) will remain the principal form of international strife, and whether the boundaries between them will continue to constitute the world's major fault lines. Certainly the outbreak of ethnonationalist conflict in the former Yugoslavia and several other former Communist states has focused fresh attention on internal warfare, as has the persistence of tribal and religious strife in such countries as Afghanistan, Burundi, Liberia, Rwanda, Somalia, Sri Lanka, and Sudan.

Nevertheless, traditional concepts retain great currency among security analysts. Although the Iron Curtain has disappeared, it is argued, similar schisms of a geographic or territorial nature will arise to take its place. Indeed, several theories have been advanced positing the likely location of these schisms.

Some analysts contend that the territorial schisms of earlier periods—notably those produced by military competition among the major powers—will be revived in the years ahead. Professor Kenneth Waltz of the University of California at Berkeley suggests that such competition will eventually reappear, with Germany, Japan, or some other rising power such as China building its military strength in order to contest America's global paramountcy. "Countries have always competed for wealth and security, and the competition has often led to conflict," he wrote in *International Security's* summer 1993 issue. "Why should the future be different from the past?"

More novel, perhaps, is the suggestion that the principal schisms of the post–Cold War era are to be found along the peripheries of the world's great civilizations: Western (including Europe and North America), Slavic-Orthodox (including Russia, Ukraine, and Serbia), Japanese, Islamic, Confucian (China), Latin American, and African. First propounded by Harvard's Samuel Huntington in the summer 1993 issue of *Foreign Affairs,* this argument

holds that the economic and ideological antagonisms of the nineteenth and twentieth centuries will be superseded in the twenty-first by antagonisms over culture and cultural identity. "Nation-states will remain the most powerful actors in world affairs," Huntington wrote, "but the principal conflicts of global politics will occur between nations and groups of different civilizations." Although the boundaries between civilizations are not as precise as those between sovereign states, he noted, these loose frontiers will be the site of major conflict. "The clash of civilizations will dominate global politics. The fault lines between civilizations will be the battle lines of the future."

Others have argued that the world's future fault lines will fall not between the major states or civilizations, but between the growing nexus of democratic, market-oriented societies and those "holdout" states that have eschewed democracy or defied the world community in other ways. Such "pariah" states or "rogue" powers are said to harbor aggressive inclinations, to support terrorism, and to seek the production of nuclear or chemical weapons. "[We] must face the reality of recalcitrant and outlaw states that not only choose to remain outside the family [of nations] but also to assault its basic values," wrote President Clinton's national security adviser, Anthony Lake, in the March–April 1994 *Foreign Affairs.* Lake placed several nations in this category—Cuba, North Korea, Iran, Iraq, and Libya—and other writers have added Sudan and Syria. But while there is disagreement about which of these states might actually fall into the "outlaw" category, Lake and other proponents of this analysis hold that the United States and its allies must work together to "contain" the rogue states and frustrate their aggressive designs.

While these assessments of the world security environment differ in many of their particulars, they share a common belief that the "battle lines of the future" (to use Huntington's expression) will fall along geographically defined boundaries, with the contending powers (and their friends and allies) arrayed on opposite sides. This, in turn, leads to similar policy recommendations that generally entail the maintenance of sufficient military strength by the United States to defeat any potential adversary or combination of adversaries.

It is certainly understandable that many analysts have proceeded from traditional assumptions regarding the nature of conflict when constructing models of future international relations, but it is not at all apparent that such assessments will prove reliable. While a number of crises since the end of the Cold War appear to have followed one of the three models described, many have not. Indeed, the most intense conflicts of the current period—including those in Algeria, Angola, Bosnia, Burma, Burundi, Haiti, Kashmir, Liberia, Rwanda, Somalia, Sri Lanka, and Sudan—cannot be fully explained using these models. Moreover, other forms of contemporary violence—terrorism, racial and religious strife, gang warfare, violence against women, and criminal violence—have shown no respect for geography or civilizational identity whatsoever, erupting in virtually every corner of the world.

THE THREAT FROM WITHIN

A fresh assessment of the world security environment suggests that the major international schisms of the twenty-first century will not always be definable in geographic terms. Many of the most severe and persistent threats to global peace and stability are arising not from conflicts between major political entities but from increased discord within states, societies, and civilizations along ethnic, racial, religious, linguistic, caste, or class lines.

The intensification and spread of internal discord is a product of powerful stresses on human communities everywhere. These stresses—economic, demographic, sociological, and environmental—are exacerbating the existing divisions within societies and creating entirely new ones. As a result, we are seeing the emergence of new or deepened fissures across international society, producing multiple outbreaks of intergroup hostility and violence. These cleavages cannot be plotted on a normal map, but can be correlated with other forms of data: economic performance, class stratification, population growth, ethnic and religious composition, environmental deterioration, and so on. Where certain conditions prevail—a widening gulf between rich and poor,

severe economic competition between neighboring ethnic and religious communities, the declining habitability of marginal lands—internal conflict is likely to erupt.

This is not to say that traditional geopolitical divisions no longer play a role in world security affairs. But it does suggest that such divisions may have been superseded in importance by the new global schisms.

FOR RICHER AND POORER: THE WIDENING GAP

The world has grown much richer over the past twenty-five years. According to the Worldwatch Institute, the world's total annual income rose from $10.1 trillion in 1970 to approximately $20 trillion in 1994 (in constant 1987 dollars). This increase has been accompanied by an improved standard of living for many of the world's peoples. But not all nations, and not all people in the richer nations, have benefited from the global increase in wealth: some countries, mostly concentrated in Africa and Latin America, have experienced a net decline in gross domestic product over the past few decades, while many of the countries that have achieved a higher GDP have experienced an increase in the number of people living in extreme poverty. Furthermore, the gap in national income between the richest and the poorest nations continues to increase, as does the gap between rich and poor people within most societies.

These differentials in economic growth rates, along with the widening gap between rich and poor, are producing dangerous fissures in many societies. As the masses of poor see their chances of escaping acute poverty diminish, they are likely to become increasingly resentful of those whose growing wealth is evident. This resentment is especially pronounced in the impoverished shantytowns that surround many of the seemingly prosperous cities of the third world. In these inhospitable surroundings, large numbers of people—especially among the growing legions of unemployed youth—are being attracted to extremist political movements like the Shining Path of Peru and the Islamic Salvation Front of Algeria, or to street gangs and drug-trafficking syndicates. The result is an increase in urban crime and violence.

Deep economic cleavages are also emerging in China and the post-Communist states of Eastern Europe and the former Soviet Union. Until the recent introduction of market reforms in these countries, the financial gap between rich and poor was kept relatively narrow by state policy, and such wealth as did exist among the bureaucratic elite was kept well hidden from public view. With the onset of capitalism the economic plight of the lowest strata of these

Sources of Human Insecurity

Income	1.3 billion people in developing countries live in poverty; 200 million people live below the poverty line in industrial countries.
Clean Water	1.3 billion people in developing countries do not have access to safe water.
Literacy	900 million adults worldwide are illiterate.
Food	800 million people in developing countries have inadequate food supplies; 500 million of this number are chronically malnourished, and 175 million are under the age of five.
Housing	500 million urban dwellers worldwide are homeless or do not have adequate housing; 100 million young people are homeless.
Preventable Death	Between 15 million and 20 million people die annually because of starvation or disease aggravated by malnutrition; 10 million people die each year because of substandard housing, unsafe water, or poor sanitation in densely populated cities.

Source: Adapted from Michael Renner, *Fighting for Survival: Environmental Decline, Social Conflict, and the New Age of Insecurity* (New York: Norton, 1996), p. 81.

societies has become considerably worse, while the newly formed entrepreneurial class has been able to accumulate considerable wealth—and to display it in highly conspicuous ways. This has generated new class tensions and provided ammunition for those who, like Gennadi Zyuganov of Russia's reorganized Communist Party, seek the restoration of the old, state-dominated system.

Equally worrisome is the impact of growing income differentials on intergroup relations in multiethnic societies. In most countries the divide between rich and poor is not the only schism that matters: of far greater significance are the divisions between various strata of the poor and lower middle class. When such divisions coincide with ethnic or religious differences—that is, when one group of poor people finds itself to be making less economic progress than a similar group of a different ethnic composition—the result is likely to be increased ethnic antagonisms and, at the extreme, increased intergroup violence. This is evident in Pakistan, where violent gang warfare in Karachi has been fueled by economic competition between the indigenous inhabitants of the surrounding region and several waves of Muslim immigrants from India and Bangladesh; it is also evident in Sri Lanka, where efforts by the Sinhalese to deny employment opportunities to the Tamils helped spark a deadly civil war.

KINDLING ETHNIC STRIFE

According to information assembled by the Stockholm International Peace Research Institute (SIPRI), ethnic and religious strife figured prominently in all but 3 of the 31 major armed conflicts underway in 1994. And while several long-running ethnic and sectarian conflicts have subsided in recent years, most analysts believe that such strife is likely to erupt repeatedly in the years ahead.

It is true that many recent ethnic and religious conflicts have their roots in clashes or invasions that occurred years ago. It is also true that the violent upheavals that broke out in the former Yugoslavia and the former Soviet Union drew upon deep-seated ethnic hostilities, even if these cleavages were not generally visible during much of the Communist era (when overt displays of ethnic antagonism were prohibited by government decree). In this sense, the ethnic fissures that are now receiving close attention from international policymakers are not really new phenomena. Nevertheless, many of these schisms have become more pronounced since the end of the Cold War, or have exhibited characteristics that are unique to the current era.

Greatly contributing to the intensity of recent ethnic and religious strife is the erosion or even disappearance of central state authority in poor third world countries experiencing extreme economic, political, and environmental stress. In such countries—especially Burundi, Liberia, Rwanda, Somalia, and Zaire—the flimsy state structures established after independence are simply unable to cope with the demands of housing and feeding their growing populations with the meager resources at hand. In such circumstances people lose all confidence in the state's ability to meet their basic needs and turn instead to more traditional, kinship-based forms of association for help in getting by—a process that often results in competition and conflict among groups over what remains of the nation's scarce resources. This shift in loyalty from the state to group identity is also evident in Bosnia and parts of the former Soviet Union, where various ethnic factions have attempted to seize or divide up the infrastructure (and in some cases the territory) left behind by the Communist regime.

Also contributing to the intensity of intergroup conflict in the current era is the spread of mass communications and other instruments of popular mobilization. These advances have contributed to what Professor James Rosenau of George Washington University calls a "skill revolution" in which individual citizens "have become increasingly competent in assessing where they fit in international affairs and how their behavior can be aggregated into significant collective outcomes." This competence can lead to calls for greater personal freedom and democracy. But it can also lead to increased popular mobilization along ethnic, religious, caste, and linguistic lines, often producing great friction and disorder within heterogeneous societies. An important case in point is India, where Hindu nationalists have proved adept at employing modern means

of communication and political organization—while retaining traditional symbols and motifs—to encourage anti-Muslim sentiment and thereby erode the authority of India's largely secular government.

DEMOGRAPHIC SCHISMS

According to the most recent UN estimates, total world population is expected to soar from approximately 5.6 billion people in 1994 to somewhere between 8 billion and 12 billion by the year 2050—an increase that will undoubtedly place great strain on the earth's food production and environmental capacity. But the threat to the world's environment and food supply is not all that we have to worry about. Because population growth is occurring unevenly in different areas, with some of the highest rates of growth to be found in countries with the slowest rates of economic growth, future population increases could combine with other factors to exacerbate existing cleavages along ethnic, religious, and class lines.

Overall, the populations of the less-developed countries (LDCS) are growing at a much faster rate than those of the advanced industrial nations. As a result, the share of world population accounted for by the LDCS rose from 69 percent in 1960 to 74 percent in 1980, and is expected to jump to nearly 80 percent in the year 2000. Among third world countries, moreover, there have been marked variations in the rate of population growth: while the newly industrialized nations of East Asia have experienced a sharp decline in the rate of growth, Africa and parts of the Middle East have experienced an increase. If these trends persist, the global distribution of population will change dramatically over the next few decades, with some areas experiencing a substantial increase in total population and others moderate or even negligible growth.

This is where other factors enter the picture. If the largest increases in population were occurring in areas of rapid economic growth, the many young adults entering the job market each year would be able to find productive employment and would thus be able to feed and house their families. In many cases, however, large increases in population are coinciding with low or stagnant economic growth, meaning that future job-seekers are not likely to find adequate employment. This will have a considerable impact on the world security environment. At the very least, it is likely to produce increased human migration from rural areas (where population growth tends to be greatest) to urban centers (where most new jobs are to be found), and from poor and low-growth countries to more affluent ones. The former process is resulting in the rapid expansion of many third world cities, with an attendant increase in urban crime and intergroup friction (especially where the new urban dwellers are of a different ethnic or tribal group from the original settlers); the latter is producing huge numbers of new immigrants in the developed and high-growth countries, often sparking hostility and sometimes violence from the indigenous populations.

Rapid population growth in poor countries with slow or stagnant economic growth has other implications for world security. In many societies it is leading to the hyperutilization of natural resources, particularly arable soil, grazing lands, forests, and fisheries, a process that severely complicates future economic growth (as vital raw materials are depleted) and accelerates the pace of environmental decline. It can also overwhelm the capacity of weak or divided governments to satisfy their citizens' basic needs, leading eventually to the collapse of states and to the intergroup competition and conflict described earlier. Finally, it could generate fresh international conflicts when states with slow population growth employ stringent measures to exclude immigrants from nearby countries with high rates of growth. While some of this is speculative, early signs of many of these phenomena have been detected. The 1994 United States intervention in Haiti, for instance, was partly motivated by a desire on Washington's part to curb the flow of Haitian "boat people" to the United States.

ENDANGERED BY ENVIRONMENT

As with massive population growth, the world has been bombarded in recent years with dire predictions about the consequences of further deterioration in the global environment. The continuing buildup of industrial gases in the earth's outer atmosphere, for example, is thought to be impeding the natural radiation of heat from the planet and thereby producing a gradual increase in global temperatures—a process known as "greenhouse warming." If such warming continues, global sea levels will rise, deserts will grow, and severe drought could afflict many important agricultural zones. Other forms of environmental degradation—the thinning of the earth's outer ozone layer, the depletion of arable soil through overcultivation, the persistence of acid rain caused by industrial emissions—could endanger human health and survival in other ways. As with population growth, these environmental effects will not be felt uniformly around the world but will threaten some states and groups more than others, producing new cleavages in human society.

The uneven impact of global environmental decline is being seen in many areas. The first to suffer are invariably those living in marginally habitable areas—arid grazing lands, coastal lowlands, tropical rain forests. As annual rainfall declines, sea levels rise, and forests are harvested, these lands become uninhabitable. The choice, for those living in such areas, is often grim: to migrate to the cities, with all of their attendant problems, or to move onto the lands of neighboring peoples (who may be of a different ethnicity or religion), producing new outbreaks of inter-group violence. This grim choice has fallen with particular severity on indigenous peoples, who in many cases were originally driven into these marginal habitats by more powerful groups. A conspicuous case in point is the Amazon region of Brazil, where systematic deforestation is destroying the habitat and lifestyle of the indigenous peoples and producing death, illness, and unwelcome migration to the cities.

States also vary in their capacity to cope with environmental crisis and the depletion of natural resources. While the wealthier countries can rebuild areas damaged by flooding or other disasters, relocate displaced citizens to safer regions, and import food and other commodities no longer produced locally, the poorer countries are much less capable of doing these things. As noted by Professor Thomas Homer-Dixon of the University of Toronto, "Environmental scarcity sharply raises financial and political demands on government by requiring huge spending on new infrastructure." Because many third world countries cannot sustain such expenditures, he notes, "we have...the potential for a widening gap between demands on the state and its financial ability to meet these demands"—a gap that could lead to internal conflict between competing ethnic groups, or significant out-migration to countries better able to cope with environmental stresses.

Finally, there is a danger that acute environmental scarcities will lead to armed interstate conflict over such vital resources as water, forests, and energy supplies. Some believe that the era of "resource wars" has already occurred in the form of recurring conflict over the Middle East's oil supplies and that similar conflicts will arise over control of major sources of water, such as the Nile, Euphrates, and Ganges rivers.

THE NEW CARTOGRAPHY

These new and growing schisms are creating a map of international security that is based on economic, demographic, and environmental factors. If this map could be represented in graphic terms, it would show an elaborate network of fissures stretching across human society in all directions—producing large concentrations of rifts in some areas and smaller clusters in others, but leaving no area entirely untouched. Each line would represent a cleavage in the human community, dividing one group (however defined) from another; the deeper and wider clefts, and those composed of many fault lines, would indicate the site of current or potential conflict.

These schisms, and their continued growth, will force policymakers to rethink their approach to international security. It is no longer possible to rely on strategies of defense and diplomacy that assume a flat, two-dimensional world of contending geopolitical actors. While such units still play a significant role in world security affairs, they are not the only actors that matter; nor is their interaction the only significant threat to peace and stability. Other actors, and other modes of interaction, are equally important. Only by considering the full range of security threats will it be possible for policymakers to design effective strategies for peace.

When the principal fault lines of international security coincided with the boundaries between countries, it was always possible for individual states to attempt to solve their security problems by fortifying their borders or by joining with other nations in regional defense systems like NATO and the Warsaw Pact. When the fault lines fall *within* societies, however, there are no clear boundaries to be defended and no role for traditional alliance systems. Indeed, it is questionable whether there is a role for military power at all: any use of force by one side in these disputes, however successful, will inevitably cause damage to the body politic as a whole, eroding its capacity to overcome the problems involved and to provide for its long-term stability. Rather than fortifying and defending borders, a successful quest for peace must entail strategies for easing and erasing the rifts in society, by eliminating the causes of dissension or finding ways to peacefully bridge the gap between mutually antagonistic groups.

The new map of international security will not replace older, traditional types. The relations between states will still matter in world affairs, and their interactions may lead, as they have in the past, to major armed conflicts. But it will not be possible to promote international peace and stability without using the new map as well, and dealing with the effects of the new global schisms. Should we fail to do so, the world of the next century could prove as violent as the present one.

STUDY QUESTIONS

1. Identify and describe several important causes of war that are not represented in this chapter.
2. Is there any fundamental sense in which the causes of war in the twenty-first century are likely to be different from those earlier in history?
3. Compare "war" among animals with war among human beings. Comment on both the advantages and dangers of looking at human war as a special case of a more general phenomenon, found in other species.
4. Discuss the advantages and *dis*advantages of looking for the causes of "war" as opposed to looking for the causes of specific wars.
5. Is there any evidence for a *dis*inclination to kill? If people are "naturally" inclined to be peaceful, why are there so many wars? If people are "naturally" inclined to be war-like, is the hope for peace unrealistic and doomed to failure?
6. Compare the basic attitudes of the political "left" and "right" with respect to war.
7. Make an argument that students of peace studies should know more about the anthropology of war—that is, "war" among nontechnological societies; make an argument that this is not terribly relevant.
8. During the nineteenth century, many people felt that nationalism could be a potent force for peace. Was it? Could it still be?
9. Make a case for (or against) the proposition that poverty is a major cause of war; similarly for population pressure, for military spending and preparation, for the role of leaders, the psychology of human decision making, for religious and ethnic orientation, and for technology.
10. It is clear that nuclear war would differ from conventional war in terms of its consequences. In what ways might nuclear war likely differ from conventional war with respect to possible *causes*? In what ways might it be similar?

SUGGESTIONS FOR FURTHER READING

Barash, David P., and C. P. Webel. 2008. *Peace and Conflict Studies*. 2nd ed. Los Angeles: Sage Publications.

Blainey, Geoffrey. 1988. *The Causes of War*. New York: Free Press.

Bramson, Leon, and George W. Goethals, eds. 1964. *War: Studies from Psychology, Sociology, Anthropology*. New York: Basic Books.

Bueno de Mesquita, Bruce. 1983. *The War Trap*. New Haven, CT: Yale University Press.

Cashman, Greg. 2007. *An Introduction to the Causes of War: Patterns of Interstate Conflict from World War I to Iraq*. Lanham, MD: Rowman & Littlefield.

Fox, Jonathan. 2005. *Religion, Civilization, and Civil War: 1945 through the New Millennium*. Lanham, MD: Lexington Books.

Frank, Jerome. 1982. *Sanity and Survival in the Nuclear Age*. New York: Random House.

Pick, Daniel. 1993. *War Machine: The Rationalisation of Slaughter in the Modern Age*. New Haven, CT: Yale University Press.

Scheff, Thomas J. 1994. *Bloody Revenge: Emotions, Nationalism, and War*. Boulder, CO: Westview Press.

Van Evera, Stephen. 2001. *Causes of War*. Ithaca, NY: Cornell University Press.

CHAPTER 2

Building "Negative Peace"

W e have looked briefly at some of the outstanding approaches to the causes of war. Now we turn to prevention.

It has often been said that war is too important to be left to the generals. By the same token, the prevention of war is too important to be left to the politicians. Similarly, study of war's prevention is too important to be left to specialists in international relations, political science, or experts in "strategic studies," especially because many of these scholars tend to be apologists for the "war system" as it has operated for centuries.

And yet, most of the world's religious and ethical traditions deplore war and profess a desire for peace. "My peace I give unto you," offers Jesus (John 14:27), along with "the peace of God, which passes all understanding" (Phil. 4:7). The Indian leader Gandhi, a devout Hindu, became perhaps the world's greatest crusader for nonviolence. The Chinese philosopher Lao Tse, founder of Taoism, emphasized that the way of war is not the "Tao," or the "Way," that human beings ought to follow.

Tennyson (who also wrote the promilitary ode "The Charge of the Light Brigade"!) expressed what is nonetheless a worldwide yearning:

> Ring out the old, ring in the new. Ring out the false, ring in the true...
> Ring out old shapes of foul disease, ring out the narrowing lust of gold.
> Ring out the thousand wars of old, ring in the thousand years of peace.[1]

Considering the positive connotations of "peace" as opposed to "war," it is only fair to ask why peace—even in its inadequate and negative form as the mere absence of war—has not yet been attained. After all, longing for a thousand years of peace when nothing like it has every been experienced seems a bit like someone who has never attended a concert looking forward to a paradise in which he or she will spend eternity listening to some heavenly choir! Most people readily give lip service to peace, but perhaps at some level, they haven't really desired it as fervently as they claim.

---

[1] "In Memoriam."

For one thing, maybe peace is boring. There are lots of war movies but precious few "peace movies"; lots of martial music but only a handful of peace songs, and so on. As with rubbernecking at the scene of a traffic accident, people's attention is drawn to extreme situations of violence, in which exciting things happen. Those who complain, for example, about a tendency for the news media to focus only on "bad news," must confront the fact that whereas people are likely to pay attention to a war or even a border clash between contending forces, they would be less than fascinated by a headline blaring, "France and Germany did not go to war today."

For another thing, many people—despite their announced abhorrence of war—make exceptions in particular cases, especially in the interest of a "greater good." Thomas Jefferson once wrote of the United States that "peace is our passion," yet he also suggested that "the tree of liberty must be refreshed from time to time with the blood of patriots and tyrants." Similarly, Benjamin Franklin wrote that "there never was a good war, or a bad peace." But Franklin also warned that "even peace can be purchased at too high a price." For all its protestations on behalf of peace, the truth is that the United States has not been especially peaceful, having intervened militarily in other countries more than a hundred times.

Theodore Roosevelt urged his fellow citizens to cherish "the great fighting masterful virtues" and to accept imperial responsibilities in Hawaii, Puerto Rico, the Philippines, and Cuba:

> I preach to you, then, my countrymen, that our country calls not for the life of ease but for the life of strenuous endeavor.... If we stand idly by, if we seek merely swollen, slothful ease and ignoble peace, if we shrink from the hard contests where men must win at hazard of their lives and at the risk of all they hold dear, then the bolder and stronger peoples will pass us by, and will win for themselves the domination of the world.[2]

It is interesting that an acknowledged embracing of war is rare in modern thinking... although war itself is not rare at all. Departments of War, common until the 1940s, have universally been replaced by Departments or Ministries of "Defense." Only ideological devotees on either extreme have embraced war as virtuous and desirable, with Chinese revolutionary leader Mao Ze-Dong, for example, having spoken for the far left when he announced that "political power grows out of the barrel of a gun.... All things grow out of the barrel of a gun..." and fascist Italian dictator Benito Mussolini, for the far right:

> War alone brings up to their highest tension all human energies and puts a stamp of nobility upon the people who have the courage to meet it.... A doctrine, therefore, which begins with a prejudice in favor of peace is foreign to Fascism.

Many have extolled the sheer intensity of confronting basic issues of life and death, exploring the boundaries of one's capacities, and often reveling in the bonding that is involved. Shakespeare's Henry V rhapsodizes about the joy a forthcoming battle holds for "We few, we happy few, we band of brothers; For he today that sheds his blood with me shall be my brother." And a combat veteran from World War II wrote,

---

[2] Theodore Roosevelt, *The Strenuous Life and Other Essays* (New York: Review of Reviews Co., 1910).

We are liberated from our individual impotence and are drunk with the power that union with our fellows brings. In moments like these many have a vague awareness of how isolated and separate their lives have hitherto been.[3]

It is said that the Inuit ("Eskimos") have about a dozen words for "snow" (distinguishing between wet, powder, icy, etc.) and that among the Bedouin there are more than a hundred words for "camel" (ornery, easy-to-ride, etc.). Similarly, in English—and most other languages—there are numerous terms referring to specific wars: the Vietnam War, Korean War, World War II, and so on. By contrast, there is only one word for "peace." Although the peace that obtained, say, between World Wars I and II was quite different from that between the Franco–Prussian War and World War I, we do not identify distinct "peaces." Maybe when—or if—peace becomes as important to English-speaking people as snow is to the Inuit or camels are to the Bedouin, we will distinguish as carefully among the different varieties of peace as we now do about different wars. For now, it must be concluded that war—for all its horrors—holds a particular interest, and even a special appeal. Hence, the need for organized opposition and for "positive approaches to negative peace."

Based on the number of national states that have existed since 1815, there have been approximately 16,000 nation-years, and during this time, war has occupied "only" 600 of these nation-years, or somewhat less that 4 percent of the possible total. The twentieth century was a comparatively warlike one, and yet modern warfare, even with its enormous capacity for devastation, was directly responsible for fewer than about 2 percent of all human deaths occurring during that time. Note, however, that there have also been many indirect casualties of war because war and preparation for war divert resources that might be directed against other causes of death, such as disease and starvation. In addition, war itself typically retards economic development, destroys existing infrastructure, devastates natural environments, renders agriculture dangerous or impossible, displaces huge numbers of people who become homeless and desperate refugees, and also creates long-lasting psychological and social wounds.

Between the years 1500 and 1942 there was an average of nearly 1 formally declared war per year, not including armed revolutions, yet between 1900 and 1965 there were approximately 350, for an average of more than 5 per year. According to peace researcher Lewis Richardson, there were at least 59 million deaths from human violence between 1820 and 1946, of which fewer than 10 million were attributable to individual and small-group violence; the remainder were due to war.[4] It is also noteworthy that historically, deaths directly attributable to disease (notably influenza, cholera, and pneumonia) as well as exposure have exceeded battle losses. In 1632, during the Thirty Years' War, the armies of Gustavus and Wallenstein faced each other outside Nuremberg, losing 18,000 men to typhus and scurvy before separating, without a shot's having been fired!

The sheer wastefulness of war has been appalling, even with nonnuclear weapons. During the Battle of the Somme (1916) in World War I, for example, the British gained a

---

[3] Glen Gray, *The Warriors: Reflections on Men in Battle* (New York: Harper & Row, 1967).
[4] Lewis Richardson, *Statistics of Deadly Quarrels* (Pittsburgh, PA.: Boxwood Press, 1960).

mere 120 square miles at a cost of 420,000 men (3,500 deaths per square mile), while the Germans lost 445,000. During World War I alone, Europe lost virtually an entire generation of young men. Here is F. Scott Fitzgerald's description of the Somme battlefield, after the war:

> See that little stream—we could walk to it in two minutes. It took the British a month to walk to it—a whole empire walking very slowly, dying in front and pushing forward behind. And another empire walked very slowly backward, a few inches a day, leaving the dead like a million bloody rugs.[5]

Of the 2,900,000 men who served in the U.S. armed forces in Vietnam (average age, 19), 300,000 were wounded and 55,000 were killed, along with an unknown number of Vietnamese (estimated at about 2 million). Yet these figures convey very little of the Vietnam War's significance, destructiveness, or horror. Numbers can be numbing.

There is no shortage of proposed solutions to the problem of war. Perhaps the simplest can be derived from the so-called war on drugs, or efforts to promote celibacy: "Just say no." But once again, this turns out to be no solution at all. "What if they had a war," goes the perennial question, "and no one came?" The problem, however, is that "they" have had many a war, and nearly always, lots of people show up. Simple condemnation of war, and/or moral exhortation for peace do not, by themselves, do the job.

Fortunately, there have been voices of sanity...indeed, many of them. Perhaps these voices, and the suggestions they give, have not been sufficiently innovative, forward thinking, or—that bugaboo of attempts to move beyond the war consensus—"realistic." Perhaps the problem is that no one solution has been pushed hard or far enough, or perhaps war is still with us because these various solutions have not been attempted in the right combination or with the right nuance. Perhaps war—like Jesus' observation about the poor—will always be with us. Perhaps, instead, the eventual prevention of war is already en route, so that peace (or rather, "negative peace") is—like Herbert Hoover's claim about prosperity during the Great Depression—just around the corner. Or perhaps something altogether new and different is needed. In any event, perhaps by reviewing some of the distilled wisdom of humanity's efforts to prevent war, we can help peacemakers of the future avoid repeating the errors of the past. And, maybe, we can inspire greater efforts and achieve greater success in the days to come.

"War is waged," wrote St. Augustine, "so that peace may prevail....But it is a greater glory to slay war with a word than people with a sword, and to gain peace by means of peace and not by means of war." In the following chapter, we examine efforts to gain peace by means of peace instead of by war or by threatening war. It is no easy quest, and there may be many routes, some of them blind alleys, others leading into thickets of mazelike complexity, whereas others may be downright dangerous. But in the interest of "realism," it should be noted that war itself is downright dangerous, too.

---

[5] F. Scott Fitzgerald, *Tender is the Night* (New York. Scribners, 1934).

William James

THE MORAL EQUIVALENT OF WAR

Famed historian Will Durant was once asked if he could summarize the history of the world in about five minutes. Responding that he could do so in even less time, he then said,

> History books describe the history of the world as a river red with blood. Running fast, it is filled with the men and events that cause bloodshed: kings and princes, diplomats and politicians. They cause revolutions and wars, violations of territory and rights. But the real history of the world takes place on the riverbanks where ordinary people dwell. They are loving one another, bearing children, and providing homes, all the while trying to remain untouched by the swiftly flowing river.[6]

Much of peace studies is concerned with efforts to build dikes—or at least, place sandbags—to channel the warlike river and keep it from people's homes; eventually, perhaps, to dry it up altogether.

But Durant's vision may be a bit romantic; after all, even though human beings have long yearned for peace, on many occasions they have also jumped rather enthusiastically into the river of war. If, as some suggest, this is at least in part because war meets certain deep-seated human needs, then it seems only reasonable to seek other, less destructive ways of satisfying those needs. If war represents what psychologist Abraham Maslow called a "peak experience," then it should be possible to achieve such experience without killing. Probably the most famous attempt to come to terms with this problem occurred in the following essay by psychologist and philosopher William James. James' suggestion has its modern counterpart in such endeavors as the Peace Corps, VISTA, and other national service programs, although its basic thrust is directed less toward social betterment per se than toward a peaceful rechanneling of human energy.

The war against war is going to be no holiday excursion or camping party. The military feelings are too deeply grounded to abdicate their place among our ideals until better substitutes are offered than the glory and shame that come to nations as well as to individuals from the ups and downs of politics and the vicissitudes of trade. There is something highly paradoxical in the modern man's relation to war. Ask all our millions, north and south, whether they would vote now (were such a thing possible) to have our war for the Union expunged from history and the record of a peaceful transition to the present time substituted for that of its marches and battles, and probably hardly a handful of eccentrics would

From "The Moral Equivalent of War" by William James, *McClure's Magazine,* August 1910.

---

[6] Quoted in Kermit Johnson, *Realism and Hope in a Nuclear Age* (Atlanta, GA: John Kow Press, 1988).

say yes. Those ancestors, those efforts, those memories and legends, are the most ideal part of what we now own together, a sacred spiritual possession worth more than all the blood poured out. Yet ask those same people whether they would be willing in cold blood to start another civil war now to gain another similar possession, and not one man or woman would vote for the proposition. In modern eyes, precious though wars may be, they must not be waged solely for the sake of the ideal harvest. Only when forced upon one, only when an enemy's injustice leaves us no alternative, is a war now thought permissible.

It was not thus in ancient times. The earlier men were hunting men, and to hunt a neighboring tribe, kill the males, loot the village, and possess the females was the most profitable, as well as the most exciting, way of living. Thus were the more martial tribes selected, and in chiefs and peoples a pure pugnacity and love of glory came to mingle with the more fundamental appetite for plunder.

Modern war is so expensive that we feel trade to be a better avenue to plunder, but modern man inherits all the innate pugnacity and all the love of glory of his ancestors. Showing war's irrationality and horror is of no effect upon him. The horrors make the fascination. War is the *strong* life; it is life *in extremis;* war taxes are the only ones men never hesitate to pay, as the budgets of all nations show us.

History is a bath of blood. The *Iliad* is one long recital of how Diomedes and Ajax, Sarpedon and Hector, *killed.* No detail of the wounds they made is spared us, and the Greek mind fed upon the story. Greek history is a panorama of jingoism and imperialism—war for war's sake, all the citizens being warriors. It is horrible reading, because of the irrationality of it all—save for the purpose of making history—and the history is that of the utter ruin of a civilization in intellectual respects perhaps the highest the earth has ever seen....

Alexander's career was piracy pure and simple, nothing but an orgy of power and plunder made romantic by the character of the hero. There was no rational principle in it, and the moment he died his generals and governors attacked one another. The cruelty of those times is incredible. When Rome finally conquered Greece, Paulus Aemilius was told by the Roman Senate to reward his soldiers for their toil by "giving" them the old kingdom of Epirus. They sacked seventy cities and carried off one hundred and fifty thousand inhabitants as slaves. How many they killed I know not, but in Aetolia they killed all the senators, five hundred and fifty in number. Brutus was "the noblest Roman of them all," but, to reanimate his soldiers on the eve of Philippi, he similarly promises to give them the cities of Sparta and Thessalonica to ravage if they win the fight.

Such was the gory nurse that trained societies to cohesiveness. We inherit the warlike type, and, for most of the capacities of heroism that the human race is full of, we have to thank this cruel history. Dead men tell no tales, and, if there were any tribes of other type than this, they have left no survivors. Our ancestors have bred pugnacity into our bone and marrow, and thousands of years of peace won't breed it out of us. The popular imagination fairly fattens on the thought of wars. Let public opinion once reach a certain fighting pitch, and no ruler can withstand it. In the Boer War both governments began with bluff but couldn't stay there; the military tension was too much for them. In 1898 our people had read the word "war" in letters three inches high for three months in every newspaper. The pliant politician McKinley was swept away by their eagerness, and our squalid war with Spain became a necessity.

At the present day, civilized opinion is a curious mental mixture. The military instincts and ideals are as strong as ever, but are confronted by reflective criticisms which sorely curb their ancient freedom. Innumerable writers are showing up the bestial side of military service. Pure loot and mastery seem no longer morally avowable motives, and pretexts must be found for attributing them solely to the enemy. England and we, our army and navy authorities repeat without ceasing, arm solely for "peace"; Germany and Japan it is who are bent on loot and glory. "Peace" in military mouths today is a synonym for "war expected." The word has become a pure provocative, and no government wishing peace sincerely should allow it ever to be printed in a newspaper. Every up-to-date dictionary should say that "peace" and "war" mean the same thing, now *in posse,* now *in actu.* It may even reasonably be said that the intensely sharp competitive *preparation* for war by the nations *is the real war,* permanent, unceasing, and that the battles are only a sort of public verification of the mastery gained during the "peace" interval.

It is plain that on this subject civilized man has developed a sort of double personality. If we take European nations, no legitimate interest of any one of them would seem to justify the tremendous destructions which a war to compass it would necessarily entail. It would seem as though common sense and reason ought to find a way to reach agreement in every conflict of honest interests. I myself think it our bounden duty to believe in such international rationality as possible. But, as things stand, I see how desperately hard it is to bring the peace party and the war party together, and I believe that the difficulty is due to certain deficiencies in the program of pacificism which set the militarist imagination strongly, and, to a certain extent, justifiably, against it. In the whole discussion both sides are on imaginative and sentimental ground. It is but one utopia against another, and everything one says must be abstract and hypothetical. Subject to this criticism and caution, I will try to characterize in abstract strokes the opposite imaginative forces and point out what to my own very fallible mind seems the best utopian hypothesis, the most promising line of conciliation.

In my remarks, pacificist though I am, I will refuse to speak of the bestial side of the war regime (already done justice to by many writers) and consider only the higher aspects of militaristic sentiment. Patriotism no one thinks discreditable, nor does anyone deny that war is the romance of history. But inordinate ambitions are the soul of every patriotism, and the possibility of violent death the soul of all romance. The militarily patriotic and romantic-minded everywhere, and especially the professional military class, refuse to admit for a moment that war may be a transitory phenomenon in social evolution. The notion of a sheep's paradise like that revolts, they say, our higher imagination. Where then would be the steeps of life? If war had ever stopped, we should have to reinvent it, on this view, to redeem life from flat degeneration.

Reflective apologists for war at the present day all take it religiously. It is a sort of sacrament. Its profits are to the vanquished as well as to the victor,

and, quite apart from any question of profit, it is an absolute good, we are told, for it is human nature at its highest dynamic. Its "horrors" are a cheap price to pay for rescue from the only alternative supposed, of a world of clerks and teachers, of coeducation and zoophily, of consumer's leagues and associated charities, of industrialism unlimited, and femininism unabashed. No scorn, no hardness, no valor anymore! Fie upon such a cattleyard of a planet!

So far as the central essence of this feeling goes, no healthy-minded person, it seems to me, can help to some degree partaking of it. Militarism is the great preserver of our ideals of hardihood, and human life with no use for hardihood would be contemptible. Without risks or prizes for the darer, history would be insipid indeed, and there is a type of military character which everyone feels that the race should never cease to breed, for everyone is sensitive to its superiority. The duty is incumbent on mankind of keeping military characters in stock—of keeping them, if not for use, then as ends in themselves and as pure pieces of perfection—so that Roosevelt's weaklings and mollycoddles may not end by making everything else disappear from the face of nature....

The virtues that prevail, it must be noted, are virtues anyhow, superiorities that count in peaceful as well as in military competition; but the strain on them, being infinitely intenser in the latter case, makes war infinitely more searching as a trial. No ordeal is comparable to its winnowings. Its dread hammer is the welder of men into cohesive states, and nowhere but in such states can human nature adequately develop its capacity. The only alternative is degeneration.

...Mankind was nursed in pain and fear and that the transition to a pleasure economy may be fatal to a being wielding no powers of defense against its disintegrative influences. If we speak of the *fear of emancipation from the fear regime,* we put the whole situation into a single phrase, fear regarding ourselves now taking the place of the ancient fear of the enemy.

Turn the fear over as I will in my mind, it all seems to lead back to two unwillingnesses of the imagination, one aesthetic and the other moral; unwillingness, first, to envisage a future in which army life, with its many elements of charm, shall be forever impossible and in which the destinies of peoples shall nevermore be decided quickly, thrillingly, and tragically by force, but only gradually and insipidly by evolution; and, second, unwillingness to see the supreme theater of human strenuousness closed and the splendid military aptitudes of men doomed to keep always in a state of latency and never show themselves in action. These insistent unwillingnesses, no less than other aesthetic and ethical insistencies, have, it seems to me, to be listened to and respected. One cannot meet them effectively by mere counterinsistency on war's expensiveness and horror. The horror makes the thrill, and, when the question is of getting the extremest and supremest out of human nature, talk of expense sounds ignominious. The weakness of so much merely negative criticism is evident— pacificism makes no converts from the military party. The military partly denies neither the bestiality nor the horror nor the expense; it only says that these things tell but half the story. It only says that war is *worth* them; that, taking human nature as a whole, its wars are its best protection against its weaker and more cowardly self and that mankind cannot *afford* to adopt a peace economy.

Pacificists ought to enter more deeply into the aesthetical and ethical point of view of their opponents. . . . So long as antimilitarists propose no substitute for war's disciplinary function, no *moral equivalent* of war, analogous, as one might say, to the mechanical equivalent of heat, so long they fail to realize the full inwardness of the situation. And as a rule they do fail. The duties, penalties, and sanctions pictured in the Utopias they paint are all too weak and tame to touch the military-minded. Tolstoi's pacificism is the only exception to this rule, for it is profoundly pessimistic as regards all this world's values and makes the fear of the Lord furnish the moral spur provided elsewhere by the fear of the enemy. But our socialistic peace advocates all believe absolutely in this world's values, and, instead of the fear of the Lord and the fear of the enemy, the only fear they reckon with is the fear of poverty if one be lazy. This weakness pervades all the socialistic literature with which I am acquainted. . . . Meanwhile men at large still live as they always have lived, under a pain-and-fear economy—for those of us who live in an ease

economy are but an island in the stormy ocean—and the whole atmosphere of present-day utopian literature tastes mawkish and dishwatery to people who still keep a sense for life's more bitter flavors. It suggests, in truth, ubiquitous inferiority.

Inferiority is always with us, and merciless scorn of it is the keynote of the military temper. "Dogs, would you live forever?" shouted Frederick the Great. "Yes," say our utopians, "let us live forever and raise our level gradually." The best thing about our "inferiors" today is that they are as tough as nails and physically and morally almost as insensitive. Utopianism would see them soft and squeamish, while militarism would keep their callousness, but transfigure it into a meritorious characteristic, needed by "the service" and redeemed by that from the suspicion of inferiority. All the qualities of a man acquire dignity when he knows that the service of the collectivity that owns him needs them. If proud of the collectivity, his own pride rises in proportion. No collectivity is like an army for nourishing such pride, but it has to be confessed that the only sentiment which the image of pacific cosmopolitan industrialism is capable of arousing in countless worthy breasts is shame at the idea of belonging to *such* a collectivity. . . . Where is the sharpness and precipitousness, the contempt for life, whether one's own, or another's? Where is the savage yes and no, the unconditional duty? Where is the conscription? Where is the blood tax? Where is anything that one feels honored by belonging to?

Having said thus much in preparation, I will now confess my own utopia. I devoutly believe in the reign of peace and in the gradual advent of some sort of a socialistic equilibrium. The fatalistic view of the war function is to me nonsense, for I know that war-making is due to definite motives and subject to prudential checks and reasonable criticisms, just like any other form of enterprise. And when whole nations are the armies and the science of destruction vies in intellectual refinement with the sciences of production, I see that war becomes absurd and impossible from its own monstrosity. Extravagant ambitions will have to be replaced by reasonable claims, and nations must make common cause against them. . . .

All these beliefs of mine put me squarely into the antimilitarist party. But I do not believe that peace either ought to be or will be permanent on this globe, unless the states pacifically organized preserve some of the old elements of army discipline. A permanently successful peace economy cannot be a simple pleasure economy. In the more-or-less socialistic future toward which mankind seems drifting, we must still subject ourselves collectively to those severities which answer to our real position upon this only partly hospitable globe. We must make new energies and hardihoods continue the manliness to which the military mind so faithfully clings. Martial virtues must be the enduring cement; intrepidity, contempt of softness, surrender of private interest, obedience to command must still remain the rock upon which states are built—unless, indeed, we wish for dangerous reactions against commonwealths fit only for contempt and liable to invite attack whenever a center of crystallization for military-minded enterprise gets formed anywhere in their neighborhood.

The war party is assuredly right in affirming and reaffirming that the martial virtues, although originally gained by the race through war, are absolute and permanent human goods. Patriotic pride and ambition in their military form are, after all, only specifications of a more general competitive passion. They are its first form, but that is no reason for supposing them to be its last form. Men now are proud of belonging to a conquering nation, and without a murmur they lay down their persons and their wealth, if by so doing they may fend off subjection. But who can be sure that *other aspects of one's country* may not, with time and education and suggestion enough, come to be regarded with similarly effective feelings of pride and shame? Why should men not someday feel that it is worth a blood tax to belong to a collectivity superior in *any* ideal respect? Why should they not blush with indignant shame if the community that owns them is vile in any way whatsoever? Individuals, daily more numerous, now feel this civic passion. It is only a question of blowing on the spark until the whole population gets incandescent and, on the ruins of the old morals of military honor, a stable system of morals of civic honor builds itself up. What the whole community comes to believe in grasps the individual as in a vise. The war function has grasped us so far, but constructive interests may someday seem no less imperative and impose on the individual a hardly lighter burden.

Let me illustrate my idea more concretely. There is nothing to make one indignant in the mere fact that life is hard, that men should toil and suffer pain. The planetary conditions once and for all are such, and we can stand it. But that so many men, by mere accidents of birth and opportunity, should have a life of *nothing else* but toil and pain and hardness and inferiority imposed upon them, should have *no* vacation, while others natively no more deserving never get any taste of this campaigning life at all—*this* is capable of arousing indignation in reflective minds. It may end by seeming shameful to all of us that some of us have nothing but campaigning and others nothing but unmanly ease. If now— and this is my idea—there were, instead of military conscription, a conscription of the whole youthful population to form for a certain number of years a part of the army enlisted against nature, the injustice would tend to be evened out, and numerous other goods to the commonwealth would follow. The military ideals of hardihood and discipline would be wrought into the growing fiber of the people; no one would remain blind, as the luxurious classes now are blind, to man's relations to the globe he lives on and to the permanently sour and hard foundations of his higher life. To coal and iron mines, to freight trains, to fishing fleets in December, to dish-washing, clothes-washing, and window-washing, to road-building and tunnel-making, to foundries and stokeholes, and to the frames of skyscrapers, would our gilded youths be drafted off, according to their choice, to get the childishness knocked out of them and to come back into society with healthier sympathies and soberer ideas. They would have paid their blood tax, done their own part in the immemorial human warfare against nature; they would tread the earth more proudly, the women would value them more highly, they would be better fathers and teachers of the following generation.

Such a conscription, with the state of public opinion that would have required it and the many moral fruits it would bear, would preserve in the midst of a pacific civilization the manly virtues which the military party is so afraid of seeing disappear in peace. We should get toughness without callousness, authority with as little criminal cruelty as possible, and painful work done cheerily because the duty is temporary and threatens not, as now, to degrade the whole remainder of one's life. I spoke of the moral equivalent of war. So far, war has been the only force that can discipline a whole community, and, until an equivalent discipline is organized, I believe that war must have its way. But I have no serious doubt that the ordinary prides and shames of social man, once developed to a certain intensity, are capable of organizing such a moral equivalent as I have sketched or some other just as effective for preserving manliness of type. It is but a question of time, of skillful propagandism, and of opinion-making men seizing historic opportunities.

The martial type of character can be bred without war. Strenuous honor and disinterestedness abound elsewhere. Priests and medical men are in a fashion educated to it, and we should all feel some degree of it imperative if we were conscious of our work as an obligatory service to the state. We should be *owned*, as soldiers are by the army, and our pride would rise accordingly. We could be poor, then, without humiliation, as army officers now are. The only thing needed henceforward is to inflame the civic temper as past history has inflamed the military temper.

Roger Fisher, William Ury, and Bruce Patton

GETTING TO YES

One way of gaining peace "by means of peace and not by means of war" is for the contending sides to reach a mutually acceptable agreement among themselves. Not surprisingly, it is easier said than done, although normal people negotiate their differences every day, typically without violence. One of the most pervasive and pernicious myths of our current culture of militarism is that war and preparation for war are natural and unavoidable, whereas peace and preparation for peace are hopelessly unrealistic activities. Peacemaking is represented as an impossible dream, the stuff of saints or the hopelessly deluded, whereas only the making of war—or at best, deterrence—is the reality. Hence, it is important to affirm and make visible the peacemaking that happens all around us, most of the time. The active field of nonviolent conflict resolution offers interesting examples of applying peace studies to interpersonal behavior as well as to international affairs.

Although ways of fighting have changed through history, the basic techniques of negotiation scarcely have. At their most contentious, negotiators have recourse only to threats or promises, and conflict resolution can be backed up by varying degrees of goodwill or ill will and based on a continuum from blind trust to ironclad verification and/or arm-twisting. Negotiations, however, can succeed only if there is a set of outcomes that each party prefers over reaching no agreement. Occasionally, participants in a dispute negotiate only to appear virtuous; but in most cases at least, it appears that a negotiated settlement is preferred over failure to agree or to using violence to force an outcome. The trick is to find a peaceful outcome that will be acceptable to all sides.

There are several ways to facilitate this "trick." One is by the involvement of highly trained third parties, who may arbitrate disputes (that is, lay down a judgment that the contenders have previously pledged to accept) or serve as mediators, whose role is to help the disputants clarify the issues and come to agreement. Third parties can help resolve disputes in several ways. For example, they can make suggestions that both sides find acceptable but which neither would be willing to offer for fear of being seen as weak. They can also help disputants go beyond the traditional, adversarial procedure of "positional bargaining" to a more creative and mutually acceptable outcome, the result of so-called integrative or principled negotiations. The following selection discusses this new and forward-looking approach, in which solving a problem takes precedence over "winning"; it was written by a highly respected team of professional negotiators.

Like it or not, you are a negotiator. Negotiation is a fact of life. You discuss a raise with your boss. You try to agree with a stranger on a price for his house. Two lawyers try to settle a lawsuit arising from a car accident. A group of oil companies plan a joint venture exploring for offshore oil. A city official meets with union leaders to avert a transit strike. The United States secretary of state sits down with his Soviet counterpart to seek an agreement limiting nuclear arms. All these are negotiations.

Everyone negotiates something every day. Like Molière's Monsieur Jourdain, who was delighted to learn that he had been speaking prose all his life, people negotiate even when they don't think of themselves as doing so. A person negotiates with his spouse about where to go for dinner and with his child about when the lights go out. Negotiation is a basic means of getting what you want from others. It is back-and-forth communication designed to reach an agreement when you and the other side have some interests that are shared and others that are opposed.

More and more occasions require negotiation; conflict is a growth industry. Everyone wants to participate in decisions that affect them; fewer and fewer people will accept decisions dictated by someone else. People differ, and they use negotiation to handle their differences. Whether in business, government, or the family, people reach most decisions through negotiation. Even when they go to court, they almost always negotiate a settlement before trial.

Although negotiation takes place every day, it is not easy to do well. Standard strategies for negotiation often leave people dissatisfied, worn out, or alienated—and frequently all three.

People find themselves in a dilemma. They see two ways to negotiate: soft or hard. The soft negotiator wants to avoid personal conflict and so makes concessions readily in order to reach agreement. He wants an amicable resolution; yet he often ends up exploited and feeling bitter. The hard negotiator sees any situation as a contest of wills in which the side that takes the more extreme positions and holds out longer fares better. He wants to win; yet he often ends up producing an equally hard response which exhausts him and his resources and harms his relationship with the other side. Other standard negotiating strategies fall between hard and soft, but each involves an attempted trade-off between getting what you want and getting along with people.

There is a third way to negotiate, a way neither hard nor soft, but rather both hard *and* soft. The method of *principled negotiation* ... is to decide issues on their merits rather than through a haggling process focused on what each side says it will and won't do. It suggests that you look for mutual gains wherever possible, and that where your interests conflict, you should insist that the result be based on some fair standards independent of the will of either side. The method of principled negotiation is hard on the merits, soft on the people. It employs no tricks and no posturing. Principled negotiation shows you

Customer	*Shopkeeper*
How much do you want for this brass dish?	That is a beautiful antique, isn't it? I guess I could let it go for $75.
Oh come on, it's dented. I'll give you $15.	Really! I might consider a serious offer, but $15 certainly isn't serious.
Well, I could go to $20, but I would never pay anything like $75. Quote me a realistic price.	You drive a hard bargain, young lady. $60 cash, right now.
$25.	It cost me a great deal more than that. Make me a serious offer.
$37.50. That's the highest I will go.	Have you noticed the engraving on that dish? Next year pieces like that will be worth twice what you pay today.

how to obtain what you are entitled to and still be decent. It enables you to be fair while protecting you against those who would take advantage of your fairness....

Every negotiation is different, but the basic elements do not change. Principled negotiation can be used whether there is one issue or several; two parties or many; whether there is a prescribed ritual, as in collective bargaining, or an impromptu free-for-all, as in talking with hijackers. The method applies whether the other side is more experienced or less, a hard bargainer or a friendly one. Principled negotiation is an all-purpose strategy. Unlike almost all other strategies, if the other side learns this one, it does not become more difficult to use; it becomes easier....

Whether a negotiation concerns a contract, a family quarrel, or a peace settlement among nations, people routinely engage in positional bargaining. Each side takes a position, argues for it, and makes concessions to reach a compromise. The classic example of this negotiating minuet is the haggling that takes place between a customer and the proprietor of a secondhand store:

And so it goes, on and on. Perhaps they will reach agreement; perhaps not.

Any method of negotiation may be fairly judged by three criteria: It should produce a wise agreement if agreement is possible. It should be efficient. And it should improve or at least not damage the relationship between the parties. (A wise agreement can be defined as one which meets the legitimate interests of each side to the extent possible, resolves conflicting interests fairly, is durable, and takes community interests into account.)

The most common form of negotiation, illustrated by the above example, depends upon successively taking—and then giving up—a sequence of positions.

Taking positions, as the customer and storekeeper do, serves some useful purposes in a negotiation. It tells the other side what you want; it provides an anchor in an uncertain and pressured situation; and it can eventually produce the terms of an acceptable agreement. But those purposes can be served in other ways. And positional bargaining fails to meet the basic criteria of producing a wise agreement, efficiently and amicably.

ARGUING OVER POSITIONS PRODUCES UNWISE AGREEMENTS

When negotiators bargain over positions, they tend to lock themselves into those positions. The more you clarify your position and defend it against attack, the more committed you become to it. The more you try to convince the other side of the impossibility of changing your opening position, the more difficult it becomes to do so. Your ego becomes identified with your position. You now have a new interest in "saving face"—in reconciling future action with past positions—making it less and less likely that any agreement will wisely reconcile the parties' original interests.

The danger that positional bargaining will impede a negotiation was well illustrated by the breakdown of the talks under President Kennedy for a comprehensive ban on nuclear testing. A critical question arose: How many on-site inspections per year should the Soviet Union and the United States be permitted to make within the other's territory to investigate suspicious seismic events? The Soviet Union finally agreed to three inspections. The United States insisted on no less than ten. And there the talks broke down—over positions—despite the fact that no one understood whether an "inspection" would involve one person looking around for one day, or a hundred people prying indiscriminately for a month. The parties had made little attempt to design an inspection procedure that would reconcile the United States's interest in verification with the desire of both countries for minimal intrusion.

As more attention is paid to positions, less attention is devoted to meeting the underlying concerns of the parties. Agreement becomes less likely. Any agreement reached may reflect a mechanical splitting of the difference between final positions rather than a solution carefully crafted to meet the legitimate interests of the parties. The result is frequently an agreement less satisfactory to each side than it could have been.

ARGUING OVER POSITIONS IS INEFFICIENT

The standard method of negotiation may produce either agreement, as with the price of a brass dish, or breakdown, as with the number of on-site inspections. In either event, the process takes a lot of time.

Bargaining over positions creates incentives that stall settlement. In positional bargaining you try to improve the chance that any settlement reached is favorable to you by starting with an extreme position, by stubbornly holding to it, by deceiving the other party as to your true views, and by making small concessions only as necessary to keep the negotiation going. The same is true for the other side. Each of those factors tends to interfere with reaching a

settlement promptly. The more extreme the opening positions and the smaller the concessions, the more time and effort it will take to discover whether or not agreement is possible.

The standard minuet also requires a large number of individual decisions as each negotiator decides what to offer, what to reject, and how much of a concession to make. Decision making is difficult and time-consuming at best. Where each decision not only involves yielding to the other side but will likely produce pressure to yield further, a negotiator has little incentive to move quickly. Dragging one's feet, threatening to walk out, stonewalling, and other such tactics become commonplace. They all increase the time and costs of reaching agreement as well as the risk that no agreement will be reached at all.

ARGUING OVER POSITIONS ENDANGERS AN ONGOING RELATIONSHIP

Positional bargaining becomes a contest of will. Each negotiator asserts what he will and won't do. The task of jointly devising an acceptable solution tends to become a battle. Each side tries through sheer willpower to force the other to change its position. "I'm not going to give in. If you want to go to the movies with me, it's *The Maltese Falcon* or nothing." Anger and resentment often result as one side sees itself bending to the rigid will of the other while its own legitimate concerns go unaddressed. Positional bargaining thus strains and sometimes shatters the relationship between the parties. Commercial enterprises that have been doing business together for years may part company. Neighbors may stop speaking to each other. Bitter feelings generated by one such encounter may last a lifetime. . . .

BEING NICE IS NO ANSWER

Many people recognize the high costs of hard positional bargaining, particularly on the parties and their relationship. They hope to avoid them by following a more gentle style of negotiation. Instead of seeing the other side as adversaries, they prefer to see them as friends. Rather than emphasizing a goal of victory, they emphasize the necessity of reaching agreement. In a soft negotiating game the standard moves are to make offers and concessions, to trust the other side, to be friendly, and to yield as necessary to avoid confrontation.

The following table illustrates two styles of positional bargaining, soft and hard. Most people see their choice of negotiating strategies as between these two styles. Looking at the table as presenting a choice, should you be a soft or a hard positional bargainer? Or should you perhaps follow a strategy somewhere in between?

PROBLEM

Positional Bargaining: Which Game Should You Play?

SOFT	HARD
Participants are friends.	Participants are adversaries.
The goal is agreement.	The goal is victory.
Make concessions to cultivate the relationship.	Demand concessions as a condition of the relationship.
Be soft on the people and the problem.	Be hard on the problem and the people.
Trust others.	Distrust others.
Change your position easily.	Dig in to your position.
Make offers.	Make threats.
Disclose your bottom line.	Mislead as to your bottom line.
Accept one-sided losses to reach agreement.	Demand one-sided gains as the price of agreement.
Search for the single answer: the one *they* will accept.	Search for the single answer: the one *you* will accept.
Insist on agreement.	Insist on your position.
Try to avoid a contest of will.	Try to win a contest of will.
Yield to pressure.	Apply pressure.

The soft negotiating game emphasizes the importance of building and maintaining a relationship. Within families and among friends much negotiation takes place in this way. The process tends to be efficient, at least to the extent of producing results quickly. As each party competes with the other in being more generous and more forthcoming, an agreement becomes highly likely. But it may not be a wise one. The results may not be as tragic as in the O. Henry story about an impoverished couple in which the loving wife sells her hair in order to buy a handsome chain for her husband's watch, and the unknowing husband sells his watch in order to buy beautiful combs for his wife's hair. However, any negotiation primarily concerned with the relationship runs the risk of producing a sloppy agreement.

More seriously, pursuing a soft and friendly form of positional bargaining makes you vulnerable to someone who plays a hard game of positional bargaining. In positional bargaining, a hard game dominates a soft one. If the hard bargainer insists on concessions and makes threats while the soft bargainer yields in order to avoid confrontation and insists on agreement, the negotiating game is biased in favor of the hard player. The process will produce an agreement, although it may not be a wise one. It will certainly be more favorable to the hard positional bargainer than to the soft one. If your response to sustained, hard positional bargaining is soft positional bargaining, you will probably lose your shirt.

THERE IS AN ALTERNATIVE

If you do not like the choice between hard and soft positional bargaining, you can change the game.

The game of negotiation takes place at two levels. At one level, negotiation addresses the substance; at another, it focuses—usually implicitly—on the procedure for dealing with the substance. The first negotiation may concern your salary, the terms of a lease, or a price to be paid. The second negotiation concerns how you will negotiate the substantive question: by soft positional bargaining, by hard positional bargaining, or by some other method. This second negotiation is a game about a game—a "meta-game." Each move you make within a negotiation is not only a move that deals with rent, salary, or other substantive questions; it also helps structure the rules of the game you are playing. Your move may serve to keep the negotiations within an ongoing mode, or it may constitute a game-changing move.

This second negotiation by and large escapes notice because it seems to occur without conscious decision. Only when dealing with someone from another country, particularly someone with a markedly different cultural background, are you likely to see the necessity of establishing some accepted process for the substantive negotiations. But whether consciously or not, you are negotiating procedural rules with every move you make, even if those moves appear exclusively concerned with substance.

The answer to the question of whether to use soft positional bargaining or hard is "neither." Change the game....We have been developing an alternative to positional bargaining: a method of negotiation explicitly designed to produce wise outcomes efficiently and amicably. This method, called *principled negotiation* or *negotiation on the merits*, can be boiled down to four basic points.

These four points define a straightforward method of negotiation that can be used under almost any circumstance. Each point deals with a basic element of negotiation, and suggests what you should do about it.

People: Separate the people from the problem.

Interests: Focus on interests, not positions.

Options: Generate a variety of possibilities before deciding what to do.

Criteria: Insist that the result be based on some objective standard.

The first point responds to the fact that human beings are not computers. We are creatures of strong emotions who often have radically different perceptions and have difficulty communicating clearly. Emotions typically become entangled with the objective merits of the problem. Taking positions just makes this worse because people's egos become identified with their positions. Hence, before working on the substantive problem, the "people problem" should be disentangled from it and dealt with separately. Figuratively if not literally, the participants should come to see themselves as working side by side, attacking the problem, not each other. Hence the first proposition: *Separate the people from the problem*.

The second point is designed to overcome the drawback of focusing on people's stated positions when the object of a negotiation is to satisfy their underlying interests. A negotiating position often obscures what you really want. Compromising between positions is not likely to produce an agreement which will effectively take care of the human needs that led people to adopt those positions. The second basic element of the method is: *Focus on interests, not positions.*

The third point responds to the difficulty of designing optimal solutions while under pressure. Trying to decide in the presence of an adversary narrows your vision. Having a lot at stake inhibits creativity. So does searching for the one right solution. You can offset these constraints by setting aside a designated time within which to think up a wide range of possible solutions that advance shared interests and creatively reconcile differing interests. Hence the third basic point: Before trying to reach agreement, *invent options for mutual gain.*

Where interests are directly opposed, a negotiator may be able to obtain a favorable result simply by being stubborn. That method tends to reward intransigence and produce arbitrary results. However, you can counter such a negotiator by insisting that his single say-so is not enough and that the agreement must reflect some fair standard independent of the naked will of either side. This does not mean insisting that the terms be based on the standard you select, but only that some fair standard such as market value, expert opinion, custom, or law determine the outcome. By discussing such criteria rather than what the parties are willing or unwilling to do, neither party need give in to the other; both can defer to a fair solution. Hence the fourth basic point: *Insist on objective criteria.*

The method of principled negotiation is contrasted with hard and soft positional bargaining in the table on the next page, which shows the four basic points of the method in boldface type....

"WINNING"

In 1964 an American father and his twelve-year-old son were enjoying a beautiful Saturday in Hyde Park,

London, playing catch with a Frisbee. Few in England had seen a Frisbee at that time and a small group of strollers gathered to watch this strange sport. Finally, one Homburg-clad Britisher came over to the father: "Sorry to bother you. Been watching you a quarter of an hour. Who's *winning?*"

In most instances to ask a negotiator, "Who's winning?" is as inappropriate as to ask who's winning a marriage. If you ask that question about your marriage, you have already lost the more important negotiation—the one about what kind of game to play, about the way you deal with each other and your shared and differing interests.

...Both theory and experience suggest that the method of principled negotiation will produce over the long run substantive outcomes as good as or better than you are likely to obtain using any other negotiation strategy. In addition, it should prove more efficient and less costly to human relationships. We find the method comfortable to use and hope you will too.

PROBLEM

Positional Bargaining: Which Game Should You Play?

SOFT	HARD
Participants are friends.	Participants are adversaries.
The goal is agreement.	The goal is victory.
Make concessions to cultivate the relationship.	Demand concessions as a condition of the relationship.
Be soft on the people and the problem.	Be hard on the problem and the people.
Trust others.	Distrust others.
Change your position easily.	Dig in to your position.
Make offers.	Make threats.
Disclose your bottom line.	Mislead as to your bottom line.
Accept one-sided losses to reach agreement.	Demand one-sided gains as the price of agreement.
Search for the single answer: the one they will accept.	Search for the single answer: the one you will accept.
Insist on agreement.	Insist on your position.
Try to avoid a contest of will.	Try to win a contest of will.
Yield to pressure.	Apply pressure.

SOLUTION

Change the Game—Negotiate on the Merits

PRINCIPLED
Participants are problem-solvers.
The goal is a wise outcome reached efficiently and amicably.
Separate the people from the problem.
Be soft on the people, hard on the problem.
Proceed independent of trust.
Focus on interests, not positions.
Explore interests.
Avoid having a bottom line.
Invent options for mutual gain.
Develop multiple options to choose from; decide later.
Insist on objective criteria.
Try to reach a result based on standards independent of will.
Reason and be open to reasons; yield to principle, not pressure.

That does not mean it is easy to change habits, to disentangle emotions from the merits, or to enlist others in the task of working out a wise solution to a shared problem. From time to time you may want to remind yourself that the first thing you are trying to win is a better way to negotiate—a way that avoids your having to choose between the satisfactions of getting what you deserve and of being decent. You can have both.

Charles Osgood

DISARMAMENT DEMANDS GRIT

"You cannot simultaneously prevent and prepare for war," wrote Albert Einstein. This sentiment can be carried further, to a more positive assertion: you can prevent war by getting rid of the weapons with which war is carried out. But not everyone would agree. Indeed, no one—not even the most ardent advocate of disarmament—claims that doing away with weapons will solve the problem of war. So long as the underlying causes persist, and so long as people have the capacity and inclination to resort to violence—especially organized violence—under certain circumstances, war will continue to haunt us.

Nonetheless, the connection between weaponry and war, although complex, is well established and legitimate. The dream of disarmament is thus an ancient one, intimately connected with the yearning for peace itself: "And they shall beat their swords into plowshares, and their spears into pruning hooks; nation shall not lift up sword against nation, neither shall they learn war any more" (Micah 4:3). The actual history of disarmament, however, is not especially encouraging. All too often, disarmament proposals have been self-serving, in which one side urges elimination of those weapons in which the other has an advantage or which are obsolete, or both sides make proposals simply for their publicity value, confident that they will be rejected.

Although general and complete disarmament has thus far eluded our grasp, there have been a number of modest successes, including prohibitions on specific weapons (dumdum bullets, biological agents, antiballistic missiles) as well as mutual agreements to forego arms races in particular places (e.g., Antarctica, the seabed). These and other accomplishments fall within the category of disarmament's "poor sister," arms control. Arms control is controversial; within the peace studies community, it is often seen as potentially pernicious, if it shifts attention from the ultimate goal of disarmament, while also seeming to legitimize various arms races and even sometimes to accelerate them in areas not explicitly prohibited. There is also a long and sorry history of using arms control negotiations as a smoke screen to build yet more weapons under the guise that one must be able to "negotiate from strength."

From "Disarmament Demands GRIT" by Charles Osgood. In E. Laszlo and D. Keys, eds., *Disarmament: The Human Factor*. 1981. New York: Pergamon Press.

However, peace specialists acknowledge four potential benefits of well-constructed arms control agreements, even if they serve largely as stopgap measures: (1) reducing the chances of war breaking out (if each side become less worried that its opponent is accumulating weapons that makes it likely to initiate an attack); (2) reducing the destructiveness of war if it does break out (say, by eliminating weapons of mass destruction or those conventional weapons that are especially brutal); (3) reducing the economic costs of preparing for war (by permitting the redirection of society's resources away from certain weapons); and (4) developing cooperation and confidence-building, which can lead to yet further agreements (assuming that the agreed measures are in fact lived up to).

Most of all, it is important to recognize that disarmament is a *process*, not an *event*, more a way of progressing than a finished masterpiece to be unveiled to the admiring world with a grand "voila!" Like perfect grace, total disarmament may never be achieved, but that doesn't diminish its worth as a goal, or rather, as a route toward possible salvation. In the twenty-first century, with the end of the Cold War, specific disarmament proposals have received considerably less attention than in the past, with the exception of some relating to nuclear weapons (taken up later in this chapter). There has been essentially no change, however, in the necessity for international communication, even as experts and ideologues disagree as to the preferred methods.

All too often, when two parties disagree, their communication is limited to threats and—more rarely—promises. Moreover, if the situation deteriorates, there can be a rapid escalation of anger and distrust—as a result of which, things can spiral out of control. But as social psychologist Charles Osgood points out, people also have other behaviors in their repertoire, by which tensions can be ratcheted down. Osgood originally presented his formulation in an influential book titled *An Alternative to War or Surrender*, and although it was especially developed with superpower tensions in mind, it is equally applicable to daily life and to nonnuclear conflicts.

...The focus of my own long-term concern at the inter-nation level has been the rationalization of a strategy...whose technical name is "Graduated and Reciprocated Initiatives in Tension-reduction." While doodling at a conference in the early 1960s, I discovered that the initials of this mind-boggling phrase spelled out GRIT, and although I generally take a dim view of acronyms, this one was not only easy for people to remember, but also suggested the kind of determination and patience required to successfully apply it. One of the aims of GRIT is to reduce and control international tension levels. Another is to create an atmosphere of mutual trust within which negotiations on critical military and political issues can have a better chance of succeeding; in other words, GRIT is not a substitute for the more familiar process of negotiation, but rather a parallel process designed to enable a nation to take the initiative in a situation where a dangerous "balance" of mutual fear exists—and, to the degree successful, GRIT smooths the path of negotiation.

However, being unconventional in international affairs, the GRIT strategy is open to suspicion abroad and resistance at home. Therefore, it is necessary to spell out the ground rules under which this particular "game" should be played, to demonstrate how national security can be maintained during the process, how the likelihood of reciprocation can be maximized, and how the genuineness of initiations and reciprocations can be evaluated. These "rules" are spelled out in detail in my "basic" pocketbook, *An Alternative to War or Surrender....*

RULES FOR MAINTAINING SECURITY

RULE 1: *Unilateral initiatives must not reduce one's capacity to inflict unacceptable nuclear retaliation should one be attacked at that level.*

Nuclear capacity can serve rational foreign policy (a) if it is viewed not only as a deterrent, but also as a security base from which to take limited risks in the direction of reducing tensions; (b) if the retaliatory, second-strike nature of the capacity is made explicit; and (c) if only the minimum capacity required for effective deterrence is maintained and the arms race damped. Needless to say, none of these conditions have been met to date by the two nuclear super-powers. Not only are nuclear weapons ambiguous as to initiation or retaliation, but both strategic and tactical weapons are redundantly deployed and in oversupply as far as capacity for graded response to aggression is concerned. Therefore, at some stage in the GRIT process, graduated and reciprocated reductions in nuclear weapons, along with the men that are assigned to them, should be initiated.

RULE 2: *Unilateral initiatives must not cripple one's capacity to meet conventional aggression with appropriately graded conventional response.*

Conventional forces are the front line of deterrence, and they must be maintained at rough parity in regions of confrontation. But the absolute level at which the balance is maintained is variable. The general rule would be to initiate unilateral moves in the regions of least tension and gradually extend them to what were originally the most tense regions.

RULE 3: *Unilateral initiatives must be graduated in risk according to the degree of reciprocation obtained from an opponent.*

This is the self-regulating characteristic of GRIT that keeps the process within reasonable limits of security. If bona fide reciprocations of appropriate magnitude are obtained, the magude and significance of

subsequent steps can be increased; if not, then the process continues with a diversity of steps of about the same magnitude of risk. The relative risk thus remains roughly constant throughout the process.

RULE 4: *Unilateral initiatives should be diversified in nature, both as to sphere of action and as to geographical locus of application.*

The reason for diversification is twofold. First, in maintaining security, diversification minimizes weakening one's position in any one sphere (such as in combat troops) or any one geographical locus. Second, in inducing reciprocation, diversification keeps applying the pressure of initiatives having a common tension-reducing intent (and, hopefully, effect), but does not "threaten" the opponent by pushing steadily in the same sphere or locus and thereby limiting his options in reciprocating.

RULES FOR INDUCING RECIPROCATION

RULE 5: *Unilateral initiatives must be designed and communicated so as to emphasize a sincere intent to reduce tensions.*

Escalation and deescalation strategies cannot be "mixed" in the sense that military men talk about the "optimum mix" of weapon systems. The reason is psychological: reactions to threats (aggressive impulses) are incompatible with reactions to promises (conciliatory impulses); each strategy thus destroys the credibility of the other. It is therefore essential that a complete shift in basic policy be clearly signaled at the beginning. The top leadership of the initiating power must establish the right atmosphere by stating the overall nature of the new policy and by emphasizing its tension-reducing intent. Early initiatives must be clearly perceived as tension reducing by the opponents in conflict situations, must be of such significance that they cannot be easily discounted as "propaganda," and they must be readily verifiable....

RULE 6: *Unilateral initiatives should be publicly announced at some reasonable interval prior to their execution and identified as part of a deliberate policy of reducing tensions.*

Prior announcements minimize the potentially unstabilizing effect of unilateral acts and their identification with total GRIT strategy helps shape the opponent's interpretation of them. However, the GRIT process cannot *begin* with a large, precipitate, and potentially destabilizing unilateral action....

RULE 7: *Unilateral initiatives should include in their announcement an explicit invitation to reciprocation in some form.*

The purpose of this "rule" is to increase pressure on an opponent by making it clear that reciprocation of appropriate form and magnitude is essential to the momentum of GRIT, and to bring to bear pressures of world opinion. However, exactly specifying the form or magnitude of reciprocation has several drawbacks: having the tone of a demand rather than an invitation, it carries an implied threat of retaliation if the demand is not met; furthermore, the specific reciprocation requested may be based on faulty perceptions of the other's situation and this may be the reason for failure to get reciprocation. It is the occurrence of reciprocation in any form, yet having the same tension-reducing intent, that is critical. Again speaking psychologically, the greatest conciliatory impact on an opponent in a conflict situation is produced by his own, voluntary act of reciprocating. Such behavior is incompatible with his Neanderthal beliefs about the unalterable hostility and aggressiveness of the initiators, and once he *has* committed a reciprocating action, all of the cognitive pressure is on modifying these beliefs.

RULES FOR DEMONSTRATING THE GENUINENESS OF INITIATIVES AND RECIPROCATIONS

RULE 8: *Unilateral initiatives that have been announced must be executed on schedule regardless of any prior commitments to reciprocate by the opponent.*

This is the best indication of the firmness and bona fides of one's own intent to reduce tensions. The control over what and how much is committed is the graduated nature of the process; at the point when each initiative is announced, the calculation has been made in terms of prior-reciprocation

history that this step can be taken within reasonable limits of security. Failure to execute an announced step, however, would be a clear sign of ambivalence in intent. This is particularly important in the early stages, when announced initiatives are liable to the charge of "propaganda."

RULE 9: *Unilateral initiatives should be continued over a considerable period, regardless of the degree or even absence of reciprocation.*

Like the steady pounding on a nail, pressure toward reciprocating builds up as one announced act follows another announced act of a tension-reducing nature, even though the individual acts may be small in significance. It is this characteristic of GRIT which at once justifies the use of the acronym and which raises the hackles of most military men. But the essence of this strategy is the calculated manipulation of the intent component of the "perceived-threat-equals-capability-times-intent" equation. It is always difficult to read the intentions of an opponent in a conflict situation and they are usually very complex. In such a situation, GRIT can be applied to consistently encourage conciliatory intents and interpretations at the expense of aggressive ones.

RULE 10: *Unilateral initiatives must be as unambiguous and as susceptible to verification as possible.*

Although actions do speak louder than words, even overt deeds are liable to misinterpretation. Inviting opponent verification via direct, on-the-spot observation or via indirect media observation (such as televising the act in question), along with requested reciprocation in the verification of his actions, is ideal; what little might be lost in the way of secrecy by both sides might be more than made up in a reduced need for secrecy on both sides.... However, the strategy of GRIT can be directly applied to this problem. Particularly in the early stages, when the risk potentials are small, observers could be publicly invited to guarantee the verifiability of doing what was announced, and although entirely *without* explicit insistence on reciprocation by the opponent, the implication would be strong indeed. Initiatives whose validities are apparently very high should be designed (for example, initial pullbacks of forces

from border confrontations), and they can operate to gradually reduce suspicion and resistance to
verification procedures. This should accelerate as the
GRIT process continues.

APPLICATIONS OF GRIT STRATEGY

Over the past fifteen years or so there has been considerable experimentation with the GRIT strategy,
but mostly in the laboratory. There have been sporadic GRIT-like moves in the real world; for example,
the graduated and reciprocated pullback of American
and Soviet tanks that had been lined up practically
snout-to-snout at the height of the Berlin Crisis. But
for the most part in recent history, these have been
one-shot affairs, always tentatively made and never
reflecting any genuine change in basic strategy.

The one exception to this dictum was "the Kennedy experiment," as documented in a significant
paper by Amitai Etzioni. The real-world test of a
strategy of calculated deescalation was conducted in
the period from June 1962 to November of 1963.
The first step was President Kennedy's speech at the
American University on June 10, in which he outlined what he called "a strategy of peace," praised
the Russians for their accomplishments, noted that
"our problems are man-made...and can be solved
by man," and then announced the first unilateral
initiative: the United States was stopping all nuclear
tests in the atmosphere, and would not resume them
unless another country did. Kennedy's speech was
published *in full* in both *Izvestia* and *Pravda*, with
a combined circulation of 10 million. On June 15
Premier Khrushchev reciprocated with a speech wel-
coming the U.S. initiative, and he announced that
he had ordered the production of strategic bombers
to be halted.

The next step was a symbolic reduction in the
trade barriers between East and West. On October
9, President Kennedy approved the sale of $250 mil-
lion worth of wheat to the Soviet Union. Although
the United States had proposed a direct America-
Russia communication link (the "hotline") in 1962,
it was not until June 20, 1963—after the "Kennedy

experiment" had begun—that the Soviets agreed to
this measure. Conclusion of a test-ban treaty, long
stalled, was apparently the main goal of the experiment. Multilateral negotiators began in earnest in
July, and on August 5, 1963, the test-ban treaty was
signed. The Kennedy experiment slowed down with
the deepened involvement in Vietnam, and it came
to an abrupt end in Dallas.

Had this real-world experiment in calculated
de-escalation been a success? To most of the initiatives taken by either side, the other reciprocated,
and the reciprocations were roughly proportional
in significance. What about psychological impact?
I do not think that anyone who lived through that
period will deny that there was a definite warming
of American attitudes toward Russians, and the same
is reported for Russian attitudes toward Americans.
The Russians even coined their own name for the
new strategy, "the policy of mutual example."

The novelty of GRIT raises shrieks of incredulity
from hawks and clucks of worry even from doves.
The question I am most often asked is this: Doesn't
any novel approach like this involve too much
risk? Anything we do in the nuclear age means taking risks. To escalate conflicts that involve another
nuclear power unquestionably carries the greatest
risk. Simply doing nothing—remaining frozen in a
status quo that is already at much too high a level
of force and tension—is certainly not without risk
over the long run. GRIT also involves risk. But the
risking comes in small packages. Looked at in a
broad perspective, the superpower confrontation
has many positive elements in it and many motivations on both sides that favor détente. It therefore
offers itself as a potential proving ground for a strategy that is novel but yet appropriate to the nuclear
age in which we are trying to survive. The assumption behind nuclear deterrence—that we can go
spinning forever into eternity, poised for mutual
annihilation and kept from it only by fragile bonds
of mutual fear—is untenable. The ultimate goal
must be to get out from under the nuclear sword of
Damocles by eliminating such weapons from the
human scene.

David Krieger and Angela McCrackien

TEN NUCLEAR MYTHS

Nuclear weapons represent the greatest of all violent threats to life on earth. With the end of the Cold War, a problem that had seemed as intractable as it was immense now offers exciting possibilities for genuine progress, including perhaps that ancient dream: disarmament. Even in the straitjacket of nuclear arms racing, treaties were negotiated that banned above-ground nuclear tests and restricted competition in antiballistic missiles as well as restraining nuclear proliferation. In 1996 a Comprehensive Test Ban Treaty was signed—its future marred, however, in 1998, when India, and then Pakistan, engaged in nuclear testing.

Not surprisingly, nuclear competition in South Asia raised the specter of nuclear proliferation generally, a danger that is especially worrisome given that unlike the United States and the former U.S.S.R., India and Pakistan share a common border and have already engaged in several wars. (This problem also applies to other potential proliferators, such as Brazil and Argentina, Israel and the Arab states, etc.) Ironically, small nuclear arsenals may also be *less* secure than large ones, because they may tempt an opponent to try a "preemptive strike"; whereas if it possessed a large supply of nuclear weapons, a country could maintain a secure "second-strike capability," being able to absorb an initial attack and still retaliate. The result, at least in theory, would be "deterrence," or at least a degree of "crisis stability." It is also possible, however, that nuclear arsenals will make hostile countries more careful and thus less likely to initiate hostilities or—if they begin—to escalate them. On the other hand, the greatest crisis stability would seem to derive from nuclear disarmament, which would have the added benefit of allowing desperately poor countries to invest in their people instead of their weapons.

With the Cold War now history, the time seems right for dramatic progress toward undoing our current reliance on nuclear weapons altogether, especially given the emergence of a new, widely recognized nuclear threat: possible use of nuclear weapons by terrorists, who might well be immune to deterrence insofar as their motivation is not traditionally "rational." In any event, despite the manifold dangers posed by nuclear weapons, combined with the opportunity offered by the end of the Cold War, some suggest that we are actually moving backward on the antinuclear front. For progress to be made, it might well be necessary for leaders as well as the public to shed some widespread nuclear myths, as identified here by David Krieger and Angela McCrackien.

———————————————————— ⌗ ————————————————————

1. *Nuclear weapons were needed to defeat Japan in World War II.* It is widely believed, particularly in the United States, that the use of nuclear weapons against the Japanese cities of Hiroshima and Nagasaki was necessary to defeat Japan in World War II. This is not, however, the opinion of the leading U.S. military figures in the war, including General Dwight Eisenhower, General Omar Bradley, General Hap Arnold, and Admiral William Leahy. General Eisenhower, for example, who was the supreme allied commander in Europe during World War II and later a U.S. president, wrote, "I had been conscious of a feeling of depression and so I voiced [to Secretary of War Stimson] my grave misgivings, first on the basis of my belief that Japan was already defeated and that dropping the bomb was completely unnecessary, and secondly because I thought that our country should avoid shocking world opinion by the use of a weapon whose employment was, I thought, no longer mandatory as a measure to save American lives. It was my belief that Japan was, at that very moment, seeking some way to surrender with a minimum loss of 'face'.... Not only was the use of nuclear force unnecessary, its destructive force was excessive, resulting in 220,000 deaths by the end of 1945.

2. *Nuclear weapons prevented a war between the United States and the Soviet Union.* Many people believe that the nuclear standoff during the Cold War prevented the two superpowers from going to war with each other for fear of mutually assured destruction. While it is true that the superpowers did not engage in nuclear warfare during the Cold War, there were many confrontations between them that came uncomfortably close to nuclear war, the most prominent being the 1962 Cuban Missile Crisis. There were also many deadly conflicts and "proxy" wars carried out by the superpowers in Asia, Africa, and Latin America. The Vietnam War, which took several million Vietnamese lives and the lives of more than 58,000 Americans, is a prominent example. These wars made the supposed nuclear peace very bloody and deadly. Lurking in the background was the constant danger of a nuclear exchange. The Cold War was an exceedingly dangerous time, with a massive nuclear arms race, and the human race was extremely fortunate to have survived it without suffering a nuclear war.

3. *Nuclear weapons prevent nuclear terrorism.* In light of the Cold War's end, many people believed that nuclear threats had gone away. While the nature of nuclear threats has changed since the end of the Cold War, these threats are far from having disappeared or even significantly diminished. During the Cold War, the greatest threat was that of a massive nuclear exchange between the United States and the Soviet Union. In the aftermath of the Cold War, a variety of new nuclear threats have emerged. Among these are the following dangers:

- increased possibilities of nuclear weapons falling into the hands of terrorists who would not hesitate to use them;
- nuclear war between India and Pakistan;
- policies of the U.S. government to make nuclear weapons smaller and more usable;
- use of nuclear weapons by accident, particularly by Russia, which has a substantially weakened early-warning system; and
- spread of nuclear weapons to other states, such as North Korea, that may perceive them to be an "equalizer" against a more powerful state.

4. *The United States needs nuclear weapons for its national security.* There is a widespread belief

in the United States that nuclear weapons are necessary for the United States to defend against aggressor states. U.S. national security, however, would be far improved if the United States took a leadership role in seeking to eliminate nuclear weapons throughout the world. Nuclear weapons are the only weapons that could actually destroy the United States, and their existence and proliferation threaten U.S. security. Continued high-alert deployment of nuclear weapons and research on smaller and more usable nuclear weapons by the United States, combined with a more aggressive foreign policy, makes many weaker nations feel threatened. Weaker states may think of nuclear weapons as an equalizer, giving them the ability to effectively neutralize the forces of a threatening nuclear weapons state. Thus, as in the case of North Korea, the U.S. threat may be instigating nuclear weapons proliferation. Continued reliance on nuclear weapons by the United States is setting the wrong example for the world and is further endangering the country rather than protecting it. The United States has strong conventional military forces and would be far more secure in a world in which no country had nuclear arms.

5. *Nuclear weapons make a country safer.* It is a common belief that nuclear weapons protect a country by deterring potential aggressors from attacking. By threatening massive retaliation, the argument goes, nuclear weapons prevent an attacker from starting a war. To the contrary, nuclear weapons are actually undermining the safety of the countries that possess them by providing a false sense of security. While deterrence can provide some psychological sense of security, there are no guarantees that the threat of retaliation will succeed in preventing an attack. There are many ways in which deterrence could fail, including misunderstandings, faulty communications, irrational leaders, miscalculations, and accidents. In addition, the possession of nuclear weapons enhances the risks of terrorism, proliferation, and ultimately nuclear annihilation.

6. *No leader would be crazy enough to actually use nuclear weapons.* Many people believe that the threat of using nuclear weapons can go on indefinitely as a means of deterring attacks, because no leader would be crazy enough to actually use them. Unfortunately, nuclear weapons have been used, and it is likely that most, if not all, leaders possessing these weapons would, under certain conditions, actually use them. U.S. leaders, considered by many to be highly rational, are the only ones who have ever actually used nuclear weapons in war, against Hiroshima and Nagasaki. Outside of these two bombings, the leaders of nuclear weapons states have repeatedly come close to using nuclear weapons. Nuclear deterrence is based upon a believable threat of nuclear retaliation, and the threat of nuclear weapons use has been constant during the post–World War II period. U.S. policy currently calls for the use of nuclear weapons in response to an attack with chemical or biological weapons against the United States, its troops, or its allies. One of the premises of the U.S. argument for preventive war is that other leaders would be willing to attack the United States with nuclear weapons. Threats of nuclear attack by India and Pakistan provide still another example of nuclear brinksmanship that could turn into a nuclear war. Globally and historically, leaders have done their best to prove that they would use nuclear weapons. Assuming that they would not do so is unwise.

7. *Nuclear weapons are a cost-effective method of national defense.* Some have argued that nuclear weapons, with their high yield of explosive power, offer the benefit of an effective defense for minimum investment. This is one reason behind ongoing research into lower-yield tactical nuclear weapons, which would be perceived as more usable. The cost of nuclear weapons research, development, testing, deployment, and maintenance, however, exceeded $5.5 trillion by 1996, according to a study by the Brookings Institution. With advances in nuclear technology and power, the costs and consequences of a nuclear war would be immeasurable.

8. *Nuclear weapons are well protected, and there is little chance that terrorists could get their hands on one.* Many people believe that nuclear weapons are well protected and that the likelihood of terrorists' obtaining these weapons is low. In the aftermath of the Cold War, however, the ability of the Russians to protect their nuclear forces has declined precipitously. In addition, a coup in a country with nuclear weapons, such as Pakistan, could lead to a government's coming to power that was willing to provide nuclear weapons to terrorists. In general, the more nuclear weapons there are in the world and the more nuclear weapons proliferate to additional countries, the greater the possibility that nuclear weapons will end up in the hands of terrorists. The best remedy for keeping nuclear weapons out of the hands of terrorists is to drastically reduce their numbers and institute strict international inspections and controls on all nuclear weapons and weapons-grade nuclear materials in all countries, until these weapons and the materials for making them can be eliminated.

9. *The United States is working to fulfill its nuclear disarmament obligations.* Most U.S. citizens believe that the United States is working to fulfill its nuclear disarmament obligations. In fact, the United States has failed to fulfill its obligations under Article VI of the Nuclear Non-Proliferation Treaty, requiring good faith efforts to achieve nuclear disarmament, for more than thirty years. The United States has failed to ratify the Comprehensive Test Ban Treaty and has withdrawn from the Anti-Ballistic Missile Treaty. The 2003 Strategic Offensive Reductions Treaty (SORT) with Russia takes strategic nuclear weapons off active deployment but has no provisions for verification or systematic reductions, and it fails to adhere to the principle of irreversibility agreed to at the 2000 Non-Proliferation Treaty Review Conference. The treaty seeks maximum flexibility for rearmament rather than irreversible reductions in nuclear arms. Nuclear weapons taken off active deployment will be put in storage, where they will actually become more vulnerable in both the United States and Russia to theft by terrorists. In the year 2012, the treaty will end, unless extended.

10. *Nuclear weapons are needed to combat threats from terrorists and "rogue states."* It has been argued that nuclear weapons are needed to protect against terrorists and "rogue states." Yet nuclear weapons, whether used for deterrence or as offensive weaponry, are not effective for this purpose. The threat of nuclear force cannot act as a deterrent against terrorists, because they do not have a territory to retaliate against. Thus, terrorists would not be prevented from attacking a country for fear of nuclear retaliation. Nuclear weapons also cannot be relied on as a deterrent against "rogue states," because their responses to a nuclear threat may be irrational and deterrence relies on rationality. If the leaders of a rogue state do not use the same calculus regarding their losses from retaliation, deterrence can easily fail. As offensive weaponry, nuclear force only promises tremendous destruction to troops, civilians, and the environment. It might work to annihilate a rogue state, but the amount of force entailed in using nuclear weaponry is indiscriminate, disproportionate, and highly immoral. It would not be useful against terrorists, because strategists could not be certain of locating an appropriate target for retaliation.

George P. Shultz, William J. Perry, Henry A. Kissinger, and Sam Nunn

A WORLD FREE OF NUCLEAR WEAPONS

Sometimes a message is less important than—or, more accurately, its impact is greatly enhanced by—the identity of the messengers. This is especially true in the case of the following article, which appeared in the *Wall Street Journal* (recognized as the leading conservative newspaper in the United States) and was written by four prominent, promilitary members of the national security "establishment." George P. Shultz was secretary of state under President Ronald Reagan; William J. Perry had been secretary of defense under President Bill Clinton; Henry A. Kissinger was national security advisor and secretary of state under Presidents Nixon and Ford; and Sam Nunn was a longtime U.S. senator and was chair of the U.S. Senate Armed Services Committee. Their endorsement in 2007 of a world free of nuclear weapons has therefore been especially influential, giving added credibility to a goal long advocated by peace activists.

Nuclear weapons today present tremendous dangers, but also an historic opportunity. U.S. leadership will be required to take the world to the next stage—to a solid consensus for reversing reliance on nuclear weapons globally as a vital contribution to preventing their proliferation into potentially dangerous hands, and ultimately ending them as a threat to the world.

Nuclear weapons were essential to maintaining international security during the Cold War because they were a means of deterrence. The end of the Cold War made the doctrine of mutual Soviet-American deterrence obsolete. Deterrence continues to be a relevant consideration for many states with regard to threats from other states. But reliance on nuclear weapons for this purpose is becoming increasingly hazardous and decreasingly effective.

North Korea's recent nuclear test and Iran's refusal to stop its program to enrich uranium—potentially to weapons grade—highlight the fact that the world is now on the precipice of a new and dangerous nuclear era. Most alarmingly, the likelihood that nonstate terrorists will get their hands on nuclear weaponry is increasing. In today's war waged on world order by terrorists, nuclear weapons are the ultimate means of mass devastation. And nonstate terrorist groups with nuclear weapons are conceptually outside the bounds of a deterrent strategy and present difficult new security challenges.

Apart from the terrorist threat, unless urgent new actions are taken, the U.S. soon will be compelled to enter a new nuclear era that will be more precarious, psychologically disorienting, and economically even more costly than was Cold War deterrence. It is far from certain that we can successfully replicate the old Soviet-American "mutually assured destruction" with an increasing number of potential nuclear enemies worldwide without dramatically increasing the risk that nuclear weapons will be used. New nuclear states do not have the benefit of years of step-by-step safeguards put in effect during the Cold War to prevent nuclear accidents, misjudgments, or unauthorized launches. The United States and the Soviet Union learned from mistakes that were less than fatal. Both countries were diligent to ensure that no nuclear weapon was used during the Cold War by design or by accident. Will new nuclear nations and the world be as fortunate in the next fifty years as we were during the Cold War?

⟨⟩

Leaders addressed this issue in earlier times. In his "Atoms for Peace" address to the United Nations in 1953, Dwight D. Eisenhower pledged America's "determination to help solve the fearful atomic dilemma—to devote its entire heart and mind to find the way by which the miraculous inventiveness of man shall not be dedicated to his death, but consecrated to his life." John F. Kennedy, seeking to break the logjam on nuclear disarmament, said, "The world was not meant to be a prison in which man awaits his execution."

Rajiv Gandhi, addressing the UN General Assembly on June 9, 1988, appealed, "Nuclear war will not mean the death of 100 million people. Or even 1,000 million. It will mean the extinction of 4,000 million: the end of life as we know it on our planet Earth. We come to the United Nations to seek your support. We seek your support to put a stop to this madness."

Ronald Reagan called for the abolishment of "all nuclear weapons," which he considered to be "totally irrational, totally inhumane, good for nothing but killing, possibly destructive of life on earth and civilization." Mikhail Gorbachev shared this vision, which had also been expressed by previous American presidents.

Although Reagan and Mr. Gorbachev failed at Reykjavik to achieve the goal of an agreement to get rid of all nuclear weapons, they did succeed in turning the arms race on its head. They initiated steps leading to significant reductions in deployed long- and intermediate-range nuclear forces, including the elimination of an entire class of threatening missiles.

What will it take to rekindle the vision shared by Reagan and Mr. Gorbachev? Can a worldwide consensus be forged that defines a series of practical steps leading to major reductions in the nuclear danger? There is an urgent need to address the challenge posed by these two questions.

The Non-Proliferation Treaty (NPT) envisioned the end of all nuclear weapons. It provides (a) that states that did not possess nuclear weapons as of 1967 agree not to obtain them, and (b) that states that do possess them agree to divest themselves of these weapons over time. Every president of both parties since Richard Nixon has reaffirmed these treaty obligations, but nonnuclear weapon states have grown increasingly skeptical of the sincerity of the nuclear powers.

Strong nonproliferation efforts are under way. The Cooperative Threat Reduction program, the Global Threat Reduction Initiative, the Proliferation Security Initiative, and the Additional Protocols are innovative approaches that provide powerful new tools for detecting activities that violate the NPT and endanger world security. They deserve full implementation. The negotiations on proliferation of nuclear weapons by North Korea and Iran, involving all the permanent members of the Security Council plus Germany and Japan, are crucially important. They must be energetically pursued.

But by themselves, none of these steps [is] adequate to the danger. Reagan and General Secretary Gorbachev aspired to accomplish more at their meeting in Reykjavik twenty years ago—the elimination of nuclear weapons altogether. Their vision shocked experts in the doctrine of nuclear deterrence, but galvanized the hopes of people around the world. The leaders of the two countries with the largest arsenals of nuclear weapons discussed the abolition of their most powerful weapons.

⟨⟩

What should be done? Can the promise of the NPT and the possibilities envisioned at Reykjavik be brought to fruition? We believe that a major effort should be launched by the United States to produce a positive answer through concrete stages.

First and foremost is intensive work with leaders of the countries in possession of nuclear weapons to turn the goal of a world without nuclear weapons into a joint enterprise. Such a joint enterprise, by involving changes in the disposition of the states possessing nuclear weapons, would lend additional weight to efforts already under way to avoid the emergence of a nuclear-armed North Korea and Iran.

The program on which agreements should be sought would constitute a series of agreed and urgent steps that would lay the groundwork for a world free of the nuclear threat. Steps would include:

- Changing the Cold War posture of deployed nuclear weapons to increase warning time and thereby reduce the danger of an accidental or unauthorized use of a nuclear weapon.
- Continuing to reduce substantially the size of nuclear forces in all states that possess them.
- Eliminating short-range nuclear weapons designed to be forward-deployed.
- Initiating a bipartisan process with the Senate, including understandings to increase confidence and provide for periodic review, to achieve ratification of the Comprehensive Test Ban Treaty, taking advantage of recent technical advances, and working to secure ratification by other key states.
- Providing the highest possible standards of security for all stocks of weapons, weapons-usable plutonium, and highly enriched uranium everywhere in the world.
- Getting control of the uranium enrichment process, combined with the guarantee that uranium for nuclear power reactors could be obtained at a reasonable price, first from the Nuclear Suppliers Group and then from the International Atomic Energy Agency (IAEA) or other controlled international reserves. It will also be necessary to deal with proliferation issues presented by spent fuel from reactors producing electricity.
- Halting the production of fissile material for weapons globally; phasing out the use of highly enriched uranium in civil commerce; and removing weapons-usable uranium from research facilities around the world and rendering the materials safe.
- Redoubling our efforts to resolve regional confrontations and conflicts that give rise to new nuclear powers.

Achieving the goal of a world free of nuclear weapons will also require effective measures to impede or counter any nuclear-related conduct that is potentially threatening to the security of any state or peoples.

Reassertion of the vision of a world free of nuclear weapons and practical measures toward achieving that goal would be, and would be perceived as, a bold initiative consistent with America's moral heritage. The effort could have a profoundly positive impact on the security of future generations. Without the bold vision, the actions will not be perceived as fair or urgent. Without the actions, the vision will not be perceived as realistic or possible.

We endorse setting the goal of a world free of nuclear weapons and working energetically on the actions required to achieve that goal, beginning with the measures outlined above.

Jonathan Schell

A POWERFUL PEACE

Jonathan Schell helped energize the antinuclear movement of the 1980s with his eloquent description of the consequences of nuclear war, *The Fate of the Earth*. In a subsequent book, *The Gift of Time*, Schell argued for a more activist antinuclear policy, distinguishing

Reprinted from "Superpower? Get Over It," the Summer 2008 *YES! Magazine,* 284 Madrona Way NE Ste 116, Bainbridge Island, WA 98110. Subscriptions: 800/937-4451. Web: www.yesmagazine.org.

between "vertical" and "horizontal" nuclear weapons accumulation, with the former referring to increased weaponry on the part of countries already possessing them, and the latter, to the proliferation of nuclear weapons among countries not currently identified as "nuclear powers." Many opponents of nuclear proliferation do not acknowledge that to a large extent, horizontal expansion of nuclear weapons is a consequence of its vertical counterpart, with previously nonnuclear countries justifying their acquisition of nuclear weapons by the refusal of nuclear-armed states to give up theirs. The following selection provides a brief, step-by-step agenda for achieving a nonnuclear world.

With each year that passes, nuclear weapons provide their possessors with less safety while provoking more danger. Possession of nuclear arms provokes proliferation. Both nourish the global nuclear infrastructure, which in turn enlarges the possibility of acquisition by terrorist groups.

The step that is needed to break this cycle can be as little doubted as the source of the problem. The double standard of nuclear "haves" and "have-nots" must be replaced by a single standard, which can only be the goal of a world free of all nuclear weapons.

What is it that prevents sensible steps toward nuclear abolition from being taken? The answer cannot be in doubt, either. It is the resolve of the world's nuclear powers to hold on to their nuclear arsenals. Countries that already have nuclear arms cite proliferation as their reason for keeping them, and those lacking nuclear arms seek them in large measure because they feel menaced by those with them.

A double-standard regime is a study in futility—a divided house that cannot stand. Its advocates preach what they have no intention of practicing. It is up to the nuclear powers to take the first step.

Their nuclear arsenals would be the largest pile of bargaining chips ever brought to any negotiating table. More powerful as instruments of peace than they ever can be for war, they would likely be more than adequate for winning agreements from the nonnuclear powers that would choke off proliferation forever.

The art of the negotiation would be to pay for strict, inspectable, enforceable nonproliferation and nuclear-materials-control agreements in the coin of existing nuclear bombs. What would be the price to the nuclear powers, for example, of a surrender by the nuclear-weapons-free states of their rights to the troublesome nuclear fuel cycle, which stands at the heart of the proliferation dilemma? Perhaps reductions by Russia and the United States from two thousand to a few hundred weapons each plus ratification of the Comprehensive Test Ban Treaty?

Further reductions, now involving the other nuclear powers, might pay for establishment and practice of inspections of ever-greater severity, and still further reductions might buy agreements on enforcement of the final ban on nuclear arms. When nuclear weapons holdings reached zero, former nuclear weapons states and nonnuclear weapons states, abolitionists all, would exercise a unanimous will to manage, control, roll back, and extirpate all nuclear weapon technology.

A world from which nuclear weapons had been banned would, of course, not be without its dangers, including nuclear ones. But we must ask how they would compare with those now approaching.

Let us suppose that the nuclear powers had agreed to move step by step toward eliminating their own arsenals. The iron chains of fear that link all the nuclear arsenals in the world would then be replaced by bonds of reassurance. Knowing that Russia and the United States were disarming, China could agree to disarm. Knowing that China was disarming, India could agree to disarm. Knowing that India was ready to disarm, Pakistan could agree to disarm as well. Any country that decided otherwise would find itself up against the sort of united global will so conspicuous by its absence today.

During the Cold War, the principal objection in the United States to a nuclear-weapon-free world was that you could not get there. That objection melted away with the Soviet Union, and today the principal objection is that even if you could get there, you would not want to be there. The arguments usually begin with the observation that nuclear weapons can never be disinvented, and that a world free of nuclear weapons is therefore at worst a mirage, at best a highly dangerous place to be. It is supposedly a mirage because, even if the hardware is removed, the know-how remains. It is said to be highly dangerous because the miscreant rearmer, now in possession of a nuclear monopoly, would be able to dictate terms to a helpless, terrorized world or, alternately, precipitate a helter-skelter, many-sided nuclear arms race.

This conclusion seems reasonable until you notice that history has taught an opposite lesson. Repeatedly, even the greatest nuclear powers have actually lost wars against tiny, backward nonnuclear adversaries without being able to extract the slightest utility from their colossal arsenals. Think of the Soviet Union in Afghanistan, or the U.S. in Vietnam, or Britian in Suez.

If, in the sixty years of the nuclear age, no great power has won a war by making nuclear threats against even tiny, weak adversaries, then how could a nuclear monopoly by a small country enable it to coerce and bully the whole world? The danger cannot be wholly discounted, but it is surely greatly exaggerated.

If the nuclear powers wish to be safe from nuclear weapons, they must surrender their own. They should collectively offer the world's nonnuclear powers a deal of stunning simplicity, inarguable fairness, and patent common sense: we will get out of the nuclear weapon business if you stay out of it. Then we will all work together to assure that everyone abides by the commitment.

The united will of the human species to save itself from destruction would be a force to be reckoned with.

HOW WE CAN DO IT

The United States, as the owner of the biggest nuclear arsenal, must take the initiative and lead the world to take these steps:

DE-ALERT. *Take nuclear weapons off high alert; separate warheads from missiles.*

NO FIRST USE. *Agree to binding bans on first use of nuclear weapons.*

NO NEW WEAPONS. *Ban research and development of all new nuclear weapons.*

BAN NUCLEAR TESTING FOREVER. *Bring into force the Comprehensive Test Ban Treaty.*

CONTROL NUCLEAR MATERIAL. *Create a verifiable treaty to bring all weapons-grade nuclear material and the technology to create it under strict international control.*

NUCLEAR WEAPONS CONVENTION. *Start negotiations, as required by the Non-Proliferation Treaty, for the phased, verifiable, and irreversible elimination of weapons.*

RESOURCES FOR PEACE. *Spend the tens of billions now spent for nuclear arms on national and global humanitarian projects.*

Lloyd J. Dumas

FINDING THE FUTURE: THE ROLE
OF ECONOMIC CONVERSION IN SHAPING
THE TWENTY-FIRST CENTURY

During the Cold War, it was routinely acknowledged that about 85 to 90 percent of the U.S. military budget was driven by competition with communism generally, and with the Soviet Union in particular. Now that the Soviet Union and the Cold War are both defunct, and only remnant Communist regimes are still in power (in Cuba, Vietnam, and North Korea), the U.S. military budget has declined, but only by about 10 percent. Clearly, any "peace dividend" has been elusive, which is troublesome for many reasons. For one thing, a militarized economy distorts and ultimately weakens any society. "Every gun that is made," said President Dwight D. Eisenhower in his 1961 Farewell Address, "every warship launched, every rocket fired signifies, in the final sense, a theft from those who hunger and are not fed, those who are cold and are not clothed."

These costs are devastating enough to warrant "economic conversion" as part of any peace-oriented future. But additionally, a war-oriented economy is probably more likely to be war-prone, so that the prevention of war may well require a reorientation of priorities away from the military and toward the domestic economy. This point has been made by many serious thinkers, including economist Joseph Schumpeter, who wrote that "the orientation toward war is mainly fostered by the domestic interests of ruling classes, but also by the influence of all those who tend to gain individually from a war policy, whether economically or socially."[7] Following World War I, concern focused increasingly on the role of the armaments industry, the so-called merchants of death, in fostering wars.

Interestingly, however, it was President Eisenhower once again—no starry-eyed idealist or softheaded pacifist—who gave voice to the most influential, critical (and regrettably accurate) description of this problem, when he warned in his Farewell Address that

> we have been compelled to create a permanent armaments industry of vast proportions....The total influence—economic, political, even spiritual—is felt in every city, every statehouse, every office of the federal government....In the councils of government, we must guard against the acquisition of unwarranted influence...by the military-industrial complex.

[7] Joseph Schumpeter, *Imperialism and Social Classes* (New York: Meridian, 1955).

This alliance of military and industrial sectors that Eisenhower so decried has now become a military-industrial-labor-science-governmental complex, and it has shown itself to be firmly entrenched indeed. But, we presume, not entrenched permanently. The stage may now be set for "economic conversion," whose long-term advantages would go beyond the immediately economic to embrace the prospect of a society, economy, and a politics oriented toward meeting human needs.

During the long Cold War, the military budget was the largest single category of federal expenditure on goods and services. For nearly half a century, with the armed might of a rival military superpower as a foil, the budget supported a large military establishment, serviced by an unparalleled system of laboratories and industrial facilities. The military budget is an expenditure, not an investment. As such, it had a particular though vaguely defined goal, to provide for the nation's security. Now the Cold War is over, the Soviet Union is no more, and the United States is the only global military superpower.

Although much has been made of the threats of international terrorism and third world conflict by those who seek to maintain as large a military as possible, these threats, such as they are, were no less serious before the demise of the Soviet Union. The "Soviet threat" was indisputably the main driver and rationale for those huge Cold War budgets, and it no longer exists. Thus, apart from the issue of whether there was ever any justification for the huge military budgets that characterized the Cold War, it is inconceivable that the continuation of military spending at anywhere near that level is justifiable today. Furthermore, many large and expensive military systems, from the MX missile to the B1 (and B2) bomber to the Trident submarine, have absolutely no relevance to dealing with third world conflict or international terrorism.

Arguments for an evenhanded approach to budget reduction, balanced between military spending and domestic programs, are simplistic and make no sense. They are appealing because they have the appearance of fairness. But fairness is not the issue. Fairness may be an appropriate criterion for judging what levels of support make sense for programs of income transfer that benefit one or another segment of the population, but it is wholly inappropriate in the case of mission-oriented programs such as education, roadbuilding, or the military. Within the bounds of affordability, levels of support for the military should be based on what is needed to achieve the mission of securing the nation against real and significant external military threats. According to such a criterion, disproportionately large cuts in the military budget are entirely sensible and justifiable. That is not a matter of ideology, it is a matter of common sense.

This situation does not call for 5 or 10 percent cuts in military spending. A military budget no larger than half, and probably more like a quarter to a third of the Cold War average, properly spent, will give us a military force strong enough to provide as much security as military forces are capable of providing in the present and foreseeable future. In any case, by some estimates more than half the United States' Cold War military budget was designed to defend other nations with standards of living comparable to our own, against a threat that no longer exists. Why then, even with all the pressures to cut the federal budget deficit, are we so reluctant to recognize the enormity of excess in present military expenditures and to do what so obviously needs doing?

This is a classic case of a set of vested interests resisting every attempt to move decisively into the future. These interests have become so intertwined with the existing political and socioeconomic structure that it is extremely difficult to disentangle them. Like a tumor that has attached itself to the body's vital organs, it cannot be safely removed by simply chopping it away. It must be detached with the care and precision of a skilled surgeon's knife....

Economic conversion is just such a careful structural approach. Conversion reaches into the economy and redirects human and capital resources from military to civilian-oriented activity. It involves the retraining and reorientation of workforces and the restructuring of organizations and facilities that have been serving the military sector so that they can *efficiently* produce civilian goods and services. It is a way of reassuring the individuals, companies, and communities whose income, profits, and economic base are currently locked into the military system that the realization of the dream of peacefully ending the Cold War need not be the beginning of an economic nightmare for them. It is a way of removing obstacles to change, of helping them let go.

But it can be much more than that. Economic conversion can play a critical role in directing key economic resources to the kinds of investment that are so important to rebuilding the competitiveness of U.S. industry and generating real economic growth that can help put an end to our trade and budget deficits. To fully understand why conversion is at the fulcrum of this important change of direction, it is first necessary to understand why the military budgets of the Cold War were so peculiarly damaging to our economic well-being.

MILITARY SPENDING AND ECONOMIC DECAY

The predominant view among economists is that money value is the arbiter of economic value. As a reflection of this, the most commonly used measure of the total economic output of a society, the gross national product (GNP) (or its close relative, the gross domestic product—GDP), includes only goods and services for which money has been paid. That goods and services produced without money exchange (for example, within the household) can be useful is not denied. But they are clearly not considered part of the "economy," and are therefore not counted as part of economic output. . . .

It is more productive to define the economy as that part of the society whose central function is to provide material well-being. It generates and distributes both the goods and services that directly satisfy

material needs (i.e., consumer goods, such as televisions and furniture) and the means required to supply them (i.e., producer goods, such as metal-cutting machines and industrial furnaces). This definition of the economy means that money value is no longer the same as economic value. The proper criterion of economic value becomes the extent to which a good or service contributes to material well-being. A bookcase made at home is just as much a part of economic output as a comparable bookcase bought from a furniture store. Whether or not it has money value, any activity that results in such a good or service contributes to the economy's goal of improving material well-being. Therefore, it makes sense to call that activity economically "contributive."

On the other hand, not all goods and services with money value add to the material standard of living. Some goods and services are created to satisfy other human wants and needs. Churches are not constructed and bibles printed to provide material well-being, but to help fulfill the need for spiritual guidance; courthouses and law books are not aimed at increasing the material wealth of society, but at providing political order and control; battle tanks and missiles do not themselves add to the material standard of living, they are produced to enhance physical security. Though these goods may carry a very hefty money price, and may be very useful for the purposes they serve, they do not directly contribute to the central purpose of the economy and so do not have any *economic* value. It is logical, then, to classify activities that result in goods or services that do not have economic value as economically "noncontributive."

Although noncontributive activities are without *economic value*, to the extent that they use productive resources they do have *economic cost*, in terms of opportunities foregone. In other words, the economic cost of a noncontributive activity is measured by the economic value that could have been created by using the same labor, machinery, and equipment to produce goods and services that have economic value.

Economically productive resources that are used for noncontributive activity can be said to be "diverted" to other than economic purposes. An economy in which significant amounts of critical economic resources have been persistently diverted to noncontributive activities will tend to experience a long-term decline in its productive competence—that is, in its ability to produce efficiently. And declining productive competence will lead to a deteriorating standard of living in the long run.

There is no question that the production of military goods and services is noncontributive activity. Whatever else may be said for such products, they do not add to the present standard of living as consumer goods do, or to the economy's capacity to produce standard-of-living goods and services in the future, as producer goods do. Military-oriented activity may be only one of many forms of noncontributive activity, but it is one of the largest and most important in the world today. And the voracious appetite of modern military sectors for both capital and engineers and scientists creates a particularly damaging kind of resource diversion. Why is the diversion of technologists and capital so damaging?

The majority of the population earns the largest part of its money income in the form of wages and salaries. Ongoing increases in wages and salaries that outrun inflation are thus key to producing sustained, broad-based improvement in the standard of living. But, since wages and salaries are the largest part of cost for most producers, increases in labor costs will squeeze profits, creating strong cost-push pressure for price increases....

The ability to offset cost-push pressures depends crucially on the rise of productivity. Although many things affect the rate of productivity increase, more than anything else, rising productivity depends on improving the techniques of production and the quantity and quality of capital available to workers. Improvements in the techniques of production come primarily from research and development (R&D) aimed at discovering and applying new civilian-oriented technology. Regardless of the amount of money spent, without a great enough quantity and quality of engineers and scientists available to perform the work, such R&D will not be successful. Money does not create technological progress, engineers and scientists do. However, if enough capital is not available, it may be difficult to provide the required research facilities, or to widely deploy the results of successful R&D to the factory floor throughout industry.

A persistent, large-scale diversion of engineers and scientists and/or capital to economically non-contributive military activity will unavoidably reduce their availability to contributive civilian activity. The stream of civilian-oriented, productivity-enhancing technological innovation will slow down, causing the rate of productivity growth to drop. Reduced productivity growth will, in turn, undermine the ability of domestic producers to offset the rising cost of labor, or for that matter, of any other input to production and supply....

How large has the diversion of technological and capital resources been in the service of the arms race? For decades now, about 30 percent of the nation's engineers and scientists (full-time equivalent) have been engaged in military R&D. Because pay has been higher and access to state-of-the-art facilities and equipment better in that arena, the military has tended to attract a disproportionate number of the "best and the brightest" technologists. Thus, although the quantitative diversion of engineers and scientists is large enough, adjusted for quality, the "brain drain" is even larger. Concerning capital diversion, as of 1990 the total book value of physical capital directly owned by the Department of Defense (DoD) (including plant equipment, structures, weapons, and related equipment and supplies) was more than 80 percent of the total book value of capital equipment and structures in all U.S. manufacturing facilities combined!

The standard of living in the United States has been declining since the mid-1970s. The failure of American industrial competitiveness has been highlighted by the replacement of more than three-quarters of a century of continuous trade surpluses (1894–1970) by decades of trade deficits. Hundreds of thousands of high-paying manufacturing jobs have been lost, while job creation has focused on "MacJobs"—low-paying, no-future jobs in the downscale part of the service sector. And all this alongside a national orgy of borrowing that quadrupled the national debt and transformed the United States from the world's largest net creditor internationally to the world's largest net debtor. Had the huge amount of capital borrowed just since 1980 been used for contributive investment and combined with the talents of otherwise diverted engineers and scientists, the

United States would have undergone an industrial renaissance. Instead, such resources were lavished on largely noncontributive activity, and all we have to show for all that debt is protracted economic decline.

One clear implication of this analysis is that not all parts of the military budget have equal economic meaning. Roughly half the military budget has traditionally been operations and maintenance expense, including the salaries and benefits of those in the armed services. Although these outlays involve a great deal of money, they have relatively little economic impact. *The main economic action lies in procurement and R&D expenditures, because those are the outlays that draw engineers and scientists, industrial capital, and other productive economic resources into the military sector.* Compared with cutbacks in military procurement and R&D, troop reductions and base closings thus do very little to release the economic resources critical to industrial renewal. Yet the military spending cuts to date have been concentrated mainly on operations and maintenance.

CONVERSION AND RECONVERSION

Economic conversion is key to economic renewal for two related reasons. First, it provides a means for efficiently reconnecting labor and capital resources released from the noncontributive military sector to contributive work in the civilian economy. It is, after all, not what diverted resources are doing (noncontributive activity), but what they are *not* doing (contributive activity) that causes economic decay. *Shrinking the military sector will do nothing to repair the economic damage of the arms race unless the released resources are reconnected to contributive civilian activity.* In economic terms, nothing will have been accomplished if those people and facilities are released from the military sector and become unemployed. Second, conversion can help reduce the natural resistance of entrenched vested interests to this restructuring by reassuring them that in fact reconnection, rather than unemployment, lies at the end of the road.

At the end of World War II, the United States faced a great challenge. A large fraction of the nation's output had to be moved from military to civilian production. With a combination of private sector and federal, state, and local government planning, the challenge was met with flying colors. Some 30 percent of U.S. output was transferred in one year without the unemployment rate ever rising above 3 percent. This experience made it clear that it is possible to redirect enormous amounts of productive resources from military to civilian activity without intolerable economic disruption. But it is an experience that must be interpreted with care.

First of all, rationing during the war combined with high incomes to create considerable pent-up demand for all manner of consumer products. When rationing ended with the war, there was a ready-made, unsatisfied market for a wide variety of goods to which war producers could turn. There was little foreign competition to challenge American producers, since every major industrial nation except the United States had been severely damaged by the war. Even more important, the companies that supplied the military during the war were basically civilian companies that shifted to military production for a few years from their normal business of making civilian products. All of their workers, including managers, engineers, and scientists, knew how to operate in a civilian commercial market environment. That is what they had spent most of their working lives doing. Though modifications had been made during the war, most production facilities and equipment had originally been designed and configured for efficient civilian production. For these firms and their workforces, this was a "reconversion"—that is, they were going back to business as usual.

The situation today is quite different. There is no deep well of unsatisfied pent-up demand, and there is fierce foreign competition. Decades, rather than a few years, of high military expenditures have drained the U.S. economy and put many domestic producers far behind their overseas rivals. It is no coincidence that the two most successful industrial economies in competition with the United States have been the two industrialized nations prevented by the World War II terms of surrender from building massive military forces—Germany and Japan.

Today there are generations of managers, engineers, scientists, and production and maintenance workers whose employment experience includes little or nothing but military-oriented work. Many present-day military-industrial firms have never operated in civilian commercial markets. Even those that are large-scale manufacturers of both military and civilian products (e.g., Boeing and Rockwell International) typically have operationally insulated military and civilian divisions functioning as separate, wholly owned subsidiaries reporting to the same overall top management.

Furthermore, during World War II, both the means of production and the technologies used in designing and manufacturing military goods were still fairly similar to those in the civilian economy. Over the past half century, the physical plant, machinery, and technologies involved in military and civilian manufacturing have sharply diverged. The technologies embodied in the designs of the products themselves are even more different. For the major military producers, moving into civilian commercial markets is most assuredly not returning to "business as usual." It is movement into new and unexplored territory. It is conversion, not reconversion.

That makes the process more difficult. But with some care and advanced planning, there is little question that it can be successful.

THE NATURE OF THE CONVERSION PROBLEM

The United States' military sector does not operate by market principles. It is the closest thing to centrally planned socialism in the United States. The nature, quantity, and price of output are not determined by impersonal market forces. They are set by the interaction of the Pentagon's central planners and the managers of military industry. The vast majority of Department of Defense business is negotiated rather than awarded through a serious and enforced competitive bidding process. In practice, virtually all major military contracts operate as if they were "cost-plus"—with producers reimbursed for whatever they have spent, "plus" a guaranteed profit. Under such a contract, the manufacturer bears virtually no risk and can increase revenues without hurting profits by high-cost, inefficient operation. In a competitive commercial marketplace, this kind of inefficient operation would cause serious, if not fatal, problems for the company. In the sheltered and subsidized

world of the centrally planned military sector, it is a recipe for growth and success....

POLICIES FOR SUCCESSFUL CONVERSION

Given a thorough understanding of the endpoints of conversion—the very different operating environments of the military and of the civilian sectors—policies can be designed to carry workers and facilities successfully through this difficult transition. For technical reasons, some things must be done regardless of the particular shape the conversion process takes. It is abundantly clear, for example, that any sensible conversion process must take seriously the need both to retrain and to reorient managers, engineers, and scientists. But other things are greatly affected by whether conversion is internal or external to the firm.

"Internal" conversion involves the transition of workforce, facilities, and equipment within a formerly military-oriented firm that is shifting to servicing a civilian market. "External" conversion involves the transition of workers, facilities, and equipment that are released by a military-oriented firm and so must find reemployment elsewhere. Internal conversion has much to recommend it. It minimizes disruption of the lives of workers and their families, since it aims at keeping as much of the workforce intact as is economically sensible. It minimizes disruption of the surrounding community as well by maintaining the tax base and the geographic patterns of living, spending, and commuting. And working within the familiar context of an existing firm and workplace means that less on-the-job adjustment is required on the part of the affected workforce. On the other hand, some external conversion is unavoidable....

Both public and private sectors have key roles to play in converting the economy. There are things they should do, and just as important, there are things they should not do. It is very helpful to have the coordination and assistance that the federal government can provide, but if the conversion process is not highly decentralized, it has very little chance of working well. The search for productive and profitable civilian activities to replace the previous military mission, and the plans for the reshaping of capital and labor they imply, must be tailored to the details of each particular facility and workplace. This is one case where a one-size-fits-all approach virtually guarantees that nothing will fit anyone. It is a mistake for the federal government to try to blueprint facility and workforce conversion. There is no good substitute for a high degree of decentralization in the detailed planning and plan implementation process. Even close oversight of microlevel conversion by the federal government is a poor idea. It is unlikely to improve the effectiveness of conversion plans and highly likely to be inefficient and expensive. Although this is more obviously true of internal conversion, it is important for external conversion as well....

It may also be time to resurrect, in updated form, one of the most successful federal investment programs in the nation's history, the World War II vintage GI Bill of Rights. Under the provisions of the GI Bill, millions of individuals who had served in the armed forces received training and educational benefits to help them improve their earning capacity and employment opportunities. According to former Senator Ralph Yarborough, who chaired a committee that evaluated the performance of the program, the GI Bill was an investment with an enormous rate of return. The extra federal taxes collected out of the higher incomes earned because of the training amounted to some thirty times the program's cost to the taxpayer. And this does not even begin to consider the plethora of other benefits to the economy and society that attend a better-trained and better-educated workforce and citizenry. A new GI Bill for all workers in the military sector would make a great deal of sense in facilitating conversion today. I see no reason why this approach could not eventually be broadened to cover all displaced workers. However, it is important to recognize that workers undergoing conversion (particularly engineers, scientists, and managers) do have special problems. Even more important, *the successful conversion of these workers,*

especially of engineers and scientists, holds the key to the kind of industrial renewal that can and will brighten the economic prospects of the entire labor force....

CONVERSION AND THE TWENTY-FIRST CENTURY

Times of transition are always difficult. They call on us to break old familiar patterns that have come to feel comfortable. Effort is required where habit and routine once carried us through. It takes some courage to face up to the need for change, even when it is clear that the patterns of the past are no longer tenable. It takes some creativity and determination to recast our lives in ways that are not just different, but better.

We are living in an era of profound change. That can be frightening, but it can also be liberating. Where the structures of the past have crumbled, there is the opportunity to create new and better structures for the future. And it is easier to build bridges when walls come down.

In the last decades of the twentieth century, structures have crumbled and walls have come down all over the world. That we are passing through a time of profound change is undeniable. What we do—or fail to do—now will change the shape of the century to come. The enormous, worldwide preemption of productive resources for military purposes over the past fifty years says a great deal about the world we have created and the priorities we have established. If we have courage, foresight, and determination, we can break with the deadly, fear-driven legacy of this tortured century. We can find a more productive, life-enhancing way to use our talents and capabilities. Conversion, properly understood and implemented, can help us work our way through the myriad details needed to build a practical path to a world that is both more prosperous and more humane.

David P. Barash

INTERNATIONAL LAW

For some people, international law is one of the great hopes of humanity, offering the prospect of subjecting the often chaotic interactions of countries to the same reason and order that—at least in theory—governs the interactions of individuals. For others, international law is laughably inadequate, primarily because it has no clear-cut enforcement mechanism. On the other hand, in the aftermath of genocidal cruelty in Bosnia and Rwanda, many of the perpetrators were declared international outlaws, and at least some have been brought before the International Court of Justice. This is a pattern that may become increasingly common in the future.

International law may be held to an unfairly strict standard. Breaches of international law, for example, are sometimes thought to show the absurdity of international law itself, perhaps because such offenses (genocide, torture, etc.) are often so egregious. But by contrast, violations of national or local law are virtually never taken as reasons to disavow legal systems. Presumably, this is because nearly everyone recognizes the need for law, even if existing laws are not perfect or perfectly complied with. The "law of nations" is and will be what we make it. Depending on our choice, international law offers the prospect of restraining, or possibly ending, war and promoting a more lawful world, which may also be more predictable, just, and peaceful.

The international community should support a system of laws to regularize international relations and maintain the peace in the same manner that law governs national order.

—Pope John Paul II

Schemes for ending war—for creating negative peace and, ultimately, positive peace as well—often founder at the level of states. By zealously guarding their sovereignty, states undermine, or at best diminish, the authority and effectiveness of international organizations such as the United Nations. Even when these organizations operate in a manner that recognizes the primacy of state sovereignty, an unavoidable tension arises between a state-centered world system and one organized around different fundamental values. By providing a unit around which dangerous and misleading notions such as peace through strength can congeal, nationalism and state-centeredness legitimize the use of violence in settling disputes. By emphasizing the similarities and often suggesting some kind of superiority on the part of each group of people, and cutting them off from others, the current political divisions of our planet make prospects for disarmament seem terribly difficult, perhaps impossible. By rewarding those who behave violently—so long as such violence, or the threat of violence, is successful—our current world system works strongly against peaceful ethical or religious resolutions of conflict. And by fraction-ating the people of the world, our current political organization makes it very difficult to deal effec-tively with problems that cross traditional borders and that require global solutions....

In short, many people are becoming increasingly aware that our current state-centric system is part of the problem, and that we must move beyond the nation-state to find the solution....All governments operate by laws, the rules of behavior that specify what is permissible and, more commonly, what is not. Even in our current system of separate states, a legal framework undergirds the relationship of states to one another. It is known as international law....

THE SOURCES OF INTERNATIONAL LAW

We are all familiar with domestic law, with its prohibitions against violent crimes such as mur-der, robbery, and assault, as well as with the way it regulates the nonviolent conduct of daily living, from the flow of traffic to the affairs of business and the standards of acceptable conduct in private and public life. Less familiar, by contrast, is interna-tional law, the acknowledged principles that guide the interactions between states, and that set limits upon what is and what is not permissible. People live within societies, not between them, so we have done far more to encourage *intra*national law than *inter*national law. And yet, international law does exist; in fact, the current body of international law is very large. Just as most daily life among individu-als within a society is peaceful, most interactions among states on the world scene is also peaceful, in accord with expectations, and thus, in a sense, "legal."

Unlike domestic law, which in the United States is codified in constitutions and amendments, as well as in the specific laws passed by federal, state, and municipal lawmaking bodies, the body of interna-tional law is relatively chaotic, spread over history and generated in many different ways. There are four major sources of international law: (1) classical writ-ings that have become widely accepted, (2) custom, (3) treaties, and (4) the rulings of international courts.

Classical Writings

In the sixteenth century, the Spanish legal scholar Francisco de Victoria developed the thesis that war must be morally justifiable, and could not simply be fought over differences of religion or for the glory of a ruler. He also maintained that soldiers were not obliged to fight in unjust wars, even if so commanded by their king. But the best-known and most influential example of classical international law is found in the work of the Dutch legal scholar Hugo Grotius. In his treatise *On the Law of War and Peace* (1625), Grotius maintained that there was a fundamental "natural law," which transcended that of nations, and which emanated from the fact that people were ultimately members of the same com-munity. Grotius argued strongly for the sovereignty of individual states, within their own realms. From this, he concluded that states must avoid interfer-ence in the internal affairs of other states. Grotius pointed to the agreements that states have made among themselves, and that have proved to be dura-ble: peace treaties, decisions as to the allocation of fishing and navigation rights, commonly accepted boundaries, and so on. The Grotian tradition thus derives the legitimacy of international law from the legitimacy of states themselves. But it goes further in seeking to derive principles whereby the behav-ior of one state toward another can be regulated, arguing that "natural right" must govern the inter-actions among states, and that this supercedes the authority of the states themselves. As Grotius saw it (and subsequent international law has affirmed), international "society" exists, which requires cer-tain norms of conduct among states, including rules governing what is acceptable during war itself. For Grotius, war was not a breakdown in the law of nations, but rather a special condition to which law still applied....

The term *international law* first appeared in 1783, with the publication of Jeremy Bentham's *Principles of International Law*. Accordingly, it is worth empha-sizing that, whatever its shortcomings, nearly all our progress in international law has taken place in just a few hundred years; in fact, things have really gath-ered steam in the last fifty years. We might therefore be on the threshold of dramatic new developments.

2 Custom

Custom is one of the most important and least appreciated sources of international law. For example, consider the "rules of diplomatic protocol," whereby diplomats from one country are considered immune to arrest or detention in another. Clearly, these "rules" are in the interest of all countries, since, if the representatives of opposing states could legally be harrassed, communication between states could quickly cease, to the disadvantage of all sides. Diplomats occasionally are expelled from a host country, usually for "activities incompatible with their diplomatic status" (that is, for spying), in which case some of the other side's diplomats typically are expelled in retaliation. But normally—that is, customarily, and thus by international law—diplomats are allowed substantial leeway, including the ability to communicate freely and secretly with their home government, as well as guarantees of their safety. (The strength of this presumption is shown by the outrage when it is violated, as when U.S. diplomats were held hostage in Iran in 1979–1980.)...

3 Treaties

International treaties are analogous to contracts among individuals. And of course, there have been many treaties, covering not only the termination of wars, but also agreements about boundaries, fishing and navigation rights, and mutually agreed restrictions as to permissible actions during war. Treaties are not always honored, but in the vast majority of cases, they have been. Backing away from treaty obligations results in a substantial loss of face, and once branded a treaty-breaker, a state may not be able to establish useful, reliable relationships with other states. Through treaties as well as customary practice, international law provides "rules of the road" by which international interaction, beneficial to each side, can be conducted. As a result, states have a strong interest in abiding by them.

4 Courts

Finally, international law—just like domestic law—requires courts to hear disputed cases and render decisions. The first example of an international court was the Central American Court of Justice, established by treaty in 1908 by five Central American republics....

Best known and most important, however, is the International Court of Justice (formerly the Permanent Court of International Justice, during its tenure under the League of Nations), located at The Hague, Netherlands, and administered by the UN. Also known as the World Court, this institution consists of a rotating membership of world jurists. It issues decisions about international law that are generally considered authoritative, although typically unenforceable. The verdict on international courts is thus mixed. On the one hand, states are gradually becoming accustomed to letting go of enough sovereignty to settle disputes in court instead of in combat. On the other, adherence to the dictates of the World Court is entirely "consensual"—it is up to the consent of those involved—whereas adherence to domestic law is obligatory. Imagine a community in which accused lawbreakers could only be brought to trial if they agreed that the laws applied to them; further, imagine that they could then decide whether or not to abide by the ruling of the courts!

ENFORCEMENT OF INTERNATIONAL LAW

The major problem with international law, therefore, aside from its diffuseness, is enforcement. Because enforcement provisions are generally lacking, some people contend that international "law" is not, strictly speaking, law at all, but rather, a set of acknowledged customs, or norms of behavior. The importance of norms alone should not be underestimated; in fact, most human behavior is conducted according to widely shared norms, not law itself. Nonetheless, domestic law is the last resort (short of violence, which domestic law typically prohibits), and law is effective at least in part because if worst comes to worst, and a lawbreaker is apprehended and found guilty of violating the law, he or she can be held accountable, suffering fines, prison terms, and the like. In the case of domestic law, individuals acknowledge (whether overtly or not) that they are subordinate to the state and its machinery of enforcement: the police, court bailiffs, the national guard, and so on. When it comes to relations among states, by contrast, the "individuals" insist on their sovereignty; they most emphatically do not recognize that any authority supercedes their own. If individual people behaved this way, domestic law could not effectively regulate their behavior. The major problem with international law, therefore, is that individual states insist on a kind of latitude that they would never allow their own citizens.

Let us briefly consider the role of sanctions (punishments for noncompliance) in law more generally. There are three primary incentives for obeying any law, domestic or international: self-interest, duty, and coercion. For example, most individuals stop at red lights not because they fear getting a traffic ticket, but rather because they know that otherwise, they are more likely to have an accident. Rules may therefore be followed out of purely utilitarian concerns, in this case, interest in one's own personal safety. Laws provide a way of regulating human conduct, for the benefit of all: You can proceed with reasonable safety through an intersection when your light is green, because you know that opposing traffic has a red light, and you have some confidence that other drivers will respect this law, just as you do.

In addition, individuals may follow the law because they feel themselves duty-bound to contribute toward an orderly society that functions with respect for authority. As members of society, who benefit from it, individuals assume a responsibility toward it. That is, some are influenced by normative considerations, or a kind of Kantian categorical imperative to do what is right and good for its own sake. And finally, some people are induced to be law-abiding by fear that "violators may be prosecuted" and forced to succumb to the state's authority if they are found guilty. Although the role of such coercive factors cannot be denied, coercion is not the only reason why most people obey the law. And similarly, the absence of such coercion does not invalidate international law, or render it toothless.

States have numerous incentives, both positive and negative, for abiding by their legal obligations to other states. If a state defects from its legal obligations, adversaries may well retaliate, one's friends and allies are liable to disapprove, and world opinion is likely to be strongly negative, leading to ostracism and possible economic, political, and cultural sanctions. Moreover, governments themselves have

a strong stake in their own legitimacy, and—even in totalitarian states—adherence to law is fundamental to such legitimacy....

THE CONFLICT WITH STATE SOVEREIGNTY

It simply isn't true that all is anarchy in the international arena, any more than it is true that all is peaceful in the domestic sphere: More than one quarter of all wars, for example, are civil wars. States generally obey the law—out of a combined sense of duty and self-interest—even though coercive sanctions, as understood in domestic law, are absent. States engage in nonviolent commerce—exchange of tourists, diplomats, ideas, trade—according to certain regulations, and usually with goodwill and amity. Moreover, states usually do not enter into treaties unless they intend to abide by them, and they only acquiesce with customary norms of behavior when they anticipate that over the long run, they will benefit by doing so. At the same time, however, they typically cling to various aspects of sovereignty. Most treaties—notably those involving nuclear weapons—include a provision permitting signatories to withdraw within a set period of time, typically three or six months, if their "supreme national interests" are jeopardized. And who makes this decision? The state itself.

We have defined states as those political entities that are granted a monopoly of legitimate violence within their borders. When they engage in what they claim is lawful violence outside their borders, states typically maintain that (1) they are acting in self-defense (the U.S.S.R. in World War II, Israel in the Six Day War), (2) they are fulfilling treaty obligations (France and Britain in World War II), (3) they are intervening on the side of legitimate authority (the United States in Vietnam, the U.S.S.R. in Afghanistan), (4) the situation is anarchic and lacks a legitimate authority (the UN in the Congo), or (5) the conflict is within the realm of international obligations (the UN in Korea). In short, state sovereignty continues to reign, although a semblance of international law is generally invoked as well. States have been especially hesitant, however, to circumscribe their day-to-day authority. It is significant that whereas the Hague Conferences produced a few halting restrictions on the waging of war, they were unable to establish any significant binding rules for peace.

States are also selective when it comes to accepting the jurisdiction of the International Court of Justice, a process known as "adjudication." Adjudication is similar to arbitration in that the decision of the third party is binding. The only difference is that in adjudication, the decision is based on international law, rather than made by an arbitrator. The Soviet Union, for example, has historically refused to submit disputes to this body, although...the United States has been no better, despite the fact that in 1946, it formally agreed to submit all of its international disputes to the International Court of Justice. At that time, the U.S. Senate attached an amendment, known as the Connally Reservation, stipulating that the Court would not have authority over any disputes that "are essentially within the domestic jurisdiction of the United States of America as determined by the United States of America." With this loophole, the United States is free to "determine" that any dispute is essentially within its domestic jurisdiction, thereby avoiding international adjudication whenever it wishes....

Law is an important part of modern human life; some would even say that it is crucial to civilization. Despite concerns about enforcement—and anxiety when, as in the case of international law, enforcement powers are lacking—law is in many ways the antithesis of rule by brute force. Might does not make right; law does (or better yet, it reflects what is right). As a result, most good, decent people are presumed to be "law-abiding," and in fact, rule by law is almost inevitably seen as preferable to rule by force. We should also be aware, however, that law can be an instrument of oppression. Laws are made by those in power, and as such, they serve to perpetuate that power, and to prevent change. Thus, laws—international as well as domestic—serve best in a conservative environment. Third world and revolutionary states often point out that international laws were established by Western powers in support of their domination. The clearest example might well be the Treaty of Tordesillas (1494), following Columbus's "discovery" of the New World, whereby the pope "legally" divided that world into Spanish and Portuguese domains...without any regard for the people already living there....

International law must be flexible, if only because of the march of technology. For several centuries, for example, ever since a Dutch ruling in 1737, "territorial waters" have been considered to extend three miles from shore; this distance was based on the effective range of shore-based cannons. Now, new guidelines are being sought, with controversy fueled by disagreement among states, especially between the exploiters and the exploited. The former, particularly the developed industrialized states with relatively little shoreline (such as Britain and Japan) argue for narrow territorial waters, while those with extensive coastal waters (like Brazil and Burma), which seek to protect their fishing industry from foreign fleets, argue for a 200-mile limit.

These issues were partly resolved by the Law of the Sea Treaty, completed after decades of wrangling. This treaty also arranged for mechanisms of dispute resolution, waste disposal, and navigation procedures, but under the Reagan administration, the United States refused to sign, maintaining that the treaty's call for an intergovernmental body to supervise mining on the deep-sea bed constituted "international socialism." This also highlights once again the susceptibility of international law to asserted claims of state sovereignty, as well as the growing pressure of north/south cleavages.

HIDDEN STRENGTHS OF INTERNATIONAL LAW

Governmental Respect for Law

Yet, governments do not routinely flout the law, not even their own domestic statutes, over which they have complete control. In most democratic countries, governments accede to legal decisions, even those that go against them. Citizens of the United States, for example, often take for granted the fact that in many cases, they can, if they wish, bring legal action against their own government. And if the courts—which are themselves organs of the government—rule against the government, citizens can receive compensation or other redress for their grievances, even though governments, not the courts, have the strong-arm potential of enforcing their will.

This emphasizes the primacy of law over force. For example, following a strike during the Korean War—an action that supposedly threatened U.S. war production at a critical time—President Truman sought to nationalize the U.S. steel industry. The Supreme Court, however, overruled this action, whereupon the government obeyed the law, albeit reluctantly. Because democratic governments have a long-range interest in settling disputes amicably that supercedes any short-term interest in winning a given dispute, they tend to abide by legal rulings, even those that they dislike.

In international affairs, as we have seen, major powers are less likely to abide by international laws...unless the opponents are so balanced that the potential costs of losing a case are less than those of further wrangling, and possibly war....

International law often appears weaker than it really is, however. This is because violations, when they occur, are often sensational and dramatic, whereas compliance is taken for granted. When domestic law is broken by individuals, only rarely are we moved to question the appropriateness of the law itself, and never to doubt the existence of such law. But a different standard seems to be applied to international law. When states violate international law, they may or may not be condemned by public opinion, but almost invariably, the law itself is called into question, and the purported weakness of international law is once again lamented. Just as we are not told about the vast majority of people who obey domestic law every day, we do not see news stories proclaiming that "Paraguay today complied with its treaty obligations regarding its border with Bolivia, and therefore, no invasion took place."

Virtually the entire civilized world was shocked, by contrast, when Chancellor Theobald von Bethmann-Hollweg justified the German invasion of Belgium in the early days of World War I by describing the international guarantee of Belgian neutrality as a "mere scrap of paper" that could readily be torn up. On the one hand, this announcement—and even more so, the brutal invasion itself—showed the truth of the chancellor's assertion: Belgian neutrality was in fact "only" an international agreement, lacking any guarantee and incapable, by itself, of keeping the invading German divisions out. On the other

hand, the level of international outrage showed that international law, even when it lacks explicit means of enforcement, has undeniable effects on public perception. (In addition, we should note that the immediate reason for Britain entering the war against Germany was the German violation of Belgian neutrality; so, in a sense, international treaty law was ultimately enforced in this case. Had Germany respected the law, it might have won the war.)

The Law of War

War—the violent resolution of conflict—can be seen as the antithesis of law, whose goal after all is the ordering of relations without recourse to violence. Cicero first wrote that *inter arma silent legis* ("in war the law is silent"). This is taken to mean that the justifiability of any given war is outside the purview of international law, since states are sovereign authorities unto themselves, and free to make war or not, as they choose. Under this view, since there is no higher authority than a state, no one can claim that a state is making war unlawfully....

Nonetheless, a body of law is widely thought to apply to states under conditions of war. War itself can even be defined as "the legal condition which equally permits two or more hostile groups to carry on a conflict by armed force." Therefore—at least according to some experts—war represents a highly formalized interval during which violence may legitimately be practiced between two opposing groups. Enough agreement exists within the community of nations that belligerents and neutrals alike recognize the existence of certain accepted standards: "Although war manifests the weakness of the community of nations, it also manifests the existence of that community."

THE NUREMBERG PRINCIPLES

States that are party to international treaties may find themselves subject, even against their will, to the legal restraints of these treaties. The losers in World War II, for example, were tried—and many were convicted—for having waged aggressive war in defiance of their obligations under the Kellogg-Briand Treaty. These trials, conducted in the German city of Nuremberg, were unique in developing the legal doctrine that individuals are personally liable to criminal prosecution for crimes against international law. This includes illegal resort to war as well as violations of accepted restraints as to appropriate conduct during war, notably the treatment of prisoners and the waging of genocide. Thus, the chief Allied prosecutor at Nuremberg wrote that

> war consists largely of acts that would be criminal if performed in time of peace—killing, wounding, kidnapping, destroying or carrying off other people's property. Such conduct is not regarded as criminal if it takes place in the course of war, because the state of war lays a blanket of immunity over the warriors. . . . But the area of immunity is not unlimited and its boundaries are marked by the laws of war.

It should also be pointed out, however, that critics objected to these proceedings, claiming that the Nuremberg Trials were simply examples of "victors' justice," and not concerned with genuine international law. Nevertheless, the so-called Nuremberg Principles have served as a benchmark in efforts to introduce humane and reasoned limits to acceptable wartime behavior. Thus, the international military tribunal that convened in Nuremberg specified a series of international crimes. Article 6 of the Nuremberg Charter identified the following:

1. Crimes against the peace, namely planning, preparation, initiation or waging of a war of aggression, or a war in violation of international treaties. . . .
2. Crimes against humanity, namely, murder, extermination, enslavement, deportation, and other inhumane acts committed against any civilian population. . . .
3. War crimes, namely, violations of the laws or customs of war. Such violations shall include, but not be limited to, murder, ill-treatment or deportation to slave labor or for any other purpose of civilian population of or in occupied territory, murder or ill-treatment of prisoners of war or persons on the seas, killing of hostages, plunder of public or private property, wanton destruction of cities, towns or villages, or devastation not justified by military necessity.

Article 7 specified that "the official position of defendants, whether as Heads of State or responsible officials of Government departments, shall not be considered as freeing them from their responsibility or mitigating their punishment." And according to Article 8, "the fact that the defendant acted pursuant to orders of this Government or of a superior shall not free him from responsibility."

Whereas the German defendants at Nuremberg were tried for crimes they had committed in violation of international law, a series of lesser-known trials were also conducted in Tokyo, of Japanese officials accused in large part of crimes of *omission*—that is, illegal failure to act.

. . . Several decades later, when U.S. army lieutenant William Calley was tried and found guilty for his role in the My Lai massacre during the Vietnam War, it marked the first time a state had accused one of its own soldiers of war crimes. Calley's highest-ranking commanding officers were not tried, however. . . . So again, whereas international laws exist, and have been enforced, such enforcement has been highly selective.

The treaties that were violated by the Nuremberg defendants, originating from the Geneva and Hague Conventions, specified limitations on such actions as naval or aerial bombardment. But they also made allowances for "military necessity," which can be stretched to permit nearly any act in wartime, however outrageous. Similarly, even the toothless Kellogg-Briand Treaty was interpreted by many as permitting "wars of self-defense," as does the current UN Charter: Article 51 grants states the "inherent right of individual or collective self-defense." Self-defense would clearly justify Poland's short-lived response in seeking to resist the German invasion in 1939, but what about France's response, namely, declaring war on Germany (France was treaty-bound to help defend Poland)? And what about the Israeli invasion of Egypt in 1967, in which Israel clearly struck first, but in which it was argued that Egyptian behavior constituted a real provocation as well as an imminent threat that justified a "preemptive" attack by Israel? Similarly, the "Brezhnev Doctrine," by which the U.S.S.R. justified its invasion of Czechoslovakia, was described as laudable pan-socialist self-defense against Western-inspired counterrevolutionaries. And the "Reagan Doctrine," under which the United States assisted right-wing revolutionaries in Marxist states such as Angola or Afghanistan, has been described by its supporters as providing aid to people seeking to defend themselves. Apologists for wars of self-defense and self-determination have thus far always been able to find loopholes in international treaties large enough to drive an army through....

A FINAL NOTE ON INTERNATIONAL LAW

International law has many imperfections. It appears to have exerted some useful restraints in some cases, while being woefully inadequate in others. The major powers give it less credence than do the lesser states, in part because the former have recourse to their military strength, whereas the latter must depend on the rule of law to offer them the possibility of a "level playing field" in contests with larger, stronger opponents. Some authorities recommend only a modest role for international law in the future, avoiding "the Charybdis of subservience to state ambitions and the Scylla of excessive pretensions of restraint," and recognizing that "it is in the interest of international law itself to put states' consciences neither to sleep nor to torture." Another view holds that international law is a beginning, something on which to build a world without boundaries, or at least, one in which the sanctity of state sovereignty is greatly curtailed in the interest of human survival as well as quality of life.

Linda Fasulo

AN INSIDER'S GUIDE TO THE UN

Conflict situations can be resolved in two basic ways: "associative" and "disassociative." The latter relies on military strength and political separation, based on the notion that "good fences make good neighbors." Associative solutions, by contrast, involve tearing down walls and joining together. As we have seen, prominent among the causes of war is the existence of feisty, sovereign states that are, by definition, disassociative relative to each other. Associative solutions include heightened reliance on international law, shared ethical norms, and the joining together of otherwise independent countries to form international organizations. As with the other "solutions" considered in this chapter, international organizations are not perfect or foolproof. Although their record is imperfect, there is much to applaud in the activities of various international organizations, especially the United Nations, which offers a way of ameliorating—although not eliminating—the often troublesome role of states.

When considering the UN, it is important to recognize what it is *not*: it is not a world government, because its members retain their sovereignty. Also, it has not proven effective in preventing conflicts among the major powers, because these powers were granted vetoes over any UN-led enforcement activities. However, the UN has been occasionally effective in peacekeeping and in monitoring compliance with cease-fires and other negotiated settlements, and often, in mediating disputes that might otherwise have turned violent. The UN also provides a valuable forum for debates in addition to the contribution of its various "functional" agencies (such as the Food and Agriculture Organization, the World Health Organization, UNESCO, UNICEF, etc.), which not only help alleviate much human misery but also help creatively undermine reliance on states as the sole unit of political/economic/social recourse.

Thus, the benefits of the United Nations go beyond simply contributing to "negative peace." It may also represent a partial step in the progression from individualism through tribalism, to nationalism and then globalism, a transition that may well be essential if we are ever to give peace a realistic chance. As might be expected, the United Nations is regularly criticized, especially by right-wing militarists and ardent nationalists...which in itself suggests that it may have a major role to play in preventing war!

The following selection focuses on UN peacekeeping operations, which have in fact achieved far more than is widely appreciated; after all, just as news reports are unlikely to announce, "War did *not* break out today between countries X and Y," people are far more aware of any failures to prevent war than of the numerous successes.

Article 43
All Members of the United Nations, in order to contribute to the maintenance of international peace and security, undertake to make available to the Security Council, on its call and in accordance with a special agreement or agreements, armed forces, assistance, and facilities, including rights of passage, necessary for the purpose of maintaining international peace and security.

—UN Charter

Although peacekeeping is one of the quintessential UN functions, it is mentioned only briefly in the Charter. Its full scope and nature have gradually emerged, through need, as a middle ground between mere arbitration of disputes, on the one hand, and use of armed force, on the other. The Security Council's first peacekeeping resolution set important precedents, establishing the United Nations Truce Supervision Organization (UNTSO) in 1948 to oversee the truce between Arabs and Jews when the United Kingdom left Palestine. Like peacekeepers today, the UNTSO troops were provided by member states. The troopers wore the blue helmets that have marked UN peacekeepers ever since. UNTSO also set the model for nomenclature: it is invariably referred to by its acronym rather than its full name. That decades-old practice has led to a roster of past and current operations that read like a chapter out of Genesis, with names that sound like the biblical Gog and Magog—actually, MOONUC and UNOMIG. UNTSO is still in operation, with an expanded mandate that includes supervising the implementation and observance of the general agreements between Israel and its four Arab neighbors.

Once the Security Council authorizes the deployment of an operation, defines its mission, and recommends how it should be carried out, the secretary general appoints a force commander and through the Secretariat's Department of Peacekeeping Operations (DPKO) arranges for management and logistics. Member states are asked to provide personnel, equipment, and logistics. The UN pays member states at the rate of $1,100 per peacekeeper per

A PEACE GLOSSARY

Just as Eskimos have many words to describe the various kinds of snow, the UN has developed words and phrases for the making and keeping of peace. Here are just a few.

Preventive diplomacy

As its name suggest, preventive diplomacy seeks to head off disputes before they become full-blown conflicts. The UN prefers this kind of diplomacy but is able to apply it in only some instances. The UN employs its extensive contacts and offices around the world to detect early signs of potential threats to international peace and security.

Peacemaking

Peacemaking involves the use of diplomacy to persuade belligerents to stop fighting and negotiate an end to their dispute.

Peace enforcement

Peace enforcement involves the use of force against one of the belligerents to enforce an end to the fighting.

Peacebuilding

Peacebuilding involves helping nations promote peace before, during, or after a conflict. Broadly defined, it employs a wide range of political, humanitarian, and human rights activities and programs.

Many parts of the UN system may join in a peacebuilding effort, as well as private bodies like nongovernmental organizations (NGOs). The secretary general often appoints representatives to coordinate the activities through special peacebuilding support offices, such as those established in Liberia, Guinea-Bissau, and the Central African Republic.

The responsibility to protect

The Charter gives the UN the right to intervene in a nation's affairs to prevent egregious human rights violations, but in recent years there has been talk about a variant on this, called the responsibility to protect. A recent international commission stated in its report that "the responsibility to protect implies an evaluation of the issues from the point of view of those seeking or needing support, rather than those who may be considering intervention."

---

month, and the governments pay the troops according to their own scales. Member states retain control over their units. Peacekeeping personnel rely less on their arms than on their international authority and their reputation for impartiality. They wear their country's uniform and are identified as peacekeepers by a UN blue helmet or a beret and a badge.

Some UN peacekeeping operations consist of military observers charged with monitoring truces, troop withdrawals, and borders or demilitarized zones. Other operations involve military formations capable of acting as buffers between hostile forces. More recently, some peacekeeping operations have combined military and police or civilian functions and personnel, with the aim of creating or strengthening political institutions, providing emergency aid, clearing land mines, or administering and monitoring free elections.

Peace-related issues have always been central to Security Council deliberations, but in the past decade they have become especially numerous and demanding of time and resources. The decade of the 1990s saw the UN launch more peace-related operations than in all the previous four decades. During the year ending June 2003, there were 14 peacekeeping missions, employing 45,000 personnel at a cost of $2.6 billion.

And the nature of the disputes has largely changed. The norm used to be that wars occurred between nation-states, which fought with field armies that were supposed to target combatants and not civilians—that was the theory, anyway. But these days nation-states have been remarkably well behaved toward one another, and in some places, like Europe, they have even forged close political ties. Instead, conflicts tend to occur within nations, in the form of civil wars (as in Rwanda, Congo, and the former Yugoslavia) or national resistance movements (like the East Timorese against Indonesian occupation, the Islamic separatists in the Philippines, the independence fighters in Kosovo, or the Palestinians against the Israelis).

THE TALKING CURE

Today, the council has to address so many requests for making or keeping peace that it usually begins by looking for a solution that does not involve a UN deployment. It starts with behind-the-scenes diplomacy, escalating to open diplomacy as needed.

A good example is the conflict between Ethiopia and its breakaway province of Eritrea, which began in the 1990s and has only recently been resolved, largely through UN and regional efforts. During the early 1980s, Ethiopia, a landlocked country, unilaterally annexed Eritrea, which gave it a port on the Red Sea; but the Eritreans resisted and finally secured their independence after a long war. Then, on May 6, 1998, the Eritrean government ordered its armed forces to occupy a slice of disputed territory on the border with Ethiopia. A regional body, the Organization of African Unity (OAU), worked out an agreement for settling the dispute, but neither side would commit to it.

In February 1999, the Security Council stepped in and urged the disputants to accept the OAU's plan. When they refused and began fighting, the council moved to its next stage of action, which was to tell the combatants to stop fighting, start talking, and arrange a cease-fire. The U.S. also joined the cease-fire efforts, and in February and March OAU special envoy Ahmed Ouyahia (of Algeria) and former U.S. national security advisor Anthony Lake visited Asmara and Addis Ababa. Algeria then brought the two parties together for talks, which broke down.

The fighting had by then stopped but seemed on the verge of resuming when, in April, the council reiterated its demand for a cease-fire and implementation of the OAU's plan. In June the council again asked the two parties to negotiate, citing a looming humanitarian crisis as drought and unrest threatened massive starvation. The U.S. sent more then 700,000 metric tons of food assistance to Ethiopia and 100,000 to Eritrea. A UN Security Council mission to Congo, led by U.S. permanent representative Richard Holbrooke, began shuttle diplomacy during several days early in May, with Holbrooke leaning on both sides not to renew the fighting.

The shuttle talks failed, the mission left, and on May 12, 2000, Ethiopia sent its forces deep into Eritrea. The Security Council passed a resolution demanding an end to military action, but the next day Ethiopia's forces made a major breakthrough and eventually advanced to within 100 kilometers of the Eritrean capital. Then the Ethiopian government, apparently satisfied it had acquired a good bargaining position, stated it was ending the war. Meanwhile, the Security Council passed another resolution, 1298, requiring that member states enforce

an arms sales embargo on both combatants. Eritrea then declared that it would move its troops back to the border that existed in May 1998.

As each combatant backed off, the OAU, UN, and other parties arranged for new talks in Algiers, which led to an agreement on June 18 for a cease-fire. Once the fighting ended, the council created the UN Mission in Ethiopia and Eritrea (UNMEE), charged with monitoring the border and ensuring that the provisions of the cease-fire were honored. The council authorized the mission at a strength of more than 4,200 military and other personnel.

By then, Ethiopia and Eritrea had been fighting or at least glaring at each other for more than two years. Why did the council wait so long? The answer is that UN peacekeepers maintain peace once it is agreed to by the combatants, but they do not create peace through military action. The main purpose of peacekeeping is simply to help prevent fighting from erupting and to give negotiators a chance to find a permanent resolution to the dispute.

A resolution seems to have been found in the Ethiopia–Eritrea border dispute. In fall 2000, the OAU envoy and Anthony Lake pursued shuttle diplomacy while members of the Security Council urged the disputants to negotiate a complete solution. At Algiers in December 2000, the two nations signed a final accord in the presence of secretary general Kofi Annan and U.S. secretary of state Madeleine Albright. The end is in sight but not quite achieved. UNMEE is expected to remain deployed until the final border between the two nations is demarcated, and until the two governments establish sufficient dialogue to ensure that they can peacefully resolve any disagreements or misunderstandings that might arise between them.

UN SANCTIONS

Sanctions are nonlethal, noninvasive mechanisms aimed at preventing a state from interacting with the outside world in certain ways, such as engaging in trade or acquiring arms. Travel bans and financial or diplomatic restrictions are also types of sanction. Although sanctions are intended to pressure governments, they may also unintentionally harm civilians too. Sometimes it is the poorest or most vulnerable members of society who are most harmed when their nation is placed under a sanction, especially one that affects trade and commerce. Consider the case of Saddam Hussein's regime in Iraq, after the Gulf War.

When Iraq invaded Kuwait in 1990, the UN imposed sweeping sanctions intended to bar the aggressor from all trade and financial dealings, except for humanitarian purposes, with the rest of the world. After the U.S. and its allies, with the blessing of the UN, routed the Iraqi armed forces and arranged a cease-fire (which the UN monitored) in 1991, the UN left the sanctions in place while stipulating that Iraq divest itself of weapons of mass destruction. Because the Iraqi government was not fully cooperating with inspections, the UN continued the sanctions throughout the years of the Saddam Hussein regime.

The Iraqi government, meanwhile, was able to partly evade the sanctions while complaining noisily that its citizens were being deprived of access to vital medicines, food, and other necessities. This effective campaign influenced the Security Council to create the Oil for Food program, which permitted the Iraqi government the option of exporting specified amounts of crude oil, under UN scrutiny, in order to pay for "humanitarian goods." Terms of the program were liberalized in 1998 and 1999, and finally in 2002, to give Iraq access to most civilian goods. The last liberalization was done through a Security Council resolution offered by the U.S. in May 2002. The idea behind the resolution was to replace typical UN sanctions with "smart sanctions" that would enable Iraqi citizens to get necessities more easily while making it more difficult for Saddam Hussein's regime to use trade in order to obtain arms and other forbidden items. On May 22, 2003, two months after the U.S.-led invasion of Iraq, the Security Council lifted sanctions, except for the sale of weapons and related materiel.

RETHINKING PEACEKEEPING

Although traditional peacekeeping remains important, it is increasingly regarded as merely the first step in a process of moving from armed conflict to political dialogue and engagement. The new approach tries to engage all stakeholders in dialogue, which means governments, of course, but also nongovernmental organizations and other groups. Among the pioneers of the new approach is Kofi Annan, who spent four years in charge of peacekeeping operations when he was undersecretary general, and one of his top aides, Shashi Tharoor. As Tharoor says of his experiences during the 1990s, when the new approach emerged, in addition to doing the usual peacekeeping tasks, they were experimenting with "all sorts of new things, everything from delivering humanitarian aid under fire, hunting down warlords, and of course monitoring no-fly zones. It was very much like fixing the engine of a moving car."

One of the places where the UN has applied its new thinking about peacekeeping is East Timor, which recently gained national independence from Indonesia. The Security Council hosted the negotiations that led in 1999 to a popular referendum in which the Timorese rejected autonomy within Indonesia and opted for complete independence. But the council had to authorize a multinational security force after Indonesian-backed militants unleashed a campaign of systematic destruction and violence in response to the Timorese referendum. Many East Timorese were killed and more than 200,000 were forced to flee, most of them to West Timor.

In October 1999, acting under Chapter VII of the UN Charter, the Security Council established the UN Transitional Administration in East Timor (UNTAET) to restore order and provide administrative services as East Timor prepared for independence. The council appointed Sergio Vieira de Mello of Brazil as the transitional administrator for East Timor. UNTAET began a program of "Timorization" of key government posts to prepare for transition to full independence. In July UNTAET established the East Timor Transitional Administration (ETTA), with a cabinet of nine ministries, five headed by East Timorese. Then UNTAET appointed a thirty-six-member National Council representing a wide spectrum of Timorese society. UNTAET began preparations for elections in late summer 2001 for a national assembly, which drew up and adopted a constitution. In 2002 the Timorese elected a president and became a new nation.

The UN's nation-building has succeeded in launching East Timor on its new path, but interestingly the effort has gotten mixed reviews. David Malone praises its director: "To make good things happen at the UN requires particular skills and qualities that may not be required in running a major corporation or running a major government. They are particular skills of endurance and determination that I think find expression in Sergio Vieira de Mello, who pulled off the East Timor operation in spite of tremendous problems on the ground and enormous bureaucratic inertia within the UN. He just has the sheer determination to get things done and they did get done." Shepard Forman concedes that the effort went fairly well but questions whether it was appropriate: "The UN as a government in Kosovo and East Timor is questionable. Few of the people that went out to govern had any more experience than any of the East Timorese. That's an example of where it [the UN] took on a role to prove itself, and it did an all right job, but we lost a year or so in terms of the Timoreses' own capacity to develop, to reconstruct."

Good, bad, or inappropriate, the UN's mission to East Timor shows that new ideas are floating about and being acted on, which is crucial if the world body is going to adapt and remain vital. Which opens up another area of change: the faces under those blue helmets.

NEW PEACEKEEPERS, NEW FACES

A relic of the colonial era, which didn't end until the 1970s, is that the Western media tend to present the European-American nations as militarily superior. This is increasingly an outdated notion. David Malone says, "It's just assumed that the West, because it is so well equipped when it goes into the peacekeeping field, is the only region providing qualified peacekeepers." Not so, he asserts. The Indians and the Pakistanis are "excellent peacekeepers," and the Bangladeshis and the Kenyans "have proved very good in the field." As proof he cites the case of the UN peacekeeping mission established in Rwanda in 1993, the same mission that was unable to stop the genocide between Hutus and Tutsis. The commander, the Canadian general Romeo Dallaire,

led a mixed force of Europeans and Ghanaians, who were outnumbered by the killers and suffered casualties as they tried to protect specific groups of victims. The Ghanaian peacekeepers saved the most lives, according to Malone, under their own brigadier general, Dallaire's deputy. "About 500 of them stayed behind and they saved at least 25,000 lives in the Kigali stadium and elsewhere," he says. "They never received any attention at all, and this tells us something about the way that peacekeeping is covered by the media. Dallaire has constantly tried to draw attention to the heroic behavior of the Ghanaians, but never with any success whatsoever."

Malone's own solution is to combine the technical prowess of the West with the commitment and courage of the Africans and other peacekeepers. "What is important in peacekeeping is that some of the Western militaries have the high-tech capacities that, say, the Ghanaian army doesn't have. So ideally a peacekeeping force in Africa will be composed of a mix of developing-country contingents and Western contingents."

Equally needed, as Malone and other insiders would agree, is a basic overhaul of how the UN constitutes and funds its peacekeeping missions. Imagine having to conduct potentially risky and difficult military operations when you don't have a standing army and lack the right to levy taxes. Understandably, the attempt to enlarge the peacekeeping concept along lines described above has stretched the peacekeeping effort sometimes beyond what it can handle. Some have likened UN peacekeeping to a volunteer fire department—but it's not that well organized, according to Kofi Annan, because for every mission it is necessary to scrounge up the fire engines and the money to pay for them "before we can start dousing any flames."

The Security Council commissioned a study led by Lakhdar Brahimi, the former foreign minister of Algeria, to examine the main shortcomings of the current operation and offer solutions for change. This so-called Brahimi report, submitted in August 2000, has become a blueprint for such efforts. The report recommends that the UN make fundamental changes in its policies and practices of peacekeeping and that it provide more financial backing. It urges an updating of the concept of peacekeeping to address modern situations where the combatants may be heavily armed and not always obedient to commanders or political leaders. In such highly charged scenarios the peacekeepers may have to choose sides, at least temporarily, in order to protect the innocent. The Security Council must therefore provide peacekeeping missions with precise instructions on how to act in a variety of possible circumstances. Equally important, according to the report, is the integration of military functions with historically civil concerns such as human rights,

policing, and food, shelter, and medical services. The UN has begun acting on the report, beginning with the Security Council's acceptance of the report's recommendations. Questions now are whether the General Assembly will deliver adequate financial support and whether the council and the secretariat have the will to follow through on the report over the long term.

STUDY QUESTIONS

1. Identify and discuss some ways of preventing war that were *not* touched upon in this chapter and that deserve consideration. Look specifically at whether the phenomenon of "asymmetric conflict" introduces qualitatively new issues or simply a different slant on the same problem.
2. Choose one or more of the selections in this chapter and disagree with it, pointing out, for example, how it is unrealistic, or undesirable, or might be counterproductive.
3. Take a current source of conflict and describe how "principled negotiation" might help both sides reach an acceptable agreement.
4. With the Cold War receding into distant memory, is arms control still important? If yes, where would you like to see it be concentrated? If no, why not?
5. Look into the current status of international organizations *other than* the United Nations. Which of these seem especially promising? Do any seem liable to be especially troublesome? Why?
6. Are there any weaknesses in international law other than the problem of enforcement? Describe them and suggest improvements.
7. What are some reasons for thinking that the current system of sovereign states is inappropriate for meeting the problems of the twenty-first century? Are there any reasons to think that this system is weakening? If so, what benefits and dangers might this pose?
8. An earlier edition of this book included a famous suggestion for world government by philosopher Immanuel Kant. Look into other schemes for world government that have been proposed since then. Are they necessarily as unrealistic as some critics suggest? (In other words, was it wise to delete consideration of world government from this chapter?)
9. Describe ways in which Osgood's strategy of GRIT might be applied to a current situation of conflict. Be specific.

10. What similarities exist between attempts to achieve negative peace on the international level and on the personal level? Differences?

SUGGESTIONS FOR FURTHER READING

Benton, Barbara, ed. 1996. *Soldiers for Peace: Fifty Years of United Nations Peacekeeping.* New York: Facts On File.

Blix, Hans. 2008. *Why Nuclear Disarmament Matters.* Cambridge, MA: MIT Press.

Cassidy, Kevin J., and Gregory A. Bischak. 1993. *Real Security: Converting the Defense Economy and Building Peace.* Albany: State University of New York Press.

Clark, Grenville, and Louis Sohn. 1966. *World Peace Through World Law: Two Alternative Plans.* Cambridge, MA: Harvard University Press.

Crocker, Chester A., Fen Osler Hampson, and Pamela R. Aall, eds. 2001. *Turbulent Peace: The Challenges of Managing International Conflict.* Washington, DC: United States Institute of Peace Press.

Findlay, Trevor, ed. 1996. *Challenges for the New Peacekeepers.* New York: Oxford University Press.

Goldman, Ralph Morris, and Willard M. Hardman.1997. *Building Trust: An Introduction to Peacekeeping and Arms Control.* Brookfield, VT: Ashgate.

Mason, David T., and James D. Meernik, eds. 2006. *Conflict Prevention and Peacebuilding in Post-War Societies: Sustaining the Peace.* New York: Routledge.

Schell, Jonathan. 2007. *The Seventh Decade: The New Shape of Nuclear Danger.* New York: Metropolitan Books.

Shaw, Malcolm. 2008. *International Law.* London: Cambridge University Press.

Sidhu, Waheguru Pal Singh, and Ramesh Chandra Thakur. 2006. *Arms Control After Iraq: Normative and Operational Challenges.* New York: United Nations University Press.

CHAPTER 3

Responding to Terrorism

F or most Americans, terrorism suddenly emerged as a major concern immediately following the terrorist attacks of 9/11. However, for many other people, terrorism has been an ever-present reality—not only terrorism perpetrated by nonstate actors (what can be designated "terrorism from below") but also terrorism brought about by the actions of states themselves ("terrorism from above"). This distinction may be jarring for readers whose understanding of terrorism is limited to the former designation: the use of violence or the threat of violence against civilians by unofficial entities seeking to influence the action of governments. But it is worth noting that official entities—namely, governments themselves—have not been reluctant to employ violence or the threat of violence against civilians in the hope of influencing the action of governments or of the civilian population: this is the essence of nuclear deterrence and, traditionally, of most counterinsurgency campaigns.

A further, potentially jarring and controversial suggestion is embodied in the saying, "One person's terrorist is another's freedom fighter." Thus, in the late eighteenth century, American revolutionaries were frequently described by the British as "terrorists," just as in the twentieth century the Irish Republican Army—substantially funded by Irish émigrés to the United States—has long been reviled, especially in England, as a terrorist organization. Even more dramatically, perhaps, a prominent "terrorist" organization (the *Irgun*), which fought on behalf of Israeli independence from British rule, subsequently contributed to the postindependence political leadership of Israel, just as the Palestinian Liberation Organization, once reviled as "terrorist," has become the recognized government on the occupied West Bank.

These issues are not raised here in order to minimize the horror derived from terrorist attacks but simply to emphasize that even such a seemingly open-and-shut case as "terrorism" warrants being understood as nuanced and not usefully categorized as a simple matter of "us" (the good guys, who are moral and law-abiding) versus "them" (the bad guys, who are immoral and unprincipled). Moreover, terrorism's history is much older and broader than most Americans assume and is not defined or constrained by considerations of religion.

This chapter is focused especially on terrorism as embodied by Islamic fundamentalism because it is largely intended for an American audience. However, it also seeks to widen the reader's perspective on this enormous and complex problem.

RAND Corporation

TERRORISM PAST AND PRESENT

Concern about future conflicts in the twenty-first century has increasingly focused on the phenomenon of "asymmetrical conflicts," among which terrorism and counterterrorism loom large. The RAND Corporation was originally formed as a semi-independent "think tank" to advise the United States Air Force ("RAND" originally stood for "research and development"). Its involvement in matters of terrorism speaks to this shift in emphasis. At the same time, the following RAND report, commissioned by the nonpartisan and highly respected League of Women Voters, provides a useful, mainstream, and comparatively uncontroversial introduction to terrorism past and present.

A BRIEF OVERVIEW OF TERRORISM

Depending on how it is defined, terrorism, both in practice and in name, dates back hundreds, even thousands, of years. In the realm of political action, the word "terrorism" was a product of the French Revolution's *régime de la terreur* (1793–1794). Ironically, "terror" initially had a positive connotation because it was associated with a struggle for democracy and a more virtuous society. That was not to last in the face of the generalized fear induced by the ever-present guillotine, and *terrorism* came to be associated with abuse of power, especially by the state.

During the nineteenth and early twentieth centuries, there was an increase in both Europe and America of the use of terror-inducing violence to promote antistate outcomes or to achieve independent statehood. Anarchists carried out a series of bombings and assassinations, the best known of which were the murders of Czar Alexander II in Russia (1881), President William McKinley in the United States (1901), and Archduke Franz Ferdinand in Sarajevo (1914). Irish, Armenian, and Bosnian insurrectionists were among the ethnoseparatist groups fighting against alien regimes. Labor uprisings in many countries were bitter and often bloody.

Beginning in about the 1930s, terrorism was turned on its head when "revolutionary" violence directed against heads of state and other persons in authority began to be replaced by "repressive" violence applied by dictators such as Adolf Hitler, Benito Mussolini, and Joseph Stalin against their own citizenry. This kind of state-directed terror, used by those in power against their own citizens, later had many counterparts in third world countries, especially in Central and South America.

Following World War II, terrorism again assumed its revolutionary connotation, most notably through the nationalist or anticolonial revolts carried out in Asia, Africa, and the Middle East in opposition to European rule. In the 1980s, there was a further expansion of the concept of terrorism in the form of state-sponsored, covert violence against other nations—such as that sponsored by Iran, Iraq, Libya, and Syria—which allowed weaker regimes to confront more powerful countries without risking large-scale retaliation.

It was primarily the activities of the Palestinian Liberation Organization (PLO) that put terrorism in the international spotlight. Although the PLO's 1968 hijacking of an Israeli El Al commercial aircraft and the 1972 attack on the Israeli Olympic team in Munich did not achieve their objectives, they did succeed in drawing world attention to their cause, which was the plight of Palestinian refugees who had either voluntarily left or had been driven from Israel and were living in overcrowded camps in neighboring countries. The PLO served as an example to other aggrieved groups, and "within the decade, the number of terrorist groups either operating internationally or committing attacks against foreign targets in their own country in order to attract international attention had more than quadrupled."[1]

Given the substantial changes that have occurred over time in the notion of what constitutes terrorism, it is important to try to pin down a definition that can act as an anchor. Bruce Hoffman, an internationally recognized authority on the subject of terrorism, suggests the following:

> [Terrorism is] the deliberate creation and exploitation of fear through violence or the threat of violence

in the pursuit of political change. All terrorist acts involve violence or the threat of violence. Terrorism is specifically designed to have far-reaching psychological effects beyond the immediate victim(s) or object of the terrorist attack. It is meant to instill fear within, and thereby intimidate, a wider "target audience" that might include a rival ethnic or religious group, an entire country, a national government or political party, or public opinion in general. Terrorism is designed to create power where there is none or to consolidate power where there is very little. Through the publicity generated by their violence, terrorists seek to obtain the leverage, influence, and power they otherwise lack to effect political change on either a local or an international scale.[2]

TERRORISM AS A RELIGIOUS IMPERATIVE

Terrorism motivated by religious belief is a centuries-old phenomenon, and scores of examples can be found in all major religions in all parts of the world. However, in the modern consciousness, the resurgence of religious terrorism is often linked to the 1979 revolution that transformed Iran into an Islamic republic. The Ayatollah Khomeini had long condemned the growing influence of the West under the government of Mohammad Reza Shah, and had called on Muslims to reject secular government in favor of the restoration of fundamental Islamic law. Moreover, Khomeini sought to extend the revolution to other Muslim countries. Violence in the service of this goal was promoted not as a tactic but, under certain conditions, as an obligation.

One of the central tenets of Islam is the duty of Muslims to engage in jihad. As Rudolph Peters, an expert on the Middle East, has explained,

> The Arabic word jihad means to strive, to exert oneself, to struggle. The word has a basic connotation of an endeavour towards a praiseworthy aim. In a religious context it may express a struggle against one's evil inclinations or an exertion for the sake of Islam and the umma [Muslim community], e.g., trying to convert unbelievers or working for the moral betterment of Islamic society ("jihad of the

[1] Bruce Hoffman, *Inside Terrorism*, 2d ed. (New York: Columbia University Press, 2006), p. 70. Hoffman goes on to say that "according to the RAND Terrorism Incident Database, the number of organizations engaged in *international* terrorism grew from only eleven in 1968 . . . to an astonishing fifty-five in 1978. Of this total, more than half (thirty, or 54 percent) were ethno-nationalist separatist movements, all seeking to copy or capitalize on the PLO's success."

[2] Hoffman, pp. 40–41.

tongue" and "jihad of the sword"). In the books on Islamic law, the word means armed struggle against the unbelievers, which is also a common meaning in the Koran.[3]

The Soviet invasion of Afghanistan further stimulated jihad and was critical to the later formation of Al Qaeda. Its leader, Osama bin Laden, has been clear and consistent in his condemnation of the West—the new Crusaders—and his desire to protect Islam from Christian aggression. Although his overarching goal is to create a worldwide, totalitarian theocracy, he has turned jihadis against the United States in particular by exploiting resentments over its military presence in the Arabian Peninsula, the war in Iraq, and American support of Israel. Bin Laden has been extremely skillful in capitalizing on the belief that engaging in defensive jihad is an individual obligation when Islam is under assault, and he has succeeded in building a broad base of support that assures a steady flow of recruits to his cause.

One of the things that make religious terrorists so formidable is their willingness to carry out operations that are far more deadly and destructive than those conducted by their secular counterparts.[4] The attacks by nineteen Al Qaeda airplane hijackers on the World Trade Center and the Pentagon are the most dramatic case in point. Including the deaths on the fourth aircraft that crashed in Pennsylvania, nearly three thousand people were killed. Until that time, no terrorist operation had killed more than five hundred.[5]

Suicide terrorism is a particularly effective and lethal form of attack. It has advantages in timing, access, and flexibility if plans have to be changed at the last minute. It is inexpensive to carry out. It results in higher death and casualty rates than other methods.[6] Since the perpetrator is not expected to survive, there is no need for a complicated getaway plan. Broad media coverage is assured; thus, the psychological, fear-inducing effects are widespread and profound.

Robert Pape argues in his study of suicide terrorism, *Dying to Win*, that contrary to what many Westerners believe, there is little connection between this phenomenon and Islamic fundamentalism or any other world religion. "Rather, what nearly all suicide terrorist attacks have in common is a specific secular and strategic goal: to compel modern democracies to withdraw military forces from territory that the terrorists consider to be their homeland."[7]

However, many terrorism specialists acknowledge a link between religion and terrorism. For example, Bruce Hoffman points to the growth in the number of religious terrorist groups during the past two decades and asserts that a major challenge facing those charged with developing effective countermeasures is to understand "why mainstream religious traditions become radicalized and co-opted by violent extremists and why "fringe" movements or hitherto peaceful religious cults suddenly embark on lethal campaigns of indiscriminate terrorism."[8]

---

[3] Rudolph Peters, *Jihad in Classical and Modern Islam: A Reader*, 2d ed. (Princeton, NJ: Markus Wiener Publishers, 2005), p.1.

[4] "Although religious terrorists committed only 6 percent of recorded terrorist incidents between 1998 and 2004, their acts were responsible for 30 percent of the total number of fatalities recorded during that time period....While Al Qaeda perpetrated only 0.1 percent of all terrorist attacks between 1998 and 2004, it was responsible for nearly 19 percent of total fatalities during that time period" (Hoffman, p. 88).

[5] Hoffman, pp. 18–19.

[6] Hoffman, pp. 132–133. "According to one estimate, the total cost of a typical Palestinian suicide operation, for example, is about one hundred fifty dollars. Yet this modest sum yields a very attractive return: on average, suicide operations worldwide kill about four times as many people as other kinds of terrorist attacks. In Israel the average is even higher, inflicting six times the number of deaths and roughly twenty-six times more casualties than other acts of terrorism" (p. 133).

[7] Robert A. Pape, *Dying to Win: The Strategic Logic of Suicide Terrorism* (New York: Random House, 2005), p. 4. Pape's study of all suicide bombings and attacks worldwide from 1980 through 2003 shows that "the leading instigators of suicide attacks are the Tamil Tigers in Sri Lanka, a Marxist-Leninist group whose members are from Hindu families but who are adamantly opposed to religion. This group committed 76 of the 315 incidents, more suicide attacks than Hamas...[and] 301 could have their roots traced to large, coherent political or military campaigns."

[8] Hoffman, p. 127. Hoffman points out that "in 1994, a third (sixteen) of the forty-nine identifiable international terrorist groups active that year could be classified as religious in character and/or motivation...." By 2004, that number had risen to nearly half (fifty-two, or 46 percent), "while thirty-two (28 percent) were left-wing groups, and twenty-four (21 percent) were ethno-nationalist/separatist organizations" (p. 86).

TRENDS IN TERRORISM

Just as the definitions of what constitutes terrorism have changed over time, so have the ways that terrorists operate. Several of the apparent trends are described below.[9]

- *Terrorism has become bloodier, and suicide terrorism is now the most deadly form.* In the period 1980–2003, suicide attacks comprised only 3 percent of all terrorist incidents but accounted for 48 percent of the fatalities.[10]
- *Terrorists have evolved new models of organization.* In place of the hierarchies of the past, terrorist groups now employ flat organizational structures and operate independent, scattered cells. They use modern communications techniques for networking across regions, and their compartmentalization makes it difficult for their enemies to penetrate their operations.
- *Terrorists have developed financial resources that make them less dependent on state sponsors.* Terrorists have become skilled in raising money, moving it, and blocking detection of their financial operations. They have direct contributors, and many groups receive financial contributions through the Internet as well. Islamic nongovernmental charity organizations are another source of funds, sometimes knowingly and sometimes not. Certain terrorist groups also engage in kidnapping for ransom, extortion, protection rackets, and drug trafficking. Others have very substantial legitimate investments that are difficult to trace.[11]

- *Terrorists have learned to effectively exploit modern communication technologies.* To reach their target audiences, terrorists no longer need to rely on underground publications and radio stations. A full range of video equipment, computers, e-mail, mass-marketed CDs and DVDs—all of the advances represented by the latest information revolution are available to them, and they are taking full advantage. They can now shape, produce, and disseminate sophisticated messages via the high-speed Internet and World Wide Web without concern for censorship and very little fear of discovery.[12]
- *Terrorists have increased their mobility and expanded their operational theater.* As a result of widespread exodus from zones of conflict, terrorists are able, on their own and through networked contact with migrating populations, to operate more extensively and effectively across borders. In addition, modern communication has also enabled transnational connectivity among terrorist groups who may not share the same ideology but do share expertise, tactics, and even technology.

THE FUTURE TERRORIST THREAT

Most people in the United States were blindsided by the September 11 attacks. Being geographically distant from most of the places in the world that foster terrorism, we did not expect such a brutal and catastrophic assault on our homeland. Perhaps that was naïve. As Michael Scheuer emphasizes in *Through Our Enemies' Eyes*, in its entire history America has

---

[9] Material for this discussion has been drawn primarily from four sources: Rohan Gunaratna, ed., *The Changing Face of Terrorism* (Singapore: Marshall Cavendish Academic, 2004), pp. 18–30; Bruce Hoffman, *Inside Terrorism*; Brian Michael Jenkins, "The New Age of Terrorism" in *Homeland Security Handbook* (New York: McGraw Hill, 2006), pp. 117–128; and Michael Scheuer, *Through Our Enemies' Eyes: Osama bin Laden, Radical Islam, and the Future of America*, 2d ed. (Washington, DC: Potomac Books, 2006).

[10] Pape, p. 6.

[11] Cindy Combs, *Terrorism in the Twenty-First Century*, 4th ed. (Upper Saddle River, NJ: Prentice Hall, 2005), p. 12. Combs states that "if the PLO [Palestinian Liberation Organization] were an American corporation, it would have been on the list of Fortune 500 companies." In the mid-1980s the organization's

financial empire was estimated to be worth $5 billion. Return on investments brought in about $1 billion a year. Most of the PLO's assets were held by private individuals or in numbered bank accounts. Its finanical advisers invested money in the European market and on Wall Street. "The PLO also held large amounts of lucrative money certificates in the United States. These and other investments were said to provide as much as 20 percent of all of the group's revenues." Like many multinational corporations, the PLO was generally involved in business ventures designed to earn money, but in some cases their purpose was primarily to generate goodwill and political support (Combs, pp. 90–91).

[12] See "The New Media, Terrorism, and the Shaping of Global Opinion" in Hoffman, pp. 197–228.

rarely had an enemy that made his plans clearer or repeated them so often:

> Osama bin Laden publicly declared war on the United States on 2 September 1996; for good measure, he did so again on 23 February 1998. Since 1996, bin Laden has repeatedly warned Americans—again always in public—that he would incrementally increase the lethality of his attacks on U.S. interests until we stopped supporting Israel, withdrew our military forces from Saudi Arabia, and ended the embargo on Iraq. During this period, he was true to his word; his forces and those he incited attacked us with steadily increasing skill, lethality, and audacity in Somalia, Saudi Arabia, Kenya, Tanzania, and Yemen. He warned that if the United States did not yield to his demands, he would bring the war he was waging into the continental United States.[13]

The fight against Al Qaeda has been called the defining conflict of the early twenty-first century. How, then, should we respond as a nation? Scheuer suggests this for a start:

> Until Americans begin to see that some of their values and goals are neither accepted or acceptable

to all races, nations, and creeds, they will not begin to understand the appeal of a person like bin Laden or be able to defend their interests against him. Indeed, they will need to go another step and recognize that, for many Muslims, U.S. foreign policy is seen as an attack on Islam...and is drawing an armed response as a matter of self-defense and scriptural requirement.[14]

It is also important to recognize that the rise of radical Islam is not confined to the Middle East. The phenomenon that we in the West associate with Al Queda has metastasized throughout the world. Muslim minorities in many countries consider themselves marginalized within their societies, and their resentment is increasingly being directed against the United States and its allies. In *The Next Attack*, Daniel Benjamin and Steven Simon observe that the "churn of local conflicts is providing soldiers for the global jihad. It may not be long before substantially more extremists from these five regions—Europe, Chechnya, Saudi Arabia, Pakistan, and Southeast Asia—are participating directly in the war against America."[15]

---

[13] Scheuer, p. xvi.

[14] Scheuer, p. 29.

[15] Daniel Benjamin and Steven Simon, *The Next Attack: The Failure of the War on Terror and a Strategy for Getting It Right* (New York: Henry Holt and Company, 2005), p. 81.

Samuel P. Huntington

THE CLASH OF CIVILIZATIONS

For some students of international affairs, the issue is less one of terrorism than of a fundamental conflict between "civilizations." This perspective was most forcefully developed by political scientist Samuel Huntington, initially in an influential article in the journal *Foreign Affairs* (excerpted here) and then later expanded into a book by the same title. Although Huntington's initial thesis was broader than simply warning about a clash between Islam and the West, that component has been the most dramatic part of his argument, one that has subsequently been taken up by many observers, especially those of a more conservative bent.

Critics of Huntington's perspective have pointed out that with the end of the U.S.–Soviet rivalry, "cold warriors" may well have felt threatened by the *absence* of a designated enemy, which led, in turn, to identifying a forthcoming "clash of civilizations" less because of its likely reality than as a form of post–Cold War job insurance. In addition, the danger exists that identifying such "clashes" may well serve as a self-fulfilling prophecy, whereby preparing for some eventualities has the effect of generating responses by the other side that cause the original prediction to become true. Moreover, others point out that "civilizations" are hardly unitary or homogeneous and that by identifying "Islam," for example, as a single entity, the "clash of civilizations" approach errs greatly by failing to recognize the complex heterogeneity of, for example, Sunni and Shiite, Arab and non-Arab, moderate and fundamentalist, and so forth.

On the other hand, it can be argued that this perspective has proven remarkably prescient: note that it initially appeared in 1993. Only time will tell whether a "clash of civilizations" explains past history, underlies current events, or—more to the point—anticipates the future. And only by understanding the argument will those seeking to pursue peace be in a good position to reject it or learn from it.

THE NEXT PATTERN OF CONFLICT

World politics is entering a new phase, and intellectuals have not hesitated to proliferate visions of what it will be—the end of history, the return of traditional rivalries between nation-states, and the decline of the nation-state from the conflicting pulls of tribalism and globalism, among others. Each of these visions catches aspects of the emerging reality. Yet they all miss a crucial, indeed a central, aspect of what global politics is likely to be in the coming years.

It is my hypothesis that the fundamental source of conflict in this new world will not be primarily ideological or primarily economic. The great divisions among humankind and the dominating source of conflict will be cultural. Nation-states will remain the most powerful actors in world affairs, but the principal conflicts of global politics will occur between nations and groups of different civilizations. The clash of civilizations will dominate global politics. The fault lines between civilizations will be the battle lines of the future.

Conflict between civilizations will be the latest phase in the evolution of conflict in the modern world. For a century and a half after the emergence of the modern international system with the Peace of Westphalia, the conflicts of the Western world were largely among princes—emperors, absolute monarchs, and constitutional monarchs attempting to expand their bureaucracies, their armies, their mercantilist economic strength and, most important, the territory they ruled. In the process they created nation-states, and beginning with the French Revolution the principal lines of conflict were between nations rather than princes. In 1793, as R. R. Palmer put it, "The wars of kings were over; the wars of peoples had begun." This nineteenth-century pattern lasted until the end of World War I. Then, as a result of the Russian Revolution and the reaction against it, the conflict of nations yielded to the conflict of ideologies, first among communism, fascism-Nazism, and liberal democracy, and then between communism and liberal democracy. During the Cold War, this latter conflict became embodied in the struggle between the two superpowers, neither of which was a nation-state in the classical European sense and each of which defined its identity in terms of its ideology.

These conflicts between princes, nation-states, and ideologies were primarily conflicts within Western civilization, "Western civil wars," as William Lind has labeled them. This was as true of the Cold War as it was of the world wars and the earlier wars of the seventeenth, eighteenth, and nineteenth centuries. With the end of the Cold War, international politics moves out of its Western phase, and its centerpiece becomes the interaction between the West and non-Western civilizations and among non-Western civilizations. In the politics of civilizations, the peoples and governments of non-Western civilizations no longer remain the objects of history as targets of Western colonialism but join the West as movers and shapers of history....

Westerners tend to think of nation-states as the principal actors in global affairs. They have been that, however, for only a few centuries. The broader reaches of human history have been the history of civilizations. In *A Study of History,* Arnold Toynbee identified twenty-one major civilizations; only six of them exist in the contemporary world.

WHY CIVILIZATIONS WILL CLASH

Civilization identity will be increasingly important in the future, and the world will be shaped in large measure by the interactions among seven or eight major civilizations. These include Western, Confucian, Japanese, Islamic, Hindu, Slavic-Orthodox, Latin American, and possibly African civilization. The most important conflicts of the future will occur along the cultural fault lines separating these civilizations from one another.

Why will this be the case?

First, differences among civilizations are not only real; they are basic. Civilizations are differentiated from each other by history, language, culture, tradition, and, most important, religion. The people of different civilizations have different views on the relations between God and man, the individual and the group, the citizen and the state, parents and children, husband and wife, as well as differing views of the relative importance of rights and responsibilities, liberty and authority, equality and hierarchy. These differences are the product of centuries. They will not soon disappear. They are far more fundamental than differences among political ideologies and political regimes. Differences do not necessarily mean conflict, and conflict does not necessarily mean violence. Over the centuries, however, differences among civilizations have generated the most prolonged and the most violent conflicts.

Second, the world is becoming a smaller place. The interactions between peoples of different civilizations are increasing; these increasing interactions intensify civilization-consciousness and awareness of differences between civilizations and commonalities within civilizations. North African immigration to France generated hostility among Frenchmen and at the same time increased receptivity to immigration by "good" European Catholic Poles. Americans react far more negatively to Japanese investment than to larger investments from Canada and European countries. Similarly, as Donald Horowitz has pointed out, "An Ibo may be…an Owerri Ibo or an Onitsha Ibo in what was the Eastern region of Nigeria. In Lagos, he is simply an Ibo. In London, he is a Nigerian. In New York, he is an African." The interactions among peoples of different civilizations enhance the civilization-consciousness of people that, in turn, invigorates differences and animosities stretching or thought to stretch back deep into history.

Third, the processes of economic modernization and social change throughout the world are separating people from long-standing local identities. They also weaken the nation-state as a source of identity. In much of the world, religion has moved in to fill this gap, often in the form of movements that are labeled "fundamentalist." Such movements are found in Western Christianity, Judaism, Buddhism, and Hinduism, as well as in Islam. In most countries and most religions, the people active in fundamentalist movements are young, college-educated, middle-class technicians, professionals, and businesspersons. The "unsecularization of the world," George Weigel has remarked, "is one of the dominant social facts of life in the late twentieth century." The revival of religion, "la revanche de Dieu," as Gilles Kepel labeled it, provides a basis for identity and commitment that transcends national boundaries and unites civilizations.

Fourth, the growth of civilization-consciousness is enhanced by the dual role of the West. On the one hand, the West is at a peak of power. At the same time, however, and perhaps as a result, a return to the roots phenomenon is occurring among non-Western civilizations. Increasingly one hears references to trends toward a turning inward and "Asianization" in Japan, the end of the Nehru legacy and the "Hinduization" of India, the failure of Western ideas of socialism and nationalism and hence "re-Islamization" of the Middle East, and now a debate over Westernization versus Russianization in Boris Yeltsin's country. A West at the peak of its power confronts non-Wests that increasingly have the desire, the will, and the resources to shape the world in non-Western ways….

Fifth, cultural characteristics and differences are less mutable and hence less easily compromised and resolved than political and economic ones. In the former Soviet Union, Communists can become Democrats, the rich can become poor and the poor rich, but Russians cannot become Estonians and Azeris cannot become Armenians. In class and ideological conflicts, the key question was "Which side are you on?" and people could and did choose sides and change sides. In conflicts between civilizations, the question is "What are you?" That is a given that cannot be changed. And as we know, from Bosnia to the Caucasus to the Sudan, the wrong answer to that question can mean a bullet in the head. Even more than ethnicity, religion discriminates sharply and exclusively among people. A person can be half-French and half-Arab and simultaneously even a citizen of two countries. It is more difficult to be half-Catholic and half-Muslim….

As people define their identity in ethnic and religious terms, they are likely to see an "us" versus "them" relation existing between themselves and people of different ethnicity or religion. The end of ideologically defined states in Eastern Europe and the former Soviet Union permits traditional ethnic identities and animosities to come to the fore. Differences in culture and religion create differences over policy issues, ranging from human rights to immigration to trade and commerce to the environment. Geographical propinquity gives rise to conflicting territorial claims from Bosnia to Mindanao. Most important, the efforts of the West to promote its values of democracy and liberalism as universal values, to maintain its military predominance and to advance its economic interests, engender countering responses from other civilizations. Decreasingly able to mobilize support and form coalitions on the basis of ideology, governments and groups will increasingly attempt to mobilize support by appealing to common religion and civilization identity.

The clash of civilizations thus occurs at two levels. At the microlevel, adjacent groups along the fault lines between civilizations struggle, often violently, over the control of territory and each other. At the macrolevel, states from different civilizations compete for relative military and economic power, struggle over the control of international institutions and third parties, and competitively promote their particular political and religious values.

THE FAULT LINES BETWEEN CIVILIZATIONS

The fault lines between civilizations are replacing the political and ideological boundaries of the Cold War as the flash points for crisis and bloodshed. The Cold War began when the Iron Curtain divided Europe politically and ideologically. The Cold War ended with the end of the Iron Curtain. As the ideological division of Europe has disappeared, the cultural division of Europe between Western Christianity, on the one hand, and Orthodox Christianity and Islam, on the other, has reemerged....

Conflict along the fault line between Western and Islamic civilizations has been going on for 1,300 years. After the founding of Islam, the Arab and Moorish surge west and north only ended at Tours in 732. From the eleventh to the thirteenth century, the Crusaders attempted with temporary success to bring Christianity and Christian rule to the Holy Land. From the fourteenth to the seventeenth century, the Ottoman Turks reversed the balance, extended their sway over the Middle East and the Balkans, captured Constantinople, and twice laid siege to Vienna. In the nineteenth and early twentieth centuries, as Ottoman power declined, Britain, France, and Italy established Western control over most of North Africa and the Middle East.

After World War II, the West, in turn, began to retreat; the colonial empires disappeared; first Arab nationalism and then Islamic fundamentalism manifested themselves; the West became heavily dependent on the Persian Gulf countries for its energy; the oil-rich Muslim countries became money-rich and, when they wished to, weapons-rich. Several wars occurred between Arabs and Israel (created by the West). France fought a bloody and ruthless war in Algeria for most of the 1950s; British and French forces invaded Egypt in 1956; American forces went into Lebanon in 1958; subsequently American forces returned to Lebanon, attacked Libya, and engaged in various military encounters with Iran; Arab and Islamic terrorists, supported by at least three Middle Eastern governments, employed the weapon of the weak and bombed Western planes and installations and seized Western hostages. This warfare between Arabs and the West culminated in 1990, when the United States sent a massive army to the Persian Gulf to defend some Arab countries against aggression by another. In its aftermath NATO planning is increasingly directed to potential threats and instability along its "southern tier."

This centuries-old military interaction between the West and Islam is unlikely to decline. It could become more virulent. The Gulf War left some Arabs feeling proud that Saddam Hussein had attacked Israel and stood up to the West. It also left many feeling humiliated and resentful of the West's military presence in the Persian Gulf, the West's overwhelming military dominance, and their apparent inability to shape their own destiny. Many Arab countries, in addition to the oil exporters, are reaching levels of economic and social development where autocratic forms of government become inappropriate and efforts to introduce democracy become stronger. Some openings in Arab political systems have already occurred. The principal beneficiaries of these openings have been Islamist movements. In the Arab world, in short, Western democracy strengthens anti-Western political forces. This may be a passing phenomenon, but it surely complicates relations between Islamic countries and the West.

Those relations are also complicated by demography. The spectacular population growth in Arab countries, particularly in North Africa, has led to increased migration to Western Europe. The movement within Western Europe toward minimizing internal boundaries has sharpened political sensitivities with respect to this development. In Italy, France, and Germany, racism is increasingly open, and political reactions and violence against Arab and Turkish migrants have become more intense and more widespread since 1990.

On both sides the interaction between Islam and the West is seen as a clash of civilizations. The West's "next confrontation," observes M. J. Akbar, an Indian Muslim author, "is definitely going to come from the Muslim world. It is in the sweep of the Islamic nations from the Maghreb to Pakistan that the struggle for a new world order will begin." Bernard Lewis comes to a similar conclusion:

We are facing a mood and a movement far transcending the level of issues and policies and the governments that pursue them. This is no less than a clash of civilizations—the perhaps irrational but surely historic reaction of an ancient rival against our Judeo-Christian heritage, our secular present, and the worldwide expansion of both.[16]

...The interactions between civilizations vary greatly in the extent to which they are likely to be characterized by violence. Economic competition clearly predominates between the American and European subcivilizations of the West and between both of them and Japan. On the Eurasian continent, however, the proliferation of ethnic conflict, epitomized at the extreme in "ethnic cleansing," has not been totally random. It has been most frequent and most violent between groups belonging to different civilizations. In Eurasia the great historic fault lines between civilizations are once more aflame. This is particularly true along the boundaries of the crescent-shaped Islamic bloc of nations from the bulge of Africa to central Asia. Violence also occurs between Muslims, on the one hand, and Orthodox Serbs in the Balkans, Jews in Israel, Hindus in India, Buddhists in Burma, and Catholics in the Philippines. Islam has bloody borders....

THE WEST VERSUS THE REST

The west is now at an extraordinary peak of power in relation to other civilizations. Its superpower opponent has disappeared from the map. Military conflict among Western states is unthinkable, and Western military power is unrivaled. Apart from Japan, the West faces no economic challenge. It dominates international political and security institutions and with Japan international economic institutions. Global political and security issues are effectively settled by a directorate of the United States, Britain, and France; world economic issues, by a directorate of the United States, Germany, and Japan, all of which maintain extraordinarily close relations with each other to the

exclusion of lesser and largely non-Western countries. Decisions made at the UN Security Council or in the International Monetary Fund that reflect the interests of the West are presented to the world as reflecting the desires of the world community. The very phrase "the world community" has become the euphemistic collective noun (replacing "the Free World") to give global legitimacy to actions reflecting the interests of the United States and other Western powers.[17] Through the IMF and other international economic institutions, the West promotes its economic interests and imposes on other nations the economic policies it thinks appropriate. In any poll of non-Western peoples, the IMF undoubtedly would win the support of finance ministers and a few others but get an overwhelmingly unfavorable rating from just about everyone else, who would agree with Georgy Arbatov's characterization of IMF officials as "neo-Bolsheviks who love expropriating other people's money, imposing undemocratic and alien rules of economic and political conduct and stifling economic freedom."

Western domination of the UN Security Council and its decisions, tempered only by occasional abstention by China, produced UN legitimation of the West's use of force to drive Iraq out of Kuwait and its elimination of Iraq's sophisticated weapons and capacity to produce such weapons. It also produced the quite unprecedented action by the United States, Britain, and France in getting the Security Council to demand that Libya hand over the Pan Am 103 bombing suspects and then to impose sanctions when Libya refused. After defeating the largest Arab army, the West did not hesitate to throw its weight around in the Arab world. The West in effect is using international institutions, military power, and economic resources to run the world in ways that will maintain Western predominance, protect Western

---

[16] Bernard Lewis, "The Roots of Muslim Rage," *The Atlantic Monthly*, Vol. 266, September 1990, p. 60; *Time*, June 15, 1992, pp. 24–28.

[17] Almost invariably, Western leaders claim they are acting on behalf of "the world community." One minor lapse occurred during the run-up to the Gulf War. In an interview on *Good Morning America*, December 21, 1990, British Prime Minister John Major referred to the actions "the West" was taking against Saddam Hussein. He quickly corrected himself and subsequently referred to "the world community." He was, however, right when he erred.

interests, and promote Western political and economic values.

That at least is the way in which non-Westerners see the new world, and there is a significant element of truth in their view. Differences in power and struggles for military, economic, and institutional power are thus one source of conflict between the West and other civilizations. Differences in culture, that is, basic values and beliefs, are a second source of conflict. V. S. Naipaul has argued that Western civilization is the "universal civilization" that "fits all men." At a superficial level, much of Western culture has indeed permeated the rest of the world. At a more basic level, however, Western concepts differ fundamentally from those prevalent in other civilizations. Western ideas of individualism, liberalism, constitutionalism, human rights, equality, liberty, the rule of law, democracy, free markets, the separation of church and state, often have little resonance in Islamic, Confucian, Japanese, Hindu, Buddhist, or Orthodox cultures. Western efforts to propagate such ideas produce instead a reaction against "human rights imperialism" and a reaffirmation of indigenous values, as can be seen in the support for religious fundamentalism by the younger generation in non-Western cultures. The very notion that there could be a "universal civilization" is a Western idea, directly at odds with the particularism of most Asian societies and their emphasis on what distinguishes one people from another. Indeed, the author of a review of a hundred comparative studies of values in different societies concluded that "the values that are most important in the West are least important worldwide."[18] In the political realm, of course, these differences are most manifest in the efforts of the United States and other Western powers to induce other peoples to adopt Western ideas concerning democracy and human rights. Modern democratic government originated in the West. When it has developed in non-Western societies it has usually been the product of Western colonialism or imposition.

The central axis of world politics in the future is likely to be, in Kishore Mahbubani's phrase, the conflict between "the West and the Rest" and the responses of non-Western civilizations to Western power and values.[19] Those responses generally take one or a combination of three forms. At one extreme, non-Western states can, like Burma and North Korea, attempt to pursue a course of isolation, to insulate their societies from penetration or "corruption" by the West, and, in effect, to opt out of participation in the Western-dominated global community. The costs of this course, however, are high, and few states have pursued it exclusively. A second alternative, the equivalent of "bandwagoning" in international relations theory, is to attempt to join the West and accept its values and institutions. The third alternative is to attempt to "balance" the West by developing economic and military power and cooperating with other non-Western societies against the West, while preserving indigenous values and institutions; in short, to modernize but not to Westernize.

IMPLICATIONS FOR THE WEST

This article does not argue that civilization identities will replace all other identities, that nation-states will disappear, that each civilization will become a single coherent political entity, that groups within a civilization will not conflict with and even fight each other. This paper does set forth the hypotheses that differences between civilizations are real and important; civilization-consciousness is increasing; conflict between civilizations will supplant ideological and other forms of conflict as the dominant global form of conflict; international relations, historically a game played out within Western civilization, will increasingly be de-Westernized and become a game in which non-Western civilizations are actors and not simply objects; successful political, security, and economic international institutions are more likely to develop within civilizations than across civilizations; conflicts between groups in different

---

[18] Harry C. Triandis, *New York Times*, December 25, 1990, p. 41, and "Cross-Cultural Studies of Individualism and Collectivism," *Nebraska Symposium on Motivation*, Vol. 37, 1989, pp. 41–133.

[19] Kishore Mahbubani, "The West and the Rest," *National Interest*, Summer 1992, pp. 3–13.

civilizations will be more frequent, more sustained, and more violent than conflicts between groups in the same civilization; violent conflict between groups in different civilizations are the most likely and most dangerous source of escalation that could lead to global wars; the paramount axis of world politics will be the relations between "the West and the Rest"; the elites in some torn non-Western countries will try to make their countries part of the West, but in most cases face major obstacles to accomplishing this; a central focus of conflict for the immediate future will be between the West and several Islamic-Confucian states.

This is not to advocate the desirability of conflicts between civilizations. It is to set forth descriptive hypotheses as to what the future may be like. If these are plausible hypotheses, however, it is necessary to consider their implications for Western policy. These implications should be divided between short-term advantage and long-term accommodation. In the short term it is clearly in the interest of the West to promote greater cooperation and unity within its own civilization, particularly between its European and North American components; to incorporate into the West societies in Eastern Europe and Latin America whose cultures are close to those of the West; to promote and maintain cooperative relations with Russia and Japan; to prevent escalation of local intercivilization conflicts into major intercivilization wars; to limit the expansion of the military strength of Confucian and Islamic states; to moderate the reduction of Western military capabilities and maintain military superiority in East and Southwest Asia; to exploit differences and conflicts among Confucian and Islamic states; to support in other civilizations groups sympathetic to Western values and interests; to strengthen international institutions that reflect and legitimate Western interests and values and to promote the involvement of non-Western states in those institutions.

In the longer term, other measures would be called for. Western civilization is both Western and modern. Non-Western civilizations have attempted to become modern without becoming Western. To date only Japan has fully succeeded in this quest. Non-Western civilizations will continue to attempt to acquire the wealth, technology, skills, machines, and weapons that are part of being modern. They will also attempt to reconcile this modernity with their traditional culture and values. Their economic and military strength relative to the West will increase. Hence the West will increasingly have to accommodate these non-Western modern civilizations whose power approaches that of the West but whose values and interests differ significantly from those of the West. This will require the West to maintain the economic and military power necessary to protect its interests in relation to these civilizations. It will also, however, require the West to develop a more profound understanding of the basic religious and philosophical assumptions underlying other civilizations and the ways in which people in those civilizations see their interests. It will require an effort to identify elements of commonality between Western and other civilizations. For the relevant future, there will be no universal civilization, but instead a world of different civilizations, each of which will have to learn to coexist with the others.

Eqbal Ahmad

TERRORISM: THEIRS AND OURS

Islamic voices are rarely heard in the West. An exception has been Eqbal Ahmad, a noted Pakistani writer and antiwar activist. In his work, Ahmad was equally critical of fundamentalist nationalism and religion in the Middle East and throughout the Islamic world, and of what he saw as the imperial policy of the West, notably the United States. The following material—a transcribed lecture—was written several years before the terrorist attacks of 2001; it is offered not only for its useful geopolitical and demographic perspective but also to emphasize the relevance of terrorism as a concern independent of 9/11.

In the 1930s and 1940s, the Jewish underground in Palestine was described as "terrorist." Then new things happened.

By 1942, the Holocaust was occurring, and a certain liberal sympathy with the Jewish people had built up in the Western world. At that point, the terrorists of Palestine, who were Zionists, suddenly started to be described, by 1944–1945, as "freedom fighters." At least two Israeli prime ministers, including Menachem Begin, you can find in books and posters with pictures, saying "Terrorists, Reward This Much." The highest reward I have noted so far was 100,000 British pounds on the head of Menachem Begin, the terrorist.

Then from 1969 to 1990, the PLO, the Palestine Liberation Organization, occupied the center stage as the terrorist organization. Yasir Arafat has been described repeatedly by the great sage of American journalism, William Safire of the *New York Times*, as the "chief of terrorism." That's Yasir Arafat.

Now, on September 29, 1998, I was rather amused to notice a picture of Yasir Arafat to the right of President Bill Clinton. To his left is Israeli Prime Minister Benjamin Netanyahu. Clinton is looking toward Arafat and Arafat is looking literally like a meek mouse. Just a few years earlier he used to appear with this very menacing look around him, with a gun appearing menacing from his belt.

You remember those pictures, and you remember the next one.

In 1985 President Ronald Reagan received a group of bearded men. They were very ferocious, with turbans, looking like they came from another century. President Reagan received them in the White House. After receiving them, he spoke to the press. He pointed toward them, I'm sure some of you will recall that moment, and said, "These are the moral equivalent of America's founding fathers." These were the Afghan Mujahiddin. They were at the time, guns in hand, battling the Evil Empire. They were the moral equivalent of our founding fathers!

In August 1998, another American president ordered missile strikes from the American navy based in the Indian Ocean to kill Osama bin Laden and his men in the camps in Afghanistan. I do not wish to embarrass you with the reminder that Mr. bin Laden, whom fifteen American missiles were fired to hit in Afghanistan, was only a few years ago the moral equivalent of George Washington and Thomas Jefferson! He got angry over the fact that he has been demoted from "moral equivalent" of your "founding fathers." So he is taking out his anger in different ways. I'll come back to that subject more seriously in a moment.

You see, I have recalled all these stories to point out to you that the matter of terrorism is rather complicated. Terrorists change. The terrorist of yesterday is the hero of today, and the hero of yesterday becomes the terrorist of today. This is a serious matter of the constantly changing world of images in which we have to keep our heads straight to know what is terrorism and what is not. But more importantly, to know what causes it and how to stop it.

The next point about our terrorism is that [a] posture of inconsistency necessarily evades definition. If you are not going to be consistent, you're not going to define. I have examined at least twenty official documents on terrorism. Not one defines the word. All of them explain it, express it emotively, polemically, to arouse our emotions rather than exercise our intelligence. I give you only one example, which is representative. October 25, 1984, George Shultz, then secretary of state of the U.S., is speaking at the New York Park Avenue Synagogue. It's a long speech on terrorism. In the State Department Bulletin of seven single-spaced pages, there is not a single definition of terrorism. What we get is the following:

Definition number one: "Terrorism is a modern barbarism that we call terrorism."

Definition number two is even more brilliant: "Terrorism is a form of political violence." Aren't you surprised? It is a form of political violence, says George Shultz, secretary of state of the U.S.

Number three: "Terrorism is a threat to Western civilization."

Number four: "Terrorism is a menace to Western moral values."

Did you notice, does it tell you anything other than arouse your emotions?

This is typical. They don't define terrorism, because definitions involve a commitment to analysis, comprehension, and adherence to some norms of consistency. That's the second characteristic of the official literature on terrorism.

The third characteristic is that the absence of [a] definition does not prevent officials from being

globalistic. We may not define terrorism, but it is a menace to the moral values of Western civilization. It is a menace also to mankind. It's a menace to good order. Therefore, you must stamp it out worldwide. Our reach has to be global. You need a global reach to kill it. Antiterrorist policies therefore have to be global. Same speech of George Shultz: "There is no question about our ability to use force where and when it is needed to counter terrorism." There is no geographical limit. On a single day the missiles hit Afghanistan and Sudan. Those two countries are 2,300 miles apart, and they were hit by missiles belonging to a country roughly 8,000 miles away. Reach is global.

A fourth characteristic: claims of power are not only globalist, they are also omniscient. We know where they are; therefore we know where to hit. We have the means to know. We have the instruments of knowledge. We are omniscient. Shultz: "We know the difference between terrorists and freedom fighters, and as we look around, we have no trouble telling one from the other."

Only, Osama bin Laden doesn't know that he was an ally one day and an enemy another. That's very confusing for Osama bin Laden. I'll come back to his story toward the end. It's a real story.

Five. The official approach eschews causation. You don't look at the causes of anybody is becoming a terrorist. Cause? What cause? They ask us to be looking, to be sympathetic to these people.

Another example. The *New York Times*, December 18, 1985, reported that the foreign minister of Yugoslavia, you remember the days when there was a Yugoslavia, requested the secretary of state of the U.S. to consider the causes of Palestinian terrorism. The secretary of state, George Shultz, and I am quoting from the *New York Times*, "went a bit red in the face. He pounded the table and told the visiting foreign minister, there is no connection with any cause. Period." Why look for causes?

Number six. The moral revulsion that we must feel against terrorism is selective. We are to feel the terror of those groups, which are officially disapproved. We are to applaud the terror of those groups of whom officials do approve. Hence, President Reagan, "I am a Contra." He actually said that. We know the Contras of Nicaragua [weren't] anything, by any definition, but terrorists. The media, to move away from the officials, heed the dominant view of terrorism.

The dominant approach also excludes from consideration, more importantly to me, the terror of friendly governments. To that question I will return because it excused among others the terror of Pinochet (who killed one of my closest friends) and Orlando Letelier; and it excused the terror of Zia ul-Haq, who killed many of my friends in Pakistan. All I want to tell you is that according to my ignorant calculations, the ratio of people killed by the state terror of Zia ul-Haq, Pinochet, Argentinian, Brazilian, Indonesian types, versus the killing of the PLO and other terrorist types is literally, conservatively, one to one hundred thousand. That's the ratio.

History unfortunately recognizes and accords visibility to power and not to weakness. Therefore, visibility has been accorded historically to dominant groups. In our time, the time that began with this day, Columbus Day.

The time that begins with Columbus Day is a time of extraordinary unrecorded holocausts. Great civilizations have been wiped out. The Mayas, the Incas, the Aztecs, the American Indians, the Canadian Indians were all wiped out. Their voices have not been heard, even to this day fully. Now they are beginning to be heard, but not fully. They are heard, yes, but only when the dominant power suffers, only when resistance has a semblance of costing, of exacting a price. When a Custer is killed or when a Gordon is besieged. That's when you know that they were Indians fighting, Arabs fighting and dying.

My last point of this section—U.S. policy in the Cold War period has sponsored terrorist regimes one after another. Somoza, Batista, all kinds of tyrants have been America's friends. You know that. There was a reason for that. I or you are not guilty. Nicaragua, Contra. Afghanistan, Mujahiddin. El Salvador, etc.

Now the second side. You've suffered enough. So suffer more.

There ain't much good on the other side either. You shouldn't imagine that I have come to praise the other side. But keep the balance in mind. Keep the imbalance in mind and first ask ourselves, What is terrorism?

Our first job should be to define the damn thing, name it, give it a description of some kind, other than "moral equivalent of [the] founding fathers" or "a moral outrage to Western civilization." *Webster's Collegiate Dictionary:* "Terror is an intense, overpowering fear." [One] uses terrorizing, terrorism, "the use of terrorizing methods of governing or resisting a government." This simple definition has one great virtue, that of fairness. It's fair. It focuses on the use of coercive violence, violence that is used illegally, extraconstitutionally, to coerce. And this definition is correct because it treats terror for what it is, whether the government or private people commit it.

Have you noticed something? Motivation is left out of it. We're not talking about whether the cause is just or unjust. We're talking about consensus, consent, absence of consent, legality, absence of legality, constitutionality, absence of constitutionality. Why do we keep motives out? Because motives differ. Motives differ and make no difference.

I have identified in my work five types of terrorism.

First, state terrorism. Second, religious terrorism; terrorism inspired by religion, Catholics killing Protestants, Sunnis killing Shiites, Shiites killing Sunnis, God, religion, sacred terror, you can call it if you wish. State, church. [Third,] crime. Mafia. All kinds of crimes commit terror. [Fourth,] there is pathology. You're pathological. You're sick. You want the attention of the whole world. You've got to kill a president. You will. You terrorize. You hold up a bus. Fifth, there is political terror of the private group; be they Indian, Vietnamese, Algerian, Palestinian, Baader-Meinhof, the Red Brigade. Political terror of the private group. Oppositional terror.

Keep these five in mind. Keep in mind one more thing. Sometimes these five can converge on each other. You start with protest terror. You go crazy. You become pathological. You continue. They converge. State terror can take the form of private terror. For example, we're all familiar with the death squads in Latin America or in Pakistan. Government has employed private people to kill its opponents. It's not quite official. It's privatized. Convergence. Or the political terrorist who goes crazy and becomes pathological. Or the criminal who joins politics. In

Afghanistan, in Central America, the CIA employed in its covert operations drug pushers. Drugs and guns often go together. Smuggling of all things often go together.

Of the five types of terror, the focus is on only one, the least important in terms of cost to human lives and human property [political terror of those who want to be heard]. The highest cost is state terror. The second highest cost is religious terror, although in the twentieth century religious terror has, relatively speaking, declined. If you are looking historically, massive costs. The next highest cost is crime. Next highest, pathology. A RAND Corporation study by Brian Jenkins, for a ten-year period up to 1988, showed [that] 50 percent of terror was committed without any political cause at all. No politics. Simply crime and pathology.

So the focus is on only one, the political terrorist, the PLO, the bin Laden, whoever you want to take. Why do they do it? What makes the terrorist tick?

I would like to knock them out quickly to you. First, the need to be heard. Imagine, we are dealing with a minority group, the political, private terrorist. First, the need to be heard. Normally, and there are exceptions, there is an effort to be heard, to get your grievances heard by people. They're not hearing it. A minority acts. The majority applauds.

The Palestinians, for example, the superterrorists of our time, were dispossessed in 1948. From 1948 to 1968 they went to every court in the world. They knocked at every door in the world. They were told that they became dispossessed because some radio told them to go away—an Arab radio, which was a lie. Nobody was listening to the truth. Finally, they invented a new form of terror, literally their invention: the airplane hijacking. Between 1968 and 1975 they pulled the world up by its ears. They dragged us out and said, Listen, Listen. We listened. We still haven't done them justice, but at least we all know. Even the Israelis acknowledge. Remember Golda Meir, prime minister of Israel, saying in 1970, "There are no Palestinians. They do not exist." They damn well exist now. We are cheating them at Oslo. At least there are some people to cheat now. We can't just push

them out. The need to be heard is essential. One motivation there.

[A] mix of anger and helplessness produces an urge to strike out. You are angry. You are feeling helpless. You want retribution. You want to wreak retributive justice. The experience of violence by a stronger party has historically turned victims into terrorists. Battered children are known to become abusive parents and violent adults. You know that. That's what happens to peoples and nations. When they are battered, they hit back. State terror very often breeds collective terror.

Do you recall the fact that the Jews were never terrorists? By and large Jews were not known to commit terror except during and after the Holocaust. Most studies show that the majority of members of the worst terrorist groups in Israel or in Palestine, the Stern and the *Irgun* gangs, were people who were immigrants from the most anti-Semitic countries of Eastern Europe and Germany. Similarly, the young Shiites of Lebanon or the Palestinians from the refugee camps are battered people. They become very violent. The ghettos are violent internally. They become violent externally when there is a clear, identifiable external target, an enemy where you can say, "Yes, this one did it to me." Then they can strike back.

Example is a bad thing. Example spreads. There was the highly publicized Beirut hijacking of a TWA plane. After that hijacking, there were hijacking attempts at nine different American airports. Pathological groups or individuals modeling on the others. Even more serious are examples [were] set by governments. When governments engage in terror, they set very large examples. When they engage in supporting terror, they engage in other sets of examples.

Absence of revolutionary ideology is central to victim terrorism. Revolutionaries do not commit unthinking terror. Those of you who are familiar with revolutionary theory know the debates, the disputes, the quarrels, the fights within revolutionary groups of Europe, the fight between anarchists and Marxists, for example. But the Marxists have always argued that revolutionary terror, if ever engaged in, must be sociologically and psychologically selective. Don't hijack a plane. Don't hold hostages. Don't kill children, for God's sake. Have you recalled also that the great revolutions, the Chinese, the Vietnamese, the Algerian, the Cuban, never engaged in hijacking? They did engage in terrorism, but it was highly selective, highly sociological, still deplorable, but there was an organized, highly limited, selective character to it. So [the] absence of revolutionary ideology that begins more or less in the post–World War II period has been central to this phenomenon.

My final question is—these conditions have existed for a long time. But why, then, this flurry of private political terrorism? Why now so much of it and so visible? The answer is modern technology. You have a cause. You can communicate it through radio and television. They will all come swarming if you have taken an aircraft and are holding 150 Americans hostage. They will all hear your cause. You have a modern weapon through which you can shoot a mile away. They can't reach you. And you have the modern means of communicating. When you put together the cause, the instrument of coercion, and the instrument of communication, politics is made. A new kind of politics becomes possible.

To this challenge, rulers from one country after another have been responding with traditional methods. The traditional method of shooting it out, whether it's missiles or some other means. The Israelis are very proud of it. The Americans are very proud of it. The French became very proud of it. Now the Pakistanis are very proud of it. The Pakistanis say, "Our commandos are the best." Frankly, it won't work. A central problem of our time, political minds, rooted in the past, and modern times, producing new realities. Therefore, in conclusion, what is my recommendation to America?

Quickly. First, avoid extremes of double standards. If you're going to practice double standards, you will be paid with double standards. Don't use it. Don't condone Israeli terror, Pakistani terror, Nicaraguan terror, El Salvadoran terror, on the one hand, and then complain about Afghan terror or Palestinian terror. It doesn't work. Try to be even-handed. A superpower cannot promote terror in one place and reasonably expect to discourage terrorism

in another place. It won't work in this shrunken world.

Do not condone the terror of your allies. Condemn them. Fight them. Punish them. Please eschew, avoid covert operations and low-intensity warfare. These are breeding grounds of terror and drugs. Violence and drugs are bred there. The structure of covert operations—I've made a film about it, which has been very popular in Europe, called *Dealing with the Demon.* I have shown that wherever covert operations have been, there has been the central drug problem. That has been also the center of the drug trade. Because the structure of covert operations, Afghanistan, Vietnam, Nicaragua, Central America, is very hospitable to drug trade. Avoid it. Give it up. It doesn't help.

Please focus on causes and help ameliorate causes. Try to look at causes and solve problems. Do not concentrate on military solutions. Do not seek military solutions. Terrorism is a political problem. Seek political solutions. Diplomacy works.

Take the example of the last attack on bin Laden. You don't know what you're attacking. They say they know, but they don't know. They were trying to kill Qadaffi. They killed his four-year-old daughter. The poor baby hadn't done anything. Qadaffi is still alive. They tried to kill Saddam Hussein. They killed Laila Bin Attar, a prominent artist, an innocent woman. They tried to kill bin Laden and his men. Not one but twenty-five other people died. They tried to destroy a chemical factory in Sudan. Now they are admitting that they destroyed an innocent factory, one-half of the production of medicine in Sudan has been destroyed, not a chemical factory. You don't know. You think you know.

Four of your missiles fell in Pakistan. One was slightly damaged. Two were totally damaged. One was totally intact. For ten years the American government has kept an embargo on Pakistan because Pakistan is trying, stupidly, to build nuclear weapons and missiles. So we have a technology embargo on my country. One of the missiles was intact. What do you think a Pakistani official told the *Washington Post?* He said it was a gift from Allah. We wanted U.S. technology. Now we have got the technology, and our scientists are examining this missile very carefully. It fell into the wrong hands. So don't do that. Look for political solutions. Do not look for military solutions. They cause more problems than they solve.

Please help reinforce, strengthen the framework of international law. There was a criminal court in Rome. Why didn't they go to it first to get their warrant against bin Laden, if they have some evidence? Get a warrant, then go after him. Internationally. Enforce the UN. Enforce the International Court of Justice. This unilateralism makes us look very stupid and them relatively larger.

Richard Falk

DEFINING A JUST WAR

Military action—whether a formally declared war or some other violent response, as to terrorism—involves one of the most drastic actions that anyone can take. Killing another human being—except by accident, self-defense, or out of insanity—is universally condemned...except during war, in which time it is not only permitted but also applauded. Nonetheless, such applause is not universal, and even when it occurs, it is rarely unequivocal. Advocates of peace have often derived strength, inspiration, and even concrete assistance from moral and ethical teaching, although to be sure, such teachings have not been unilaterally antiwar. There have been concerted and influential efforts to support the ethical legitimacy of war under certain circumstances, and indeed, even though violence is perhaps the most frequent target of the world's moral systems, and although war in general is widely criticized, it is debatable whether such systems have been more likely to oppose or to support *specific* wars.

Perhaps it avails nothing if moralists condemn war in general but lend their approval to each particular war as it comes along. But this conclusion omits a potentially important characteristic of moral thought: a continuing predisposition *against* violence and killing. There is little room, after all, to criticize the horrors of Auschwitz or the bombing of Hiroshima from an engineering standpoint—these events were technical triumphs. Only by applying moral judgments, can outrage—and from such outrage, a determination to change—be developed.

The most carefully enunciated and influential moral approach to war in the Western tradition, so-called just war doctrine, is largely the result of Catholic social teaching, derived especially from the writing of St. Augustine. This approach, sometimes called "Christian realism," can be criticized as unacceptably apologetic when it comes to warmaking. Certainly, it cannot by itself be counted on as a bulwark against war, if only because the "just war" doctrine is specifically concerned with identifying circumstances under which war is permissible. But its approach is nuanced and, if anything, biased against war except under carefully defined conditions and in carefully restricted ways. Thus, it offers some potential assistance in preventing war...or at least in making it less destructive or even less likely.

Writing in the immediate aftermath of the 9/11 terrorist attacks on the United States, noted legal scholar and antiwar activist Richard Falk sought to illuminate a "just" response. Note that this article was written while the U.S. military action against Afghanistan was in its early stages and well before the invasion of Iraq.

I have never since my childhood supported a shooting war in which the United States was involved, although in retrospect I think the NATO war in Kosovo achieved beneficial results. The war in Afghanistan against apocalyptic terrorism qualifies in my understanding as the first truly just war since World War II. But the justice of the cause and of the limited ends is in danger of being negated by the injustice of improper means and excessive ends. Unlike World War II and prior just wars, this one can be won only if tactics adhere to legal and moral constraints on the means used to conduct it, and to limited ends.

The perpetrators of the September 11 attack cannot be reliably neutralized by nonviolent or diplomatic means; a response that includes military action is essential to diminish the threat of repetition, to inflict punishment, and to restore a sense of security at home and abroad. The extremist political vision held by Osama bin Laden, which can usefully be labeled "apocalyptic terrorism," places this persisting threat well outside any framework of potential reconciliation, or even negotiation, for several reasons: its genocidal intent is directed generically against Americans and Jews; its proclaimed goal is waging an unconditional civilizational war—Islam against the West—without drawing any distinction between civilian and military targets; it has demonstrated a capacity and willingness to inflict massive and traumatizing damage on our country and a tactical ingenuity and ability to carry out its missions of destruction by reliance on the suicidal devotion of its adherents.

There are three types of responses to the attack, each of which contains some merit and enjoys some support. None of them is adequate, however.

ANTIWAR/PACIFIST APPROACH

The pacifist position opposing even limited military action overlooks the nature of the threat and is thus irrelevant to meeting the central challenge of restoring some sense of security among our citizenry and in the world generally.

Also, in the current setting, unlike in the civil rights movement and the interventionist conflicts of the Cold War era (especially Vietnam), antiwar and pacifist stands possess little or no cultural resonance with the overwhelming majority of Americans. It may be that at later stages of the war this assessment will prove to have been premature, and even now Quaker, Christian, Gandhian, and Buddhist forms of pacifism offer a profound critique of wars. These critiques should be seriously heeded, since they lend weight to the the view that the use of force should be marginal and kept to an absolute minimum. Certainly the spiritually motivated pacifist witness can be both inspirational and instructive, and help to mitigate and interrogate militarist postures.

Another form of antiwar advocacy rests on a critique of the United States as an imperialist superpower or empire. This view also seems dangerously inappropriate in addressing the challenge posed by the massive crime against humanity committed on September 11. Whatever the global role of the United States—and it is certainly responsible for much global suffering and injustice, giving rise to widespread resentment that at its inner core fuels the terrorist impulse—it cannot be addressed so long as this movement of global terrorism is at large and prepared to carry on with its demonic work. These longer-term concerns—which include finding

From "Defining a Just War" by Robert Falk. Reprinted with permission from the October 11, 2001, issue of *The Nation*. For subscription information, call 1-800-333-8536. Portions of each week's *Nation* magazine can be accessed at http://www.thenation.com.

ways to promote Palestinian self-determination, the internationalization of Jerusalem, and a more equitable distribution of the benefits of global economic growth and development—must be addressed. Of course, much of the responsibility for the failure to do so lies with the corruption and repressive policies of governments, especially in the Middle East, outside the orbit of U.S. influence. A distinction needs to be drawn as persuasively as possible between inherently desirable lines of foreign policy reform and retreating in the face of terrorism.

LEGALIST/UN APPROACH

International treaties that deal with terrorism on civil aircraft call for cooperation in apprehending suspects and allow for their subsequent indictment and prosecution by national courts. Such laws could in theory be invoked to capture Osama bin Laden and his leading associates and charge them with international crimes, including crimes against humanity. A tribunal could be constituted under the authority of the United Nations, and a fair trial could then be held that would avoid war and the ensuing pain, destruction, and associated costs. The narrative of apocalyptic terrorism could be laid before the world as the crimes of Nazism were bared at Nuremberg.

But this course is unlikely to deal effectively with the overall threat. A public prosecution would give bin Laden and associates a platform to rally further support among a large constituency of sympathizers, and conviction and punishment would certainly be viewed as a kind of legal martyrdom....

Undoubtedly, the world would be safer and more secure with a stronger UN that had the support of the leading states in the world. The United States has for years acted more to obstruct than to foster such a transformation. Surely the long-term effects of this crisis should involve a new surge of support for a reformed UN that would have independent means of financing its operations, with its own peacekeeping and enforcement capabilities backed up by an international criminal court. Such a transformed UN would generate confidence that it could and would uphold its charter in an even-handed manner that treats people equally. But it would be foolish to pretend that the UN today, even

if it were to enjoy a far higher level of U.S. support than it does, could mount an effective response to the September 11 attacks.

MILITARIST APPROACH

Unlike pacifism and legalism, militarism poses a practical danger of immense proportions. Excessive reliance on the military will backfire badly, further imperiling the security of Americans and others, spreading war and destruction far afield, as well as emboldening the government to act at home in ways that weaken U.S. democracy....

To expand war objectives...would be full of risks, require massive military strikes inflicting much destruction and suffering, and would create a new wave of retaliatory violence directed against the United States and Americans throughout the world. If military goals overshoot, either by becoming part of a design to destroy Israel's enemies or to solve the problem of proliferation of weapons of mass destruction, the war against global terrorism will be lost, and badly.

Just as the pacifist fallacy involves unrealistic exclusion of military force from an acceptable response, the militarist fallacy involves an excessive reliance on military force in a manner that magnifies the threat it is trying to diminish or eliminate. It also expands the zone of violence in particularly dangerous ways that are almost certain to intensify and inflame anti-Americanism. It should be kept in mind that war occasions deep suffering, and recourse to international force should be both a last resort and on as limited a scale as possible.

But there is a fourth response, which has gained support among foreign policy analysts and probably a majority of Americans.

LIMITING MEANS AND ENDS

Unlike in major wars of the past, the response to this challenge of apocalyptic terrorism can be effective only if it is also widely perceived as legitimate. And legitimacy can be attained only if the role of military force is marginal to the overall conduct of the war and if the relevant frameworks of moral, legal, and religious restraint are scrupulously respected.

Excessive use of force in pursuing the perpetrators of September 11 will fan the flames of Islamic militancy and give credence to calls for holy war. What lent the WTC/Pentagon attack its quality of sinister originality was the ability of a fanatical political movement to take advantage of the complex fragility and vulnerability of advanced technology. Now that this vulnerability has been exposed to the world, it is impossible to ensure that other extremists will not commit similar acts—even if Osama bin Laden is eliminated.

The only way to wage this war effectively is to make sure that force is used within relevant frameworks of restraint. Excessive force can take several forms, like the pursuit of political movements remote from the WTC attack, especially if such military action is seen as indirectly doing the dirty work of eliminating threats to Israel's occupation of Palestinian territories and Jerusalem. Excessiveness would also be attributed to efforts to destroy and restructure regimes, other than the Taliban, that are hostile to the United States but not significantly connected with either the attack or Al Qaeda.

The second, closely related problem of successfully framing a response is related to the U.S. manner of waging war: the U.S. temperament has tended to approach war as a matter of confronting evil. In such a view, victory can be achieved only by the total defeat of the other, and with it, the triumph of good.

In the current setting, goals have not been clarified, and U.S. leaders have used grandiose language about ending terrorism and destroying the global terrorist network. The idea of good against evil has been a consistent part of the process of public mobilization, with the implicit message that nothing less than a total victory is acceptable. What are realistic ends? Or put differently, what ends can be reconciled with a commitment to achieve an effective response? What is needed is extremely selective uses of force... combined with criminal law enforcement operations—cutting off sources of finance, destroying terrorist cells, using policing techniques abetted, to the extent necessary, by paramilitary capabilities.

Also troubling is the Bush administration's ingrained disdain for multilateralism and its determination to achieve security for the United States by military means—particularly missile defense and space weaponization. This unilateralism has so far been masked by a frantic effort to forge a global coalition, but there is every indication that the U.S. government will insist on complete operational control over the war and will not be willing to accept procedures of accountability within the UN framework.

The administration has often said that many of the actions in this war will not be made known to the public. But an excessive emphasis on secrecy in the conduct of military operations is likely to make the uses of force more difficult to justify to those who are skeptical about U.S. motives and goals, thus undercutting the legitimacy of the war.

in building a global coalition for cooperative action, especially with respect to law enforcement in countries where Al Qaeda operates, the U.S. government has struck a number of Faustian bargains. It may be necessary to enter into arrangements with governments that are themselves responsible for terrorist policies and brutal repression, such as Russia in Chechnya and India in Kashmir. But the cost of doing so is to weaken claims that a common antiterrorist front is the foundation of this alliance. For some governments the war against apocalyptic terrorism is an opportunity to proceed with their own repressive policies free from censure and interference. The U.S. government should weigh the cost of writing blank checks against the importance of distinguishing its means and ends from the megaterrorist ethos that animated the September 11 attacks. There are some difficult choices ahead, including the extent to which Afghan opposition forces—particularly the Northern Alliance—should be supported, in view of their own dubious human rights record.

How, then, should legitimacy be pursued in the current context? The first set of requirements is essentially political: to disclose goals that seem reasonably connected with the attack and with the threat posed by those who planned, funded, and carried it out.... We must make a distinction between those individuals and entities that have been actively engaged in the perpetration of the visionary program of international, apocalyptic terrorism uniquely Al Qaeda's and those who have used funds or training to advance more traditional goals relating to griev-ances associated with the governance of a particular country and have limited their targets largely to the authorities in their countries, like the ETA in Spain and the IRA in Ireland and Britain.

Legitimacy with respect to the use of force in international settings derives from the mutually reinforcing traditions of the "just war" doctrine, international law, and the ideas of restraint embed-ded in the great religions of the world. The essen-tial norms are rather abstract in character, and lend themselves to debate and diverse interpretation. The most important ideas are:

- the principle of discrimination: force must be directed at a military target, with damage to civilians and civilian society being incidental;
- the principle of proportionality: force must not be greater than that needed to achieve an accept-able military result and must not be greater than the provoking cause;

- the principle of humanity: force must not be directed even against enemy personnel if they are subject to capture, wounded, or under con-trol (as with prisoners of war);
- the principle of necessity: force should be used only if nonviolent means to achieve military goals are unavailable.

These abstract guidelines for the use of force do not give much operational direction. In each situation we must ask, Do the claims to use force seem reason-able in terms of the ends being pursued, including the obligation to confine civilian damage as much as possible? Such assessments depend on interpretation, but they allow for debate and justification, and clear instances of violative behavior could be quickly iden-tified. The justice of the cause and of the limited ends will be negated by the injustice of improper means and excessive ends. Only the vigilance of an active cit-izenry, alert to this delicate balance, has much hope of helping this new war to end in a true victory.

Robert Pape

DYING TO WIN: THE STRATEGIC LOGIC
OF SUICIDE TERRORISM

Concern about terrorism as a general phenomenon has typically eclipsed interest in the actual motivations of individual terrorists, who, after all, are human beings with their own goals, hopes, fears, angers, and other driving forces. Just as peace activists like to ask, What if they had a war and no one came? we might inquire, What if they called for a terrorist attack and no one volunteered? Or similarly, What makes individuals "volunteer"—not only to engage in lethal violence toward presumably innocent victims but also to willingly give up their lives in the process? Discussion of the causes of war often revolve around a presumed tension between causation at the level of individuals (the role of personal aggressiveness, frustration, anger, greed, obedience to authority, etc.) and at the level of states (realpolitik, institutionalized decision making, the influence of history, socioeco-nomic or geopolitical considerations, etc.) The following selection represents one of the more notable efforts to rectify this omission and to introduce a personalized interpretive level into what is otherwise a diffuse geopolitical and ideological debate.

Suicide terrorism is rising around the world, but there is great confusion as to why. Since many such attacks—including, of course, those of September 11, 2001—have been perpetrated by Muslim terrorists professing religious motives, it might seem obvious that Islamic fundamentalism is the central cause. This presumption has fueled the belief that future 9/11s can be avoided only by a wholesale transformation of Muslim societies, a core reason for broad public support in the United States for the recent conquest of Iraq.

However, the presumed connection between suicide terrorism and Islamic fundamentalism is misleading and may be encouraging domestic and foreign policies likely to worsen America's situation and needlessly harm many Muslims.

I have compiled a database of every suicide bombing and attack around the globe from 1980 through 2003—315 attacks in all. It includes every attack in which at least one terrorist killed himself or herself while attempting to kill others; it excludes attacks authorized by a national government, for example by North Korea against the South. This database is the first complete universe of suicide terrorist attacks worldwide. I have amassed and independently verified all the relevant information that could be found in English and other languages (for example, Arabic, Hebrew, Russian, and Tamil) in print and online. The information is drawn from suicide terrorist groups themselves, from the main organizations that collect such data in target countries, and from news media around the world. More than a "list of lists," this database probably represents the most comprehensive and reliable survey of suicide terrorist attacks that is now available.

The data show that there is little connection between suicide terrorism and Islamic fundamentalism, or any one of the world's religions. In fact, the leading instigators of suicide attacks were the liberation tigers of Tamil Eelam (the "Tamil Tigers") in Sri Lanka, a Marxist-Leninist group whose members are from Hindu families but who are adamantly opposed to religion. This group committed 76 of the 315 incidents, more suicide attacks than Hamas.

Rather, what nearly all suicide terrorist attacks have in common is a specific secular and strategic goal: to compel modern democracies to withdraw military forces from territory that the terrorists consider to be their homeland. Religion is rarely the root cause, although it is often used as a tool by terrorist organizations in recruiting and in other efforts in service of the broader strategic objective.

Three general patterns in the data support my conclusions. First, nearly all suicide terrorist attacks occur as part of organized campaigns, not as isolated or random incidents. Of the 315 separate attacks in the period I studied, 301 could have their roots traced to large, coherent political or military campaigns.

Second, democratic states are uniquely vulnerable to suicide terrorists. The United States, France, India, Israel, Russia, Sri Lanka, and Turkey have been the targets of almost every suicide attack of the past two decades, and each country has been a democracy at the time of the incidents.

Third, suicide terrorist campaigns are directed toward a strategic objective. From Lebanon to Israel to Sri Lanka to Kashmir to Chechnya, the sponsors of every campaign have been terrorist groups trying to establish or maintain political self-determination by compelling a democratic power to withdraw from the territories it claims. Even Al Qaeda fits this pattern: although Saudi Arabia is not under American military occupation per se, a principal objective of Osama bin Laden is the expulsion of American troops from the Persian Gulf and the reduction of Washington's power and influence in the region.

Understanding suicide terrorism is essential for the promotion of American security and international peace after September 11, 2001. On that day, nineteen Al Qaeda terrorists hijacked four airlines and destroyed the World Trade Center towers and part of the Pentagon, killing nearly three thousand innocent people. This episode awakened

Americans and the world to a new fear that previously we had barely imagined: that even at home in the United States, we were vulnerable to devastating attack by determined terrorists, willing to die to kill us.

What made the September 11 attack possible—and so unexpected and terrifying—was that willingness to die to accomplish the mission. The final instructions found in the luggage of several hijackers leave little doubt about their intentions, telling them to make

> an oath to die.... When the confrontation begins, strike like champions who do not want to go back to this world.... Check your weapons long before you leave;...you must make your knife sharp and must not discomfort your animal during the slaughter.... Afterwards, we will all meet in the highest heaven....

The hijackers' suicide was essential to the terrible lethality of the attack, making it possible to crash airplanes into populated buildings. It also created an element of surprise, allowing the hijackers to exploit the counterterrorism measures and mindset that had evolved to deal with ordinary terrorist threats. Perhaps most jarring, the readiness of the terrorists to die in order to kill Americans amplified our sense of vulnerability. After September 11, Americans knew that we must expect that future Al Qaeda or other anti-American terrorists may be equally willing to die, and so not deterred by fear of punishment or of anything else. Such attackers would not hesitate to kill more Americans, and could succeed in carrying out equally devastating attacks—or worse—despite our best efforts to stop them.

September 11 was monstrous and shocking in scale, but it was not fundamentally unique. For more than twenty years, terrorist groups have been increasingly relying on suicide attacks to achieve major political objectives. From 1980 to 2003, terrorists across the globe waged seventeen separate campaigns of suicide terrorism, including those by Hezbollah to drive the United States, French, and Israeli forces out of Lebanon; by Palestinian terrorist groups to force Israel to abandon the West Bank and Gaza; by the Tamil Tigers to compel the Sri Lankan government to accept an independent Tamil homeland; by Al Qaeda to pressure the United States to withdraw from the Persian Gulf region. Since August of 2003, an eighteenth campaign has begun, aimed at driving the United States out of Iraq; as of this writing, it is not yet clear how much this effort owes to indigenous forces and how much to foreigners, possibly including Al Qaeda.

More worrying, the raw number of suicide terrorist attacks is climbing. At the same time that terrorist incidents of all types have declined by nearly half, from a peak of 666 in 1987 to 348 in 2001, suicide terrorism has grown, and the trend is continuing. Suicide terrorist attacks have risen from an average of 3 per year in the 1980s to about 10 per year in the 1990s to more than 40 each year in 2001 and 2002, and nearly 50 in 2003. These include continuing campaigns by Palestinian groups against Israel and by Al Qaeda and Taliban-related forces in Saudi Arabia and Afghanistan, as well as at least 20 attacks in Iraq against U.S. troops, the United Nations, and Iraqis collaborating with the American occupation.

Although many Americans have hoped that Al Qaeda has been badly weakened by U.S. counterterrorism efforts since September 11, 2001, the data show otherwise. In 2002 and 2003, Al Qaeda conducted 15 suicide terrorist attacks, more than in all the years before September 11 combined, killing 439 people.

Perhaps most worrying of all, suicide terrorism has become the most deadly form of terrorism. Suicide attacks amount to just 3 percent of all terrorist incidents from 1980 through 2003, but account for 48 percent of all fatalities, making the average suicide terrorist attack twelve times deadlier than other forms of terrorism—even if the immense losses of September 11 are not counted. If a terrorist group does get its hands on a nuclear weapon, suicide attack is the best way to ensure the bomb will go off and the most troublesome scenario for its use.

Since September 11, 2001, the United States has responded to the growing threat of suicide terrorism by embarking on a policy to conquer Muslim countries—not simply rooting out existing havens for terrorists in Afghanistan but going further to remake Muslim societies in the Persian Gulf. To be sure, the United States must be ready to use force to protect Americans and their allies, and must do so when necessary. However, the close association between foreign military occupations and the growth of suicide terrorist movements in the occupied regions should make us hesitate over any strategy centering on the transformation of Muslim societies by means of heavy military power. Although there may still be good reasons for such a strategy, we should recognize that the sustained presence of heavy American combat forces in

Muslim countries is likely to increase the odds of the next 9/11.

To win the war on terrorism, we must have a new conception of victory. The key to lasting security lies not only in rooting out today's generation of terrorists who are actively planning to kill Americans, but also in preventing the next, potentially larger generation from rising up. America's overarching purpose must be to achieve the first goal without failing at the second. To achieve that purpose, it is essential that we understand the strategic, social, and individual logic of suicide terrorism.

Our enemies have been studying suicide terrorism for over twenty years. Now is the time to level the playing field.

Charles P. Webel

TERROR: THE NEGLECTED BUT INESCAPABLE CORE OF TERRORISM

Most considerations of terrorism focus on its geopolitical impact, underlying causes, or various recommended antiterrorism tactics and strategies. Notably lacking has been consideration of its *effects* upon victims. When examined in this way, a striking and often ignored similarity emerges between terrorism as precipitated by comparatively weak, unorganized, nonstate actors and that of powerful, officially sanctioned governments themselves. The former is (rightly) condemned by nearly everyone in the West; only rarely is the latter placed in the same category. To do so, however, is to experience a potentially valuable shift in perspective, helping us to—as the poet Robert Burns put it—"see ourselves as others see us." The result may be troubling…but then again, so is terrorism itself.

*We are determined to answer the call of history and we
will defeat terror.*
                                    —U.S. President George W. Bush

*Only by the elimination of terrorism's root causes can the
world hope to succeed in greatly reducing it if not putting
an end to it.*
                                    —Haig Khatchadourian, *The Morality of Terrorism*

What can be done against force, without force?
                                    —Cicero, Letter to His Friends

THE SETTING

On Sept. 11, 2001, during the first year of this new
millennium, the cities of New York and Washington, DC, were attacked by terrorists. The loss of
life—approximately 3,000 civilians—was exceeded
in American history only by battles during the Civil
War, although cities in other countries experienced
far greater civilian casualties during World War II.

A number of factors make the events of September 11, 2001, and their aftermath unprecedented in
American history: First, the attacks were perpetrated
by foreign terrorists on American soil. Second, U.S.
civilian airplanes were transformed into weapons of
mass destruction. Third, the U.S. was not in a declared
state of war at the time. Fourth, the identities of the
perpetrators were unknown and were probably "nonstate actors." Fifth, no one has claimed responsibility
for the events of 9/11, in contrast to most other terrorist attacks and acts of violence committed against
civilian populations during wartime and since 1945.
Finally, millions of Americans, as well as many civilians in other countries, have felt unprecedented levels of stress, anxiety, trauma, and related feelings of
having been "terrorized" by these attacks.

According to a study conducted by the RAND
Corporation and published in the November 15,
2001, issue of *The New England Journal of Medicine*,
90 percent of the people surveyed reported they had
experienced at least some degree of stress three to
five days after the initial attacks on 9/11, while 44
percent were trying to cope with "substantial symptoms." These symptoms include the respondents'

feeling "very upset" when they were reminded
of what happened on 9/11; repeated, disturbing
memories, thoughts, and/or dreams; difficulty concentrating; trouble falling and/or staying asleep;
and feelings of anger and/or angry outbursts. Furthermore, the RAND study found that 47 percent of
interviewed parents reported that their children were
worried about their own safety and/or the safety of
loved ones, and that 35 percent of the respondents'
children had one or more clear symptoms of stress.
The survey concluded with a list of measures taken
by these randomly selected American adults to cope
with their feelings of anxiety and stress.

How generalizable are these findings? Would
these findings be comparable to studies of other
populations terrorized and traumatized by political
attacks? How long will people feel this way, even in
the unlikely event that no significant additional acts
of terrorist violence are perpetrated on American
soil? And how will everyday citizens and policymakers behave if there are more events like September
11, 2001?

How might we try to account for the usage of
"terrorism" as a political tactic and of terror as a predictable human response to the violence, and threats
of violence, employed by terrorists against innocent
people? And what might we all learn about terror
from the experiences of people around the world
who underwent and survived terrifying acts of political violence during the twentieth century?

Is there a common core experience of terror that
links the victims of contemporary terrorist attacks to
populations who were terrorized during the twentieth century? For example, are the survivors of terrifying acts of political violence committed during
the Second World War psychologically and ethically
similar to the concentration camp survivors of the
Nazi and Stalinist periods? To what degree do their
experiences resemble those of the surviving victims
of acts of state-sponsored terrorism, such as "ethnic
cleansing" and genocide, committed in Eastern and
Central Europe during the twentieth century? And
what measures—psychotherapeutic, socioeconomic,
legal, political, and diplomatic—should be taken to
aid the victims of terrorism, to prosecute the perpetrators of mass political violence, and to minimize
the risks of future terrorist attacks?

These are the questions that orient my phenomenological and cross-cultural inquiry into terror and terrorism. In this essay and in...*Terror, Terrorism, and the Human Condition* (St. Martin's/Palgrave/Macmillan Press, 2004), I...report and analyze the feelings and thoughts of survivors of terrorist and related attacks, both in the Western Hemisphere and in Europe.

UNRAVELING THE HISTORY AND SCOPE OF TERROR AND TERRORISM

The events of 9/11 and their aftermath constitute a unique variation on an all-too-common historical theme, one played out in terrifying variations in Europe during the twentieth century. These historical events offer us the opportunity to explore and to try to come to terms with our most basic needs, feelings, thoughts, and desires—including vulnerability, rage, meaninglessness, dread, revenge, hostility, conviction, hope, fortitude, courage, faith, and solidarity.

I take a novel approach to understanding the multiple dimensions of terror and terrorism, and I situate and assess the diverse and often divergent meanings and interpretations of these terms, experiences, and events within a comparative and historical framework.

My methods for approaching terror and terrorism are multidisciplinary. They are drawn from phenomenological and trauma psychology, psychoanalytic and political theory, comparative politics, ethnography, and oral history. They are informed and undergirded by a conviction that the kinds of nonviolent theory and practices articulated and exemplified by Gandhi and Martin Luther King, as well as by the peace movements of the early 1980s and by the "velvet revolutions" in Germany and Eastern Europe in the late 1980s and early 1990s, offer us today a practicable model for confronting both the terrorist "wars" outside our persons, and the terrors inside us as well.

The similarities and differences among American, European, Latin American, and Asian interpretations and experiences of terror and terrorism are intriguing and important, especially if we hope to devise culturally appropriate ways of treating the victims of political terror and to facilitate prosecution of the perpetrators of political terrorism.

WHAT IS "'TERRORISM'"?

The term "terrorism" means premeditated, politically motivated violence perpetrated against noncombatant targets by subnational groups or clandestine agents, usually intended to influence an audience.

> DCI Counterterrorist Center, Central Intelligence Agency, p. 3

...it [terrorism] is distinguished from all other kinds of violence by its "bifocal" character; namely, by the fact that the immediate acts of terrorist violence, such as shootings, bombings, kidnappings, and hostage-taking, are intended as means to certain goals, which vary with the particular terrorist acts or series of such acts...the concept of terrorism is a "family resemblance" concept....Consequently, the concept as a whole is an "open" or "open-textured" concept, nonsharply demarcated from other types/forms of individual or collective violence. The major types of terrorism are: predatory, retaliatory, political, and political-moralistic/religious. The terrorism may be domestic or international, "from above"—i.e., state or state-sponsored terrorism, or "from below."

> Haig Khatchadourian, *The Morality of Terrorism*, p. 11

...terrorism is fundamentally a form of psychological warfare. Terrorism is designed, as it has always been, to have profound psychological repercussions on a target audience. Fear and intimidation are precisely the terrorists' timeless stock-in-trade....It is used to create unbridled fear, dark insecurity, and reverberating panic. Terrorists seek to elicit an irrational, emotional response.

> Bruce Hoffman, "Lessons of 9/11," RAND, CT-201, October 2002

Etymologically, "terrorism" derives from "terror." Originaliy the word meant a system, or regime, of terror: at first imposed by the Jacobins, who applied the word to themselves without any negative connotations, subsequently it came to be applied to any policy or regime of the sort and to suggest a strongly negative attitude, as it generally does today....Terrorism is meant to cause terror (extreme fear) and, when successful, does so. Terrorism is intimidation with a purpose: the terror is meant to cause others to do things they would otherwise not do. Terrorism is coercive intimidation.

Igor Primoratz, "What is Terrorism?" *Journal of Applied Philosophy*, Vol. 7, No. 2, 1990, pp. 129–30

All wars are terrorism!

Political Slogan

In searching for a universal definition of "terrorism," a concept that is as contested ("one man's terrorist is another man's freedom fighter...") as it is "open," I found that "terrorism" has been used most often to denote politically-motivated attacks by *subnational* agents (this part is virtually uncontested in the relevant scholarly literature) *and/or states* (this is widely debated, but increasingly accepted) on noncombatants, usually in the context of war, revolution, and struggles for national liberation. In this sense, "terrorism" is as old as human conflict.

However, "terrorism" and "terrorists" have become relativized in recent times, since there is very little consensus on who, precisely, is or is not a "terrorist," or what is or is not an act of terrorism. Thus, who is or is not a "terrorist," and what may or may not be "acts of terrorism," depend largely on the perspective of the group or the person using (or abusing) those terms.

"Terrorism" is clearly a subcategory of political violence in particular, and of violence in general. Almost all current definitions of terrorism known to me focus on the violent acts committed (or threatened) by "terrorists," and neglect *the effects of those acts on their victims*. My focus is on the *terrifying effects* of certain violent acts on the victims of those acts, rather than on continuing the never-ending debate as to who is, or is not, a "terrorist." Nonetheless, for functional purposes, I propose the following definition of "terrorism":

Terrorism is a premeditated, usually politically motivated, use, or threatened use, of violence,

in order to induce a state of terror in its immediate victims, usually for the purpose of influencing another, less reachable audience, such as a government.

Note that under this definition, states—which commit "terrorism from above" (TFA)—and subnational entities, individuals and groups alike—which engage in "terrorism from below" (TFB)—may commit acts of terrorism. Note, as well, that the somewhat artificial distinction between "combatants" and "noncombatants" does not come into play here, since *both* groups may be terrorized by acts of political violence.

My underlying assumption is that unless necessary and sufficient conditions can be provided by perpetrators of "terrorism from above" (i.e., state actors using "terror bombing" to attempt to break the morale of a civilian population and its government, as has been done numerous times since the Italians bombed Tripoli in 1911), and by "terrorists from below" (ranging from the Russian revolutionaries and defenders of "Red Terror" during the late nineteenth and early twentieth centuries to Al Qaeda) to justify their acts, *any* act that deliberately inculcates terror is, more or less, unethical. However, there are of course *degrees* of moral culpability. The decisions by Churchill to target the civilian populations (especially the working class neighborhoods of industrial cities) of Germany for "terror bombings" during World War II, and by Truman to "nuke" Hiroshima and Nagasaki (which had no military significance) are, by this criterion, acts of "terrorism from above." But they are not morally equivalent to such acts of "terrorism from below" as the terrorist attacks of September 11, 2001, on the United States, or of the acts of other terrorist groups (such as the "Red Army Faction") during the late twentieth century who targeted civilians as means to achieving perceived political ends. This is not because they are "less unethical," but, on the contrary, because they are *more* unethical, for both consequentialist and deontological reasons.

From a consequentialist perspective, terror bombings of civilians during wartime have resulted in many *more* casualties (millions of dead and wounded) than *all* acts of "terrorism from below" combined. Furthermore, they have rarely resulted in achieving their declared political objectives: the firebombings of German and Japanese cities did *not* by themselves significantly induce the German and Japanese governments to surrender; rather, they tended to harden to resolve of the indigenous populations to fight harder (as did the German *Blitz* of England during 1940). Even the nuclear bombings of Hiroshima and Nagasaki did not significantly influence, or accelerate, the outcome of the war in the Pacific, because the Japanese government seems willing to have surrendered *before* the bombings. On the other hand, the terror bombing of Rotterdam in 1940 (which, apparently, may not have been intended by the *Luftwaffe*) was followed almost immediately by the surrender of the Dutch to the Germans; and Serbia did withdraw from Kosovo soon after Belgrade and other Yugoslavian cities were bombed by NATO in 1999. But in these two cases, the bombing was brief and civilian casualties were probably in the hundreds, and not in the hundreds of thousands, as they were in Germany and Japan during World War II.

Accordingly, the terror bombings committed by Great Britain and the United States, as well as by Nazi Germany and by Japan (principally in China), are classic examples of "terrorism from above" (TFA) or "state terrorism" (ST) and they resulted in millions of civilian casualties, without accomplishing their most important political objectives, viz., the profound demoralization of the civilian populations and prompt surrender of their antagonists. But what these state terrorists *did* accomplish, like their "terrorist from below" counterparts, was the *terrorization* of huge numbers of people, the use of persons as means to alleged political ends, and the dehumanization and denial of dignity to the objects of their terror bombings. And this is unethical by any known moral criterion.

To sum up the commonalities and differences between TFA and TFB in terms of their respective degrees of moral culpability for terrorizing and/or killing many innocent (and possibly a few "guilty") people, while both are unethical, TFA usually *exceeds* TFB in its moral reprehensibility in terms of

1. *The magnitude, or scale, of terror.* TFA, or ST, is immeasurably more pernicious than TFB, since nation-states under Hitler and Stalin killed and/

or terrorized tens of millions of their own citizens in the 1930s and 1940s and slaughtered millions of "enemies" during the Second World War. Japan, Great Britain, and the United States also killed and/ or terrorized millions of "enemies" in Chinese and German cities during that war. Latin American, African, and Asian despots and dictators, many with American support, killed and/or terrorized many thousands of their own citizens during the twentieth century. And the United States has used "precision bombing" and "counterinsurgency" campaigns to kill and/or terrorize millions of Vietnamese and other Southeast Asians, as well as civilians in countries ranging from Afghanistan to Somalia. In comparison, the collective efforts of TFB groups, ranging from the IRA and PFLP[20] to Al Qaeda, have probably resulted in fewer than ten thousand casualties—a tragedy for all the victims and their families, but in scale not comparable to TFA "collateral damage."

2. *The culpability, or degree of legal and/or ethical responsibility*, of the people who made the decisions to terrorize and/or kill people unfortunate enough to be living in states at war with their own is also disproportionately skewed toward TFA. Such decision-makers as Hitler, Stalin, Truman, Churchill, Pol Pot, and L. B. Johnson, who collectively issued orders resulting in the deaths of tens of millions of non-combatants and the terrorization of millions of their compatriots, rarely if ever engaged in personally overseeing the soldiers, sailors, and bombardiers who "were just following" (their) "orders." On the contrary: they were distant and detached from the mass killings that resulted from their policies, and would probably have refused to acknowledge their culpability for any "war crimes" and/or "crimes against humanity"—had they ever been called before an institution such as the International Court of Justice. In contrast, most leaders of TFB subnational groups are themselves directly involved in the terrorist operations, and may even put their lives at risk "for the sake of the cause." They may rationalize what they do, and justify mass murder by appeals to political motives (as do TFA decision-makers), but they would be, and have been, held individually legally culpable for their "crimes against humanity,"

---

[20] People's Front for the Liberation of Palestine.

unlike their TFB counterparts (the trials of Serbian leaders may set a notable precedent for a TFA decision-maker to be held legally culpable for crimes against humanity, in this case Bosnians).

TFA and TFB *share comparable degrees* of moral culpability because

1. They *instrumentalize* the victims of their terrorist tactics. Both TFA and TFB turn civilian noncombatants and combatants alike into disposable means to be used (or terrorized) in order to achieve perceived political ends. Along the way,

2. They *dehumanize, objectify, and demonize* their real and perceived "enemies," including the leaders of other nations or groups ("The Great Satan," "The Evil One," etc.). They also frequently polarize the conflicting parties, esteeming themselves and their followers as "good and virtuous," with "God on our side," and denigrating their opponents as "wicked," "evil," and frequently "in-" (or sub-) "human." Citizens of other states who are killed and/or terrorized by their subordinates' tactics are denoted as "collateral damage," and "body counts" of those killed are often employed as quantitative measures of an "operation's" "success."

3. They use or threaten to use *violence on a mass scale*, often disregarding and/or prematurely discarding nonviolent means of conflict resolution. From a crude utilitarian perspective, the "costs" of "inadvertent" and/or "unintentional"—but *nevertheless predictable and foreseeable* "friendly fire" and/ or "collateral damage" are reflexively seen by many decision-makers to be outweighed by the perceived "benefits" of "victory." Dialogue, negotiation, diplomacy, compromise, the use of nonviolent tactics and/or of nonlethal force, and the recourse to international institutions, are often regarded by both TFA and TFB as, at best, futile and, at worst, weak and defeatist.

4. *Weapons of mass destruction (WMD)*, including but not limited to chemical, biological, and nuclear weapons, are desirable "assets" to both TFA and TFB, even though the use of such weapons on a significant scale may have global—even omnicidal and therefore suicidal—consequences. WMD terrorism is the logical extension of the "logic of deterrence" and the "ethics of retaliation" (a version of *lex talionis*, "an eye for an eye").

Consequently, this "Age of Global Terrorism," dating from the early twentieth century, when "total war" and "strategic bombing" became acceptable components of military and diplomatic strategy, has culminated in the progressive obliteration of important previously-held distinctions. Most notably, there has been a gradual collapse of the distinction between "illegitimate" (i.e. civilian noncombatants) and "legitimate" (i.e. military) "targets," as well as of the distinction between "terrorists" and "the states" (and peoples…) that allegedly "support them."

Finally, this century-long process is leading to the erosion of the boundary between "terrorism" and "war," to such a degree that, since at least the early days of World War II, for the civilian populations of the affected states, war has, ipso facto, become indistinguishable from terrorism. Terror, or *psychological* warfare, has become a predictable tool to be employed by war planners and policymakers. This turn of events is on the one hand a regression to the kind of "barbarism" that preceded the rise of "civilization" about five thousand years ago in the Ancient Near East, and on the other hand is a seemingly inevitable consequence of technological "progress" *un*accompanied by a comparable "moral evolution" on the parts of the proponents, practitioners, and apologists for TFA and TFB alike. . . .

STUDY QUESTIONS

1. In what ways does twenty-first-century terrorism confront the world with issues that are historically unique? In what ways is it essentially a continuation of the past?

2. Familiarize yourself with the "just war" tradition, especially as developed by Christian ethicists. To what extent do these considerations apply to terrorism?

3. Make a case that terrorism is best confronted by international police work and law enforcement rather than by military action. Make the opposite case.

4. It has sometimes been claimed that terrorists are simply "evil" and/or that they are motivated by hatred of "our freedom." Agree or disagree, and provide reasons for your position.

5. Are there other potential "clashes of civilizations" beyond those enumerated by Samuel Huntington? Does his approach provide insight into terrorism specifically, as distinct from other conflicts? Discuss some issues that might be misrepresented by Huntington's argument.

6. Make a case for (or against) considering "terrorism from above" as in any way connected to "terrorism from below."

7. What are some consequences of analyzing the motivations of individual terrorists as opposed to looking at "terrorism" more generally?

8. Develop a menu of possible nonviolent responses to the problem of terrorism.

9. It has been said that the Bush administration's "war on terror" is merely an excuse for a never-ending militarization of U.S. foreign policy. Agree or disagree, and backup your position.

10. Does the struggle against terrorism require policies that differ from the struggle against other forms of violence? Why or Why not? Be specific.

SUGGESTIONS FOR FURTHER READING

Allison, Graham. 2005. *Nuclear Terrorism: The Ultimate Preventable Catastrophe*. New York: Holt.

Bobbitt, Philip. 2008. *Terror and Consent: The Wars for the Twenty-First Century*. New York: Alfred A. Knopf.

Chaliand, Gérard, and Arnaud Blin, eds. 2007. *The History of Terrorism: From Antiquity to Al Qaeda*. Berkeley: University of California Press.

Chomsky, Noam. 2003. *Pirates and Emperors, Old and New: International Terrorism in the Real World*. Boston: South End Press.

Coll, Steven. 2004. *Ghost Wars: The Secret History of the CIA, Afghanistan, and bin Laden, from the Soviet Invasion to September 10, 2001*. New York: Penguin Books.

Keefer, Philip, and Norman Loayza, eds. 2008. *Terrorism, Economic Development, and Political Openness*. New York: Cambridge University Press.

Laqueur, Walter. 2004. *No End to War: Terrorism in the Twenty-First Century*. New York: Continuum.

Miller, Seamus. 2008. *Terrorism and Counter-Terrorism: Ethics and Liberal Democracy*. New York: Wiley-Blackwell.

Scheuer, Michael, and Bruce Hoffman. 2007. *Through Our Enemies' Eyes: Osama bin Laden, Radical Islam, and the Future of America*. Washington, DC: Potomac Books.

Smelser, Neil J. 2007. *The Faces of Terrorism: Social and Psychological Dimensions*. Princeton, NJ: Princeton University Press.

CHAPTER 4

Building "Positive Peace"

I t is important to be against war. But it is not enough. We also need to be
in favor of something—something positive and affirming: namely, peace.
Peace studies is unique not only because it is multidisciplinary and forth-
rightly proclaims its adherence to "values" but also because it identifies positive visions of
peace as being greater than the absence of war.

The "positive peace" toward which peace studies strives may be, if anything, even
more challenging than the prevention of war. It is a variation on what has been called the
"dog–car problem." Imagine a dog that has spent years barking and running after cars.
Then, one day, it catches one. What does it *do* with it? What would devotees of peace *do*
with the world if they had the opportunity?

This is not a useless exercise, as before any future can be established, it must first
be imagined. And moreover, unlike our hypothetical car-chasing dog, the establishment
of positive peace is not an all-or-nothing phenomenon. The movement toward positive
peace is likely to be halting and fragmentary, with substantial success along certain dimensions, likely failures along others. On balance, the project is formidable, nothing less than
a fundamental effort to rethink the relationship of human beings to each other and to
their shared planet. If war and its causes are difficult to define—and this is assuredly the
case—positive peace is even more elusive. (It can even be dangerous, because disagreements over what constitutes a desirable "peace" can lead to war.)

Earlier, we briefly considered "just war" doctrine. The conditions for a "just peace"
are no less strenuous or important. The relevant issues include—but are not limited to—
aspirations for human rights, economic fairness and opportunity, democratization, and
environmental well-being and sustainability. Nonetheless, there is no agreement as to
what, specifically, is desired or how much emphasis to place on each goal.

The pursuit of positive peace nonetheless leads to certain agreed principles, one of
which is a minimization of violence, not only the overt violence of war, but also what has
been called "structural violence," a condition that is typically built into many social and

cultural institutions. A slaveholding society may be at "peace" in that it is not literally at war, but it is also rife with structural violence. Structural violence has the effect of denying people important rights such as economic opportunity, social and political equality, a sense of fulfillment and self-worth, and access to a healthy natural environment. When people starve to death, or even go hungry, a kind of violence is taking place. Similarly, when human beings suffer from diseases that are preventable, when they are denied a decent education, housing, an opportunity to play, to grow, to work, to raise a family, to express themselves freely, to organize peacefully, or to participate in their own governance, a kind of violence is occurring, even if bullets or clubs are not being used. Society visits violence on human rights and dignity when it forcibly stunts the optimum development of each human being, whether because of race, religion, sex, sexual preference, age, ideology, and so on. In short, structural violence is another way of identifying oppression, and positive peace would be a situation in which structural violence and oppression are minimized.

In addition, social injustice is important not only in its contribution to structural violence but also as a major contributor to war, often in unexpected ways. For many citizens of the United States and Europe, as well as privileged people worldwide, current lifestyles are fundamentally acceptable. Hence, peace for them has come to mean the continuation of things as they are, with the additional hope that overt violence will be prevented. For others—perhaps the majority on our planet—change of one sort or another is desired. And for a small minority, peace is something to fight for! A Central American peasant was quoted in the *New York Times* as saying, "I am for peace, but not peace with hunger."

There is a long tradition suggesting that injustice is a primary cause of war. The French philosopher Denis Diderot, for example, was convinced that a world of justice and plenty would mean a world free of tyranny and war. Hence, in his eighteenth-century treatise, the *Encyclopedia*, Diderot sought to establish peace by disseminating all the world's technical information, from beekeeping to iron forging. And, of course, similar efforts continue today, although few advocates of economic and social development claim that the problem of violence can be solved simply by spreading knowledge or even by keeping everyone's belly full.

The troubling relationship of human beings to their natural environment must also be reworked, perhaps in fundamental ways. A world at peace must be one in which environmental, human rights, and economic issues all cohere to foster maximum well-being; ecological harmony cannot realistically be separated from questions of human rights or economic justice (or, for that matter, from the issues of democratization and demilitarization).

In relation to the environment, political or economic ideology do not appear to be significant. Environmental degradation is, to be sure, intimately connected to poverty: wealthy states often export their most odious environmental abuses, and impoverished states are often forced by their poverty to accept the situation. Moreover, within any given state, wealthy people are able to purchase certain amenities, while the poor find themselves living in degraded, and often downright dangerous, surroundings. But in general, left-leaning governments have not shown themselves to be more environmentally sensitive than their right-leaning counterparts. In avowedly Socialist or Communist societies, for example, "production goals" typically replaced the capitalist pursuit of "profit" as the "bottom line" to which environmental values were all too frequently sacrificed.

A very important shift in human consciousness—intimately related to the agenda of peace studies—is the realization that "national security" must be defined in ways that go far beyond military strength and that as our planet becomes increasingly interconnected politically, economically, and socially, and also as our global environment is increasingly endangered, the health, well-being, and security of every individual becomes inseparable from the health, well-being, and security of the earth itself.

Aldo Leopold

THE LAND ETHIC

An ecological perspective demands that we recognize the reality of connectedness, which, as the poet Francis Thompson put it, "all things...near and far, hiddenly to each other, connected are, that thou canst not stir a flower without the troubling of a star." This is true not only for biology, but also for social, political, and economic systems. Thus, not only do wars ruin the environment, but environmental destruction—and its threat—can lead to wars. Millions of refugees regularly flee environmental disasters such as drought, floods, famine, and disease. These refugees, who constitute a humanitarian disaster in themselves, can also raise international tensions.

The destruction of rain forests, for example, is not only a deeply troubling environmental issue with worldwide implications, but it arises from particular economic systems (notably a free-market free-for-all), with no small dose of racism (devaluing the rights of indigenous peoples). The poverty resulting from deforestation and displacement leads to land degradation and the growing problem of desertification as hungry, desperate people clear and cultivate regions that should be left untouched. This in turn leads to yet more poverty and social unrest. Intensive farming of highly erodable land permanently destroys soil; large-scale intrusions into wildlife habitat (which contribute to species extinction) are in large part responses to land hunger in rural, developing countries, where a small minority of wealthy people own most of the arable land, thereby pushing others to environmentally abusive behavior. Worldwide, the burning of fossil fuels produces greenhouse gases; resulting global climate warming may increase food insecurity by reducing agricultural productivity. All of these factors—plus many others—are intertwined in complex ways with the exponential growth of the human population.

There is an enormous and growing literature on specific solutions to environmental problems, such as mass transportation; improved energy efficiency and cogeneration; "soft" energy paths such as solar, wind, and tidal power; organic agriculture; enhanced recycling; eating "lower on the food chain"; and an enlightened population policy that encourages family planning, especially by empowering women.

The word "ecology" derives from the Greek *oikos*, meaning house. It refers to the interrelations between living things and their environment, with the latter including other living things (plants, animals, microorganisms) as well as inanimate objects and processes such as climate, rock, water, and air. Despite dreams of space travel and the colonization of other planets, the fact remains that human beings have only one home, and good planets are hard to find.

In the final analysis, a world at peace must be one in which all living things experience themselves as being "at home." In recent times, some of the crucial relationships among the world's species, and between those species and their environments, have become increasingly tenuous, which in turn has begun to threaten the quality of life, and even its continuation. At risk is nothing less than the integrity of various life-support systems: the air we breathe, the water we drink, the food we eat, as well as the diverse fabric of life that provides emotional and spiritual sustenance.

The following selection—written by one of the great figures in ecology, and the founder of "wildlife management"—attempts to look broadly at the problem and to suggest the beginning of a solution: notably, a code of environmental ethics.

When godlike Odysseus returned from the wars in Troy, he hanged all on one rope a dozen slave-girls of his household whom he suspected of misbehavior during his absence.

This hanging involved no question of propriety. The girls were property. The disposal of property was then, as now, a matter of expedience, not of right and wrong.

Concepts of right and wrong were not lacking from Odysseus' Greece: witness the fidelity of his wife through the long years before at last his black-prowed galleys clove the wine-dark seas for home. The ethical structure of that day covered wives, but had not yet been extended to human chattels. During the three thousand years which have since elapsed, ethical criteria have been extended to many fields of conduct, with corresponding shrinkages in those judged by expediency only.

THE ETHICAL SEQUENCE

This extension of ethics, so far studied only by philosophers, is actually a process in ecological evolution. Its sequences may be described in ecological as well as in philosophical terms. An ethic, ecologically, is a limitation on freedom of action in the struggle for existence. An ethic, philosophically, is a differentiation of social from antisocial conduct. These are two definitions of one thing. The thing has its origin in the tendency of interdependent individuals or groups to evolve modes of cooperation. The ecologist calls these symbioses. Politics and economics are advanced symbioses in which the original free-for-all competition has been replaced, in part, by cooperative mechanisms with an ethical content.

The complexity of cooperative mechanisms has increased with population density, and with the efficiency of tools. It was simpler, for example, to define the anti-social uses of sticks and stones in the days of the mastodons than of bullets and billboards in the age of motors.

The first ethics dealt with the relation between individuals; the Mosaic Decalogue is an example. Later accretions dealt with the relation between the individual and society. The Golden Rule tries to integrate the individual to society; democracy to integrate social organization to the individual.

There is as yet no ethic dealing with man's relation to land and to the animals and plants which grow upon it. Land, like Odysseus' slave-girls, is still property. The land-relation is still strictly economic, entailing privileges but not obligations.

The extension of ethics to this third element in human environment is, if I read the evidence correctly, an evolutionary possibility and an ecological necessity. It is the third step in a sequence. The first two have already been taken. Individual thinkers since the days of Ezekiel and Isaiah have asserted that the despoliation of land is not only inexpedient but wrong. Society, however, has not yet affirmed their belief. I regard the present conservation movement as the embryo of such an affirmation.

An ethic may be regarded as a mode of guidance for meeting ecological situations so new or intricate, or involving such deferred reactions, that the path of social expediency is not discernible to the average individual. Animal instincts are modes of guidance for the individual in meeting such situations. Ethics are possibly a kind of community instinct in-the-making.

THE COMMUNITY CONCEPT

All ethics so far evolved rest upon a single premise: that the individual is a member of a community of interdependent parts. His instincts prompt him to compete for his place in that community, but his ethics prompt him also to cooperate (perhaps in order that there may be a place to compete for).

The land ethic simply enlarges the boundaries of the community to include soils, waters, plants, and animals, or collectively: the land.

This sounds simple: do we not already sing our love for and obligation to the land of the free and the home of the brave? Yes, but just what and whom do we love? Certainly not the soil, which we are sending helter-skelter downriver. Certainly not the waters, which we assume have no function except to turn turbines, float barges, and carry off sewage. Certainly not the plants, of which we exterminate whole communities without batting an eye. Certainly not the animals, of which we have already extirpated many of the largest and most beautiful species. A land ethic of course cannot prevent the alteration, management, and use of these "resources," but it does affirm their right to continued existence, and, at least in spots, their continued existence in a natural state.

In short, a land ethic changes the role of *Homo sapiens* from conqueror of the land-community to plain member and citizen of it. It implies respect for his fellow-members, and also respect for the community as such.

In human history, we have learned (I hope) that the conqueror role is eventually self-defeating. Why? Because it is implicit in such a role that the conqueror knows, *ex cathedra,* just what makes the community clock tick, and just what and who is valuable, and what and who is worthless, in community life. It always turns out that he knows neither, and this is why his conquests eventually defeat themselves.

In the biotic community, a parallel situation exists. Abraham knew exactly what the land was for: it was to drip milk and honey into Abraham's mouth. At the present moment, the assurance with which we regard this assumption is inverse to the degree of our education.

The ordinary citizen today assumes that science knows what makes the community clock tick; the scientist is equally sure that he does not. He knows that the biotic mechanism is so complex that its workings may never be fully understood....

THE ECOLOGICAL CONSCIENCE

Conservation is a state of harmony between men and land. Despite nearly a century of propaganda, conservation still proceeds at a snail's pace; progress still consists largely of letterhead pieties and convention oratory. On the back forty we still slip two steps backward for each forward stride.

The usual answer to this dilemma is "more conservation education." No one will debate this, but is it certain that only the *volume* of education needs stepping up? Is something lacking in the *content* as well?

It is difficult to give a fair summary of its content in brief form, but, as I understand it, the content is substantially this: obey the law, vote right, join some organizations, and practice what conservation is profitable on your own land; the government will do the rest.

Is not this formula too easy to accomplish anything worthwhile? It defines no right or wrong, assigns no obligation, calls for no sacrifice, implies no change in the current philosophy of values. In respect of land-use, it urges only enlightened self-interest. Just how far will such education take us?

No important change in ethics was ever accomplished without an internal change in our intellectual emphasis, loyalties, affections, and convictions. The proof that conservation has not yet touched these foundations of conduct lies in the fact that philosophy and religion have not yet heard of it. In our attempt to make conservation easy, we have made it trivial.

SUBSTITUTES FOR A LAND ETHIC

When the logic of history hungers for bread and we hand out a stone, we are at pains to explain how much the stone resembles bread. I now describe some of the stones which serve in lieu of a land ethic.

One basic weakness in a conservation system based wholly on economic motives is that most members of the land community have no economic value. Wildflowers and songbirds are examples. Of the 22,000 higher plants and animals native to Wisconsin, it is doubtful whether more than 5 percent can be sold, fed, eaten, or otherwise put to economic use. Yet these creatures are members of the biotic community, and if (as I believe) its stability depends on its integrity, they are entitled to continuance.

When one of these non-economic categories is threatened, and if we happen to love it, we invent subterfuges to give it economic importance. At the beginning of the century songbirds were supposed to be disappearing. Ornithologists jumped to the rescue with some distinctly shaky evidence to the effect that insects would eat us up if birds failed to control them. The evidence had to be economic in order to be valid.

It is painful to read these circumlocutions today. We have no land ethic yet, but we have at least drawn nearer the point of admitting that birds should continue as a matter of biotic right, regardless of the presence or absence of economic advantage to us.

A parallel situation exists in respect of predatory mammals, raptorial birds, and fish-eating birds. Time was when biologists somewhat overworked the evidence that these creatures preserve the health of game by killing weaklings, or that they control rodents for the farmer, or that they prey only on "worthless" species. Here again, the evidence had to be economic in order to be valid. It is only in recent years that we hear the more honest argument that predators are members of the community, and that no special interest has the right to exterminate them for the sake of a benefit, real or fancied, to itself....

Lack of economic value is sometimes a character not only of species or groups, but of entire biotic communities: marshes, bogs, dunes, and "deserts" are examples. Our formula in such cases is to relegate their conservation to government as refuges, monuments, or parks. The difficulty is that these communities are usually interspersed with more valuable private lands; the government cannot possibly own or control such scattered parcels. The net effect is that we have relegated some of them to ultimate extinction over large areas....

Industrial landowners and users, especially lumbermen and stockmen, are inclined to wail long and loudly about the extension of government ownership and regulation to land, but (with notable exceptions) they show little disposition to develop the only visible alternative: the voluntary practice of conservation on their own lands.

When the private landowner is asked to perform some unprofitable act for the good of the community, he today assents only with outstretched palm. If the act costs him cash this is fair and proper, but when it costs only forethought, open-mindedness, or time, the issue is at least debatable. The overwhelming growth of land-use subsidies in recent years must be ascribed, in large part, to the government's own agencies for conservation education: the land bureaus, the agricultural colleges, and the extension services. As far as I can detect, no ethical obligation toward land is taught in these institutions.

To sum up: a system of conservation based solely on economic self-interest is hopelessly lopsided. It tends to ignore, and thus eventually to eliminate, many elements in the land community that lack commercial value, but that are (as far as we know) essential to its healthy functioning. It assumes, falsely, I think, that the economic parts of the biotic clock will function without the uneconomic parts. It tends to relegate to government many functions eventually too large, too complex, or too widely dispersed to be performed by government.

An ethical obligation on the part of the private owner is the only visible remedy for these situations.

THE LAND PYRAMID

An ethic to supplement and guide the economic relation to land presupposes the existence of some mental image of land as a biotic mechanism. We can be ethical only in relation to something we can see, feel, understand, love, or otherwise have faith in.

The image commonly employed in conservation education is "the balance of nature." For reasons too lengthy to detail here, this figure of speech fails to describe accurately what little we know about the land mechanism. A much truer image is the one employed in ecology: the biotic pyramid. I shall first sketch the pyramid as a symbol of land, and later develop some of its implications in terms of land-use.

Plants absorb energy from the sun. This energy flows through a circuit called the biota, which may be represented by a pyramid consisting of layers. The bottom layer is the soil. A plant layer rests on the soil, an insect layer on the plants, a bird and rodent layer on the insects, and so on up through various animal groups to the apex layer, which consists of the larger carnivores.

The species of a layer are alike not in where they came from, or in what they look like, but rather in what they eat. Each successive layer depends on those below it for food and often for other services, and each in turn furnishes food and services to those above. Proceeding upward, each successive layer decreases in numerical abundance. Thus, for every carnivore there are hundreds of his prey, thousands of their prey, millions of insects, uncountable plants. The pyramidal form of the system reflects this numerical progression from apex to base. Man shares an intermediate layer with the bears, raccoons, and squirrels which eat both meat and vegetables.

The lines of dependency for food and other services are called food chains. Thus soil-oak-deer-Indian is a chain that has now been largely converted to soil-corn-cow-farmer. Each species, including ourselves, is a link in many chains. The deer eats a hundred plants other than oak, and the cow a hundred plants other than corn. Both, then, are links in a hundred chains. The pyramid is a tangle of chains so complex as to seem disorderly, yet the stability of the system proves it to be a highly organized structure. Its functioning depends on the cooperation and competition of its diverse parts.

In the beginning, the pyramid of life was low and squat; the food chains short and simple. Evolution has added layer after layer, link after link. Man is one of thousands of accretions to the height and complexity of the pyramid. Science has given us many doubts, but it has given us at least one certainty: the trend of evolution is to elaborate and diversify the biota.

Land, then, is not merely soil; it is a fountain of energy flowing through a circuit of soils, plants, and animals. Food chains are the living channels which conduct energy upward; death and decay return it to the soil. The circuit is not closed; some energy is dissipated in decay, some is added by absorption from the air, some is stored in soils, peats, and long-lived forests; but it is a sustained circuit, like a slowly augmented revolving fund of life. There is always a net loss by downhill wash, but this is normally small and offset by the decay of rocks. It is deposited in the ocean and, in the course of geological time, raised to form new lands and new pyramids.

The velocity and character of the upward flow of energy depend on the complex structure of the plant and animal community, much as the upward flow of sap in a tree depends on its complex cellular organization. Without this complexity, normal circulation would presumably not occur. Structure means the characteristic numbers, as well as the characteristic kinds and functions, of the component species. This interdependence between the complex structure of the land and its smooth functioning as an energy unit is one of its basic attributes.

When a change occurs in one part of the circuit, many other parts must adjust themselves to it. Change does not necessarily obstruct or divert the flow of energy; evolution is a long series of self-induced changes, the net result of which has been to elaborate the flow mechanism and to lengthen the circuit. Evolutionary changes, however, are usually slow and local. Man's invention of tools has enabled him to make changes of unprecedented violence, rapidity, and scope.

One change is in the composition of floras and faunas. The larger predators are lopped off the apex of the pyramid; food chains, for the first time in history, become shorter rather than longer. Domesticated species from other lands are substituted for wild ones, and wild ones are moved to new habitats. In this worldwide pooling of faunas and floras, some species get out of bounds as pests and diseases, others are extinguished. Such effects are seldom intended or foreseen; they represent unpredicted and often untraceable readjustments in the structure. Agricultural science is largely a race between the emergence of new pests and the emergence of new techniques for their control.

Another change touches the flow of energy through plants and animals and its return to the soil. Fertility is the ability of soil to receive, store, and release energy. Agriculture, by overdrafts on the soil, or by too radical a substitution of domestic for native species in the superstructure, may derange the channels of flow or deplete storage. Soils depleted of their storage, or of the organic matter which anchors it, wash away faster than they form. This is erosion.

Waters, like soil, are part of the energy circuit. Industry, by polluting waters or obstructing them with dams, may exclude the plants and animals necessary to keep energy in circulation.

Transportation brings about another basic change: the plants or animals grown in one region are now consumed and returned to the soil in another.

Transportation taps the energy stored in rocks, and in the air, and uses it elsewhere; thus we fertilize the garden with nitrogen gleaned by the guano birds from the fishes of seas on the other side of the Equator. Thus the formerly localized and self-contained circuits are pooled on a worldwide scale.

The process of altering the pyramid for human occupation releases stored energy, and this often gives rise, during the pioneering period, to a deceptive exuberance of plant and animal life, both wild and tame. These releases of biotic capital tend to becloud or postpone the penalties of violence.

This thumbnail sketch of land as an energy circuit conveys three basic ideas:

1. That land is not merely soil.
2. That the native plants and animals kept the energy circuit open; others may or may not.
3. That man-made changes are of a different order than evolutionary changes, and have effects more comprehensive than is intended or foreseen.

These ideas, collectively, raise two basic issues: Can the land adjust itself to the new order? Can the desired alterations be accomplished with less violence? . . .

The combined evidence of history and ecology seems to support one general deduction: the less violent the man-made changes, the greater the probability of successful readjustment in the pyramid. Violence, in turn, varies with human population density; a dense population requires a more violent conversion. In this respect, North America has a better chance for permanence than Europe, if she can contrive to limit her density.

This deduction runs counter to our current philosophy, which assumes that because a small increase in density enriched human life, that an indefinite increase will enrich it indefinitely. Ecology knows of no density relationship that holds for indefinitely wide limits. All gains from density are subject to a law of diminishing returns.

Whatever may be the equation for men and land, it is improbable that we as yet know all its terms. Recent discoveries in mineral and vitamin nutrition reveal unsuspected dependencies in the up-circuit: incredibly minute quantities of certain substances determine the value of soils to plants, of plants to animals. What of the down-circuit? What of the vanishing species, the preservation of which we now regard as an esthetic luxury? They helped build the soil; in what unsuspected ways may they be essential to its maintenance? [It has been proposed]...that we use prairie flowers to reflocculate the wasting soils of the dust bowl; who knows for what purpose cranes and condors, otters and grizzlies may some day be used?

LAND HEALTH AND THE A-B CLEAVAGE

A land ethic, then, reflects the existence of an ecological conscience, and this in turn reflects a conviction of individual responsibility for the health of the land. Health is the capacity of the land for self-renewal. Conservation is our effort to understand and preserve this capacity.

Conservationists are notorious for their dissensions. Superficially these seem to add up to mere confusion, but a more careful scrutiny reveals a single plane of cleavage common to many specialized fields. In each field one group (A) regards the land as soil, and its function as commodity-production; another group (B) regards the land as a biota, and its function as something broader. How much broader is admittedly in a state of doubt and confusion.

In my own field, forestry, Group A is quite content to grow trees like cabbages, with cellulose as the basic forest commodity. It feels no inhibition against violence; its ideology is agronomic. Group B, on the other hand, sees forestry as fundamentally different from agronomy because it employs natural species, and manages a natural environment rather than creating an artificial one. Group B prefers natural reproduction on principle. It worries on biotic as well as economic grounds about the loss of species like chestnut, and the threatened loss of the white pines. It worries about a whole series of secondary forest functions: wildlife, recreation, watersheds, wilderness areas. To my mind, Group B feels the stirrings of an ecological conscience.

In the wildlife field, a parallel cleavage exists. For Group A the basic commodities are sport and meat; the yardsticks of production are ciphers of take in pheasants and trout. Artificial propagation is acceptable as a permanent as well as a temporary recourse—if its unit costs permit. Group B, on the other hand, worries about a whole series of biotic side-issues. What is the cost in predators of producing a game crop? Should we have further recourse to exotics? How can management restore the shrinking species, like prairie grouse, already hopeless as shootable game? How can management restore the threatened rarities, like trumpeter swan and whooping crane? Can management principles be extended to wildflowers? Here again it is clear to me that we have the same A-B cleavage as in forestry....

The ecological fundamentals of agriculture are just as poorly known to the public as in other fields of land-use. For example, few educated people realize that the marvelous advances in technique made during recent decades are improvements in the pump, rather than the well. Acre for acre, they have barely sufficed to offset the sinking level of fertility.

In all of these cleavages, we see repeated the same basic paradoxes: man the conqueror *versus* man the biotic citizen; science the sharpener of his sword *versus* science the searchlight on his universe; land the slave and servant *versus* land the collective organism. Robinson's injunction to Tristram may well be applied, at this juncture, to *Homo sapiens* as a species in geological time:

> Whether you will or not
> You are a King, Tristram, for you are one
> Of the time-tested few that leave the world,
> When they are gone, not the same place it was.
> Mark what you leave.

THE OUTLOOK

It is inconceivable to me that an ethical relation to land can exist without love, respect, and admiration for land, and a high regard for its value. By value, I of course mean something far broader than mere economic value; I mean value in the philosophical sense.

Perhaps the most serious obstacle impeding the evolution of a land ethic is the fact that our educational and economic system is headed away from, rather than toward, an intense consciousness of land. Your true modern is separated from the land by many middlemen, and by innumerable physical gadgets. He has no vital relation to it; to him it is the space between cities on which crops grow. Turn him loose for a day on the land, and if the spot does not happen to be a golf links or a "scenic" area, he is bored stiff. If crops could be raised by hydroponics instead of farming, it would suit him very well. Synthetic substitutes for wood, leather, wool, and other natural land products suit him better than the originals. In short, land is something he has "outgrown."

Almost equally serious as an obstacle to a land ethic is the attitude of the farmer for whom the land is still an adversary, or a taskmaster that keeps him in slavery. Theoretically, the mechanization of farming ought to cut the farmer's chains, but whether it really does is debatable.

One of the requisites for an ecological comprehension of land is an understanding of ecology, and this is by no means co-extensive with "education"; in fact, much higher education seems deliberately to avoid ecological concepts. An understanding of ecology does not necessarily originate in courses bearing ecological labels; it is quite as likely to be labeled geography, botany, agronomy, history, or economics. This is as it should be, but whatever the label, ecological training is scarce.

The case for a land ethic would appear hopeless but for the minority which is in obvious revolt against these "modern" trends.

The "key-log" which must be moved to release the evolutionary process for an ethic is simply this: quit thinking about decent land-use as solely an economic problem. Examine each question in terms of what is ethically and esthetically right, as well as what is economically expedient. A thing is right when it tends to preserve the integrity, stability, and beauty of the biotic community. It is wrong when it tends otherwise.

It of course goes without saying that economic feasibility limits the tether of what can or cannot be done for land. It always has and it always will. The fallacy the economic determinists have tied around our collective neck, and which we now need to cast off, is the belief that economics determines *all* land-use. This is simply not true. An innumerable host of actions and attitudes, comprising perhaps the bulk of all land relations, is determined by the land-user's tastes and predilections, rather than by his purse. The bulk of all land relations hinges on investments of time, forethought, skill, and faith rather than on investments of cash. As a land-user thinketh, so is he.

I have purposely presented the land ethic as a product of social evolution because nothing so important as an ethic is ever "written." Only the most superficial student of history supposes that Moses "wrote" the Decalogue; it evolved in the minds of a thinking community, and Moses wrote a tentative summary of it for a "seminar." I say tentative because evolution never stops.

The evolution of a land ethic is an intellectual as well as emotional process. Conservation is paved with good intentions which prove to be futile, or even dangerous, because they are devoid of critical understanding either of the land, or of economic land-use. I think it is a truism that as the ethical frontier advances from the individual to the community, its intellectual content increases.

The mechanism of operation is the same for any ethic: social approbation for right actions: social disapproval for wrong actions.

By and large, our present problem is one of attitudes and implements. We are remodeling the Alhambra with a steam shovel, and we are proud of our yardage. We shall hardly relinquish the shovel, which after all has many good points, but we are in need of gentler and more objective criteria for its successful use.

Al Gore

NOBEL PRIZE ACCEPTANCE SPEECH

To be sure, global warming isn't the only environmental issue that must be confronted by advocates of positive peace: the world faces a dramatic and potentially catastrophic reduction in biodiversity, the variety and abundance of living species. Economic exploitation of nature is becoming increasingly unsustainable, especially given the incontrovertible fact that many resources are finite and not renewable. Energy in particular poses thorny problems, especially insofar as use patterns remain tethered to fossil fuels. Population pressure seems unrelenting and, paradoxically, is most concentrated in third world countries that are least capable of absorbing its social and economic impact, not to mention the environmental costs. And the aforementioned is but a small sample, beyond the general pespective advocated by Aldo Leopold.

Looming above these issues, however, is the increasingly evident fact that human beings are dramatically and perhaps irreversibly changing the climate of planet Earth. And responsible for many of the warnings about this potential catastrophe has been Al Gore, former vice president of the United States, whose efforts in this regard earned him a Nobel Peace Prize in 2007. Following is Gore's Nobel Prize acceptance speech, delivered on December 10, 2007, in Oslo, Norway.

SPEECH BY AL GORE ON THE ACCEPTANCE OF THE NOBEL PEACE PRIZE, DECEMBER 10, 2007, OSLO, NORWAY

We, the human species, are confronting a planetary emergency—a threat to the survival of our civilization that is gathering ominous and destructive potential even as we gather here. But there is hopeful news as well: we have the ability to solve this crisis and avoid the worst—though not all—of its consequences, if we act boldly, decisively, and quickly.

However, despite a growing number of honorable exceptions, too many of the world's leaders are still best described in the words Winston Churchill applied to those who ignored Adolf Hitler's threat: "They go on in strange paradox, decided only to be undecided, resolved to be irresolute, adamant for drift, solid for fluidity, all powerful to be impotent."

So today, we dumped another 70 million tons of global-warming pollution into the thin shell of atmosphere surrounding our planet, as if it were an open sewer. And tomorrow we will dump a slightly larger amount, with the cumulative concentrations now trapping more and more heat from the sun.

As a result, the earth has a fever. And the fever is rising. The experts have told us it is not a passing affliction that will heal by itself. We asked for a second opinion. And a third. And a fourth. And the consistent conclusion, restated with increasing alarm, is that something basic is wrong.

We are what is wrong, and we must make it right.

Last September 21, as the Northern Hemisphere tilted away from the sun, scientists reported with unprecedented distress that the North Polar ice cap is "falling off a cliff." One study estimated that it could be completely gone during summer in less than twenty-two years. Another new study, to be presented by U.S. Navy researchers later this week, warns it could happen in as little as seven years.

Seven years from now.

In the last few months, it has been harder and harder to misinterpret the signs that our world is spinning out of kilter. Major cities in North and South America, Asia, and Australia are nearly out of water due to massive droughts and melting glaciers. Desperate farmers are losing their livelihoods. Peoples in the frozen Arctic and on low-lying Pacific islands are planning evacuations of places they have long called home. Unprecedented wildfires have forced a half million people from their homes in one country and caused a national emergency that almost brought down the government in another. Climate refugees have migrated into areas already inhabited by people with different cultures, religions, and traditions, increasing the potential for conflict. Stronger storms in the Pacific and Atlantic have threatened whole cities. Millions have been displaced by massive flooding in South Asia, Mexico, and eighteen countries in Africa. As temperature extremes have increased, tens of thousands have lost their lives. We are recklessly burning and clearing our forests and driving more and more species into extinction. The very web of life on which we depend is being ripped and frayed.

We never intended to cause all this destruction, just as Alfred Nobel never intended that dynamite be used for waging war. He had hoped his invention would promote human progress. We shared that same worthy goal when we began burning massive quantities of coal, then oil and methane.

Even in Nobel's time, there were a few warnings of the likely consequences. One of the very first winners of the prize in chemistry worried that, "We are evaporating our coal mines into the air." After performing ten thousand equations by hand, Svante Arrhenius calculated that the earth's average temperature would increase by many degrees if we doubled the amount of CO_2 in the atmosphere.

Seventy years later, my teacher, Roger Revelle, and his colleague, Dave Keeling, began to precisely document the increasing CO_2 levels day by day.

But unlike most other forms of pollution, CO_2 is invisible, tasteless, and odorless—which has helped keep the truth about what it is doing to our climate out of sight and out of mind. Moreover, the catastrophe now threatening us is unprecedented—and we often confuse the unprecedented with the improbable.

We also find it hard to imagine making the massive changes that are now necessary to solve the crisis. And when large truths are genuinely inconvenient, whole societies can, at least for a time, ignore them. Yet as George Orwell reminds us: "Sooner or later a false belief bumps up against solid reality, usually on a battlefield."

In the years since this prize was first awarded, the entire relationship between humankind and the earth has been radically transformed. And still, we have remained largely oblivious to the impact of our cumulative actions.

Indeed, without realizing it, we have begun to wage war on the earth itself. Now, we and the earth's climate are locked in a relationship familiar to war planners: "Mutually assured destruction."

More than two decades ago, scientists calculated that nuclear war could throw so much debris and smoke into the air that it would block life-giving sunlight from our atmosphere, causing a "nuclear winter." Their eloquent warnings here in Oslo helped galvanize the world's resolve to halt the nuclear arms race.

Now science is warning us that if we do not quickly reduce the global warming pollution that is trapping so much of the heat our planet normally radiates back out of the atmosphere, we are in danger of creating a permanent "carbon summer."

As the American poet Robert Frost wrote, "Some say the world will end in fire; some say in ice." Either, he notes, "would suffice."

But neither need be our fate. It is time to make peace with the planet.

We must quickly mobilize our civilization with the urgency and resolve that has previously been seen only when nations mobilized for war. These prior struggles for survival were won when leaders found words at the eleventh hour that released a mighty surge of courage, hope, and readiness to sacrifice for a protracted and mortal challenge.

These were not comforting and misleading assurances that the threat was not real or imminent;

that it would affect others but not ourselves; that ordinary life might be lived even in the presence of extraordinary threat; that Providence could be trusted to do for us what we would not do for ourselves.

No, these were calls to come to the defense of the common future. They were calls upon the courage, generosity, and strength of entire peoples, citizens of every class and condition who were ready to stand against the threat once asked to do so. Our enemies in those times calculated that free people would not rise to the challenge; they were, of course, catastrophically wrong.

Now comes the threat of climate crisis—a threat that is real, rising, imminent, and universal. Once again, it is the eleventh hour. The penalties for ignoring this challenge are immense and growing, and at some near point would be unsustainable and unrecoverable. For now, we still have the power to choose our fate, and the remaining question is only this: Have we the will to act vigorously and in time, or will we remain imprisoned by a dangerous illusion?

Mahatma Gandhi awakened the largest democracy on earth and forged a shared resolve with what he called "Satyagraha"—or "truth force."

In every land, the truth—once known—has the power to set us free.

Truth also has the power to unite us and bridge the distance between "me" and "we," creating the basis for common effort and shared responsibility.

There is an African proverb that says, "If you want to go quickly, go alone. If you want to go far, go together." We need to go far, quickly.

We must abandon the conceit that individual, isolated, private actions are the answer. They can and do help. But they will not take us far enough without collective action. At the same time, we must ensure that in mobilizing globally, we do not invite the establishment of ideological conformity and a new lockstep "ism."

That means adopting principles, values, laws, and treaties that release creativity and initiative at every level of society in multifold responses originating concurrently and spontaneously.

This new consciousness requires expanding the possibilities inherent in all humanity. The innovators who will devise a new way to harness the sun's energy for pennies or invent an engine that's carbon negative may live in Lagos or Mumbai or Montevideo. We must ensure that entrepreneurs and inventors everywhere on the globe have the chance to change the world.

When we unite for a moral purpose that is manifestly good and true, the spiritual energy unleashed can transform us. The generation that defeated fascism throughout the world in the 1940s found, in rising to meet their awesome challenge, that they had gained the moral authority and long-term vision to launch the Marshall Plan, the United Nations, and a new level of global cooperation and foresight that unified Europe and facilitated the emergence of democracy and prosperity in Germany, Japan, Italy, and much of the world. One of their visionary leaders said, "It is time we steered by the stars and not by the lights of every passing ship."

In the last year of that war, you gave the Peace Prize to a man from my hometown of two thousand people, Carthage, Tennessee. Cordell Hull was described by Franklin Roosevelt as the "Father of the United Nations." He was an inspiration and hero to my own father, who followed Hull in the Congress and the U.S. Senate and in his commitment to world peace and global cooperation.

My parents spoke often of Hull, always in tones of reverence and admiration. Eight weeks ago, when you announced this prize, the deepest emotion I felt was when I saw the headline in my hometown paper that simply noted I had won the same prize that Cordell Hull had won. In that moment, I knew what my father and mother would have felt were they alive.

Just as Hull's generation found moral authority in rising to solve the world crisis caused by fascism, so too can we find our greatest opportunity in rising to solve the climate crisis. In the Kanji characters used in both Chinese and Japanese, "crisis" is written with two symbols, the first meaning "danger," the second "opportunity." By facing and removing the danger of the climate crisis, we have the opportunity to gain the moral authority and vision to vastly increase our own capacity to solve other crises that have been too long ignored.

We must understand the connections between the climate crisis and the afflictions of poverty, hunger, HIV-AIDS, and other pandemics. As these problems are linked, so too must be their solutions. We must begin by making the common rescue of the global environment the central organizing principle of the world community.

Fifteen years ago, I made that case at the "Earth Summit" in Rio de Janeiro. Ten years ago, I presented it in Kyoto. This week, I will urge the delegates in Bali to adopt a bold mandate for a treaty that establishes a universal global cap on emissions and uses the market in emissions trading to efficiently allocate resources to the most effective opportunities for speedy reductions.

This treaty should be ratified and brought into effect everywhere in the world by the beginning of 2010—two years sooner than presently contemplated. The pace of our response must be accelerated to match the accelerating pace of the crisis itself.

Heads of state should meet early next year to review what was accomplished in Bali and take personal responsibility for addressing this crisis. It is not unreasonable to ask, given the gravity of our circumstances, that these heads of state meet every three months until the treaty is completed.

We also need a moratorium on the construction of any new generating facility that burns coal without the capacity to safely trap and store carbon dioxide.

And most important of all, we need to put a price on carbon—with a CO_2 tax that is then rebated back to the people, progressively, according to the laws of each nation, in ways that shift the burden of taxation from employment to pollution. This is by far the most effective and simplest way to accelerate solutions to this crisis.

The world needs an alliance—especially of those nations that weigh heaviest in the scales where earth is in the balance. I salute Europe and Japan for the steps they've taken in recent years to meet the challenge, and the new government in Australia, which has made solving the climate crisis its first priority.

But the outcome will be decisively influenced by two nations that are now failing to do enough: the United States and China. While India is also growing fast in importance, it should be absolutely clear that it is the two largest CO_2 emitters—most of all, my own country—that will need to make the boldest moves, or stand accountable before history for their failure to act.

Both countries should stop using the other's behavior as an excuse for stalemate and instead develop an agenda for mutual survival in a shared global environment.

These are the last few years of decision, but they can be the first years of a bright and hopeful future if we do what we must. No one should believe a solution will be found without effort, without cost, without change. Let us acknowledge that if we wish to redeem squandered time and speak again with moral authority, then these are the hard truths:

The way ahead is difficult. The outer boundary of what we currently believe is feasible is still far short of what we actually must do. Moreover, between here and there, across the unknown, falls the shadow.

That is just another way of saying that we have to expand the boundaries of what is possible. In the words of the Spanish poet Antonio Machado, "Path-walker, there is no path. You must make the path as you walk."

We are standing at the most fateful fork in that path. So I want to end as I began, with a vision of two futures—each a palpable possibility—and with a prayer that we will see with vivid clarity the necessity of choosing between those two futures, and the urgency of making the right choice now.

The great Norwegian playwright Henrik Ibsen wrote, "One of these days, the younger generation will come knocking at my door."

The future is knocking at our door right now. Make no mistake, the next generation will ask us one of two questions. Either they will ask, "What were you thinking; why didn't you act?"

Or they will ask instead, "How did you find the moral courage to rise and successfully resolve a crisis that so many said was impossible to solve?"

We have everything we need to get started, save perhaps political will, but political will is a renewable resource.

So let us renew it, and say together, "We have a purpose. We are many. For this purpose we will rise, and we will act."

P. Freire

THE PEDAGOGY OF THE OPPRESSED

Peace implies a state of satisfaction. But it is very difficult to be satisfied when denied basics such as food, clothing, shelter, education, medical care, and hope. Not surprisingly, therefore, there is little peace in a world characterized by painful differences between the rich and poor, between the haves and the have-nots. Poverty and social oppression may not lead directly to war, but they certainly are not conducive to peace. Indeed, a substantial motivation for military expenditures may well be concern on the part of the "haves" with preventing any fundamental reorganization in the worldwide distribution of power and wealth.

And yet, fundamental changes have begun. With the end of the Cold War, the primary division among the world's inhabitants has shifted from an East-West to a North-South axis. The search for peace must therefore include a search for economic and social betterment.

Measured by life expectancy, calories consumed, years of education, per capita gross domestic product, and so forth, there are extraordinary disparities in wealth, both within and between countries. Especially in so-called third world countries, grinding poverty is persistent, degrading, miserable, life shortening, life threatening, and life denying. Although "development" has long been the preferred solution for poverty among Western elites, others have criticized such approaches as mere masks for continued oppression. Thus, "dependencia" theory—based on the Spanish word for "dependency"—suggests that indigenous peoples and resources are simply being exploited by the wealthier, industrialized states of the North and that poor people and poor countries are not so much underdeveloped as overexploited, such that poverty results not from neglect but from altogether too much attention! Dependencia theorists point out, for example, that Indonesia, Brazil, and Sudan are rich; only their people are poor.

Poverty is fundamental to the appeal long exerted by communism. Once again, however, our focus is less on specific, ideological proposals than on understanding some of the background issues. One of the most stimulating (and radical) approaches to the issue of poverty is found in the work of revolutionary Brazilian educator and social theorist Paulo Freire, who has long been concerned with those who are oppressed. Freire explores how to break down the wall between the oppressed and their oppressors, between theory and practice, between teacher and those taught—to achieve true "dialogue," with the goal of moving toward a more egalitarian society.

While the problem of humanization has always, from an axiological point of view, been humankind's central problem, it now takes on the character of an inescapable concern.[1] Concern for humanization leads at once to the recognition of dehumanization, not only as an ontological possibility but as an historical reality. And as an individual perceives the extent of dehumanization, he or she may ask if humanization is a viable possibility. Within history, in concrete, objective contexts, both humanization and dehumanization are possibilities for a person as an uncompleted being conscious of their incompletion.

But while both humanization and dehumanization are real alternatives, only the first is the people's vocation. This vocation is constantly negated, yet it is affirmed by that very negation. It is thwarted by injustice, exploitation, oppression, and the violence of the oppressors; it is affirmed by the yearning of the oppressed for freedom and justice, and by their struggle to recover their lost humanity.

Dehumanization, which marks not only those whose humanity has been stolen, but also (though in a different way) those who have stolen it, is a *distortion* of the vocation of becoming more fully human. This distortion occurs within history; but it is not an historical vocation. Indeed, to admit of dehumanization as an historical vocation would lead either to cynicism or total despair. The struggle for humanization, for the emancipation of labor, for the overcoming of alienation, for the affirmation of men and women as persons would be meaningless. This struggle is possible only because dehumanization, although a concrete historical fact, is *not* a given destiny but the result of an unjust order that engenders violence in the oppressors, which in turn dehumanizes the oppressed.

Because it is a distortion of being more fully human, sooner or later being less human leads the oppressed to struggle against those who made them so. In order for this struggle to have meaning, the oppressed must not, in seeking to regain their humanity (which is a way to create it), become in turn oppressors of the oppressors, but rather restorers of the humanity of both.

This, then, is the great humanistic and historical task of the oppressed: to liberate themselves and their oppressors as well. The oppressors, who oppress, exploit, and rape by virtue of their power, cannot find in this power the strength to liberate either the oppressed or themselves. Only power that springs from the weakness of the oppressed will be sufficiently strong to free both. Any attempt to "soften" the power of the oppressor in deference to the weakness of the oppressed almost always manifests itself in the form of false generosity; indeed, the attempt never goes beyond this. In order to have the continued opportunity to express their "generosity," the oppressors must perpetuate injustice as well. An unjust social order is the permanent fount of this "generosity," which is nourished by death, despair, and poverty. That is why the dispensers of false generosity become desperate at the slightest threat to its source.

True generosity consists precisely in fighting to destroy the causes which nourish false charity. False charity constrains the fearful and subdued, the "rejects of life," to extend their trembling hands. True generosity lies in striving so that these hands—whether of individuals or entire peoples—need be extended less and less in supplication, so that more and more they become human hands which work and, working, transform the world.

This lesson and this apprenticeship must come, however, from the oppressed themselves and from those who are truly in solidarity with them. As individuals or as peoples, by fighting for the restoration

---

[1] The current movements of rebellion, especially those of youth, while they necessarily reflect the peculiarities of their respective settings, manifest in their essence this preoccupation with people as beings in the world and with the world—preoccupation with *what* and *how* they are "being." As they place consumer civilization in judgment, denounce bureaucracies of all types, demand the transformation of the universities (changing the rigid nature of the teacher-student relationship and placing that relationship within the context of reality), propose the transformation of reality itself so that universities can be renewed, attack old orders and established institutions in the attempt to affirm human beings as the Subjects of decision, all these movements reflect the style of our age, which is more anthropological than anthropocentric.

of their humanity they will be attempting the restoration of true generosity. Who is better prepared than the oppressed to understand the terrible significance of an oppressive society? Who suffers the effects of oppression more than the oppressed? Who can better understand the necessity of liberation? They will not gain this liberation by chance but through the praxis of their quest for it, through their recognition of the necessity to fight for it. And this fight, because of the purpose given it by the oppressed, will actually constitute an act of love opposing the lovelessness which lies at the heart of the oppressors' violence, lovelessness even when clothed in false generosity.

But almost always, during the initial stage of the struggle, the oppressed, instead of striving for liberation, tend themselves to become oppressors, or "sub-oppressors." The very structure of their thought has been conditioned by the contradictions of the concrete, existential situation by which they were shaped. Their ideal is to be men; but for them, to be men is to be oppressors. This is their model of humanity. This phenomenon derives from the fact that the oppressed, at a certain moment of their existential experience, adopt an attitude of "adhesion" to the oppressor. Under these circumstances they cannot "consider" him sufficiently clearly to objectivize him—to discover him "outside" themselves. This does not necessarily mean that the oppressed are unaware that they are downtrodden. But their perception of themselves as oppressed is impaired by their submersion in the reality of oppression. At this level, their perception of themselves as opposites of the oppressor does not yet signify engagement in a struggle to overcome the contradiction;[2] the one pole aspires not to liberation, but to identification with its opposite pole.

In this situation the oppressed do not see the "new man" as the person to be born from the resolution of this contradiction, as oppression gives way to liberation. For them, the new man and woman themselves become oppressors. Their vision of the new man or woman is individualistic; because of their identification with the oppressor, they have no consciousness of themselves as persons or as members of an oppressed class. It is not to become free that they want agrarian reform, but in order to acquire land and thus become landowners—or, more precisely, bosses over other workers. It is a rare peasant who, once "promoted" to overseer, does not become more of a tyrant toward his former comrades than the owner himself. This is because the context of the peasant's situation, that is, oppression, remains unchanged. In this example, the overseer, in order to make sure of his job, must be as tough as the owner—and more so. Thus is illustrated our previous assertion that during the initial stage of their struggle the oppressed find in the oppressor their model of "manhood."

Even revolution, which transforms a concrete situation of oppression by establishing the process of liberation, must confront this phenomenon. Many of the oppressed who directly or indirectly participate in revolution intend—conditioned by the myths of the old order—to make it their private revolution. The shadow of their former oppressor is still cast over them.

The "fear of freedom" which afflicts the oppressed,[3] a fear which may equally well lead them to desire the role of oppressor or bind them to the role of oppressed, should be examined. One of the basic elements of the relationship between oppressor and oppressed is *prescription*. Every prescription represents the imposition of one individual's choice upon another, transforming the consciousness of the person prescribed to into one that conforms with the prescriber's consciousness. Thus, the behavior of the oppressed is a prescribed behavior, following as it does the guidelines of the oppressor.

The oppressed, having internalized the image of the oppressor and adopted his guidelines, are fearful of freedom. Freedom would require them to eject this image and replace it with autonomy and responsibility. Freedom is acquired by conquest, not by gift. It must be pursued constantly and responsibly. Freedom is not an ideal located outside of man; nor is it an idea which becomes myth. It is rather

---

[2] The term "contradiction" denotes the dialectical conflict between opposing social forces.—Translator's note.

[3] This fear of freedom is also to be found in the oppressors, though, obviously, in a different form. The oppressed are afraid to embrace freedom; the oppressors are afraid of losing the "freedom" to oppress.

the indispensable condition for the quest for human completion.

To surmount the situation of oppression, people must first critically recognize its causes, so that through transforming action they can create a new situation, one which makes possible the pursuit of a fuller humanity. But the struggle to be more fully human has already begun in the authentic struggle to transform the situation. Although the situation of oppression is a dehumanized and dehumanizing totality affecting both the oppressors and those whom they oppress, it is the latter who must, from their stifled humanity, wage for both the struggle for a fuller humanity; the oppressor, who is himself dehumanized because he dehumanizes others, is unable to lead this struggle.

However, the oppressed, who have adapted to the structure of domination in which they are immersed, and have become resigned to it, are inhibited from waging the struggle for freedom so long as they feel incapable of running the risks it requires. Moreover, their struggle for freedom threatens not only the oppressor, but also their own oppressed comrades who are fearful of still greater repression. When they discover within themselves the yearning to be free, they perceive that this yearning can be transformed into reality only when the same yearning is aroused in their comrades. But while dominated by the fear of freedom they refuse to appeal to others, or to listen to the appeals of others, or even to the appeals of their own conscience. They prefer gregariousness to authentic comradeship; they prefer the security of conformity with their state of unfreedom to the creative communion produced by freedom and even the very pursuit of freedom.

The oppressed suffer from the duality which has established itself in their innermost being. They discover that without freedom they cannot exist authentically. Yet, although they desire authentic existence, they fear it. They are at one and the same time themselves and the oppressor whose consciousness they have internalized. The conflict lies in the choice between being wholly themselves or being divided; between ejecting the oppressor within or not ejecting them; between human solidarity or alienation; between following prescriptions or having choices; between being spectators or actors; between acting or having the illusion of acting through the action of the oppressors; between speaking out or being silent, castrated in their power to create and re-create, in their power to transform the world. This is the tragic dilemma of the oppressed which their education must take into account....

The central problem is this: How can the oppressed, as divided, unauthentic beings, participate in developing the pedagogy of their liberation? Only as they discover themselves to be "hosts" of the oppressor can they contribute to the midwifery of their liberating pedagogy. As long as they live in the duality in which *to be* is *to be like,* and *to be like* is *to be like the oppressor,* this contribution is impossible. The pedagogy of the oppressed is an instrument for their critical discovery that both they and their oppressors are manifestations of dehumanization....

Any situation in which "A" objectively exploits "B" or hinders his or her pursuit of self-affirmation as a responsible person is one of oppression. Such a situation in itself constitutes violence, even when sweetened by false generosity, because it interferes with the individual's ontological and historical vocation to be more fully human. With the establishment of a relationship of oppression, violence has *already* begun. Never in history has violence been initiated by the oppressed. How could they be the initiators, if they themselves are the result of violence? How could they be the sponsors of something whose objective inauguration called forth their existence as oppressed? There would be no oppressed had there been no prior situation of violence to establish their subjugation.

Violence is initiated by those who oppress, who exploit, who fail to recognize others as persons—not by those who are oppressed, exploited, and unrecognized. It is not the unloved who initiate disaffection, but those who cannot love because they love only themselves. It is not the helpless, subject to terror, who initiate terror, but the violent, who with their power create the concrete situation which begets the "rejects of life." It is not the tyrannized who initiate despotism, but the tyrants. It is not the despised who initiate hatred, but those who despise. It is not those whose humanity is denied them who negate humankind, but those who denied that humanity (thus negating their own as well). Force is used not by those who have become weak under the preponderance of the strong, but by the strong who have emasculated them.

For the oppressors, however, it is always the oppressed (whom they obviously never call "the oppressed" but—depending on whether they are fellow countrymen or not—"those people" or "the blind and envious masses" or "savages" or "natives" or "subversives") who are disaffected, who are "violent," "barbaric," "wicked," or "ferocious" when they react to the violence of the oppressors.

Yet it is—paradoxical though it may seem—precisely in the response of the oppressed to the violence of their oppressors that a gesture of love may be found. Consciously or unconsciously, the act of rebellion by the oppressed (an act which is always, or nearly always, as violent as the initial violence of the oppressors) can initiate love. Whereas the violence of the oppressors prevents the oppressed from being fully human, the response of the latter to this violence is grounded in the desire to pursue the right to be human. As the oppressors dehumanize others and violate their rights, they themselves also become dehumanized. As the oppressed, fighting to be human, take away the oppressors' power to dominate and suppress, they restore to the oppressors the humanity they had lost in the exercise of oppression.

It is only the oppressed who, by freeing themselves, can free their oppressors. The latter, as an oppressive class, can free neither others nor themselves. It is therefore essential that the oppressed wage the struggle to resolve the contradiction in which they are caught; and the contradiction will be resolved by the appearance of the new man: neither oppressor nor oppressed, but man in the process of liberation. If the goal of the oppressed is to become fully human, they will not achieve their goal by merely reversing the terms of the contradiction, by simply changing poles.

…An act is oppressive only when it prevents people from being more fully human. Accordingly, these necessary restraints do not *in themselves* signify that yesterday's oppressed have become today's oppressors. Acts which prevent the restoration of the oppressive regime cannot be compared with those which create and maintain it, cannot be compared

with those by which a few men and women deny the majority their right to be human.

However, the moment the new regime hardens into a dominating "bureaucracy" the humanist dimension of the struggle is lost and it is no longer possible to speak of liberation. Hence our insistence that the authentic solution of the oppressor-oppressed contradiction does not lie in a mere reversal of position, in moving from one pole to the other. Nor does it lie in the replacement of the former oppressors with new ones who continue to subjugate the oppressed—all in the name of their liberation....

A careful analysis of the teacher-student relationship at any level, inside or outside the school, reveals its fundamentally *narrative* character. This relationship involves a narrating Subject (the teacher) and patient, listening objects (the students). The contents, whether values or empirical dimensions of reality, tend in the process of being narrated to become lifeless and petrified. Education is suffering from narration sickness.

The teacher talks about reality as if it were motionless, static, compartmentalized, and predictable. Or else he expounds on a topic completely alien to the existential experience of the students. His task is to "fill" the students with the contents of his narration—contents which are detached from reality, disconnected from the totality that engendered them and could give them significance. Words are emptied of their concreteness and become a hollow, alienated, and alienating verbosity.

The outstanding characteristic of this narrative education, then, is the sonority of words, not their transforming power. "Four times four is sixteen; the capital of Pará is Belém." The student records, memorizes, and repeats these phrases without perceiving what four times four really means, or realizing the true significance of "capital" in the affirmation "the capital of Pará is Belém," that is, what Belém means for Pará and what Pará means for Brazil.

Narration (with the teacher as narrator) leads the students to memorize mechanically the narrated content. Worse yet, it turns them into "containers," into "receptacles" to be "filled" by the teacher. The more completely she fills the receptacles, the better a teacher she is. The more meekly the receptacles permit themselves to be filled, the better students they are.

Education thus becomes an act of depositing, in which the students are the depositories and the teacher is the depositor. Instead of communicating, the teacher issues communiqués and makes deposits which the students patiently receive, memorize, and repeat. This is the "banking" concept of education, in which the scope of action allowed to the students extends only as far as receiving, filing, and storing the deposits. They do, it is true, have the opportunity to become collectors or cataloguers of the things they store. But in the last analysis, it is the people themselves who are filed away through the lack of creativity, transformation, and knowledge in this (at best) misguided system. For apart from inquiry, apart from the praxis, individuals cannot be truly human. Knowledge emerges only through invention and re-invention, through the restless, impatient, continuing, hopeful inquiry human beings pursue in the world, with the world, and with each other.

In the banking concept of education, knowledge is a gift bestowed by those who consider themselves knowledgeable upon those whom they consider to know nothing. Projecting an absolute ignorance onto others, a characteristic of the ideology of oppression, negates education and knowledge as processes of inquiry. The teacher presents himself to his students as their necessary opposite; by considering their ignorance absolute, he justifies his own existence. The students, alienated like the slave in the Hegelian dialectic, accept their ignorance as justifying the teacher's existence—but, unlike the slave, they never discover that they educate the teacher.

The *raison d'être* of libertarian education, on the other hand, lies in its drive toward reconciliation. Education must begin with the solution of the teacher-student contradiction, by reconciling the poles of the contradiction so that both are simultaneously teachers *and* students....

Dialogue cannot exist,...in the absence of a profound love for the world and for people. The naming of the world, which is an act of creation and re-creation, is not possible if it is not infused with love. Love is at the same time the foundation of dialogue and dialogue itself. It is thus necessarily the task of responsible Subjects and cannot exist in a relation of domination. Domination reveals the pathology of love: sadism in the dominator and masochism in the dominated. Because love is an act of courage, not of fear, love is commitment to others. No matter where the oppressed are found, the act of love is commitment to their cause—the cause of liberation. And this commitment, because it is loving, is dialogical. As an act of bravery, love cannot be sentimental; as an act of freedom, it must not serve as a pretext for manipulation. It must generate other acts of freedom; otherwise, it is not love. Only by abolishing the situation of oppression is it possible to restore the love which that situation made impossible. If I do not love the world—if I do not love life—if I do not love people—I cannot enter into dialogue.

On the other hand, dialogue cannot exist without humility. The naming of the world, through which people constantly re-create that world, cannot be an act of arrogance. Dialogue, as the encounter of those addressed to the common task of learning and acting, is broken if the parties (or one of them) lack humility. How can I dialogue if I always project ignorance onto others and never perceive my own? How can I dialogue if I regard myself as a case apart from others—mere "its" in whom I cannot recognize other "I"s? How can I dialogue if I consider myself a member of the in-group of "pure" men, the owners of truth and knowledge, for whom all non-members are "these people" or "the great unwashed"? How can I dialogue if I start from the premise that naming the world is the task of an elite and that the presence of the people in history is a sign of deterioration, thus to be avoided? How can I dialogue if I am closed to—and even offended by—the contribution of others? How can I dialogue if I am afraid of being displaced, the mere possibility causing me torment and weakness? Self-sufficiency is incompatible with dialogue. Men and women who lack humility (or have lost it) cannot come to the people, cannot be their partners in naming the world. Someone who cannot acknowledge himself to be as mortal as everyone else still has a long way to go before he can reach the point of encounter. At the point of encounter there are neither utter ignoramuses nor perfect sages; there are only people who are attempting, together, to learn more than they now know.

Dialogue further requires an intense faith in humankind, faith in their power to make and remake, to create and re-create, faith in their vocation to be more fully human (which is not the privilege of an elite, but the birthright of all). Faith in people is an *a priori* requirement for dialogue; the "dialogical man" believes in others even before he meets them face-to-face. His faith, however, is not naïve. The "dialogical man" is critical and knows that although it is within the power of humans to create and transform, in a concrete situation of alienation individuals may be impaired in the use of that power. Far from destroying his faith in the people, however, this possibility strikes him as a challenge to which he must respond. He is convinced that the power to create and transform, even when thwarted in concrete situations, tends to be reborn. And that rebirth can occur—not gratuitously, but in and through the struggle for liberation—in the supersedence of slave labor by emancipated labor which gives zest to life. Without this faith in people, dialogue is a farce which inevitably degenerates into paternalistic manipulation.

Founding itself upon love, humility, and faith, dialogue becomes a horizontal relationship of which mutual trust between the dialoguers is the logical consequence. It would be a contradiction in terms if dialogue—loving, humble, and full of faith—did not produce this climate of mutual trust, which leads the dialoguers into ever closer partnership in the naming of the world. Conversely, such trust is obviously absent in the anti-dialogics of the banking method of education. Whereas faith in humankind is an *a priori* requirement for dialogue, trust is established by dialogue. Should it founder, it will be seen that the preconditions were lacking. False love, false humility, and feeble faith in others cannot create trust. Trust is contingent on the evidence which one party provides the others of his true, concrete intentions; it cannot exist if that party's words do not coincide with their actions. To say one thing and do another—to take one's own word lightly—cannot inspire trust. To glorify democracy and to silence the people is a farce; to discourse on humanism and to negate people is a lie.

Nor yet can dialogue exist without hope. Hope is rooted in men's incompletion, from which they move out in constant search—a search which can be carried out only in communion with others. Hopelessness is a form of silence, of denying the world and fleeing from it. The dehumanization resulting from an unjust order is not a cause for despair but for hope, leading to the incessant pursuit of the humanity denied by injustice. Hope, however, does not consist in crossing one's arms and waiting. As long as I fight, I am moved by hope; and if I fight with hope, then I can wait.

Jeffrey Sachs

GLOBAL ECONOMIC SOLIDARITY

Poverty persists as an underlying cause as well as effect of structural violence. It also lurks behind much of the world's overt violence and is, in any event, a constant rebuke to any conception of human dignity and positive peace. Although the world as a whole is, in a sense, wealthy, great disparities exist, and in some places, those disparities have been increasing. Many factors contribute to this, including (but not limited to) population pressure, environmental degradation, governmental corruption, traditions of helplessness and hopelessness, and exploitation by local socioeconomic systems as well as by foreign countries and multinational corporations.

The struggle against world poverty and economic injustice is intimately connected with efforts toward positive peace and has been undertaken not only by nongovernmental organizations but also by increasing numbers of prominent economists. Among them, one of the most effective and influential is Jeffrey Sachs. Here is an excerpt from a lecture by Professor Sachs.

The end of poverty—by the year 2025. It's seems like an outlandish claim, an impossible dream. But it's within reach. It is a scientifically sound objective. And it is the most urgent challenge of our generation.

In fact, if we in the rich world fail to take up this challenge, we will imperil ourselves and the world. A crowded world, one that is "bursting at the seams," cannot afford to leave millions to die each year of extreme poverty without imperiling all the rest.

John F. Kennedy...put it this way in his inaugural address in 1961:

> To those peoples in the huts and villages across the globe struggling to break the bonds of mass misery, we pledge our best efforts to help them help themselves, for whatever period is required—not because the Communists may be doing it, not because we seek their votes, but because it is right. If a free society cannot help the many who are poor, it cannot save the few who are rich.

In my last lecture, in New York, I talked about war and peace and about our extremely dangerous tendency to define the world as "us versus them." Because of that tendency, war can erupt as a self-fulfilling prophecy of conflict between mutually suspicious groups.

...War can...erupt as a result of the collapse of an impoverished society, one suffering the scourges of drought, hunger, lack of jobs, and lack of hope. Ending poverty is therefore a basic matter of our own security.

Darfur, Somalia, Afghanistan. These are all, at their core, wars of extreme poverty. So too, quite obviously, were the recent wars of Liberia, Sierra Leone, Haiti, and many others. The U.S. has just established a new military command in Africa, declaring Africa to pose new security threats to the U.S. But even as the U.S. spends more than $600 billion on the military, and even as U.S. counterinsurgency forces spread out across the impoverished stretches of the Sahel, the U.S. will never achieve peace if it continues to spend less than one hundredth of the military budget on Africa's economic development. An army can never pacify a hungry, disease-ridden, and impoverished population.

We need to understand the challenge of extreme poverty not only as a matter of ethics and politics, but also as a matter of science. We can and must achieve a much clearer understanding of how to end poverty, based on the best scientific evidence. We have powerful technologies that can be mobilized, and which can make a remarkable difference at a remarkable speed.

We can usefully start our diagnosis by understanding the progress that has been made. When John Kennedy spoke of the bonds of mass misery in 1961, close to half the planet was in extreme poverty, measured by the traditional standard of living of $1 per day or less. Today, the proportion of the world's population in extreme poverty is down to around one-sixth, approximately 1 billion of the world's 6.6 billion people. The absolute numbers of the poor are declining, and their proportion is declining even faster. Globalization has, on balance, helped the poor, especially in Asia, where economic growth and poverty reduction are proceeding at historically unprecedented rates. We have the wind in our sails, since world markets give a powerful impetus to the spread of technologies and the rise of income. Once countries get on to the ladder of development—exporting manufactures and services in world markets, and linked to the world in networks of production, trade, finance, and technology—they tend to make continued progress up the ladder. Market forces, based on saving, investment, trade, and technological advance take hold. The crisis of extreme poverty is centered in those regions not yet on the development ladder, stuck in extreme poverty and hunger, with only the weakest of links to global production—through primary agricultural goods and mineral resources.

Poverty is not yet declining in tropical Africa and a few other places. Africa has not so much been harmed by globalization, as bypassed by it. The basic challenge is to help Africa and other still-impoverished regions onto the development ladder.

Consider some recent data, this time using the metrics of life and death rather than dollars. Life expectancy at birth is probably the best single indicator of overall human well-being that we have. Life expectancy is not only a crucially important goal in its own right, but is also an excellent indicator of overall social organization—for example, the quality of the health system, the presence or absence of war, the reach of infrastructure, and the extent of food insecurity. Life expectancy at birth is also relatively easy to measure and to compare across countries.

The worldwide improvements in life expectancy on the planet have been dramatic. In 1960, 105 countries, with two-thirds of the world's population, had a life expectancy at birth of less than 60 years. By 2004, that list had shrunk to only 47 countries, with a mere 12 percent of the world's population. And virtually all of those 47 countries are in Africa (with the exceptions being Afghanistan, Cambodia, Haiti, Laos, and Papua New Guinea).

Why does Africa lag? Here is where the scientific evidence on extreme poverty is vital. The overwhelming nonscientific assumption held in our societies is that Africa suffers mainly from the corruption and mismanagement of its leaders. With the viciousness and despotism of Robert Mugabe in Zimbabwe, it's an understandable view. Yet this seemingly self-evident view is wrong as a generalization. Zimbabwe may get the headlines, but there are many countries in Africa, like Tanzania and Mozambique just nearby, that have talented and freely elected governments struggling against poverty. But they too face great obstacles, and their people too continue to suffer from extreme deprivation.

Consider the fact that nine developing countries—with two in Africa—were tied with exactly the same corruption score in this year's Transparency International index. Specifically, Ghana and Senegal were assessed to be at the same level of corruption as Brazil, China, Egypt, India, Mexico, Peru, and Saudi Arabia. Yet the two African countries have life expectancies of around fifty-six years, while all but one of the other countries have life expectancies of more than seventy years. On average, for countries with comparable corruption levels, Africa's life expectancy rates are nearly twenty years below the rest of the world's.

Africa's problems are not due mainly to corruption, but to its ecology, history, weak infrastructure, and burgeoning population growth. Moreover, once those underlying sources of extreme poverty and disease are scientifically identified, we can also identify the practical technologies and strategies needed to solve these problems, and thereby enable Africa like the rest of the world to break free of the poverty trap.

Africa, compared with other poor regions of the world, suffers from four enormous burdens, all of which are solvable with proven and relatively low-cost technologies.

The first is low food production. Africa is a hungry continent, with grain yields roughly one-third of other developing regions of the planet. Part of the problem is Africa's age-old dependence on rain-fed agriculture in a savanna climate, where the risks of drought are ever present. Sub-Saharan Africa lacks the river-based irrigation systems of South and East Asia. Another urgent problem with Africa's agriculture is that Africa's soils have been depleted of nutrients because impoverished farmers have been unable to afford fertilizers to replenish their soils. Older techniques for replenishing soil nutrients, such as the rotation of farmlands, allowing the replenishment of nutrients on land left fallow for ten or twenty years, are no longer feasible. Rising land scarcity because of Africa's burgeoning population means that scarce arable land can no longer be left fallow even for one year, much less a generation.

The second challenge is Africa's disease ecology, which leads to uniquely high burdens of tropical diseases, especially malaria. This again is a matter of ecology. Africa has a climate and species of disease vectors that contribute to its unique burden of tropical infectious diseases. These are controllable, but at much greater effort than is needed in other parts of the world.

The third challenge is Africa's miserably deficient infrastructure, with the world's poorest network of roads, power, rail, and fiber-optic cables for Internet. For many historical and geographical reasons, Africa's colonial powers did not build the roads, rail, and power grids that they did in other parts of the world.

The fourth challenge is the continuing surge of population, in which poor families are still having six or more children in rural areas. Fertility rates are still so high in rural Africa that populations are doubling each generation.

These challenges—food production, disease control, weak infrastructure, burgeoning populations—are not caused by corruption but by ecology, by history, and by the vicious cycle of extreme poverty itself. Each of these challenges is susceptible to utterly practical solutions, and in short order, but they require public-sector investments beyond the levels that impoverished African countries can afford.

African countries, in short, face a poverty trap. They can overcome impoverishment through identifiable and proven public investments, but these countries are simply too poor to undertake those investments out of their own resources. Nor are they creditworthy enough to borrow those resources from global capital markets, though these markets can help.

This litany of problems may seem overwhelming. Left alone, they will be. But each is actually solvable, and much more easily than is typically imagined. We've seen what can be done, for example, in our own Millennium Villages, a project that applies proven techniques to these very challenges in villages across a dozen countries of Africa. Here is what can be accomplished.

Powerful technologies, as simple as insecticide-treated bed nets and a new generation of anti-malaria medicines, can control malaria by 90 percent or more. Antiretroviral medicines can make AIDS a chronic rather than fatal disease, and one with reduced stigma and much more chance of prevention. These successes, and many like them, have been accomplished in countless specific projects where donor funds have been made available, but not on a country scale or regional scale.

Current agronomic technologies can triple food production. The key in that case is to get smallholder farms the vital inputs of high-yield seeds, fertilizers, and small-scale water management techniques that can dramatically boost farm yields. Africa can and must have a "green revolution" as India initiated nearly forty years ago. Malawi has started this year, with a program to guarantee vital inputs for the poorest farmers. Food yields have soared in a neighborhood of acute food shortages. And we should certainly remember that India's green revolution also depended on international aid in its early years. Virtually every country has needed a helping hand at some point. It's a rule of life.

Current technologies can extend roads, rail, power, and the Internet even to the most remote regions. A satellite dish, or a mobile phone tower, can end isolation that might have seemed irremediable a generation ago.

The fourth challenge, excessive population growth, is similarly susceptible to practical and proven solutions. Fertility rates in rural Africa are still around six children or more. This is understandable, if disastrous. Poor families are worried about the high rates of child mortality, and compensate by having large families. Poor families lack access to contraception and family planning. Girls often are deprived of even a basic education, because the family cannot afford it, and are instead forced into early marriage rather than encouraged to stay in school. And the value placed on mothers' time is very low, in part because agricultural productivity is itself so low. With few opportunities to earn remunerative income, mothers are pushed—often by their husbands or the community—to have more children.

Yet, as shown by countless countries around the world, fertility rates will fall rapidly, and on a voluntary basis, if an orderly effort is led by government with adequate resources. Investments in child survival, contraceptive availability, schooling of children—especially girls—and higher farm productivity can result in a voluntary decline in total fertility from around six to perhaps three or lower within a single decade. But these things will not happen by themselves. They require resources, which impoverished Africa lacks.

The world has committed, time and again, to help Africa accomplish these development objectives. We are pledged, all countries on the planet, to support the Millennium Development Goals (MDGs), the internationally agreed goals set in the year 2000 to cut poverty, hunger, and disease decisively by the year 2015. We are halfway to 2015, but still far off the mark. Our governments talk, and they even begin to act, but they fail to act with the urgency and decisiveness required by the circumstances, and commensurate with our promises. And the urgency will grow as climate stresses multiply. The longer we wait, the greater is the suffering and the larger are the long-term risks and costs.

Success in the MDGs will require stronger actions on all fronts—by civil society, by businesses, by African governments and communities....But success will also require finance, at a scale that can only be provided by official development assistance by rich country governments. Our governments have long promised to deliver 0.7 percent of rich-world GNP as official aid, but so far have consistently failed to do so.

The situation is absurd in many ways—at least 10 million people dying each year because the rich world refuses to spend 0.7 percent of GNP on aid! For Africa specifically, we would need around $70 billion per year to enable Africa to get onto the ladder of development. That's $70 per person per year from each of us in the rich countries. It's about 0.2 per cent of our annual income. It's well under the annual cost of the Iraq War. Indeed, it's about 2 percent of the estimated wealth of the world's 1,000 billionaires. And consider that Wall Street and the City of London together took home Christmas bonuses of some $40 billion this past holiday season.

The deep question is why the rich countries, with so much wealth, are so irresponsibly and relentlessly neglectful, when the amounts needed are so small and the consequences of inaction are so catastrophic for all. Is this the fate of modern societies? Are our politicians inevitably distracted by local concerns, or by the illusions of war? Are our populations so jaded and cynical and uncaring as to make this neglect inevitable? The answer, thankfully, is no. Let's not overgeneralize. Several of the world's wealthiest countries do honor their commitments. The key for us is to understand why they do, while the rest do not.

Five countries of Northern Europe have long met the 0.7 percent of GNP commitment. These are Denmark, Luxembourg, the Netherlands, Norway, and Sweden. The European Union has now promised, once again, to do so by 2015. Yet the European Union obviously agonizes in this promise. The U.S. doesn't even agonize. It doesn't even try. The U.S. will spend $600 billion on the military this year, but only $4 billion on African development. Moreover, senior U.S. officials vigorously reject the global standard of 0.7 percent in aid, even though the U.S. government signed on to that international target.

The striking thing about the aid performance is the very strong correlation between a country's international aid and its care for the poor at home. Countries that take care of their own poor also tend to help the world's poor. Countries that neglect their own poor tend to walk away from their international responsibilities as well.

In brief, the social welfare model of Northern Europe helps the poor both at home and abroad. The U.S. model, alas, leaves the poor to suffer their fate, both at home and abroad. Americans, as a result, are fearful of their economic future, as they are left to fend for themselves. They have little time for others. The world is seen as filled with threats, and of "us versus them," rather than with opportunities in an interconnected global society. The Nordic countries, by contrast, have the domestic security of social protection, which they then seek to extend to the world.

The successes of the Nordic system are crucial for us to understand. Many on the political left admire the Nordic social welfare state, as do I. Yet they mistakenly believe that the Nordic countries are somehow antimarket and antiglobalization.

Nothing could be further from the truth. Denmark, Finland, the Netherlands, Norway, and Sweden are all market-based economies, competing fiercely in world markets. They believe in open trade and invest heavily in high technology and in R&D to keep their international competitiveness. But they have discovered that it is possible to combine market efficiency and open trade with strong social services and social protection. They have achieved, in short, a system of "economic solidarity" within a market economy. Rather than compromising their economic well-being, these institutions of economic solidarity have strengthened the market system itself. The Nordic countries have not only eliminated poverty in their midst and achieved the best health outcomes in the world, they have also fostered the confidence to extend such solidarity to the rest of the world.

No doubt, the Nordic successes have depended, in part, on their relatively small size and social homogeneity. Their levels of internal social trust are very high. Migration is putting that social trust under challenge. But even if their social homogeneity is not replicable elsewhere, their social trust can be. Perhaps the key to success, after all, in the twenty-first century will be building trust across ethnic and cultural lines within our own societies, as well as across societies.

We can end poverty, at home and abroad, with the technologies and tools that we have, if we trust each other sufficiently, at home and abroad. As John F. Kennedy said in the context of war and peace, we need not talk about blind trust, a naïve trust, a trust of dreamers or fanatics. We must seek a practical trust, built on specific institutions and specific ways of delivering help for the poor. Our economic solidarity must rely on scientific evidence and rigorous audits as much as on trust. But at the core of such institutions is the trust that we are all in this together, that our fates, economic and otherwise, are shared, and that the defeat of poverty will be a victory of security for all on the planet.

My suggestions on economic solidarity therefore are the following:

First, let us embrace market economics—yes—but also recognize that free-market economics are passé. We need an active role of the state, to help the poorest to break free of the poverty trap, and to help narrow the inequalities of a high-income market society.

Let us understand that economic solidarity is insurance for all, the poor and the rich. Our societies can be both productive and safe. If we invest in solidarity, we will also end up with a more caring society. It's not our poor versus the poor abroad. It is help and solidarity with both.

Let us resolve to honor our commitments in the fight against poverty, hunger, and disease. Our commitments are small compared with our vast wealth, and the benefits will be vast. We have the power to save millions of lives each year, to help slow a burgeoning population growth in the poorest countries, and to reduce, if not end, the conflicts and wars caused by extreme poverty, which threaten peace everywhere. This, truly, is the work of our generation.

Martin Luther King, Jr.

LETTER FROM A BIRMINGHAM JAIL

Martin Luther King, Jr., was especially concerned with racial prejudice and the absence of civil rights for African Americans in the United States. (As time went on, he expanded this focus to include the problems of poverty and the war in Vietnam.) His "Letter from a Birmingham Jail," one of the signal documents of the U.S. civil rights movement, was originally written on the margins of a local newspaper that had published a statement by a number of Georgia ministers denouncing the civil rights campaign in which Reverend King, and many others, had been engaged. This selection could also have been placed in the next chapter on nonviolence. As a passionate and influential call for social justice, it seems equally appropriate to any consideration of positive peace.

My Dear Fellow Clergymen:
...I am in Birmingham because injustice is here. Just as the prophets of the eighth century BC left their villages and carried their "thus saith the Lord" far beyond the boundaries of their home towns, and just as the apostle Paul left his village of Tarsus and carried the gospel of Jesus Christ to the far corners of the Greco-Roman world, so am I compelled to carry the gospel of freedom beyond my own hometown. Like Paul, I must constantly respond to the Macedonian call for aid.

Moreover, I am cognizant of the interrelatedness of all communities and states. I cannot sit idly by in Atlanta and not be concerned about what happens in Birmingham. Injustice anywhere is a threat to justice everywhere. We are caught in an inescapable network of mutuality, tied in a single garment of destiny. Whatever affects one directly affects all indirectly. Never again can we afford to live with the narrow, provincial "outside agitator" idea. Anyone who lives inside the United States can never be considered an outsider anywhere within its bounds.

...You may well ask, "Why direct action? Why sit-ins, marches and so forth? Isn't negotiation a better path?" You are quite right in calling for negotiation. Indeed, this is the very purpose of direct action. Nonviolent direct action seeks to create such a crisis and foster such a tension that a community which has constantly refused to negotiate is forced to confront the issue. It seeks so to dramatize the issue that it can no longer be ignored. My citing the creation of tension as part of the work of the nonviolent-resister may sound rather shocking. But I must confess that I am not afraid of the word "tension." I have earnestly

opposed violent tension, but there is a type of constructive, nonviolent tension which is necessary for growth. Just as Socrates felt that it was necessary to create a tension in the mind so that individuals could rise from the bondage of myths and half-truths to the unfettered realm of creative analysis and objective appraisal, so must we see the need for nonviolent gadflies to create the kind of tension in society that will help men rise from the dark depths of prejudice and racism to the majestic heights of understanding and brotherhood....

Lamentably, it is an historical fact that privileged groups seldom give up their privileges voluntarily. Individuals may see the moral light and voluntarily give up their unjust posture; but, as Reinhold Niebuhr has reminded us, groups tend to be more immoral than individuals.

We know through painful experience that freedom is never voluntarily given by the oppressor; it must be demanded by the oppressed. Frankly, I have yet to engage in a direct-action campaign that was "well timed" in the view of those who have not suffered unduly from the disease of segregation. For years now I have heard the word "Wait!" It rings in the ear of every Negro with piercing familiarity. This "Wait" has almost always meant "Never." We must come to see, with one of our distinguished jurists, that "justice too long delayed is justice denied."

We have waited for more than 340 years for our constitutional and God-given rights. The nations of Asia and Africa are moving with jetlike speed toward gaining political independence, but we still creep at horse-and-buggy pace toward gaining a cup of coffee at a lunch counter. Perhaps it is easy for those who have never felt the stinging darts of segregation to say, "Wait." But when you have seen vicious mobs lynch your mothers and fathers at will and drown your sisters and brothers at whim; when you have seen hate-filled policemen curse, kick, and even kill your black brothers and sisters; when you see the vast majority of your 20 million Negro brothers smothering in an airtight cage of poverty in the midst of an affluent society; when you suddenly find your tongue twisted and your speech stammering as you seek to explain to your six-year-old daughter why she can't go to the public amusement park that has just been advertised on television, and see tears welling up in her eyes when she is told that Funtown is closed to colored children, and see ominous clouds of inferiority beginning to form in her little mental sky, and see her beginning to distort her personality by developing an unconscious bitterness toward white people; when you have to concoct an answer for a five-year-old son who is asking, "Daddy, why do white people treat colored people so mean?"; when you take a cross-country drive and find it necessary to sleep night after night in the uncomfortable corners of your automobile because no motel will accept you; when you are humiliated day in and day out by nagging signs reading "white" and "colored"; when your first name becomes "nigger," your middle name becomes "boy" (however old you are) and your last name becomes "John," and your wife and mother are never given the respected title "Mrs."; when you are harried by day and haunted by night by the fact that you are a Negro, living constantly at tiptoe stance, never quite knowing what to expect next, and are plagued with inner fears and outer resentments; when you are forever fighting a degenerating sense of "nobodiness"—then you will understand why we find it difficult to wait. There comes a time when the cup of endurance runs over, and men are no longer willing to be plunged into the abyss of despair. I hope, sirs, you can understand our legitimate and unavoidable impatience.

You express a great deal of anxiety over our willingness to break laws. This is certainly a legitimate concern. Since we so diligently urge people to obey the Supreme Court's decision of 1954 outlawing segregation in the public schools, at first glance it may seem rather paradoxical for us consciously to break laws. One may well ask, "How can you advocate breaking some laws and obeying others?" The answer lies in the fact that there are two types of laws: just and unjust. I would be the first to advocate obeying just laws. One has not only a legal but a moral responsibility to obey just laws. Conversely, one has a moral responsibility to disobey unjust laws. I would agree with St. Augustine that "an unjust law is no law at all."

Now, what is the difference between the two? How does one determine whether a law is just or unjust? A just law is a man-made code that squares with the moral law or the law of God. An unjust law is a code that is out of harmony with the moral law. To put it in the terms of St. Thomas Aquinas: An unjust law is a human law that is not rooted in eternal law and natural law. Any law that uplifts human personality is just. Any law that degrades human personality is unjust. All segregation statutes are unjust because segregation distorts the soul and damages the personality. It gives the segregator a false sense of superiority and the segregated a false sense of inferiority. Segregation, to use the terminology of the Jewish philosopher Martin Buber, substitutes an "I–it" relationship for an "I–thou" relationship and ends up relegating persons to the status of things. Hence segregation is not only politically, economically, and sociologically unsound, it is morally wrong and sinful. Paul Tillich has said that sin is separation. Is not segregation an existential expression of man's tragic separation, his awful estrangement, his terrible sinfulness? Thus it is that I can urge men to obey the 1954 decision of the Supreme Court, for it is morally right; and I can urge them to disobey segregation ordinances, for they are morally wrong.

Let us consider a more concrete example of just and unjust laws. An unjust law is a code that a numerical or power majority group compels a minority group to obey but does not make binding on itself. This is *difference* made legal. By the same token, a just law is a code that a majority compels a minority to follow and that it is willing to follow itself. This is *sameness* made legal.

Let me give another explanation. A law is unjust if it is inflicted on a minority that, as a result of being denied the right to vote, had no part in enacting or devising the law. Who can say that the legislature of Alabama which set up that state's segregation laws was democratically elected? Throughout Alabama all sorts of devious methods are used to prevent Negroes from becoming registered voters, and there are some counties in which, even though Negroes constitute a majority of the population, not a single Negro is registered. Can any law enacted under such circumstances be considered democratically structured?...

We should never forget that everything Adolf Hitler did in Germany was "legal," and everything the Hungarian freedom fighters did in Hungary was "illegal." It was "illegal" to aid and comfort a Jew in Hitler's Germany. Even so, I am sure that, had I lived in Germany at the time, I would have aided and comforted my Jewish brothers. If today I lived in a Communist country where certain principles dear to the Christian faith are suppressed, I would openly advocate disobeying that country's antireligious laws....

I had hoped that the white moderate would understand that law and order exist for the purpose of establishing justice and that when they fail in this purpose they become the dangerously structured dams that block the flow of social progress. I had hoped that the white moderate would understand that the present tension in the South is a necessary phase of the transition from an obnoxious negative peace, in which the Negro passively accepted his unjust plight, to a substantive and positive peace, in which all men will respect the dignity and worth of human personality. Actually, we who engage in nonviolent direct action are not the creators of tension. We merely bring to the surface the hidden tension that is already alive. We bring it out in the open, where it can be seen and dealt with. Like a boil that can never be cured so long as it is covered up but must be opened with all its ugliness to the natural medicines of air and light, injustice must be exposed, with all the tension its exposure creates, to the light of human conscience and the air of national opinion before it can be cured.

...Human progress never rolls in on wheels of inevitability; it comes through the tireless efforts of men willing to be co-workers with God, and without

this hard work, time itself becomes an ally of the forces of social stagnation. We must use time creatively, in the knowledge that the time is always ripe to do right. Now is the time to make real the promise of democracy and transform our pending national elegy into a creative psalm of brotherhood. Now is the time to lift our national policy from the quicksand of racial injustice to the solid rock of human dignity....

Oppressed people cannot remain oppressed forever. The yearning for freedom eventually manifests itself, and that is what has happened to the American Negro. Something within has reminded him of his birthright of freedom, and something without has reminded him that it can be gained. Consciously or unconsciously, he has been caught up by the *Zeitgeist*, and with his black brothers of Africa and his brown and yellow brothers of Asia, South America, and the Caribbean, the United States Negro is moving with a sense of great urgency toward the promised land of racial justice. If one recognizes this vital urge that has engulfed the Negro community, one should readily understand why public demonstrations are taking place. The Negro has many pent-up resentments and latent frustrations, and he must release them. So let him march; let him make prayer pilgrimages to the city hall; let him go on freedom rides—and try to understand why he must do so. If his repressed emotions are not released in nonviolent ways, they will seek expression through violence; this is not a threat but a fact of history. So I have not said to my people, "Get rid of your discontent." Rather, I have tried to say that this normal and healthy discontent can be channeled into the creative outlet of nonviolent direct action. And now this approach is being termed extremist.

But though I was initially disappointed at being categorized as an extremist, as I continued to think about the matter I gradually gained a measure of satisfaction from the label. Was not Jesus an extremist for love: "Love your enemies, bless them that curse you, do good to them that hate you, and pray for them which despitefully use you, and persecute you." Was not Amos an extremist for justice: "Let justice roll down like waters and righteousness like an ever-flowing stream." Was not Paul an extremist for the Christian gospel: "I bear in my body the marks of the Lord Jesus." Was not Martin Luther an extremist: "Here I stand; I cannot do otherwise, so help me God." And John Bunyan: "I will stay in jail to the end of my days before I make a butchery of my conscience." And Abraham Lincoln: "This nation cannot survive half slave and half free." And Thomas Jefferson: "We hold these truths to be self-evident, that all men are created equal...." So the question is not whether we will be extremists, but what kind of extremists we will be. Will we be extremists for hate or for love? Will we be extremists for the preservation of injustice or for the extension of justice? In that dramatic scene on Calvary's hill three men were crucified. We must never forget that all three were crucified for the same crime—the crime of extremism. Two were extremists for immorality, and thus fell below their environment. The other, Jesus Christ, was an extremist for love, truth and goodness, and thereby rose above his environment. Perhaps the South, the nation, and the world are in dire need of creative extremists.

I had hoped that the white moderate would see this need. Perhaps I was too optimistic; perhaps I expected too much. I suppose I should have realized that few members of the oppressor race can understand the deep groans and passionate yearnings of the oppressed race, and still fewer have the vision to see that injustice must be rooted out by strong, persistent, and determined action. I am thankful, however, that some of our white brothers in the South have grasped the meaning of this social revolution and committed themselves to it.

...I hope the church as a whole will meet the challenge of this decisive hour. But even if the church does not come to the aid of justice, I have no despair about the future. I have no fear about the outcome of our struggle in Birmingham, even if our motives are at present misunderstood. We will reach the goal of freedom in Birmingham and all over the nation, because the goal of America is freedom. Abused and scorned though we may be, our destiny is tied up with America's destiny. Before the pilgrims landed at Plymouth, we were here. Before the pen of Jefferson etched the majestic words of the Declaration of Independence across the pages of history, we were here. For more than two centuries our forebears labored in this country without wages; they made cotton king; they built the homes of their masters while suffering gross injustice and shameful humiliation—and yet out of a bottomless vitality they continued to thrive and develop. If the inexpressible cruelties of slavery could not stop us, the opposition we now face will surely fail. We will win our freedom because the sacred heritage of our nation and the eternal will of God are embodied in our echoing demands.

...One day the South will recognize its real heroes. They will be the James Merediths, with the noble sense of purpose that enables them to face jeering and hostile mobs, and with the agonizing loneliness that characterizes the life of the pioneer. They will be old, oppressed, battered Negro women, symbolized in a seventy-two-year-old woman in Montgomery, Alabama, who rose up with a sense of dignity and with her people decided not to ride segregated buses, and who responded with ungrammatical profundity to one who inquired about her weariness: "My feets is tired, but my soul is at rest." They will be the young high school and college students, the young ministers of the gospel and a host of their elders, courageously and nonviolently sitting in at lunch counters and willingly going to jail for conscience' sake. One day the South will know that when these disinherited children of God sat down at lunch counters, they were in reality standing up for what is best in the American dream and for the most sacred values in our Judaeo-Christian heritage, thereby bringing our nation back to those great wells of democracy which were dug deep by the founding fathers in their formulation of the Constitution and the Declaration of Independence.

Never before have I written so long a letter. I'm afraid it is much too long to take your precious time. I can assure you that it would have been much shorter if I had been writing from a comfortable desk, but what else can one do when he is alone in a narrow jail cell, other than write long letters, think long thoughts, and pray long prayers?

If I have said anything in this letter that overstates the truth and indicates an unreasonable impatience, I beg you to forgive me. If I have said anything that understates the truth and indicates my having a patience that allows me to settle for anything less than brotherhood, I beg God to forgive me.

I hope this letter finds you strong in the faith. I also hope that circumstances will soon make it possible for me to meet each of you, not as an integrationist or a civil-rights leader but as a fellow clergyman and a Christian brother. Let us all hope that the dark clouds of racial prejudice will soon pass away and the deep fog of misunderstanding will be lifted from our fear-drenched communities, and in some not too distant tomorrow the radiant stars of love and brotherhood will shine over our great nation with all their scintillating beauty.

Yours for the cause of
Peace and Brotherhood,
Martin Luther King, Jr.

David P. Barash

HUMAN RIGHTS

Like Mark Twain's celebrated remark about the weather, it sometimes appears that everyone talks about human rights, but no one does anything about it. The truth, fortunately, is otherwise. To some extent, moreover, talking about human rights *is* doing something about it, because in many cases a focused attention to human rights, combined with the power of the international community's approval or disapproval, can be surprisingly effective.

The situation, however, is rather grim: nearly half the world's people are denied democratic freedoms and participation; more than half of Asia and black Africa do not have access to safe water; jails are filled with political prisoners, many of them held without trial and victimized by torture; child labor is widespread; women are often deprived of the economic, social, and political rights that men take for granted; many workers are not only nonunionized but prohibited even from forming unions; the right of conscientious objection to military service is not recognized in most countries; censorship is widespread; many millions of people are illiterate, chronically sick, without adequate shelter, and just plain hungry; the basic rights of homosexuals, indigenous people, the elderly, and the deviant are routinely trampled. And yet, concern with human rights has been growing, and real progress is being made, with more anticipated.

A BRIEF HISTORY OF HUMAN RIGHTS

It is tempting to claim that human rights are as old as the human species, but in truth, this is not so. Even if human rights themselves are God-given, inalienable, and fundamental, the conception of human rights as such—and respect for them—is relatively new. Individuals may possess rights and privileges, but these have traditionally been considered the province of society, to be bestowed or revoked by the larger unit (band, tribe, village, city, state) at will. In virtually all societies, for virtually all of human

From *Introduction to Peace Studies* by David P. Barash. 1991. Belmont, CA: Wadsworth. Used by permission.

history, ultimate value derived from the social order, not the individual. Hence, an individual human being could not claim entitlement to very much, if anything, simply because he or she existed as a human being....

It was not until the Enlightenment, particularly in Europe, that the concept of universal human rights for all people first gained prominence. It had existed before, but primarily as a smattering of isolated thought rather than a consistent, widespread trend.

According to this new perspective, a body of human rights exists that are intrinsic and not provable; they stem ultimately from the natural order of things, not from the laws of society or from human logic. Hence, this approach derives human rights from what is called "natural law," with its implication that such rights are established by an authority even higher than that of governments. Heraclitus (about 500 B.C.) wrote that "all human laws are nourished by one, which is divine. For it governs as far as it will, and is sufficient for all, and more than enough." And Aristotle, in his *Ethics*, advanced the notion that "of political justice, part is natural, part legal—natural, that which everywhere has the same force and does not exist by people's thinking this or that." When the natural law viewpoint reappeared during the Enlightenment, it was used especially to counter claims that kings ruled with absolute authority and by divine right. Finally, by the seventeenth and eighteenth centuries, the concept crystalized that people possess inherent rights, and that it is society's job to *recognize* these preexisting rights, not to create them.

The idea of human rights as currently understood...is largely a Western tradition, deriving especially from the work of John Locke and John Stuart Mill. Locke maintained that the fundamental human right was the right to property, the primary one being the right to the secure ownership of one's own body; civil and political rights flowed, in his view, from this. And Mill strove to identify a set of rights not covered by the state. Thus, there is some truth to the criticism that Western human rights advocates may occasionally be guilty of moral arrogance, seeking to export their own rather

culture-bound ideas, especially their emphasis on civil/political freedom.

It should also be emphasized that Western political thought is not limited to individualism and human rights; rather, it coexists with respect for—and often, virtual worship of—the state. According to influential theorists such as Hegel and Herder, rights are enlarged and created for individuals only through the actions of the state. And for orthodox Marxists, value derives only from the social order; in Marxist analysis, individual rights do not exist unless they are explicitly granted by society. Although Communist societies are supposedly designed to maximize the benefits of every person, the "rights" of each individual come to naught if they run counter to the greater good of society as a whole. Individuals can expect to receive benefits from a community only insofar as they participate in it, and further its goals. And as we shall see, even today—with ever-increasing agreement on the meaning and desirability of human rights—there continues to be substantial disagreement as to priorities.

Human Rights in the Twentieth Century

Internationally, there was very little concern with human rights until quite recently, after World War II. Despite the Enlightenment, despite capitalism's emphasis on individual property rights, and despite democracy's emphasis on individual political rights, as a practical matter, state sovereignty has long superseded human rights. When the worldwide state system was established in the mid-seventeenth century, governments agreed—ostensibly in the interest of world peace—not to concern themselves very much with how other governments treated their own citizens. Within its own boundaries, each state was supreme and could do as it wished.

Gradually, however, human rights law developed, initially out of concern for protecting persons during armed conflict. The Geneva Convention of 1864, for example, sought to establish standards for treatment of wounded soldiers and of prisoners. (It is ironic that war—the most inhumane of situations—should have led to the first organized recognition of shared humanitarian values.) The International Committee of the Red Cross is a notable nongovernmental organization long concerned with international human rights; it was organized by a group of Swiss citizens, involved in the 1864 Geneva Conference....

Following World War I, there was widespread recognition that one cause of that conflict had been the denial of national rights within large empires such as Austria's. Hence, human rights received explicit attention from the League of Nations, which emphasized that the rights of minorities must be respected by larger federal governments. Labor rights—the right to organize and to decent working conditions and wages, and restrictions on child labor—were the focus of the International Labor Organization, which later functioned within the United Nations. Opposition to slavery catalyzed numerous early human rights organizations, such as the Anti-Slavery League. (Most Americans do not realize that in many countries, slavery was only abolished during the 1950s; some claim that it is still being practiced today, in Mauritania and Pakistan.)

Organized, worldwide concern for human rights did not really coalesce until after World War II, perhaps in part as a reaction to the devastating denials of rights that occurred in association with that conflict. In the aftermath of the Nazi Holocaust most especially, the world's conscience was finally activated—partly out of regret for those who had suffered, and partly, too, out of enlightened self-interest. Martin Niemoeller put it memorably:

> First they came for the Jews and I did not speak out—because I was not a Jew. Then they came for the Communists and I did not speak out—because I was not a Communist. Then they came for the trade unionists and I did not speak out—because I was not a trade unionist. Then they came for me—and there was no one left to speak out for me.[4]

In recent decades, the world's people have begun to speak out for themselves and for human rights of every sort. Before we review some of the legal protections, conventions, and treaties that have resulted, let us consider the question of what

is meant by human rights, and how they have come to be asserted.

THE POLITICAL PHILOSOPHY OF HUMAN RIGHTS

Human rights implies a new way of viewing the relationship of governments and their peoples, whereby governance is intended to enhance the dignity of human beings, not exploit them. With this in mind, let us examine three major political philosophies of human rights, each of which is divisible into two branches.

Liberalism

In traditional liberal thought, human rights exist not only because of their contribution to human dignity, but also because human beings, themselves, naturally possess such rights. "The object of any obligation," wrote the philosopher Simone Weil,

> in the realm of human affairs, is always the human being as such. There exists an obligation towards every human being for the sole reason that he or she is a human being,...

In Jefferson's phrase, people have certain "inalienable rights" that may not be denied. The liberal view of human rights thus corresponds to the "natural law" perspective. One of the great classical liberals, John Locke, argued that civil law, to be valid, must be tested against this "natural law," which is the ultimate arbiter of justice. And when the framers of the Declaration of Independence complained of a "long train of abuses and usurpations" on the part of King George III, it was precisely natural law that they believed was being abused and usurped.

Another liberal theory of human rights derives from "utilitarianism," especially the works of John Stuart Mill and Jeremy Bentham. The idea here is that society should value whatever is utilitarian, or useful, in maximizing human happiness and freedom. The best-known motto of utilitarianism is "the greatest good for the greatest number," although individual freedom and equality are recognized as well, so as to prevent tyranny by the majority. Social betterment is to be achieved through equality and maximum personal liberty....

---

[4] In fact, Pastor Niemoeller himself became a victim of the Nazis.

Conservatism

Traditional conservatism is rarely articulated today with respect to human rights, because it is in large part a philosophy of unequal rights and privileges, and as such, difficult to defend in an avowedly egalitarian age. But the unspoken tenets of conservatism are nonetheless influential in actual practice. Classical conservatism can be said to have originated with Plato, who argued in *The Republic* that all people are not equal, and that the best form of government is therefore not democracy, but rule by a philosopher–king. This belief in unequal rights underpins many right-wing governments, from the "classical conservatism" of the military juntas that ruled Brazil and Greece, as well as the various U.S.-sponsored Central American governments (Guatemala, Honduras, Panama), to the neo-fascist dictatorships that arose in Chile and Paraguay, where rights were reserved only for the most powerful.

Group-oriented Philosophies

Finally, there is a third branch of human rights philosophy, which, for want of a better term, might be called "group oriented." It can be subdivided into two branches, Marxist and nationalist. For Karl Marx, individuals were not independent actors; rather, they were controlled by economic forces, pawns in a relentless class struggle. In the Marxist view, the liberal emphasis on individual rights is therefore misplaced, a bourgeois luxury, form without substance. Instead, rights are conferred by society, and they should belong exclusively to the proletariat (the working class). Such an approach leads automatically to an embrace of socioeconomic rights and material equality, with a downplaying of civil/political rights. Thus, in Marxist societies, freedom of speech and opinion are permitted insofar as they do not conflict with the stated goals of group advancement and welfare. The state, and not the working class, typically becomes paramount....

The second version of group-oriented human rights has a leftist flavor, but is not, strictly speaking, Marxist. It originates instead in the experience of national liberation movements, and places special emphasis on the right to national self-determination and economic development, from

which all other rights are then derived. Believers in the human right to national self-determination downplay the individual as well as the social class, although they remain committed to equal rights. Emphasis instead is on the rights of a national grouping. This approach lay behind the "Universal Declaration of the Rights of Peoples," which grew out of a meeting of highly regarded, nongovernmental third world spokespersons in 1976. The first three articles in this thirty-article document read as follows:

1. Every people has the right to existence.
2. Every people has the right to the respect of its national and cultural identity.
3. Every people has the right to retain peaceful possession of its territory and to return to it if it is expelled.

...The emphasis on "people's rights" clearly distinguishes this approach from the Western focus on "individual rights."

Nationalist group-oriented regimes are found in many third world states, such as Algeria and Zimbabwe, which are often leftist, but rarely Communist. Tanzanian president Julius Nyerere was one of the most articulate spokespersons for the nationalist group-oriented point of view:

> For what do we mean when we talk of freedom? First, there is national freedom; that is, the ability of the citizens of Tanzania to determine their own future, and to govern themselves without interference from non-Tanzanians. Second, there is freedom from hunger, disease, and poverty. And third, there is personal freedom for the individual; that is, his right to live in dignity and equality with all others, his right to freedom of speech.

The difference between this viewpoint and the others (classical and egalitarian liberal, classical and neo-fascist conservative, Marxist group-oriented) is more one of emphasis than of absolutes. But the "rights" associated with individual competition—so dear to the liberal conception of human rights—are devalued. "The important thing for us," explains Nyerere, "is the extent to which we succeed in preventing the exploitation of one man by another, and in spreading the concept of working together cooperatively for the common good instead of competitively for individual private gain."...

On balance, capitalist democracies give insufficient attention to socioeconomic rights, while socialist governments take inadequate account of civil/political ones. Recent evidence suggests that economic development is more rapid under capitalism: but relatively little benefit from such development actually reaches the poorest citizens....

Those who are wealthy and privileged characteristically favor maximum freedom (especially, freedom of economic competition) and a minimal role for government, which, at least in the United States, often leads in turn to opposition to the "welfare state" or resistance to affirmative action plans. Those lacking in wealth and power are typically more in need of laws and specified rights, to be assured by society. Hence, Western governments tend to describe socioeconomic rights as not really "human rights" at all, but rather, goals or aspirations for society.

As we shall see, human rights can be characterized in many ways, although a global consensus has been developing that incorporates not only the traditional American concern with political liberty, but also the second and third world concern with socioeconomic rights, as well as additional values that are difficult to pigeonhole. Many other rights are also asserted—states' rights, consumer rights—but to suggest that something is a "human right" is to claim something particularly fundamental and weighty, and should not be done lightly....

Citizens of the United States need to recognize the importance that large numbers of people, especially in the second and third worlds, attribute to socioeconomic rights. In the words of Leopold Senghor, former president of Senegal, "human rights begin with breakfast." Without such an awareness, relatively well-off Westerners too quickly sneer at the poor "rights" records of other countries, oblivious to their own shortcomings in the eyes of others. In addition, once we recognize the validity of socioeconomic rights, then governments such as Libya under Qaddafi or Cuba under Castro—which to many in the West are failures in the civil/political sphere because of their lack of representative government, widespread censorship, and torture and abuse of political prisoners—can be recognized as effective, even admirable, in other domains, such as public health or literacy. (This is not to claim that success in some dimensions of human rights cancels outrages in another; rather, it helps permit a more balanced perception of systems that might otherwise seem unidimensionally evil, and whose high level of domestic acceptance would otherwise be difficult for Americans to understand.) Thus, in an effort to identify basic human rights, Richard Falk has proposed the following:

1. *Basic human needs:* the rights of individuals and groups to food, housing, health, and education; the duty of governments to satisfy these rights...
2. *Basic decencies:* the rights of individuals and groups to be protected against genocide, torture, arbitrary arrest, detention, and execution, or their threat;...
3. *Participatory rights:* the rights of individuals and groups to participate in the processes that control their lives, including choice of political leadership, of job, of place of residence, or cultural activity and orientation;...
4. *Security rights:* the rights of individuals and groups (including those of unborn generations) to be reasonably secure about their prospects of minimal physical well-being and survival; the duty of governments and peoples to uphold this right by working to achieve sustainable forms of national and ecological security....

The Rights of Categories of People

We have thus far focused on the various rights themselves (civil, political, social, economic, and so on), rather than on the categories of people in whom such rights are supposed to inhere. But these categories are in many cases so important that, by themselves, they constitute major areas of concern. Women's rights is one example. Women comprise more than 50 percent of the world's population, and yet they are without doubt an oppressed group. For centuries, women have suffered from patriarchal social structures that devalue their personhood and deny many of their basic human rights. This includes a diverse array of abuses, such as footbinding in pre-Communist China, the forced seclusion and isolation of women in certain modern-day Hindu and Moslem societies, sexual mutilation as currently practiced on millions of young women in several African societies, polygamy, restricted or nonexistent choice as to marriage, and—even in ostensibly "liberated" societies such as those of the United States and Great Britain—greatly restricted economic and professional opportunities along with underrepresentation in political life.

Other groups also deserve attention. There are about 200 million indigenous people worldwide, representing national majorities in such states as Guatemala and Bolivia, and small minorities in such states as Brazil, Australia, and the United States. Regardless of their numbers, indigenous people are generally in dire straits, sometimes—as in Guatemala or Brazil—being subjected to outright genocide. In other cases, they are severely maltreated, and/or they enjoy dramatically fewer opportunities and privileges than their nonnative counterparts. Australian aborigines are the most imprisoned people on Earth, with an incarceration rate sixteen times that of the Caucasian population; the life expectancy of Mayan Indians in Guatemala is eleven years shorter than that of the nonindigenous population; the average per capita income of native Americans is one-half that of the rest of the U.S. population; large dams have devastated the homelands of indigenous peoples in Canada, Brazil, Norway, the Philippines, and India, depriving them of an arguably crucial human right: to live in their ancestral homelands. And this is but a partial list.

Other groups can also be identified as having particular human rights claims and vulnerabilities: the mentally ill, children, the homeless, racial minorities, the handicapped, convicts, unskilled workers, migrant laborers, refugees, political dissidents, the elderly, and so on. Ideally, human rights such as civil freedoms, economic opportunity, protection from mass destruction, and the right to a safe and clean environment will be equally shared by all people. In practice, these rights must often be defended most vigilantly for those groups that have thus far been the most victimized. . . .

It seems unavoidable that various rights will conflict. In a famous opinion, U.S. Supreme Court justice Oliver Wendell Holmes concluded that the right to free speech did not extend to yelling "Fire" in a crowded theater. The "right" to a drug-free environment may conflict with the "rights" to privacy, just as the "right" of third world people to healthy babies has already been found to conflict with the "right" of the Nestlé company to market substandard infant formula. In Islamic states, women's "rights" are often subordinated to the "rights" of people to practice the religion of their choice. A woman's "right" to control her own body, including an abortion if she desires, runs contrary to a fetus's "right" to life; the "right" of religious freedom can conflict with a child's "right" to necessary medical care, as when fundamentalist parents refuse lifesaving treatment for their child; the public's "right" to safe air travel appears to have triumphed over individual "rights" not to be searched without a warrant; and the list goes on. . . .

However they are sliced, many human rights are essentially claims against the authority of governments. As such, they are freedoms *from*—guarantees that governments will refrain from behaving badly toward their own people. These can be distinguished from freedoms *to*—the asserted obligations of society to help its members to achieve a better life. This distinction somewhat parallels the one between negative and positive peace—between those rights asserted *against* governments (no war, no intrusions into personal freedom) and those expected *of* them (establish positive peace, provide for basic human needs). In most cases, the first category (negative rights) seems easier for governments to achieve; certain states may simply lack the resources to make substantial improvements in socioeconomic conditions, but they all can stop torturing, murdering, and otherwise oppressing their people. . . .

UN-Related Agreements

In assessing the legal status of human rights, the UN Charter represents a useful starting point. Its major reference to human rights appears in Article 55:

> With a view to the creation of conditions of stability and well-being which are necessary for peaceful

and friendly relations among nations based on respect for the principle of equal rights and self-determination of peoples, the United Nations shall promote: a. higher standards of living, full employment, and conditions of economic and social progress and development; b. solutions of international economic, social, health, and related problems, and international cultural and educational cooperation; and c. universal respect for, and observance of, human rights and fundamental freedoms for all without distinction as to race, sex, language, or religion.

But if the UN Charter serves as a constitution, it lacks a bill of rights, specifying which human rights are to be "respected" and "observed." This was accomplished largely by the UN-sponsored Universal Declaration of Human Rights (UDHR), passed unanimously in 1948. Thus, after the UN Charter endorsed human rights, the Universal Declaration went ahead and enumerated them. The United States was a major contributor to the UDHR; much of its impetus came from Eleanor Roosevelt, widow of the late U.S. president. The UDHR consists of thirty articles, of which the first twenty-one are primarily civil/political, prohibiting torture and arbitrary arrest, and guaranteeing freedom of assembly, religion, speech, emigration, and even the right to vote by secret ballot. The remaining articles are concerned with socioeconomic and cultural rights, including the right to work, to an "adequate" standard of living, to an education, and to some form of social security, and even specifying the right to vacations with pay.

The Universal Declaration is not technically binding in the sense of an international treaty; it is a recommendation only, and makes no provisions for enforcement. Nonetheless, it has had substantial impact on thinking worldwide. The UDHR is widely respected, and has legitimated concern with human rights; it has even been incorporated into many national constitutions. To some degree, it has become part of customary international law; accordingly, many judicial scholars argue that it has the literal force of law, although it is often violated. (It should be noted that customary law is more universal and more durable than treaty law.)...

People dispute precisely what obligations member states undertake when, in the UN Charter, they agree to "promote universal respect for and observance" of human rights. Nonetheless, an underlying consensus has emerged. The accepted phrase is that governments have no business engaging in a "consistent pattern of gross violations of human rights." Thus, isolated incidents are unlikely to generate worldwide outrage. By contrast, "gross violations"—that is, serious, recurring acts—merit condemnation and, ultimately, such actions as censure, economic boycott, and possibly even military intervention. Abuses of this sort could include widespread torture, mass arrests and imprisonment without trial, genocide, and vicious policies of racial segregation and debasement....

The Problem of Enforcement

Faced with the awesome, sovereign power of states, the international human rights regime can seem woefully inadequate, based as it is on mere legalisms or exhortations, and devoid of enforcement mechanisms. But legal systems always have difficulty controlling powerful actors—labor unions in Britain, for example, or large corporations in the United States. And ultimately, most of them rely on voluntary compliance. Some states have in fact complied voluntarily with international human rights norms, largely to achieve international legitimacy as well as to avoid ostracism.

Frustration with the rights-denying policies of states occasionally spills over into efforts to transcend the authority of states. Although lacking in legal authority, individuals of high moral and international standing have on occasion gathered together to fill what they see as a vacuum in the protection of human rights. So-called people's tribunals have periodically convened to draw attention to various human rights abuses. Most notable of these was the Russell Tribunal, which roundly criticized U.S. policy during the Vietnam War. The League for the Rights of Peoples, established in Rome in 1976, has held numerous sessions, evaluating repression under Marcos in the Philippines, offering a retrospective on Turkish genocide against Armenians from 1915 to 1916, and criticizing Brazil's behavior toward its indigenous Amazonian population, Indonesia's strong-arm tactics in East Timor, U.S. intervention in Central America, and Soviet intervention in Afghanistan, as well as questioning the legitimacy of nuclear weapons. Such actions are of uncertain effectiveness, but they do attract a degree of public attention, while also serving to undercut the presumption that only state-centered approaches are relevant in dealing with violations of human rights. . . .

An approach that emphasizes human rights represents a fundamentally new way of thinking about human dignity and world politics, reflecting as it does the determination that states must meet certain standards, both in their own domestic affairs and in their international relations. Even today, after several decades of vigorous prohuman rights advocacy, states typically act with primary regard to their power and perceived national interests, rather than according to the ideals of human rights. There is, as a result, the constant danger that concern for human rights will be sacrificed on the altar of state sovereignty, expediency, and realpolitik.

Human rights advocacy involves a different perspective from which to view the human condition and the goals of society and politics—as citizens of a larger community than individual states or nation-states. As opposed to the relatively narrow focus of states, concern with superordinate human rights requires that political barriers be transcended, in the search for human dignity on the widest possible scale. . . .

HUMAN RIGHTS AND PEACE

Human rights and peace are inextricably connected, in several ways. First, the denial of human rights is itself a denial of peace. A world in which there is no armed conflict, but in which fundamental human rights are thwarted, could not in any meaningful sense be considered peaceful. Speaking at the United Nations, Pope John Paul II explicitly linked human rights and war:

> The Universal Declaration of Human Rights has struck a real blow against the many deep roots of war since the spirit of war in its basic primordial meaning springs up . . . where the inalienable rights of men are violated. This is a new and deeply

relevant vision of the cause of peace. One that goes deeper and is more radical.

The pope's perspective applies to socioeconomic rights no less than civil/political ones. As one Scandinavian peace researcher has noted, "Whether a child dies in infancy due to poverty and consequent malnutrition and lack of hygiene, or if it grows up and at a later stage is executed as a political opponent, the society in which this happens must be considered hostile to human rights." And, we might add, to peace as well.

Second, there appears to be a connection between the way a state treats its own population and its inclinations toward other states. As Franklin Roosevelt put it, "We in this nation still believe that it [self-determination] should be predicated on certain freedoms which we think are essential everywhere. We know that we ourselves will never be wholly safe at home unless other governments recognize such freedoms." . . .

Third, a denial of human rights can provoke breaches of the peace, if other states become involved. Humanitarian intervention of this sort may be legal; certainly, there is ample precedent in the classical writings of international law. . . .

On the other hand, claims of humanitarian intervention have often been used as an excuse for aggression (of which the Spanish–American War may well be an example). Hitler claimed that dismemberment of Czechoslovakia and, later, the invasion of Poland were warranted to stop the persecution of both countries' German-speaking minorities. Vietnam invaded Cambodia ostensibly to oust the genocidal Khmer Rouge regime, and the United States explained its invasion of Grenada at least partly as a response to human rights violations on that Caribbean island. . . . (No comparable justifications were ever used by the United States to overthrow rightist regimes, including the Somoza dictatorship, which was far more abusive of human rights, or the government of El Salvador. . . .)

Finally, one of the widely recognized human rights—specified in the first articles of both 1966 human rights conventions—is that of national self-determination. Abuses of this right often lead directly to war, especially civil war . . . which makes this issue a difficult one. The pursuit of human rights may in fact lead more to violence than to peace, since human rights often are won by struggle and confrontation. Furthermore, it is not obvious whether all claims for national self-determination are worthy of success. Should there be independent states for…Basques, Welsh, Scots, Quebecois, and Native Americans? For its part, the UN Security Council has determined that, at least in certain cases, such as anticolonial struggles, a continuing denial of human rights constitutes a formal threat to international peace (this was applied to Zimbabwe, Namibia, and South Africa).

In summary, the connection between human rights and peace is complex and multifaceted. It is useful to claim that human rights contribute to peace, but the most fundamental connection may well be that such claims encourage adherence to human rights, for their own sake, regardless of whether this actually promotes peace as narrowly defined.

THE FUTURE

What of the future? Several things can be said with confidence. The first is that the question of human rights will continue to demand attention on the international agenda.…

A second safe conclusion is that the question of human rights will continue to be controversial, with different conceptions competing with one another, while the very notion of human rights competes with the basic inclination of states to engage in amoral, realpolitik maneuverings. The dilemma may be profound. Consider these realpolitik questions, for example, from the perspective of a government leader. What should a state do when confronted with this choice it desires a particular strategic relationship with another state, but that other state engages in human rights abuses. Which should be sacrificed, national strategy or a commitment to human rights?…

Perhaps, on the other hand, the "natural law" school is correct, and support of human rights is simply the right thing to do, period, regardless of its practical consequences.…

There is yet another possibility, a way station between the amorality of realpolitik and the absolutism of morality for its own sake. Some argue that power (or at least, security) can readily be

reconciled with human rights.…Former secretary of state Cyrus Vance echoed this sentiment when he observed: "We pursue our human rights objectives, not only because they are right, but because we have a stake in the stability that comes when people can express their hopes and find their futures freely. Our ideals and our interests coincide."

Promoting Human Rights

It is difficult to imagine exactly what a U.S. foreign policy would be if it was organized primarily around the promotion of human rights worldwide. However, the following specific actions, which have already been taken at different times in support of human rights, suggest the benefits to be gained from a continuation, to say nothing of an expansion, of such policies:

- *Subtle diplomacy.* Quiet, persistent pressure raised with offending governments has the advantage that the government in question need not worry about losing face if and when abuses are corrected. A disadvantage, beyond the high chance of being ignored, is that a government may claim that it is employing subtle diplomacy while it is actually doing nothing.
- *Public statements.* This involves drawing world attention to specific abuses and to governments that violate human rights. It may involve publicly dissociating one's own government from the unacceptable behavior of another. Human rights compliance can be promoted by publicizing violations through the publication of reports conducted by respected, impartial investigative commissions; especially in a world climate committed to human rights, most governments seek to avoid the embarrassment that comes with being branded a violator of these rights.
- *Symbolic acts.* Sending support to dissidents, either by words, by contact with opposition figures, or by otherwise indicating disapproval of abuses, is a way of emphasizing to both the offending government and its people that human rights violations are noticed and rejected.
- *Cultural penalties.* By isolating offenders at international cultural events, including athletic

contests and other exchanges, such governments are made to feel like pariahs. Although it is easy to scoff at such minimal "penalties," pride and the universal desire to be accepted enhance the impact of such actions.

- *Economic penalties.* Applying trade embargoes, renouncing investment in the offending country, refusing development loans and other forms of foreign aid—these actions can hurt the economy of offending countries, thereby putting pressure (often on the more wealthy and influential citizens) to modify policies and/or oust the government....

- *Immigration.* Human rights activists, dissidents, and those being deprived of their human rights can be permitted to enter the United States. In the recent past, the "right" of immigration has been applied quite selectively, facilitating immigration by people fleeing leftist countries whose human rights policies the United States wishes to criticize, while making it very difficult for refugees from rightist countries that are allied to the United States, and whose human rights policies it is inclined to ignore or whitewash.

- *Legal approaches.* International law can be applied more vigorously, by indicting violators of human rights overseas, just as people involved in the international drug trade have occasionally been indicted and, when possible, extradited for trial.

- *Multilateral approaches.* The United States can commit itself to the various human rights organizations now ac-tive worldwide, especially the United Nations Commission on Human Rights....

- *Destabilization and belligerency.* The United States has actively sought to destabilize the governments of certain countries—for example, Nicaragua—at least in part, we are told, for their human rights abuses. This remains an option, although of questionable legality or morality, unless the abuses are sufficiently flagrant, and unless the policy is applied evenhandedly to all regimes, regardless of ideology. Certainly, the human rights abuses of Nazi Germany and imperial Japan were influential in the U.S. decision to make war upon them, although these abuses actually became more serious after war was declared. The Tanzanian invasion of Uganda, which ultimately toppled the government of Idi Amin, won widespread support because that regime's human rights record was particularly atrocious....

We conclude our discussion of human rights with an account by Jerome Shestack, a longtime human rights activist. Shestack recognizes the extraordinarily difficult and seemingly hopeless task of securing human rights worldwide, in the face of human cruelty, frailty, misunderstandings, and the power of states. He conjures up the Greek myth of Sisyphus, who was condemned to spend eternity pushing a boulder up a hill, only to have it roll back again just as he reached the top. Sisyphus' task is absurd, and yet—echoing the existential philosopher Albert Camus—Shestack points out that

> Sisyphus may turn out to be a more enduring hero than Hercules. For if, as Camus taught, life itself is absurd, Sisyphus represents the only triumph possible over that absurdity. In his constancy to reach that summit, even with failure preordained, Sisyphus demonstrated that the human spirit is indomitable and that dedication to a higher goal is in itself man's reason for living....The realities of the world may foredoom a great part of the struggle and make most of the effort seem abysmal. Yet, the very struggle itself takes on symbolic meaning, enhancing human dignity. And when all is said and done, there is no other humane course to pursue.

STUDY QUESTIONS

1. Discuss connections between overpopulation, poverty, and environmental destruction.
2. In some ways, "human rights" is like Mom and apple pie: everyone is in favor. But in fact, the question of human rights can be enormously controversial. Explain.
3. Martin Luther King, Jr., once said that "injustice anywhere is an affront to justice everywhere." The merits of this statement are—or should be—obvious. But is there any sense in which this idea could be troublesome?
4. Agree or disagree with the notion that human rights is a Western concept that should not be applied to other societies. Take "female circumcision" as an example.
5. Look into the question of whether ecological stability and sustainability conflicts with economic growth and development.
6. It is often said that one cannot make omelets without breaking eggs. Propose some guidelines as to how many eggs, and of what sort, might legitimately be "broken" in order to establish positive peace.
7. Positive peace is as much a matter of national security as is negative peace. Agree or disagree, trying to be specific and "hardheaded" in your response.
8. Compare and contrast differences in wealth within a country with differences in wealth between countries; is the solution to such differences simply a matter of "development"?
9. When peace becomes a positive goal (as opposed to war prevention), then people feel inclined to fight for it; hence, it is better to aim "lower." Agree or disagree, using historical examples and/or plausible future scenarios.
10. Describe some successes in achieving positive peace. What can we learn from them? Do the same with some failures.

SUGGESTIONS FOR FURTHER READING

Barry, Brian. 2005. *Why Social Justice Matters*. New York: Polity Press.

Collier, Paul. 2008. *The Bottom Billion: Why the Poorest Countries Are Failing and What Can Be Done About It*. New York: Oxford University Press.

Donnelly, Jack. 2002. *Universal Human Rights in Theory and Practice*. Ithaca, NY: Cornell University Press.

Hunt, Lynn. 2008. *Inventing Human Rights: A History*. New York: W. W. Norton.

Lockwood, Bert B., ed. 2006. *Women's Rights: A Human Rights Quarterly Reader*. Baltimore, MD: The Johns Hopkins University Press.

Philander, S. George. 2008. *Encyclopedia of Global Warming and Climate Change*. Los Angeles: Sage Publications.

Pojman, Louis P., and Paul Pojman. 2007. *Environmental Ethics: Readings in Theory and Application.* Belmont, CA: Wadsworth.

Renner, Michael. 1996. *Fighting for Survival: Environmental Decline, Social Conflict, and the New Age of Insecurity.* New York: Norton.

Tietenberg, Tom. 2006. *Environmental Economics and Policy.* Boston: Addison-Wesley.

Todaro, Michael P., and Stephen C. Smith. 2008. *Economic Development.* Boston: Addison-Wesley.

CHAPTER 5

Nonviolence

Much of the human world is structured by violence—the international political and military system perhaps most of all. Hence, a commitment to nonviolence is necessarily radical. Nonviolence is not limited to tactics for overcoming any one oppressive system—whether colonial domination, denial of civil rights, and so forth—but rather it seeks to overthrow all relationships based on violence, oppression, and the unfair domination of some by others. Thus, nonviolence is directly relevant not only to the prevention of war but also to the establishment of social justice, environmental protection, and the securing of human rights. Nonviolence seeks to change the terms whereby individuals and groups interact: not only with each other but even with planet Earth.

It can be argued, for example, that the destructive patterns whereby people and states interact violently with one another are also reflected in the destructive style that characterizes so much of the interaction of people with their environment: the burning of rain forests, the clear-cutting of temperate woodlands, the gouging of the earth during strip mining, the pollution of water and air, the extinction of plant and animal species. All these can be seen as deriving from a lack of what Gandhi called *ahimsa*, best translated into English, perhaps, as "nonviolent love." This is not love of the sloppy, sentimental kind but is closer to the Christian concept of *agape*, a transcending love of connection and mutual commitment. It is also similar to Albert Schweitzer's concept of "reverence for life."

The poet Walt Whitman had this love in mind when he wrote the following:

> Were you looking to be held together by lawyers?
> Or by an agreement on paper? Or by arms?
> Nay, nor the world, nor any living thing, will so cohere.
> Only those who love each other shall become indivisible.

It must be emphasized that nonviolence has emerged as a definite, defiant, hard-headed strategy of social transformation. The very word "nonviolence" is thus unfortunate because it evokes images of passivity, especially in its regrettable counterpart, "passive resistance." This is akin to translating *light* as "nondarkness" or defining *good* as merely the absence of evil. Mohandas Gandhi, the greatest twentieth-century apostle of nonviolence, coined the word *satyagraha*, which can be translated literally from the Sanskrit as "soul-force" or "soul-truth." It incorporates such positive traits as courage, directness, friendly civility, absolute honesty, respect for other living creatures, and willingness to suffer in pursuit of deeply felt goals.

Traditionally, when conflicts are resolved by violence, they simply involve the triumph of one protagonist over the other. Such a "resolution" may occur via threat, persuasion, or compulsion by naked force, but, in any event, the presumption is that one side wins and the other loses: what mathematicians call a "zero sum game." (In most competitive sports, for example, for every winner there is a loser, so the sum total of wins and losses equals zero.) By contrast, devotees of nonviolence seek to resolve the conflict at its source rather than to defeat or annihilate the opponent. The goal is to persuade the adversary that all parties have more to gain by acting in harmony and love than by persevering in discord and violence: that is, that the parties are not really adversaries at all!

As we shall see, there have been numerous spokespeople for nonviolence and for creative nonviolent resistance. It was Gandhi, however, who most closely wedded theory to practice, employing nonviolence as a coherent approach to peace. For nonviolent activists in the Gandhian mold, violence itself is the enemy, and, thus, there is no room for violence in the arsenal of those who would effect creative, peaceful change. If the goal is a genuine social revolution, then the more violence, the less revolution: "The practice of violence, like all action, changes the world," wrote social philosopher Hannah Arendt. "But the most probable change is to a more violent world."[1]

For practitioners of nonviolence, therefore, it is crucially important to recognize the interdependence of means and ends: a goal of peace can only be achieved by the use of nonviolence. For example, by using violent methods, revolutions (even the most well-meaning ones) and even antiwar movements can build up reservoirs of resentment and hatred, thereby laying the foundations for additional injustice and yet more violence. Political activists of the far left and far right are generally prone to make compromises with violence, convinced that their vision of the world-as-it-should-be justifies virtually any means of attaining it. Lenin announced, for example, that "to achieve our ends, we will unite even with the Devil."

Similarly, ideologues of the far right did not hesitate to make common cause with oppressive dictatorships—such as Somoza in Nicaragua, Marcos in the Philippines, Chun doo Hwan in South Korea, Pinochet in Chile, Duvalier in Haiti, the Shah in Iran, Suharto in Indonesia, Botha in South Africa—in the interest of a presumed greater good, the defeat or containment of international communism.

Cicero, in *The Letters to His Friends*, asks, "What can be done against force, without force?" Students of nonviolence would answer, "Plenty." They would, in fact, question whether anything effective, lasting, or ultimately worthwhile can be done against force,

---

[1] Hannah Arendt, *On Violence* (New York: Harcourt, Brace and World, 1969).

with force. The Rev. Martin Luther King, Jr., nonviolent leader of the civil rights movement in the United States—and a visionary who, like Gandhi, was also intensely practical and result-oriented—wrote that "returning violence for violence multiplies violence, adding deeper darkness to a night already devoid of stars. Darkness cannot drive out darkness; only light can do that. Hate cannot drive out hate; only love can do that." This does not mean that the practitioner of nonviolence is forbidden anger, even hate; rather, these feelings must be redirected creatively against various *systems* of evil rather than individuals.

What, then, does nonviolence look like in practice? It takes many forms: marches; boycotts; picketing; leafleting; strikes; civil disobedience; the peaceful occupation of various government facilities; vigils and fasts; mass imprisonment; tax resistance; and a willingness to be abused by the authorities and yet to respond nonviolently, with courage and determination, even politeness. Thus, the nonviolent struggle is if anything more intense and difficult than its violent counterpart. It is not an alternative to fighting, but rather, a different (nonviolent and loving) way of doing so.

When a victim responds to violence with yet more violence, he or she is reacting in predictable, perhaps even instinctive ways. Violent responses validate the original attacker, even, in a way, vindicating the original violence as far as the attacker is concerned: because the opponent is so violent, then presumably he or she "deserved it." Thus, there is a widespread expectation of countervailing power analogous in the social sphere to Newton's first law, which states that for every action there is an equal and opposite reaction. Accustomed to counterviolence—and even, perhaps, hoping for it—the violent person who encounters a nonviolent opponent who is courageous and respectful, even loving, becomes a "victim" of a kind of moral judo in which the attacker's own energy is redirected, knocking him or her off balance.

It is said of some people and some nations that "they only understand force," and, therefore, they cannot be moved by anything other than force or the threat of force. The truth, however, may be precisely the opposite: those who understand and expect force can generally deal with it effectively. By contrast, the British authorities in India, like supporters of segregation laws in the U.S. South, were consistently off balance and flustered by the creative nonviolent tactics employed against their regime.

Historically, violent governmental overreaction has often worked to the ultimate detriment of the perpetrators, transforming victims into martyrs who became symbols of their regime's callous wrongheadedness. In 1819, for example, a nonviolent crowd in Manchester, England, was attacked by soldiers while listening to speeches calling for the repeal of the Corn Laws; this so-called Peterloo Massacre became a rallying cry for radicals who eventually succeeded in their demands. The slaughter of participants in the Paris Commune of 1871 led to greater solidarity among the French working class. In 1905, a large gathering of nonviolent Russian peasants in St. Petersburg, led by Father Gapon, attempted to submit a petition to Czar Nicholas, whose troops responded by slaughtering hundreds of unarmed people. This led to a general strike, which ushered in some limited democratic reforms but, more important, also signaled the beginning of the end for czarist tyranny. When the Russian Revolution finally took place, thirteen years later, it was in many ways the culmination of mounting popular revulsion at the czar's wanton violence toward his own people.

The arrest and beating of U.S. civil rights protesters during the 1950s and early 1960s, along with the murder of civil rights workers and innocent bystanders (including children), was instrumental in bringing about desegregation and the passing of the subsequent Civil Rights and Voting Rights Acts. The "police riot" at the 1968 Democratic Party Convention in Chicago led to widespread condemnation of the political system, just as the killing of four unarmed students at Kent State University in 1970 galvanized sentiment against the Vietnam War. The 1988 Israeli policy of beating Palestinian protesters who sought an end to Israeli occupation of the West Bank led to solidification of Palestinian sentiment and subjected the Israeli government to greater pressure for a negotiated agreement. In 1989, when nonviolent protesters—mostly students—occupied Tiananmen Square and demanded political reforms, the Chinese government responded with tanks and the slaughter of hundreds, perhaps thousands of protesters. Although the Chinese government has thus far survived this episode, it seems clear that when nonviolent protesters are abused, the world's conscience is aroused, and significant changes are often set in motion.

Nonviolent protest has accomplished much more than the creation of martyrs. In 1986, for example, the corrupt dictatorship of Ferdinand Marcos in the Philippines was toppled, largely due to "people power," the persistent nonviolence of Filipino civilians. Strongly supported by the Catholic church, crowds of unarmed Filipinos at one point interposed themselves between a small number of dissident troops and those ostensibly loyal to Marcos, who had been ordered to suppress their opponents. When it became evident that his own military would not fire on the nonviolent, unarmed populace, it was clear that the end of the Marcos regime had come. Similar campaigns caused the ouster of the long-lasting Duvalier regime in Haiti and produced the first ever democratic government in South Korea. And the prodemocracy movement in Eastern Europe succeeded in throwing off Communist domination with essentially nonviolent techniques (except in Romania). It is also notable that in many countries, this "velvet revolution"—so named because of the virtual absence of bloodshed—was hastened by instances in which the repressive government reacted violently to nonviolent protesters...which in turn served to delegitimate the government itself.

This pattern continued into the 21st century as well, with the so-called Rose Revolution in Georgia, the Orange Revolution in Ukraine, and the Tulip Revolution in Kyrgyzstan, among others.

This is but a small and highly selective sampling. It is noteworthy that examples of "successful" violence are far better known—although not necessarily more numerous or important—than their successful nonviolent counterparts. The argument can in fact be made that violent outcomes are, by definition, failures and that nonviolence represents the best in our politics and in human potential.

Henry David Thoreau

CIVIL DISOBEDIENCE

Henry David Thoreau was not, strictly speaking, an advocate of nonviolence. However, he was deeply troubled by government misbehavior, notably the institution of slavery and the Mexican–American War, which he saw as a blatant act of imperialist aggression by the United States. Thoreau protested by famously refusing to pay taxes and was imprisoned as a result. He was influential in developing the concept of civil disobedience and had a powerful effect on the thinking of Leo Tolstoy and Mohandas Gandhi, among many others. Thoreau, in turn—like Gandhi after him—had been influenced by the Bhagavad Gita, the great Hindu epic that emphasized the importance of renouncing personal possessiveness and striving in pursuit of greater aims.

Advocates of civil disobedience have long been considered unpatriotic, not only because they recommend a less bellicose stand toward proclaimed national "enemies" but also because their efforts are in some ways subversive of accepted national values. When, in the 1960s, Black Power advocate H. Rap Brown pointed out that violence was "as American as cherry pie," he spoke a part of the truth. So did theologian and peace activist Thomas Merton, when he warned that the sources of violence can be found

> not in esoteric groups but in the very culture itself, its mass media, its extreme individualism and competitiveness, its inflated myths of virility and toughness, and its overwhelming preoccupation [with means of destruction].[2]

Thoreau's call for civil disobedience and for the priority of conscience, combined with the image of him living in relative isolation by the shores of Walden Pond, challenge us to consider the position of the peace activist as principled outsider. Thus, pacifism and tax resistance, for example, are warily tolerated in the United States so long as they are performed by small and uninfluential groups. But as Thomas Merton pointed out,

> There is also an implication that any minority stand against war on grounds of conscience is *ipso facto* a kind of deviant and morally eccentric position, to be tolerated only because there are always a few religious half-wits around in any case, and one has to humor them in order to preserve the nation's reputation for respecting individual liberty.[3]

The following selection is from Thoreau's essay "Civil Disobedience."

— ⬡ —

From *Civil Disobedience: Theory and Practice* by Henry David Thoreau.

[2] Thomas Merton, *The Non-Violent Alternative* (New York: Farrar, Straus & Giroux, 1980).
[3] Merton, *Non-Violent Alternative.*

heartily accept the motto—"That government is best which governs least"; and I should like to see it acted up to more rapidly and systematically. Carried out, it finally amounts to this, which also I believe—"That government is best which governs not at all"; and when men are prepared for it, that will be the kind of government which they will have. Government is at best but an expedient; but most governments are usually, and all governments are sometimes, inexpedient. The objections which have been brought against a standing army, and they are many and weighty, and deserve to prevail, may also at last be brought against a standing government. The standing army is only an arm of the standing government. The government itself, which is only the mode which the people have chosen to execute their will, is equally liable to be abused and per-verted before the people can act through it. Witness the present Mexican war, the work of comparatively a few individuals using the standing government as their tool; for, in the outset, the people would not have consented to this measure.

This American government—what is it but a tradition, though a recent one, endeavoring to transmit itself unimpaired to posterity, but each instant losing some of its integrity? It has not the vitality and force of a single living man; for a single man can bend it to his will. It is a sort of wooden gun to the people themselves. But it is not the less necessary for this; for the people must have some complicated machinery or other, and hear its din, to satisfy that idea of government which they have. Governments show thus how successfully men can be imposed on, even impose on themselves, for their own advantage. It is excellent, we must all allow. Yet this government never of itself furthered any enterprise, but by the alacrity with which it got out of its way. *It* does not keep the country free. *It* does not settle the West. *It* does not educate. The character inherent in the American people has done all that has been accomplished; and it would have done somewhat more, if the government had not sometimes got in its way. For government is an expedient by which men would fain succeed in let-ting one another alone; and, as has been said, when it is most expedient, the governed are most let alone by it. . . .

But, to speak practically and as a citizen, unlike those who call themselves no-government men, I ask for, not at once no government, but *at once* a better government. Let every man make known what kind of government would command his respect, and that will be one step toward obtaining it.

. . . I think that we should be men first, and subjects afterward. It is not desirable to cultivate a respect for the law, so much as for the right. The only obligation which I have a right to assume, is to do at any time what I think right. It is truly enough said, that a corporation has no conscience; but a corporation of conscientious men is a corporation *with* a conscience. Law never made men a whit more just; and, by means of their respect for it, even the well-disposed are daily made the agents of injustice. A common and natural result of an undue respect for law is, that you may see a file of soldiers, colonel, captain, corporal, privates, powder monkeys, and all, marching in admirable order over hill and dale to the wars, against their wills, ay, against their com-mon sense and consciences, which makes it very steep marching indeed, and produces a palpitation of the heart. They have no doubt that it is a dam-nable business in which they are concerned; they are all peaceably inclined. Now, what are they? Men at all? or small movable forts and magazines, at the service of some unscrupulous man in power? . . .

The mass of men serve the state thus, not as men mainly, but as machines, with their bodies. They are the standing army, and the militia, jailers, constables, posse comitatus, & c. In most cases there is no free exercise whatever of the judgment or of the moral sense; but they put themselves on a level with wood and earth and stones; and wooden men can perhaps be manufactured that will serve the pur-pose as well. Such command no more respect than men of straw or a lump of dirt. They have the same sort of worth only as horses and dogs. Yet such as these even are commonly esteemed good citizens. Others—as most legislators, politicians, lawyers, ministers, and officeholders—serve the state chiefly with their heads; and, as they rarely make any moral distinctions, they are as likely to serve the Devil, without *intending* it, as God. A very few, as heroes, patriots, martyrs, reformers in the great sense, and *men*, serve the state with the consciences also, and so necessarily resist it for the most part; and they are commonly treated as enemies by it....

How does it become a man to behave toward this American government to-day? I answer, that he cannot without disgrace be associated with it. I cannot for an instant recognize the political organization as *my* government which is the *slave's* government also.

All men recognize the right of revolution; that is, the right to refuse allegiance to, and to resist, the government, when its tyranny or its inefficiency are great and unendurable. But almost all say that such is not the case now. But such was the case, they think, in the Revolution of '75. If one were to tell me that this was a bad government because it taxed certain foreign commodities brought to its ports, it is most probable that I should not make an ado about it, for I can do without them. All machines have their friction; and possibly this does enough good to counterbalance the evil. At any rate, it is a great evil to make a stir about it. But when the friction comes to have its machine, and oppression and robbery are organized, I say, let us not have such a machine any longer. In other words, when a sixth of the population of a nation which has undertaken to be the refuge of liberty are slaves, and a whole country is unjustly overrun and conquered by a foreign army, and subjected to military law, I think that it is not too soon for honest men to rebel and revolutionize. What makes this duty the more urgent is the fact, that the country so overrun is not our own, but ours is the invading army.

...I quarrel not with far-off foes, but with those who, near at home, cooperate with, and do the bidding of, those far away, and without whom the latter would be harmless. We are accustomed to say, that the mass of men are unprepared; but improvement is slow, because the few are not materially wiser or better than the many. It is not so important that many should be as good as you, as that there be some absolute goodness somewhere; for that will leaven the whole lump. There are thousands who are *in opinion* opposed to slavery and to the war, who yet in effect do nothing to put an end to them; who, esteeming themselves children of Washington and Franklin, sit down with their hands in their pockets, and say that they know not what to

do, and do nothing; who even postpone the question of freedom to the question of free-trade, and quietly read the prices-current along with the latest advices from Mexico, after dinner, and, it may be, fall asleep over them both. What is the price-current of an honest man and patriot to-day? They hesitate, and they regret, and sometimes they petition; but they do nothing in earnest and with effect. They will wait, well disposed, for others to remedy the evil, that they may no longer have it to regret....

It is not a man's duty, as a matter of course, to devote himself to the eradication of any, even the most enormous wrong; he may still properly have other concerns to engage him; but it is his duty, at least, to wash his hands of it, and, if he gives it no thought longer, not to give it practically his support. If I devote myself to other pursuits and contemplations, I must first see, at least, that I do not pursue them sitting upon another man's shoulders. I must get off him first, that he may pursue his contemplations too. See what gross inconsistency is tolerated. I have heard some of my townsmen say, "I should like to have them order me out to help put down an insurrection of the slaves, or to march to Mexico— see if I would go"; and yet these very men have each, directly by their allegiance, and so indirectly, at least, by their money, furnished a substitute....

How can a man be satisfied to entertain an opinion merely, and enjoy *it*? Is there any enjoyment in it, if his opinion is that he is aggrieved? If you are cheated out of a single dollar by your neighbor, you do not rest satisfied with knowing that you are cheated, or with saying that you are cheated, or even with petitioning him to pay you your due; but you take effectual steps at once to obtain the full amount, and see that you are never cheated again. Action from principle, the perception and the performance of right, changes things and relations; it is essentially revolutionary, and does not consist wholly with anything which was. It not only divides states and churches, it divides families; ay, it divides the *individual*, separating the diabolical in him from the divine.

Unjust laws exist: shall we be content to obey them, or shall we endeavor to amend them, and obey them until we have succeeded, or shall we transgress them at once? Men generally, under such a government as this, think that they ought to wait until they have persuaded the majority to alter them. They think that, if they should resist, the remedy would be worse than the evil. But it is the fault of the government itself that the remedy *is* worse than the evil. *It* makes it worse. Why is it not more apt to anticipate and provide for reform? Why does it not cherish its wise minority? Why does it cry and resist before it is hurt? Why does it not encourage its citizens to be on the alert to point out its faults, and *do* better than it would have them? Why does it always crucify Christ, and excommunicate Copernicus and Luther, and pronounce Washington and Franklin rebels?...

If the injustice is part of the necessary friction of the machine of government, let it go, let it go: perchance it will wear smooth—certainly the machine will wear out. If the injustice has a spring, or a pulley, or a rope, or a crank, exclusively for itself, then perhaps you may consider whether the remedy will not be worse than the evil; but if it is of such a nature that it requires you to be the agent of injustice to another, then, I say, break the law. Let your life be a counter friction to stop the machine. What I have to do is to see, at any rate, that I do not lend myself to the wrong which I condemn....

I do not hesitate to say, that those who call themselves Abolitionists should at once effectually withdraw their support, both in person and property, from the government of Massachusetts, and not wait till they constitute a majority of one, before they suffer the right to prevail through them. I think that it is enough if they have God on their side, without waiting for that other one. Moreover, any man more right than his neighbors constitutes a majority of one already.

...I know this well, that if one thousand, if one hundred, if ten men whom I could name—if ten *honest* men only—ay, if *one* HONEST man, in this State of Massachusetts, *ceasing to hold slaves*, were actually to withdraw from this copartnership, and be locked up in the county jail therefore, it would be the abolition of slavery in America. For it matters not how small the beginning may seem to be: what is once well done is done forever....

Under a government which imprisons any unjustly, the true place for a just man is also a prison.

The proper place to-day, the only place which Massachusetts has provided for her freer and less desponding spirits, is in her prisons, to be put out and locked out of the State by her own act, as they have already put themselves out by their principles. It is there that the fugitive slave, and the Mexican prisoner on parole, and the Indian come to plead the wrongs of his race, should find them; on that separate, but more free and honorable ground, where the State places those who are not *with* her, but *against* her—the only house in a slave State in which a free man can abide with honor. If any think that their influence would be lost there, and their voices no longer afflict the ear of the State, that they would not be as an enemy within its walls, they do not know by how much truth is stronger than error, nor how much more eloquently and effectively he can combat injustice who has experienced a little in his own person. Cast your whole vote, not a strip of paper merely, but your whole influence. A minority is powerless while it conforms to the majority; it is not even a minority then; but it is irresistible when it clogs by its whole weight. If the alternative is to keep all just men in prison, or give up war and slavery, the State will not hesitate which to choose. If a thousand men were not to pay their tax-bills this year, that would not be a violent and bloody measure, as it would be to pay them, and enable the State to commit violence and shed innocent blood. This is, in fact, the definition of a peaceable revolution, if any such is possible. If the tax-gatherer, or any other public officer, asks me, as one has done, "But what shall I do?" my answer is, "If you really wish to do anything, resign your office." When the subject has refused allegiance, and the officer has resigned his office, then the revolution is accomplished. But even suppose blood should flow. Is there not a sort of bloodshed when the conscience is wounded? Through this wound a man's real manhood and immortality flow out, and he bleeds to an everlasting death. I see this blood flowing now....

I have paid no poll-tax for six years. I was put into a jail once on this account, for one night; and, as I stood considering the walls of solid stone, two or three feet thick, the door of wood and iron, a foot thick, and the iron grating which strained the light, I could not help being struck with the foolishness of that institution which treated me as if I were mere flesh and blood and bones, to be locked up.

I wondered that it should have concluded at length that this was the best use it could put me to, and had never thought to avail itself of my services in some way. I saw that, if there was a wall of stone between me and my townsmen, there was a still more difficult one to climb or break through, before they could get to be as free as I was. I did not for a moment feel confined, and the walls seemed a great waste of stone and mortar. I felt as if I alone of all my townsmen had paid my tax. They plainly did not know how to treat me, but behaved like persons who are underbred. In every threat and in every compliment there was a blunder; for they thought that my chief desire was to stand the other side of that stone wall. I could not but smile to see how industriously they locked the door on my meditations, which followed them out again without let or hindrance, and *they* were really all that was dangerous. As they could not reach me, they had resolved to punish my body; just as boys, if they cannot come at some person against whom they have a spite, will abuse his dog. I saw that the State was half-witted, that it was timid as a lone woman with her silver spoons, and that it did not know its friends from its foes, and I lost all my remaining respect for it, and pitied it.

Thus the State never intentionally confronts a man's sense, intellectual or moral, but only his body, his senses. It is not armed with superior wit or honesty, but with superior physical strength. I was not born to be forced. I will breathe after my own fashion. Let us see who is the strongest. What force has a multitude? They can only force me who obey a higher law than I. They force me to become like themselves. I do not hear of *men* being *forced* to live this way or that by masses of men. What sort of life were that to live? When I meet a government which says to me, "Your money or your life," why should I be in haste to give it my money? It may be in a great strait, and not know what to do: I cannot help that. It must help itself; do as I do. It is not worth the while to snivel about it. I am not responsible for the successful working of the machinery of society. I am not the son of the engineer. I perceive that, when an acorn and a chestnut fall side by side, the one does not remain inert to make way for the other, but both obey their own laws, and spring and grow and flourish as best they can, till one, perchance, overshadows

and destroys the other. If a plant cannot live according to its nature, it dies; and so a man.

...I have never declined paying the highway tax, because I am as desirous of being a good neighbor as I am of being a bad subject; and, as for supporting schools, I am doing my part to educate my fellow-countrymen now. It is for no particular item in the tax-bill that I refuse to pay it. I simply wish to refuse allegiance to the State, to withdraw and stand aloof from it effectually. I do not care to trace the course of my dollar, if I could, till it buys a man or a musket to shoot one with—the dollar is innocent—but I am concerned to trace the effects of my allegiance. In fact, I quietly declare war with the State, after my fashion, though I will still make what use and get what advantage of her I can, as is usual in such cases.

...I sometimes say to myself, When many millions of men, without heat, without ill will, without personal feeling of any kind, demand of you a few shillings only, without the possibility, such is their constitution, of retracting or altering their present demand, and without the possibility, on your side, of appeal to any other millions, why expose yourself to this overwhelming brute force? You do not resist cold and hunger, the winds and the waves, thus obstinately; you quietly submit to a thousand similar necessities. You do not put your head into the fire. But just in proportion as I regard this as not wholly a brute force, but partly a human force, and consider that I have relations to those millions as to so many millions of men, and not of mere brute or inanimate things, I see that appeal is possible, first and instantaneously, from them to the Maker of them, and secondly, from them to themselves. But, if I put my head deliberately into the fire, there is no appeal to fire or to the Maker of fire, and I have only myself to blame....

I do not wish to quarrel with any man or nation. I do not wish to split hairs, to make fine distinctions, or set myself up as better than my neighbors. I seek rather, I may say, even an excuse for conforming to the laws of the land. I am but too ready to conform to them. Indeed, I have reason to suspect myself on this head; and each year, as the tax-gatherer comes round, I find myself disposed to review the acts and position of the general and State governments, and the spirit of the people, to discover a pretext for conformity....

The authority of government, even such as I am willing to submit to—for I will cheerfully obey those who know and can do better than I, and in many things even those who neither know nor can do so well—is still an impure one: to be strictly just, it must have the sanction and consent of the governed. It can have no pure right over my person and property but what I concede to it. The progress from an absolute to a limited monarchy, from a limited monarchy to a democracy, is a progress toward a true respect for the individual. Even the Chinese philosopher was wise enough to regard the individual as the basis of the empire. Is a democracy, such as we know it, the last improvement possible in government? Is it not possible to take a step further toward recognizing and organizing the rights of man? There will never be a really free and enlightened State, until the State comes to recognize the individual as a higher and independent power, from which all its own power and authority are derived, and treats him accordingly. I please myself with imagining a State at last which can afford to be just to all men, and to treat the individual with respect as a neighbor; which even would not think it inconsistent with its own repose, if a few were to live aloof from it, not meddling with it, nor embraced by it, who fulfilled all the duties of neighbors and fellow-men. A State which bore this kind of fruit, and suffered it to drop off as fast as it ripened, would prepare the way for a still more perfect and glorious State, which also I have imagined, but not yet anywhere seen.

Leo Tolstoy

LETTER TO ERNEST HOWARD CROSBY

As a young man, Leo Tolstoy served in the Russian army during the Crimean War. In his later years, however, Tolstoy increasingly adopted a unique brand of Christianity, embracing personal nonviolence and especially the first commandment, "Thou shalt not kill," so vigorously that he was widely hailed as the thirteenth apostle. Tolstoy was especially concerned about personal compliance with war, which he denounced as nothing less than murder. As such, his writings stand in marked contrast to the "Christian realist" tradition, which sought to elaborate situations under which recourse to war was acceptable.

Tolstoy maintained a kind of principled anarchism, opposing not only participation in war but the very workings of government, whose institutionalized violence he considered inimical to peace and to religious conscience. In his "Letter on the Peace Conference," Tolstoy wrote,

> Armies can be reduced and abolished only in opposition to the will, but never by the will, of government. Armies will only be diminished and abolished when people cease to trust governments, and themselves seek salvation from the miseries that oppress them, and seek that safety, not by the complicated and delicate combinations of diplomats, but in the simple fulfillment of that law, binding upon every man, inscribed in all religious

From "Letter to Ernest Howard Crosby" by Leo Tolstoy. In *Writings on Civil Disobedience and Nonviolence,* translated by Aylmer Mude. 1987. Philadelphia: New Society Publishers.

teachings, and present in every heart, not to do to others what you wish them not to do to you—above all, not to slay your neighbors.

Armies will first diminish, and then disappear, only when public opinion brands with contempt those who, whether from fear, or for advantage, sell their liberty and enter the ranks of those murderers, called soldiers; and when the men now ignored and even blamed—who, in despite of all the persecution and suffering they have borne—have refused to yield the control of their actions into the hands of others, and become the tools of murder—are recognized by public opinion to be the foremost champions and benefactors of mankind. Only then will armies first diminish and then quite disappear, and a new era in the life of mankind will commence. And that time is near.

Tolstoy was convinced that the common people are as responsible for war as their leaders. This, in turn, contributed to his determination that individuals have the opportunity—indeed, the responsibility—to take things into their own hands and refuse to fight.

In the following selection, the influence of Eastern thought can be seen in Tolstoy's embrace of nonviolence, notably his rejection of ethical egoism and even utilitarianism: "the greatest good for the greatest number."

———————————————— ⟨⟩ ————————————————

"What would happen if people were all obliged to obey the law of nonresistance?"

But, in the first place, it is impossible to oblige every one to accept the law of nonresistance. Secondly, if it were possible to do so, such compulsion would in itself be a direct negation of the very principle set up. Oblige all men to refrain from violence? Who then should enforce the decision? Thirdly, and this is the chief point, the question, as put by Christ, is not at all, "Can nonresistance become a general law for humanity?" but, "How much each man act to fulfil his allotted task, to save his soul, and to do the will of God, three things which are really one and the same thing?"...

Tradition—the collective wisdom of my greatest forerunners—tells me that I should do unto others as I would that they should do unto me. My reason shows me that only by all men acting thus is the highest happiness for all men attainable. Only when I yield myself to that intuition of love which demands obedience to this law is my own heart happy and at rest. And not only can I then know how to act, but I can and do discern that work, to cooperate in which my activity was designed and is required. I cannot fathom God's whole design, for the sake of which the universe exists and lives; but the divine work which

is being accomplished in this world, and in which I participate by living, is comprehensible to me.

This work is the annihilation of discord and strife among men, and among all creatures; and the establishment of the highest unity, concord, and love. It is the fulfilment of the promises of the Hebrew prophets, who foretold a time when all men should be taught by truth, when spears should be turned into reaping-hooks, swords be beaten to plowshares, and the lion lie down with the lamb. So that a man of Christian intelligence not only knows what he has to do, but he also understands the work he is doing. He has to act so as to cooperate toward the establishment of the kingdom of God on earth. For this, a man must obey his intuition of God's will, i.e., he must act lovingly toward others, as he would that others should act toward him. Thus the intuitive demands of man's soul coincide with the external aim of life which he sees before him....

And yet, in spite of such a twofold indication, clear and indubitable to a man of Christian understanding of what is the real aim and meaning of human life, and of what men should do and should not do, we find people (and people calling themselves Christians) who decide that in such and such circumstances men ought to abandon God's law and reason's guidance, and act in opposition to them; because, according to their concep-tion, the effects of actions performed in submission to God's law may be detrimental or inconvenient.

According to the law, contained alike in tradi-tion, in our reason, and in our hearts, man should always do unto others as he would that they should do unto him; he should always cooperate in the development of love and union among created beings. But on the contrary, in the judgment of these people who look ahead, as long as it is premature, in their opinion, to obey this law, man should do violence, imprison or kill people, and thereby evoke anger and venom instead of loving union in the hearts of men. It is as if a bricklayer, set to do a par-ticular task, and knowing that he was cooperating with others to build a house, after receiving clear and precise instructions from the master himself how to build a certain wall, should receive from some fellow bricklayers (who like himself knew neither the plan of the house nor what would fit in with it) orders to cease building his wall, and instead rather to pull down a wall which other workmen had erected.

Astonishing delusion! A being who breathes one day and vanishes the next receives one definite, indubitable law to guide him through the brief term of his life; but instead of obeying that law he prefers to fancy that he knows what is necessary, advanta-geous, and well-timed for men, for all the world—this world which continually shifts and evolves; and for the sake of some advantage (which each man pictures after his own fancy) he decides that he and other people should temporarily abandon the indubitable law given to one and to all, and should act, not as they would that others should act toward them, bringing love into the world, but instead do violence, imprison, kill, and bring into the world enmity whenever it seems profitable to do so. And he decides to act thus, though he knows that the most horrible cruelties, martyrdoms, and mur-ders—from the inquisitions, and the murders, and horrors of all the revolutions, down to the violences of contemporary anarchists, and their slaughter by the established authorities—have only occurred because people will imagine that they know what is necessary for mankind and for the world. But are there not always, at any given moment, two opposite parties, each of which declares that it is necessary to use force against the other—the "law and order" party against the "anarchist"; the "anarchist" against the "law and order" men; English against Americans, and Americans against English, and English against Germans; and so forth in all possible combinations and rearrangements?

A man enlightened by Christianity sees that he has no reason to abandon the law of God, given to enable him to walk with sure foot through life, in order to follow the chance, inconstant, and often contradictory demands of men. But besides this, if he has lived a Christian life for some time, and has developed in himself a Christian moral sensibility, he literally cannot act as people demand of him. Not this reason only, but his feeling also, makes it impossible. To many people of our society it would be impossible to torture or kill a baby, even if they were told that by so doing they could save hundreds of people. And in the same way a man, when he has developed a Christian sensibility of heart, finds a whole series of actions are become impossible for him. For instance, a Christian who is obliged to take part in judicial proceedings in which a man may be sentenced to death, or who is obliged to take part in evictions, or in debating a proposal leading to war, or to participate in preparations for war (not to mention war itself), is in a position parallel to that of a kindly man called on to torture or to kill a baby. It is not reason alone that forbids him to do what is demanded of him; he feels instinctively that he can-not do it. For certain actions are morally impossible, just as others are physically impossible. As a man cannot lift a mountain, and as a kindly man can-not kill an infant, so a man living the Christian life cannot take part in deeds of violence. Of what value then to him are arguments about the imaginary advantages of doing what is morally impossible for him to do?

But how is a man to act when he sees clearly an evil in following the law of love and its corollary law of nonresistance? How (to use the stock example) is a man to act when he sees a criminal killing or outraging a child, and he can only save the child by killing the criminal? When such a case is put, it is generally assumed that the only possible reply is that one should kill the assailant to save the child.

But this answer is given so quickly and decidedly only because we are all so accustomed to the use of violence, not only to save a child, but even to prevent a neighboring government altering its frontier at the expense of ours, or to prevent some one from smuggling lace across that frontier, or even to defend our garden fruit from a passerby. It is assumed that to save the child, the assailant should be killed.

But it is only necessary to consider the question, "On what grounds ought a man, whether he be or be not a Christian, to act so?" in order to come to the conclusion that such action has no reasonable foundation, and only seems to us necessary because up to two thousand years ago such conduct was considered right, and a habit of acting so had been formed. Why should a non-Christian, not acknowledging God, and not regarding the fulfilment of His will as the aim of life, decide to kill the criminal in order to defend the child? By killing the former he kills for certain; whereas he cannot know positively whether the criminal would have killed the child or not. But letting that pass, who shall say whether the child's life was more needed, was better, than the other's life? Surely, if the non-Christian knows not God, and does not see life's meaning to be in the performance of His will, the only rule for his actions must be a reckoning, a conception, of which is more profitable for him and for all men, a continuation of the criminal's life or of the child's. To decide that, he needs to know what would become of the child whom he saves, and what, had he not killed him, would have been the future of the assailant. And as he cannot know this, the non-Christian has no sufficient rational ground for killing a robber to save a child.

If a man be a Christian, and consequently acknowledges God, and sees the meaning of life in fulfilling His will, then, however ferocious the assailant, however innocent and lovely the child, he has even less ground to abandon the God-given law, and to do to the criminal as the criminal wishes to do to the child. He may plead with the assailant, may interpose his own body between the assailant and the victim; but there is one thing he cannot do—he cannot deliberately abandon the law he has received from God, the fulfilment of which alone gives meaning to his life. Very probably bad education, or his

animal nature, may cause a man, Christian or non-Christian, to kill an assailant, not to save a child, but even to save himself or to save his purse. But it does not follow that he is right in acting thus, or that he should accustom himself or others to think such conduct right. What it does show is that, notwithstanding a coating of education and of Christianity, the habits of the stone age are yet so strong in man that he still commits actions long since condemned by his reasonable conscience.

I see a criminal killing a child, and I can save the child by killing the assailant—therefore, in certain cases, violence must be used to resist evil. A man's life is in danger, and can be saved only by my telling a lie—therefore, in certain cases, one must lie. A man is starving, and I can only save him by stealing—therefore, in certain cases, one must steal. . . . There is no moral law concerning which one might not devise a case in which it is difficult to decide which is more moral, to disobey the law or to obey it? But all such devices fail to prove that the laws, "Thou shalt not lie, steal, or kill," are invalid.

It is thus with the law of nonresistance. People know it is wrong to use violence, but they are so anxious to continue to live a life secured by "the strong arm of the law," that, instead of devoting their intellects to the elucidation of the evils which have flowed, and are still flowing, from admitting that man has a right to use violence to his fellow-men, they prefer to exert their mental powers in defense of that error. *Fais ce que dois, advienne que pourra*—"Do what's right, come what may"—is an expression of profound wisdom. We each can know indubitably what we ought to do, but what results will follow from our actions we none of us either do or can know. Therefore it follows that, besides feeling the call of duty, we are further driven to act as duty bids us by the consideration that we have no other guidance, but are totally ignorant of what will result from our action.

Christian teaching indicates what a man should do to perform the will of Him who sent him into life; and discussion as to what results we anticipate from such or such human actions have nothing to do with Christianity, but are just an example of the error which Christianity eliminates. None of us has ever yet met the imaginary criminal with the imaginary child, but all the horrors which fill the annals of history and of our own times came, and come, from this one thing, namely, that people will believe they really foresee speculative future results of actions.

The case is this. People once lived an animal life, and violated or killed whom they thought well to violate or to kill. They even ate one another, and public opinion approved of it. Thousands of years ago, as far back as the times of Moses, a day came when people had realized that to violate or kill one another is bad. But there were people for whom the reign of force was advantageous, and these did not approve of the change, but assured themselves and others that to do deeds of violence and to kill people is not always bad, but that there are circumstances when it is necessary and even moral. And violence and slaughter, though not so frequent or so cruel as before, continued, only with this difference, that those who committed or commended such acts excused themselves by pleading that they did it for the benefit of humanity.

It was just this sophistical justification of violence that Christ denounced. When two enemies fight, each may think his own conduct justified by the circumstances. Excuses can be made for every use of violence, and no infallible standard has ever been discovered by which to measure the worth of these excuses. Therefore Christ taught us to disbelieve in any excuse for violence, and (contrary to what had been taught by them of old times) never to use violence. One would have thought that those who have professed Christianity would be indefatigable in exposing deception in this matter; for in such exposure lay one of the chief manifestations

of Christianity. What really happened was just the reverse. People who profited by violence, and who did not wish to give up their advantages, took on themselves a monopoly of Christian preaching, and declared that, as cases can be found in which non-resistance causes more harm than the use of violence (the imaginary criminal killing the imaginary child), therefore Christ's doctrine of non-resistance need not always be followed; and that one may deviate from His teaching to defend one's life or the life of others; or to defend one's country, to save society from lunatics or criminals, and in many other cases.

The decision of the question in what cases Christ's teaching should be set aside was left to the very people who employed violence. So that it ended by Christ's teaching on the subject of not resisting evil by violence being completely annulled....The real question is not whether it will be good or bad for a certain human society that people should follow the law of love and the consequent law of non-resistance. But it is this: Do you, who today live and tomorrow will die, you who are indeed tending deathward every moment, do you wish now, immediately and entirely, to obey the law of Him who sent you into life, and who clearly showed you His will, alike in tradition and in your mind and heart; or do you prefer to resist His will? And as soon as the question is put thus, only one reply is possible: I wish now, this moment, without delay or hesitation, to the very utmost of my strength, neither waiting for one or counting the cost, to do that which alone is clearly demanded by Him who sent me into the world; and on no account, and under no conditions, do I wish to, or can I, act otherwise—for herein lies my only possibility of a rational and unharassed life.

Edna St. Vincent Millay

CONSCIENTIOUS OBJECTOR

Nonviolent antiwar protest takes many forms. Much has been written by way of specific advice for individuals contemplating tax resistance, draft resistance, organized opposition to various government policies, and so forth. Consistent with the goal of this book, however, which is to focus on general principles and to provide lasting food for thought, we present "Conscientious Objector," a remarkable and timeless poem by Edna St. Vincent Millay.

I shall die,
 but that is all that I shall do for Death.
I hear him leading his horse out of the stall; I hear
 the clatter on the barn floor.
He is in haste; he has business in Cuba, business
 in the Balkans, many calls to make this
 morning.
But I will not hold the bridle
 while he cinches the girth.
And he may mount by himself:
 I will not give him a leg up.

Though he flick my shoulders with his whip, I will
 not tell him which way the fox ran.

With his hoof on my breast, I will not tell him where
 the black boy hides in the swamp.
I shall die, but that is all I shall do for Death; I am
 not on his payroll.

I will not tell him the whereabouts of my friends
 nor of my enemies either.
Though he promise me much,
 I will not map him the route to any man's door.
Am I a spy in the land of the living,
 that I should deliver men to Death?
Brother, the password and the plans of our city are
 safe with me; never through me Shall you be
 overcome.

Albert Camus

NEITHER VICTIMS NOR EXECUTIONERS

Personal commitment to nonviolence takes many forms. To complement Millay's statement in poetry, and Tolstoy's Christian-based faith, we present a prose, secular selection, from a renowned essay by French philosopher-novelist-playwright Albert Camus. Ironically, "Neither Victims nor Executioners" first appeared in a magazine titled *Combat*, which was edited by Camus on behalf of the anti-Nazi French Resistance during World War II. Somewhat like Tolstoy—although without the latter's religious motivation—Camus eventually committed himself to nonviolence. He was especially concerned with denying the legitimacy of violence on behalf of political ideologies of any persuasion.

The seventeenth century was the century of mathematics, the eighteenth that of the physical sciences, and the nineteenth that of biology.

Our twentieth century is the century of fear. I will be told that fear is not a science. But science must be somewhat involved since its latest theoretical

From Albert Camus, "Neither Victims nor Executioners," *Combat*, fall 1946. Translated by Dwight MacDonald, 1947. *Politics*, July–August, 1947.

advances have brought it to the point of negating itself while its perfected technology threatens the globe itself with destruction. Moreover, although fear itself cannot be considered a science, it is certainly a technique.

The most striking feature of the world we live in is that most of its inhabitants—with the exception of pietists of various kinds—are cut off from the future. Life has no validity unless it can project itself toward the future, can ripen and progress. Living against a wall is a dog's life.

…I once said that, after the experiences of the last two years, I could no longer hold to any truth which might oblige me, directly or indirectly, to demand a man's life. Certain friends whom I respected retorted that I was living in Utopia, that there was no political truth which could not one day reduce us to such an extremity, and that we must therefore either run the risk of this extremity or else simply put up with the world as it is.

They argued the point most forcefully. But I think they were able to put such force into it only because they were unable to really *imagine* other people's death. It is a freak of the times. We make love by telephone, we work not on matter but on machines, and we kill and are killed by proxy. We gain in cleanliness, but lose in understanding.

But the argument has another, indirect meaning: it poses the question of utopia. People like myself want not a world in which murder no longer exists (we are not so crazy as that!) but rather one in which murder is not legitimate. Here indeed we are utopian—and contradictory. For we do live, it is true, in a world where murder is legitimate, and we ought to change it if we do not like it. But it appears that we cannot change it without risking murder. Murder thus throws us back on murder, and we will continue to live in terror whether we accept the fact with resignation or wish to abolish it by means which merely replace one terror with another.

It seems to me every one should think this over. For what strikes me, in the midst of polemics, threats, and outbursts of violence, is the fundamental good will of every one. From Right to Left, every one, with the exception of a few swindlers, believes that his particular truth is the one to make men happy. And yet the combination of all these good intentions has produced the present infernal world, where men are killed, threatened, and deported, where war is prepared, where one cannot speak freely without being insulted or betrayed.…

Little is to be expected from present-day governments, since these live and act according to a murderous code. Hope remains only in the most difficult task of all: to reconsider everything from the ground up, so as to shape a living society inside a dying society. Men must therefore, as individuals, draw up among themselves, within frontiers and across them, a new social contract which will unite them according to more reasonable principles.

More precisely, the latter's task would be to speak out clearly against the confusions of the Terror and at the same time to define the values by which a peaceful world may live. The first objectives might be the drawing up of an international code of justice whose Article No. 1 would be the abolition of the death penalty, and an exposition of the basic principles of a sociable culture ("*civilisation du dialogue*"). Such an undertaking would answer the needs of an era which has found no philosophical justification for that thirst for fraternity which today burns in Western man. There is no idea, naturally, of constructing a new ideology, but rather of discovering a style of life.

Let us suppose that certain individuals resolve that they will consistently oppose to power the force of example; to authority, exhortation; to insult, friendly reasoning; to trickery, simple honor. Let us suppose they refuse all the advantages of present-day society and accept only the duties and obligations which bind them to other men. Let us suppose they devote themselves to orienting education, the press, and public opinion toward the principles outlined here. Then I say that such men would be acting not as utopians but as honest realists. They would be preparing the future and at the same time knocking down a few of the walls which imprison us today. If realism be the art of taking into account both the present and the future, of gaining the most while sacrificing the least, then who can fail to see the positively dazzling realism of such behavior?

Whether these men will arise or not I do not know. It is probable that most of them are even now thinking things over, and that is good. But one thing is sure: their efforts will be effective only to the degree they have the courage to give up, for the present, some of their dreams, so as to grasp the more firmly the essential point on which our very lives depend. Once there, it will perhaps turn out to be necessary, before they are done, to raise their voices....

To save what can be saved so as to open up some kind of future—that is the prime mover, the passion and the sacrifice that is required. It demands only that we reflect and then decide, clearly, whether humanity's lot must be made still more miserable in order to achieve far-off and shadowy ends, whether we should accept a world bristling with arms where brother kills brother; or whether, on the contrary, we should avoid bloodshed and misery as much as possible so that we give a chance for survival to later generations better equipped than we are.

For my part, I am fairly sure that I have made the choice. And, having chosen, I think that I must speak out, that I must state that I will never again be one of those, whoever they be, who compromise with murder, and that I must take the consequences of such a decision....

We are asked to love or to hate such and such a country and such and such a people. But some of us feel too strongly our common humanity to make such a choice. Those who really love the Russian people, in gratitude for what they have never ceased to be— that world leaven which Tolstoy and Gorky speak of—do not wish for them success in power-politics, but rather want to spare them, after the ordeals of the past, a new and even more terrible bloodletting. So, too, with the American people, and with the peoples of unhappy Europe. This is the kind of elementary truth we are liable to forget amidst the furious passions of our time.

Yes, it is fear and silence and the spiritual isolation they cause that must be fought today. And it is sociability ("*le dialogue*") and the universal intercommunication of men that must be defended. Slavery, injustice, and lies destroy this intercourse and forbid this sociability; and so we must reject them. But these evils are today the very stuff of history, so that many consider them necessary evils. It is true that we cannot "escape history," since we are in it up to our necks. But one may propose to fight within history

to preserve from history that part of man which is not its proper province. That is all I have tried to say here. The "point" of this article may be summed up as follows:

Modern nations are driven by powerful forces along the roads of power and domination. I will not say that these forces should be furthered or that they should be obstructed. They hardly need our help and, for the moment, they laugh at attempts to hinder them. They will, then, continue. But I will ask only this simple question: what if these forces wind up in a dead end, what if that logic of history on which so many now rely turns out to be a will-o'-the-wisp? What if, despite two or three world wars, despite the sacrifice of several generations and a whole system of values, our grandchildren—supposing they survive— find themselves no closer to a world society? It may well be that the survivors of such an experience will be too weak to understand their own sufferings. Since these forces are working themselves out and since it is inevitable that they continue to do so, there is no reason why some of us should not take on the job of keeping alive, through the apocalyptic historical vista that stretches before us, a modest thoughtfulness which, without pretending to solve everything, will constantly be prepared to give some human meaning to everyday life. The essential thing is that people should carefully weigh the price they must pay.

To conclude: all I ask is that, in the midst of a murderous world, we agree to reflect on murder and to make a choice. After that, we can distinguish those who accept the consequences of being murderers themselves or the accomplices of murderers, and those who refuse to do so with all their force and being. Since this terrible dividing line does actually exist, it will be a gain if it be clearly marked. Over the expanse of five continents throughout the coming years an endless struggle is going to be pursued between violence and friendly persuasion, a struggle in which, granted, the former has a thousand times the chances of success than that of the latter. But I have always held that, if he who bases his hopes on human nature is a fool, he who gives up in the face of circumstances is a coward. And henceforth, the only honorable course will be to stake everything on a formidable gamble: that words are more powerful than munitions.

Mohandas Gandhi

AHIMSA, OR THE WAY OF NONVIOLENCE

Mohandas Gandhi is the preeminent figure of nonviolence, at least in the twentieth century, if not future centuries. (The word "Mahatma" is an honorific title in the Hindi language, meaning "great soul.") Gandhi may have been the first person—certainly, he was the most effective and influential—to extend nonviolence from a principle of individual behavior to a concerted strategy grounded in a search for political and social justice.

Gandhi's teachings—as well as his practical example—have been carefully studied by many nonviolent leaders, including the Rev. Martin Luther King, Jr., who patterned his leadership of the civil rights struggle in the United States after Gandhi's decades-long efforts in South Africa and then India. (Gandhian thought and practice has also influenced human rights crusaders in China, Burma, Indonesia, and indeed, around the globe.)

"With the increased velocity of modern changes we do not know what the world will be a hundred years hence," wrote S. Radhakrishnan, vice president and later president of India, in the introduction to Gandhi's book of autobiographical reflections, *All Men Are Brothers.*

> We cannot anticipate the future currents of thought and feeling. But years may go their way, yet the great principles of *satya* and *ahimsa*, truth and nonviolence, are there to guide us. They are the silent stars keeping holy vigil above a tired and turbulent world. Like Gandhi we may be firm in our conviction that the sun shines above the drifting clouds.
>
> We live in an age which is aware of its own defeat and moral coarsening, an age in which old certainties are breaking down, the familiar patterns are tilting and cracking. There is increasing intolerance and embitterment.... It is our pride that one of the greatest figures of history lived in our generation, walked with us, spoke to us, taught us the way of civilized living. He who wrongs no one fears no one. He has nothing to hide and so is fearless. He looks everyone in the face. His step is firm, his body upright, and his words are direct and straight. Plato said long ago: "There always are in the world a few inspired men whose acquaintance is beyond price."

Gandhi explained that *ahimsa* "does not mean meek submission to the will of the evildoer, but it means pitting of one's whole soul against the will of the tyrant. Working under this law of our being, it is possible for a single individual to defy the whole might of an unjust empire..." In addition to *ahimsa* and *satya* (or *satyagraha*), another Gandhian term is crucially important: *tapasya*, a willingness to undergo suffering oneself and not to shift it onto another—including the opponent—as a consequence of one's commitment to the truth of nonviolence.

Although *tapasya* may be especially difficult for many people to accept or understand (not to mention, to practice!), it should not be especially foreign, especially if one substitutes "courage" for "willingness to suffer," which has the added benefit of helping dispel the frequent misunderstanding that practitioners of nonviolence are lazy or cowardly, seeking an easy way out of conflict.

The courage and commitment of *satyagrahis* come at a price, as revealed in this eyewitness account of the famous "salt *satyagraha*" of 1930. Gandhi and twenty-five hundred peaceful marchers arrived at a police stockade near the Dharasana Salt Works, in defiance of law and in complete silence, approaching and in turn being battered on the head with steel-shod clubs, while no one even raised an arm in self-protection: "From where I stood I heard the sickening whack of the clubs on unprotected skulls....The survivors, without breaking ranks, silently and doggedly marched on until struck down."[4] In the long run, such techniques have in fact been overwhelmingly successful, in no small part because of their powerful appeal to shared human conscience. (Once, when visiting England, Gandhi was asked his impression of Western civilization, to which he replied "It would be a good idea.")

It may be that—as is frequently pointed out—Gandhian nonviolence would not have succeeded against, say, a nuclear-armed Hitler. Perhaps it requires a degree of underlying humanity and goodwill on the other side. But it is also true that the British empire had not been especially gentle or humane in its treatment of colonial subjects and, in the end, persistent nonviolent tactics succeeded in liberating a nation of (at that time) more than 400 million people, without firing a shot.

Gandhi himself pointed out that nonviolence is more pervasive in ordinary human life than most of us realize and far more frequently (and successfully) employed than is violence.

It is hoped that the following selections will help acquaintant the reader with the remarkable, inspired person Gandhi was, and, in the process, reveal the potential for nonviolence as an approach to peace.

Nonviolence is the greatest force at the disposal of mankind. It is mightier than the mightiest weapon of destruction devised by the ingenuity of man. Destruction is not the law of the humans. Man lives freely by his readiness to die, if need be, at the hands of his brother, never by killing him. Every murder or other injury, no matter for what cause, committed or inflicted on another is a crime against humanity.

Harijan, July 20, 1931

The first condition of nonviolence is justice all round in every department of life. Perhaps, it is too much to expect of human nature. I do not, however, think so. No one should dogmatize about the capacity of human nature for degradation or exaltation.

Mahatma, V, April, 1940

Just as one must learn the art of killing in the training for violence, so one must learn the art of dying in the training for nonviolence. Violence does not mean emancipation from fear, but discovering the means of combating the cause of fear. Nonviolence, on the other hand, has no cause for fear. The votary of nonviolence has to cultivate the capacity for sacrifice

---

[4] Quoted in Erik Erikson, *Gandhi's Truth* (New York: W. W. Norton, 1969).

of the highest type in order to be free from fear. He recks not if he should lose his land, his wealth, his life. He who has not overcome all fear cannot practise *ahiṃsā* to perfection. The votary of *ahiṃsā* has only one fear, that is of God. He who seeks refuge in God ought to have a glimpse of the *Atma* that transcends the body; and the moment one has a glimpse of the imperishable *Atma* one sheds the love of the perishable body. Training in nonviolence is thus diametrically opposed to training in violence. Violence is needed for the protection of things external, nonviolence is needed for the protection of the *Atma*, for the protection of one's honour.

Harijan, September 1, 1940

It is no nonviolence if we merely love those that love us. It is nonviolence only when we love those that hate us. I know how difficult it is to follow this grand law of love. But are not all great and good things difficult to do? Love of the hater is the most difficult of all. But by the grace of God even this most difficult thing becomes easy to accomplish if we want to do it.

Letter of December 31, 1934

I have found that life persists in the midst of destruction and therefore there must be a higher law than that of destruction....

It is not that I am incapable of anger, for instance, but I succeed on almost all occasions to keep my feelings under control. Whatever may be the result, there is always in me conscious struggle for following the law of nonviolence deliberately and ceaselessly. Such a struggle leaves one stronger for it. The more I work at this law, the more I feel the delight in my life, the delight in the scheme of the universe. It gives me a peace and a meaning of the mysteries of nature that I have no power to describe.

Young India, October 1, 1931

If we turn our eyes to the time of which history has any record down to our own time, we shall find that man has been steadily progressing towards *ahiṃsā*. Our remote ancestors were cannibals. Then came a time when they were fed up with cannibalism and they began to live on chase. Next came a stage when man was ashamed of leading the life of

a wandering hunter. He therefore took to agriculture and depended principally on mother earth for his food. Thus from being a nomad he settled down to civilized stable life, founded villages and towns, and from member of a family he became member of a community and a nation. All these are signs of progressive *ahiṃsā* and diminishing *hiṃsā*. Had it been otherwise, the human species should have been extinct by now, even as many of the lower species have disappeared.

Prophets and *avatārs* have also taught the lesson of *ahiṃsā* more or less. Not one of them has professed to teach *hiṃsā*. And how should it be otherwise? *Hiṃsā* does not need to be taught. Man as animal is violent, but as Spirit is nonviolent. The moment he awakes to the Spirit within, he cannot remain violent. Either he progresses towards *ahiṃsā* or rushes to his doom. That is why the prophets and *avatārs* have taught the lesson of truth, harmony, brotherhood, justice, etc. all attributes of *ahiṃsā*.

Harijan, August 11, 1940

I have never claimed to present the complete science of nonviolence. It does not lend itself to such treatment. So far as I know, no single physical science does, not even the very exact science of mathematics. I am but a seeker.

Harijan, February 22, 1942

In the application of *Satyāgraha*, I discovered in the earliest stages that pursuit of truth did not admit of violence being inflicted on one's opponent but that he must be weaned from error by patience and sympathy. For, what appears to be truth to the one may appear to be error to another. And patience means self-suffering. So the doctrine came to mean vindication of truth, not by infliction of suffering on the opponent, but on one's self.

Young India, November, 1919

In this age of wonders no one will say that a thing or idea is worthless because it is new. To say it is impossible because it is difficult, is again not in consonance with the spirit of the age. Things undreamt of are daily being seen, the impossible is ever becoming possible. We are constantly being astonished these days at the amazing discoveries in the field of violence. But I maintain that far more undreamt of and seemingly impossible discoveries will be made in the field of nonviolence.

Harijan, August 25, 1940

Nonviolence is a universal principle and its operation is not limited by a hostile environment. Indeed, its efficacy can be tested only when it acts in the midst of and in spite of opposition. Our nonviolence would be a hollow thing and worth nothing, if it depended for its success on the goodwill of the authorities.

Harijan, November 12, 1938

No man could be actively nonviolent and not rise against social injustice no matter where it occurred.

Harijan, April 20, 1940

Passive resistance is a method of securing rights by personal suffering; it is the reverse of resistance by arms. When I refuse to do a thing that is repugnant to my conscience, I use soul-force. For instance, the government of the day has passed a law which is applicable to me. I do not like it. If by using violence I force the government to repeal the law, I am employing what may be termed body-force. If I do not obey the law and accept the penalty for its breach, I use soul-force. It involves sacrifice of self.

Everybody admits that sacrifice of self is infinitely superior to sacrifice of others. Moreover, if this kind of force is used in a cause that is unjust, only the person using it suffers. He does not make others suffer for his mistakes. Men have before now done many things which were subsequently found to have been wrong. No man can claim that he is absolutely in the right or that a particular thing is wrong because he thinks so, but it is wrong for him so long as that is his deliberate judgement. It is therefore meet that he should not do that which he knows to be wrong, and suffer the consequence whatever it may be. This is the key to the use of soul-force.

Indian Home Rule, 1909

You might of course say that there can be no nonviolent rebellion and there has been none known to history. Well, it is my ambition to provide an instance, and it is my dream that my country may

win its freedom through nonviolence. And, I would like to repeat to the world times without number, that I will not purchase my country's freedom at the cost of nonviolence. My marriage to nonviolence is such an absolute thing that I would rather commit suicide than be deflected from my position. I have not mentioned truth in this connexion, simply because truth cannot be expressed except by nonviolence.

Young India, November 12, 1931

The conviction has been growing upon me, that things of fundamental importance to the people are not secured by reason alone but have to be purchased with their suffering. Suffering is the law of human beings; war is the law of the jungle. But suffering is infinitely more powerful than the law of the jungle for converting the opponent and opening his ears, which are otherwise shut, to the voice of reason. Nobody has probably drawn up more petitions or espoused more forlorn causes than I and I have come to this fundamental conclusion that if you want something really important to be done you must not merely satisfy the reason, you must move the heart also. The appeal of reason is more to the head but the penetration of the heart comes from suffering. It opens up the inner understanding in man. Suffering is the badge of the human race, not the sword.

Young India, November 4, 1931

Nonviolence is a power which can be wielded equally by all—children, young men and women, or grown up people—provided they have a living faith in the God of Love and have therefore equal love for all mankind. When nonviolence is accepted as the law of life it must pervade the whole being and not be applied to isolated acts.

Harijan, September 5, 1936

Perfect nonviolence is impossible so long as we exist physically, for we would want some space at least to occupy. Perfect nonviolence whilst you are inhabiting the body is only a theory like Euclid's point or straight line, but we have to endeavour every moment of our lives.

Harijan, July 21, 1940

Taking life may be a duty. We do destroy as much life as we think necessary for sustaining our body. Thus for food we take life, vegetable and other, and for health we destroy mosquitoes and the like by the use of disinfectants, etc., and we do not think that we are guilty of irreligion in doing so . . . for the benefit of the species, we kill carnivorous beasts. . . . Even man-slaughter may be necessary in certain cases. Suppose a man runs amuck and goes furiously about, sword in hand, and killing anyone that comes in his way, and no one dares to capture him alive. Anyone who despatches this lunatic will earn the gratitude of the community and be regarded as a benevolent man.

Young India, November 4, 1926

A man cannot practise *ahiṃsā* and be a coward at the same time. The practice of *ahiṃsā* calls forth the greatest courage.

Speeches and Writings of Mahatma Gandhi,
no date given

Nonviolence is "not a resignation from all real fighting against wickedness." On the contrary, the nonviolence of my conception is a more active and real fight against wickedness than retaliation whose very nature is to increase wickedness. I contemplate a mental and therefore a moral opposition to immoralities. I seek entirely to blunt the edge of the tyrant's sword, not by putting up against it a sharper-edged weapon, but by disappointing his expectation that I would be offering physical resistance. The resistance of the soul that I should offer would elude him. It would at first dazzle him and at last compel recognition from him, which recognition would not humiliate but would uplift him. It may be urged that this is an ideal state. And so it is.

Young India, October 8, 1925

I object to violence because when it appears to do good, the good is only temporary; the evil it does is permanent. I do not believe that the killing of even every Englishman can do the slightest good to India. The millions will be just as badly off as they are today, if someone made it possible to kill off every Englishman tomorrow. The responsibility is more ours than that of the English for the present state of things. The English will be powerless to do evil if we

will but be good. Hence my incessant emphasis on reform from within.

Young India, May 21, 1925

History teaches one that those who have, no doubt with honest motives, ousted the greedy by using brute force against them, have in their turn become a prey to the disease of the conquered.

Young India, May 6, 1926

It is to me a matter of perennial satisfaction that I retain generally the affection and trust of those whose principles and policies I oppose. The South Africans gave me personally their confidence and extended their friendship. In spite of my denunciation of British policy and system I enjoy the affection of thousands of Englishmen and women, and in spite of unqualified condemnation of modern materialistic civilization, the circle of European and American friends is ever widening. It is again a triumph of nonviolence.

Young India, March 17, 1927

My experience, daily growing stronger and richer, tells me that there is no peace for individuals or for nations without practising truth and nonviolence to the uttermost extent possible for man. The policy of retaliation has never succeeded.

Young India, December 15, 1927

I have been practising with scientific precision nonviolence and its possibilities for an unbroken period of over fifty years. I have applied it in every walk of life—domestic, institutional, economic and political. I know of no single case in which it has failed. Where it has seemed sometimes to have failed, I have ascribed it to my imperfections. I claim no perfection for myself. But I do claim to be a passionate seeker after Truth, which is but another name for God. In the course of that search the discovery of nonviolence came to me. Its spread is my life mission. I have no interest in living except for the prosecution of that mission.

Harijan, July 6, 1940

I do not want to live at the cost of the life even of a snake. I should let him bite me to death rather than kill him. But it is likely that if God puts me to that cruel test and permits a snake to assault me, I may not have the courage to die, but that the beast in me may assert itself and I may seek to kill the snake in defending this perishable body. I admit that my belief has not become so incarnate in me as to warrant my stating emphatically that I have shed all fear of snakes so as to befriend them as I would like to be able to.

An Autobiography

Ahiṃsā is soul-force and the soul is imperishable, changeless, and eternal. The atom bomb is the acme of physical force and, as such, subject to the law of dissipation, decay, and death that governs the physical universe. Our scriptures bear witness that when soul-force is fully awakened in us, it becomes irresistible. But the test and condition of full awakening is that it must permeate every pore of our being and emanate with every breath that we breathe.

But no institution can be made nonviolent by compulsion. Nonviolence and truth cannot be written into a constitution. They have to be adopted of one's own free will. They must sit naturally upon us like next-to-skin garments or else they become a contradiction in terms.

Mahatma Gandhi, The Last Phase, II, circa 1947

My creed of nonviolence is an extremely active force. It has no room for cowardice or even weakness. There is hope for a violent man to be some day nonviolent, but there is none for a coward. I have therefore said more than once in these pages that if we do not know how to defend ourselves, our women, and our places of worship by the force of suffering, i.e., nonviolence, we must, if we are men, be at least able to defend all these by fighting.

Young India, June 16, 1927

In life, it is impossible to eschew violence completely. Now the question arises, where is one to draw the line? The line cannot be the same for everyone. For, although, essentially the principle is the same, yet everyone applies it in his or her own way. What is one man's food can be another's poison. Meat-eating is a sin for me. Yet, for another person, who has always lived on meat and never seen anything

wrong in it, to give it up, simply in order to copy me, will be a sin.

If I wish to be an agriculturist and stay in a jungle, I will have to use the minimum unavoidable violence, in order to protect my fields. I will have to kill monkeys, birds, and insects, which eat up my crops. If I do not wish to do so myself, I will have to engage someone to do it for me. There is not much difference between the two. To allow crops to be eaten up by animals, in the name of *ahiṃsā*, while there is a famine in the land, is certainly a sin. Evil and good are relative terms. What is good under certain conditions can become an evil or a sin, under a different set of conditions....

Mahatma, VII, 1946

The people of a village near Bettia told me that they had run away whilst the police were looting their houses and molesting their womenfolk. When they said that they had run away because I had told them to be nonviolent, I hung my head in shame. I assured them that such was not the meaning of my nonviolence. I expected them to intercept the mightiest power that might be in the act of harming those who were under their protection, and draw without retaliation all harm upon their own heads even to the point of death, but never to run away from the storm centre. It was manly enough to defend one's property, honour, or religion at the point of the sword. It was manlier and nobler to defend them without seeking to injure the wrongdoer. But it was unmanly, unnatural, and dishonourable to forsake the post of duty and, in order to save one's skin, to leave property, honour, or religion to the mercy of the wrongdoer. I could see my way of delivering *ahiṃ sā* to those who knew how to die, not to those who were afraid of death.

Gandhiji in Indian Villages, published in 1927

My nonviolence does not admit of running away from danger and leaving dear ones unprotected. Between violence and cowardly flight, I can only prefer violence to cowardice. I can no more preach nonviolence to a coward than I can tempt a blind man to enjoy healthy scenes. Nonviolence is the summit of bravery. And in my own experience, I have had no difficulty in demonstrating to men trained in the school of violence the superiority of nonviolence. As a coward, which I was for years, I harboured violence. I began to prize nonviolence only when I began to shed cowardice.

Young India, May 28, 1924

Nonviolence cannot be taught to a person who fears to die and has no power of resistance. A helpless mouse is not nonviolent because he is always eaten by pussy. He would gladly eat the murderess if he could, but he ever tries to flee from her. We do not call him a coward, because he is made by nature to behave no better than he does. But a man who, when faced by danger, behaves like a mouse, is rightly called a coward. He harbours violence and hatred in his heart and would kill his enemy if he could without hurting himself. He is a stranger to nonviolence. All sermonizing on it will be lost on him. Bravery is foreign to his nature. Before he can understand nonviolence he has to be taught to stand his ground and even suffer death, in the attempt to defend himself against the aggressor who bids fair to overwhelm him. To do otherwise would be to confirm his cowardice and take him farther away from nonviolence. Whilst I may not actually help anyone to retaliate, I must not let a coward seek shelter behind nonviolence so-called. Not knowing the stuff of which nonviolence is made, many have honestly believed that running away from danger every time was a virtue compared to offering resistance, especially when it was fraught with danger to one's life. As a teacher of nonviolence I must, so far as it is possible for me, guard against such an unmanly belief.

Harijan, July 20, 1935

I am not a visionary. I claim to be a practical idealist. Religion of nonviolence is not meant merely for the *rishis* and saints. It is meant for the common people as well. Nonviolence is the law of our species as violence is the law of the brute. The spirit lies dormant in the brute, and he knows no law but that of physical might. The dignity of man requires obedience to a higher law, to the strength of the spirit.

I have ventured to place before India the ancient law of self-sacrifice. For *Satyāgraha* and its offshoots, noncooperation and civil resistance are nothing but new names for the law of suffering. The *rishis,* who

discovered the law of nonviolence in the midst of violence, were greater geniuses than Newton. They were themselves greater warriors than Wellington. Having themselves known the use of arms, they realized their uselessness and taught a weary world that its salvation lay not through violence but through nonviolence.

Nonviolence in its dynamic condition means conscious suffering. It does not mean meek submission to the will of the evildoer, but it means putting of one's whole soul against the will of the tyrant. Working under this law of our being, it is possible for a single individual to defy the whole might of an unjust empire to save his honour, his religion, his soul, and lay the foundation for that empire's fall or its regeneration.

And so I am not pleading for India to practise nonviolence because it is weak. I want her to practise nonviolence being conscious of her strength and power. No training in arms is required for realization of her strength. We seem to need it, because we seem to think that we are but a lump of flesh. I want to recognize that she has a soul that cannot perish and that can rise triumphant above every physical weakness and defy the physical combination of a whole world....If India takes up the doctrine of the sword, she may gain momentary victory. Then India will cease to be the pride of my heart. I am wedded to India because I owe my all to her. I believe absolutely that she has a mission for the world. She is not to copy Europe blindly. India's acceptance of the doctrine of the sword will be the hour of my trial. I hope I shall not be found wanting. My religion has no geographical limits. If I have a living faith in it, it will transcend my love for India herself. My life is dedicated to the service of India through the religion of nonviolence which I believe to be the root of Hinduism.

Mahatma, II, *Young India,* August 11, 1920

I must continue to argue till I convert opponents or I own defeat. For my mission is to convert every Indian, even Englishmen, and finally the world to nonviolence for regulating mutual relations whether political, economic, social, or religious. If I am accused of being too ambitious, I should plead guilty. If I am told that my dream can never materialize, I would answer, "That is possible," and go my way. I am a seasoned soldier of nonviolence, and I have evidence enough to sustain my faith. Whether, therefore, I have one comrade or more or none, I must continue my experiment.

Mahatma, V, Harijan, January 13, 1940

It has been suggested by American friends that the atom bomb will bring in *ahiṃsā,* as nothing else can. It will, if it is meant that its destructive power will so disgust the world, that it will turn it away from violence for the time being. And this is very like a man glutting himself with the dainties to the point of nausea, and turning away from them only to return with redoubled zeal after the effect of nausea is well over. Precisely in the same manner will the world return to violence with renewed zeal, after the effect of disgust is worn out.

Often does good come out of evil. But that is God's, not man's plan. Man knows that only evil can come out of evil, as good out of good....The moral to be legitimately drawn from the supreme tragedy of the atom bomb is that it will not be destroyed by counter bombs, even as violence cannot be by counter violence. Mankind has to go out of violence only through nonviolence. Hatred can be overcome only by love. Counter hatred only increases the surface, as well as the depth of hatred....

Mahatma, VII, *Harijan,* July 1946

Gene Sharp

CIVILIAN RESISTANCE AS A NATIONAL DEFENSE

Could nonviolence be applied, as a practical matter, to the defense strategy of modern governments? One of the most seriously considered applications involves civilian-based defense, or CBD, which embraces a variety of nonviolent techniques intended to make it very difficult, if not impossible, for a conquering state to govern another and to gain any benefit from its "victory." CBD must be distinguished from "civil defense," the much less realistic government plan for protecting citizenry in the event of nuclear war, widely derided as neither civil nor defense. CBD is also different from so-called nonprovocative defense (NPD), which emphasizes "defensive defense" via such armaments as antitank devices, antiaircraft munitions, and mobile infantry, as opposed to potentially provocative, offensive weaponry such as bombers, tanks, and other "power-projecting" technology. NPD is a potential way of helping countries avoid the "security dilemma" whereby the pursuit of military security by one country induces insecurity on the part of others; nonetheless, it clearly fails the test of true nonviolence.

The major theorist of CBD, Gene Sharp, has identified specific tactics of nonviolent action. Civilian defenders would not violently resist the occupation of their country; moreover, they would willingly expose themselves to the possibility of substantial hardship, suffering, and even death. But traditional military defenders, too, must anticipate great hardship and suffering, and sometimes death, even in a "successful," violent war. Advocates of CBD emphasize that substantial training of committed citizens would

From Gene Sharp, *Civilian Resistance as a National Defense: Nonviolent Action Against Aggression.* A. Roberts, ed. 1968, Harrisburg, PA: Stackpole Books.

be required. But again, traditional military training in the ways of violence also requires time, effort, and sacrifice as well as commitment. Moreover, most efforts at nonviolent resistance—Hungary in the mid-nineteenth century, Norway in World War II, Eastern Europe in 1989—were spontaneous, unplanned, and largely leaderless. Serious CBD, well rehearsed and supported by material resources, has never been tried. Given its impressive track record as a form of resistance when it was essentially extemporized, the future of CBD might be bright indeed if it were ever actually carried out by a well-trained populace. And the prospect of facing a determined and highly disciplined citizenry, committed to denying the invader virtually all fruits of conquest, might deter invasion no less effectively than the amassing of military forces and at substantially less cost and risk of provocation.

As weapons become ever more destructive, doctrines of national security based on traditional military techniques offer less and less prospect of defense. During the Vietnam War, for example, a U.S. major claimed that the village of Ben Tre "had to be destroyed in order for us to save it." Gene Sharp has pointed out that by contrast, CBD alters this dynamic in a crucial way, because it would seek nonviolently to "deny the attackers their objectives and to make society politically indigestible and ungovernable."[5]

It is widely believed that military combat is the only effective means of struggle in a wide variety of situations of acute conflict. However, there is another whole approach to the waging of social and political conflict. Any proposed substitute for war in the defense of freedom must involve wielding power, confronting and engaging an invader's military might, and waging effective combat. The technique of nonviolent action, although relatively ignored and undeveloped, may be able to meet these requirements and provide the basis for a defense policy.

ALTERNATIVE APPROACH TO THE CONTROL OF POLITICAL POWER

Military action is based largely on the idea that the most effective way of defeating an enemy is by inflicting heavy destruction on his armies, military equipment, transport system, factories, and cities. Weapons are designed to kill or destroy with maximum efficiency. Nonviolent action is based on a different approach: to deny the enemy the human assistance and cooperation which are necessary if he is to exercise control over the population. It is thus based on a more fundamental and sophisticated view of political power.

A ruler's power is ultimately dependent on support from the people he would rule. His moral authority, economic resources, transport system, government bureaucracy, army, and police—to name but a few immediate sources of his power—rest finally upon the cooperation and assistance of other people. If there is general conformity, the ruler is powerful.

But people do not always do what their rulers would like them to do. The factory manager recognizes this when he finds his workers leaving their jobs and machines, so that the production line ceases operation, or when he finds the workers persisting in doing something on the job which he has forbidden them to do. In many areas of social and political life comparable situations are commonplace....

NONVIOLENT ACTION

The "technique" of "nonviolent action," which is based on this approach to the control of political power and the waging of political struggles, has been the subject of many misconceptions. For the

---

[5] Gene Sharp, *Making Europe Unconquerable: The Potential of Civilian-based Deterrence and Defense* (Cambridge, MA: Ballinger, 1985).

sake of clarity, the two terms are defined in this section.

The term *technique* is used here to describe the overall means of conducting an action or struggle. One can therefore speak of the technique of guerrilla warfare, of conventional warfare, and of parliamentary democracy.

The term *nonviolent action* refers to those methods of protest, noncooperation, and intervention in which the actionists, without employing physical violence, refuse to do certain things which they are expected, or required, to do, or do certain things which they are not expected, or are forbidden, to do. In a particular case there can of course be a combination of acts of omission and acts of commission.

Nonviolent action is a generic term; it includes the large class of phenomena variously called "nonviolent resistance," "satyagraha," "passive resistance," "positive action," and "nonviolent direct action." While it is not violent, it *is* action, and not inaction; passivity, submission, and cowardice must be surmounted if it is to be used. It is a means of conducting conflicts and waging struggles and is not to be equated with (though it may be accompanied by) purely verbal dissent or solely psychological influence. It is not "pacifism," and in fact has in the vast majority of cases been applied by nonpacifists. The motives for the adoption of nonviolent action may be religious or ethical, or they may be based on considerations of expediency. Nonviolent action is not an escapist approach to the problem of violence, for it can be applied in struggles against opponents relying on violent sanctions. The fact that in a conflict one side is nonviolent does not imply that the other side will also refrain from violence. Certain forms of nonviolent action may be regarded as efforts to persuade by action, while others are more coercive.

METHODS OF NONVIOLENT ACTION

There is a very wide range of methods, or forms, of nonviolent action, and at least 125 have been identified. They fall into three classes—nonviolent protest, noncooperation, and nonviolent intervention.

Generally speaking, the methods of *nonviolent protest* are symbolic in their effect and produce an awareness of the existence of dissent. Under tyrannical regimes, however, where opposition is stifled, their impact can in some circumstances be very great. Methods of nonviolent protest include marches, pilgrimages, picketing, vigils, "haunting" officials, public meetings, issuing and distributing protest literature, renouncing honors, voluntary emigration, and humorous pranks.

The methods of *nonviolent noncooperation*, if sufficient numbers take part, are likely to present the opponent with difficulties in maintaining the normal efficiency and operation of the system, and in extreme cases the system itself may be threatened. Methods of nonviolent noncooperation include various types of strike (such as general strike, sit-down strike, industry strike, go-slow, and work-to-rule), various types of boycott (such as economic boycott, consumers' boycott, traders' boycott, rent refusal, international economic embargo, and social boycott), and various types of political noncooperation (such as boycott of government employment, boycott of elections, revenue refusal, civil disobedience, and mutiny).

The methods of *nonviolent intervention* have some features in common with the first two classes but also challenge the opponent more directly, and, assuming that fearlessness and discipline are maintained, relatively small numbers may have a disproportionately large impact. Methods of nonviolent intervention include sit-ins, fasts, reverse strikes, nonviolent obstruction, nonviolent invasion, and parallel government.

The exact way in which methods from each of the three classes are combined varies considerably from one situation to another. Generally speaking, the risks to the actionists on the one hand, and to the system against which they take action on the other, are least in the case of nonviolent protest and greatest in the case of nonviolent intervention. The methods of noncooperation tend to require the largest numbers but not to demand a large degree of special training from all participants. The methods of nonviolent intervention are generally effective if the participants possess a high degree of internal discipline and are willing to accept severe repression; the tactics must also be selected and carried out with particular care and intelligence....

NONVIOLENT ACTION VERSUS VIOLENCE

There can be no presumption that an opponent, faced with an opposition relying solely on nonviolent methods, will suddenly renounce his capacity for violence. Instead, nonviolent action can operate against opponents able and willing to use violent sanctions and can counter their violence in such a way that they are thrown politically off balance in a kind of political *jiu-jitsu*.

Instead of confronting the opponent's police and troops with the same type of forces, nonviolent actionists counter these agents of the opponent's power indirectly. Their aim is to demonstrate that repression is incapable of cowing the populace and to deprive the opponent of his existing support, thereby undermining his ability or will to continue with the repression. Far from indicating the failure of nonviolent action, repression often helps to make clear the cruelty of the political system being opposed, and so to alienate support from it. Repression is often a kind of recognition from the opponent that the nonviolent action constitutes a serious threat to his policy or regime, one which he finds it necessary to combat.

Just as in war danger from enemy fire does not always force frontline soldiers to panic and flee, so in nonviolent action repression does not necessarily produce submission. True, repression *may* be effective, but it may fail to halt defiance, and in this case the opponent will be in difficulties. Repression against a nonviolent group which persists in face of it and maintains nonviolent discipline may have the following effects: it may alienate the general population from the opponent's regime, making them more likely to join the resistance; it may alienate the opponent's usual supporters and agents, and their initial uneasiness may grow into internal opposition and at times into noncooperation and disobedience; and it may rally general public opinion (domestic or international) to the support of the nonviolent actionists. Though the effectiveness of this last factor varies greatly from one situation to another, it may produce various types of supporting actions. If repression thus produces larger numbers of nonviolent action-ists, thereby increasing the defiance, and if it leads to internal dissent among the opponent's

supporters, thereby reducing his capacity to deal with the defiance, it will clearly have rebounded against the opponent.

Naturally, with so many variables (including the nature of the contending groups, the issues involved, the context of the struggle, the means of repression, and the methods of nonviolent action used), in no two instances will nonviolent action "work" in exactly the same way. However, it is possible to indicate in very general terms the ways in which it does achieve results. It is, of course, sometimes defeated: no technique of action can guarantee its user short-term victory in every instance of its use. It is important to recognize, however, that failure in nonviolent action may be caused not by an inherent weakness of the technique but by weakness in the movement employing it, or in the strategy and tactics used....

THE INDIRECT APPROACH
TO THE OPPONENT'S POWER

The technique of nonviolent action, and the policy of civilian defense relying upon it, can be regarded as extreme forms of the "strategy of indirect approach" which Liddell Hart has propounded in the sphere of military strategy. He has argued that a direct strategy—confronting the opponent head-on—consolidates the opponent's strength. "To move along the line of natural expectation consolidates the opponent's balance and thus increases his resisting power." An indirect approach, he argues, is militarily more sound, and generally effective results have followed when the plan of action has had "such indirectness as to ensure the opponent's unreadiness to meet it." "Dislocation" of the enemy is crucial, he insists, to achieve the conditions for victory, and the dislocation must be followed by "exploitation" of the opportunity created by the position of insecurity. It thus becomes important "to nullify opposition by paralyzing the power to oppose" and to make "the enemy do something wrong."

These general, and at first glance abstract, principles of strategy can take a concrete form not only in certain types of military action but also in nonviolent action, and therefore in civilian defense. An invader, or other usurper, is likely to be best equipped to apply, and to combat, military and other violent means of combat and repression. Instead of meeting him directly on that level, nonviolent actionists and civilian defenders rely on a totally different technique of struggle, or "weapons system." The whole conflict takes on a very special character: the combatants fight, but with different weapons. Given an extensive, determined, and skillful application of nonviolent action, the opponent is likely to find that the nonviolent actionists' insistence on fighting with their chosen "weapons system" will cause him very special problems which frustrate the effective utilization of his own forces. As indicated above, the opponent's unilateral use of violent repression may only increase the resistance and win new support for the resisters, and even the opponent's supporters, agents, and soldiers may first begin to doubt the rightness of his policies and finally undertake internal opposition.

The use of nonviolent action may thus reduce or remove the very sources of the opponent's power without ever directly confronting him with the same violent means of action on which he had relied. The course of the struggle may be viewed as an attempt by the nonviolent actionists to increase their various types of strength, not only among their usual supporters but also among third parties and in the opponent's camp, and to reduce by various processes the strength of the opponent. This type of change in the relative power positions will finally determine the outcome of the struggle.

Success in nonviolent struggle depends to a very high degree on the persistence of the nonviolent actionists in fighting with *their own* methods and opposing all pressures—whether caused by emotional hostility to the opponent's brutalities, temptations of temporary gains, or *agents provocateurs* employed by the opponent (of which there have been examples)—to fight with the opponent's own, violent, methods. Violence by, or in support of, their side will sharply counter the operation of the very special mechanisms of change in nonviolent action—even when the violence is on a relatively small scale, such as rioting, injury, violent sabotage involving loss of life, or individual assassinations. The least amount of violence will, in the eyes of many, justify severe repression, and it will sharply reduce the tendency for such repression to bring

sympathy and support for the nonviolent actionists, and it may well, for several reasons, reduce the number of resisters. Violence will also sharply reduce sympathy and support in the opponent's own camp.

The use of violence by, or in support of, the resisters, has many effects. Its dangers are indicated by, among other things, an examination of the likely effect on the opponent's soldiers and police, who may have become sympathetic to the resisters and reluctant to continue as opposition agents. It is well known that ordinary soldiers will fight more persistently and effectively if it is a matter of survival, and if they and their comrades are being shot, bombed, wounded, or killed. Soldiers and police acting against a nonviolent opposition and not facing such dangers may at times be inefficient in carrying out repression—for example by slackness in searches for "wanted" resisters, firing over the heads of demonstrators, or not shooting at all. In extreme cases they may openly mutiny. When such inefficiency or mutiny occurs, the opponent's power is severely threatened: this will often be an objective of nonviolent actionists or civilian defenders.

The introduction of violence by their side, however, will sharply reduce their chances of undermining opposition loyalty, as the influences producing sympathy are removed and their opponents' lives become threatened. This is simply an illustration of the point that it is very dangerous to believe that one can increase one's total combat strength by combining violent sabotage, assassinations, or types of guerrilla or conventional warfare with civilian defense, which relies on the very different technique of nonviolent action.

DEVELOPMENT OF THE TECHNIQUE

Nonviolent action has a long history, but because historians have often been more concerned with other matters much information has undoubtedly been lost. Even today, this field is largely ignored, and there is no good history of the practice and development of the technique. But it clearly began early.

A very significant pre-Gandhian expansion of the technique took place in the nineteenth and early twentieth centuries. The technique received impetus from three groups during this period: first, from trade unionists and other social radicals who sought a means of struggle—largely strikes, general strikes, and boycotts—against what they regarded as an unjust social system, and for an improvement in the condition of working men; second, from nationalists who found the technique useful in resisting a foreign enemy; and third, on the level of ideas and personal example, from individuals who wanted to show how a better society might be created....

Since Gandhi's time, the use of nonviolent action has spread throughout the world at an unprecedented rate. In some cases it was stimulated by Gandhi's thought and practice, but where this was so the technique was often modified in new cultural and political settings; in these cases it has already moved beyond Gandhi.

Quite independently of the campaigns led by Gandhi, important nonviolent struggles emerged under exceedingly difficult circumstances in Nazi-occupied and Communist countries: nonviolent action was used to a significant extent in the Norwegian and Danish resistance in the Second World War, in the East German uprising in 1953, in the Hungarian revolution in 1956, and in the strikes in the Soviet political prisoner camps, especially in 1953. There have been other important developments in Africa, Japan, and elsewhere. There have, of course, been setbacks, and the limited and sporadic use of nonviolent action in South Africa, for example, has been followed by advocacy of violence. However, when seen in historical perspective, there is no doubt that the technique of nonviolent action has developed very rapidly in the twentieth century.

In this same perspective, it is only recently that nonviolent resistance has been seen as a possible substitute for war in deterring or defeating invasion and other threats. It is even more recently that any attempt has been made to work out this policy—now called "civilian defense"—in any detail and that an examination of its merits and problems has been proposed.

It is inconceivable that any country will in the foreseeable future permanently abandon its defensive capacity. Threats—some genuine, some exaggerated—are too real to people; there has been too much aggression and seizure of power by dictators

to be forgotten. But while defense and deterrence inevitably rely on sanctions and means of struggle, there is much reason for dissatisfaction with the usual military means. The question therefore arises whether there exists an alternative means of struggle which could be the basis of a new defense policy. Nonviolent action is an alternative means of struggle; in this, it has more in common with military struggle than with conciliation and arbitration. Could there then be a policy of civilian defense which relies on this nonviolent technique? The question must be answered, not in terms of philosophy and dogma, but in the practical examination of concrete strategies through which it might operate, the problems which might be faced, and alternative ways in which these might possibly be solved. All this will depend to a large degree on an understanding of the technique of nonviolent action, its methods, dynamics, mechanisms, and requirements.

LEARNING FROM THE PAST

Generally speaking, very little effort has been made to learn from past cases of nonviolent action with a view to increasing our understanding of the nature of the technique, and gaining knowledge which might be useful in future struggles, or which might contribute to an expansion of the use of nonviolent action instead of violence. Study of past cases could provide the basis for a more informed assessment of the future political potentialities of the technique.

There are far too few detailed documentary accounts of past uses of nonviolent action; such accounts can provide raw material for analyses of particular facets of the technique and help in the formulation of hypotheses which might be tested in other situations. An important step, therefore, in the development of research in this field is the preparation of purely factual accounts of a large number of specific cases of nonviolent action, accompanied if possible with collections of existing interpretations and explanations of the events....

Another subject which deserves careful study is the meaning of, and conditions for, success in nonviolent action. The varying meanings of the terms "success" and "defeat" need to be distinguished, and consideration given to concrete achievements in particular struggles. The matter is much more complex than may at first appear. For example, failure within a short period of time to get an invader to withdraw fully from an occupied country may nevertheless be accompanied by the frustration of several of the invader's objectives, the maintenance of a considerable degree of autonomy within the "conquered" country, and the furtherance of a variety of changes in the invader's own regime and homeland; these changes may themselves later lead either to the desired full withdrawal, or to further relaxation of occupation rule. When various types of "success" and "defeat" have been distinguished, it would be desirable to have a study of the conditions under which they have occurred in the past and seem possible in the future. These conditions would include factors in the social and political situation, the nature of the issues in the conflict, the type of opponent and his repression, the type of group using nonviolent action, the type of nonviolent action used (taking into account quality, extent, strategy, tactics, methods, persistence in face of repression, etc.), and lastly the possible role and influence of "third parties."

The question of the viability and political practicality of the technique of nonviolent action is one which can be investigated by research and analysis, and it is possible that the efficiency and political potentialities of this technique can be increased by deliberate efforts.

STUDY QUESTIONS

1. What is meant by Gandhi's insistence that *satyagraha* must be done by the strong, rather than the weak?

2. Suggest nonreligious bases for nonviolence as a social practice and as a way of life.

3. Black Power advocate H. Rap Brown once wrote that violence was "as American as cherry pie." Agree or disagree.

4. "Let no man pull you so low," wrote Martin Luther King, Jr., "as to make you hate him." Analyze and interpret this observation.

5. "My creed of nonviolence is an extremely active force," wrote Gandhi. "It has no room for cowardice or even weakness. There is hope for a violent man to be some day nonviolent, but there is none for a coward." Why not?

6. According to Victor Hugo (and many others), "No army can withstand the force of an idea whose time has come." Is there any evidence that nonviolence is such an idea? Or could this simply be wishful thinking?

7. What about "selective nonviolence," that is, using violence in some circumstances and nonviolence in others?

8. Can you find any examples of nonviolence among animals? Can we learn from it?

9. What about the oft-cited problem of how nonviolence (Gandhian or otherwise) would fare if it had to face, for example, a nuclear-armed Hitler? Similarly, is there anything in the events and issues of the twenty-first century that renders nonviolence especially compelling—or, alternatively, less appropriate than in the past?

10. Compare the nonviolent conceptions of Gandhi, Tolstoy, King, and one or more modern leaders.

SUGGESTIONS FOR FURTHER READING

Ackerman, Peter, and Christopher Kruegler. 1994. *Strategic Nonviolent Conflict: The Dynamics of People Power in the Twentieth Century.* Westport, CT: Praeger.

Burrowes, Robert J. 1996. *The Strategy of Nonviolent Defense: A Gandhian Approach.* Albany: State University of New York Press.

Hanigan, James P. 1984. *Martin Luther King, Jr., and the Foundations of Nonviolence.* Lanham, MD: University Press of America.

Kurlansky, Mark. 2008. *Nonviolence: The History of a Dangerous Idea.* New York: Modern Library.

Lakey, George. 1987. *Powerful Peacemaking: A Strategy for a Living Revolution.* Philadelphia: New Society Publishers.

Merton, Thomas. 1980. *The Nonviolent Alternative.* New York: Farrar, Straus & Giroux.

Moses, Greg. 1997. *Revolution of Conscience: Martin Luther King, Jr., and the Philosophy of Nonviolence.* New York: Guilford Press.

Schell, Jonathan. 2004. *The Unconquerable World: Power, Nonviolence, and the Will of the People.* New York: Henry Holt.

Sharp, Gene, and Joshua Paulson. 2005. *Waging Nonviolent Struggle: 20th Century Practice and 21st Century Potential.* Manchester, NH: Extending Horizons Books.

Zinn, Howard. 2002. *The Power of Nonviolence: Writings by Advocates of Peace.* Boston: Beacon Press.

CHAPTER 6

Religious Inspiration

R eligious teachings are primarily concerned with humanity's relationship with God. But the world's religions invariably devote substantial
attention, as well, to the way human beings treat each other. They
are inevitably drawn to questions of war and peace, the former because the taking of life
is one of the most intense and consequential human acts, and the latter because systems
of "peace" are fundamental to the basic condition of human life, spiritual no less than
material or social.

We turn to religious inspiration with hope and gratitude (it is noteworthy, for example, that nonviolence, both in theory and practice, has largely been motivated by religious
teaching). Nonetheless, it must also be acknowledged that when it comes to matters of war
and peace, religion has been a double-edged sword. It may be that on balance, religious
tradition has been as likely to support militarism as to oppose it. Sometimes, religious
authorities have been among the most outspoken cheerleaders for war-making; at other
times, even if not vigorously supporting prevailing government policy, they have passively
acquiesced in the status quo. Historically, religions have buttressed bloodthirsty and unjust
activities either from belief that the appropriate stance is to "render unto Caesar that which
is Caesar's" and/or out of self-protective or self-serving motives. The following inscription
(loosely translated) is commonly seen even today on houses in certain small villages of
Bavaria: "Saint Florian, protect our town, pass by my house, burn others down."

The Old Testament is replete with bloody accounts of the so-called commanded
wars in which God urged his people to destroy others: "When the Lord your God gives
them over to you, and you defeat them, then you must utterly destroy them; you shall
make no covenant with them, and show no mercy to them" (Deuteronomy 7:2). Other
religious traditions also have displayed a positive attitude toward war. Best known among
these is the *jihad*, or holy war, among Muslims, in which fallen warriors are guaranteed
entry into heaven. Although Hinduism contributed mightily to Gandhian nonviolence, it
also has a vigorous military tradition, reflected in such texts as the *Mahabharata*, in which
the devout are urged to fight, even for a cause with which they might disagree. By contrast,

peace has long been central to Buddhism, although war resistance as such has not been especially prominent among Buddhist teachings.

Christianity has a complex relationship with war. Because it is the predominant religious tradition of the United States, it deserves special attention here. Although many of its founding principles emphasize pacifism, turning the other cheek, and loving one's neighbor, the reality is that mainstream Christianity has been one of the great warrior religions of history (along with Islam, Hinduism, and Shintoism, the predominant religious tradition of Japan). There is a fundamental Christian ambiguity toward war, reflected in the attitude toward the cross. On the one hand, it is supposed to be the ultimate symbol of peace and love, something with which to replace violence and sin; on the other hand, it has long been seen as a sword with which to smite the forces of evil.

Christians were the eventual heirs of the dying Roman empire, fighting numerous—and increasingly unsuccessful—wars. The "holy war" tradition in Christianity is a direct descendant of the commanded wars of the Old Testament. This tradition was especially virulent during the Middle Ages, most dramatically during the Crusades, which were fought in an attempt to drive Muslims from Palestine. "Deus Vult" (God wills it) was the battle cry of the Crusaders. "A new sort of army has appeared," preached Saint Bernard of Clairvaux, in the twelfth century.

> It fights a double war; first, the war of the flesh and blood against enemies; second, the war of the spirit against Satan and vice.... The soldier of Christ kills with safety; he dies with more safety still. He serves Christ when he kills. He serves himself when he is killed.

And as recently as 1914, the bishop of London urged his countrymen to

> kill Germans. Kill them, not for the sake of killing, but to save the world, to kill the good as well as the bad, to kill the young men as well as the old...I look upon it as a war for purity, I look upon everyone who dies in it as a martyr.[1]

At the same time, not surprisingly, German soldiers were marching into battle with the assurance "Gott mit uns" (God is with us).

Perhaps the final word on this paradox belongs to Blaise Pascal, brilliant mathematician and devout Catholic: "Men never do evil so completely and cheerfully, as when they do it from religious conviction."

Two other aspects of Christian religious tradition—both nearly as troublesome as holy wars from the perspective of peace studies—warrant mention. One is an approach that (like the commanded wars) dates from the Old Testament and was revived especially during the sixteenth to eighteenth centuries. This view teaches that war is undesirable, but deservedly so: a war is a retribution upon the ungodly and the unrighteous, whose function is to chastise those who have displeased God. War was thus seen as God's vengeance upon the wicked but also a kind of penance for the war-maker, who is thus reminded of his or her sinfulness and of God's greatness. This view is not currently popular.

---

[1] Quoted in Roland Bainton, *Christian Attitudes Toward War and Peace* (Nashville, TN: Abingdon Press, 1960).

Another troublesome aspect of the Christian religious tradition has an equally long history while remaining currently influential, especially among the more conservative wing of religious orthodoxy. It applies more directly to efforts at achieving positive peace than to opposing war. This approach is essentially to support the status quo, to counsel submission on the part of people—especially the poor and those otherwise oppressed—to existing social and economic conditions, while trusting to eternal salvation in the afterlife. Not surprisingly, Communist doctrine was especially critical of…this aspect of religion, referring to it as the "opiate of the masses." Karl Marx had this to say:

> The social principles of Christianity justified the slavery of antiquity, glorified the serfdom of the Middle Ages, and equally know, when necessary, how to defend the oppression of the proletariat.…The social principles of Christianity preach the necessity of a ruling and an oppressed class, and all they have for the latter is the pious wish the former will be charitable.…The social principles of Christianity declare all vile acts of the oppressors against the oppressed to be either the just punishment of original sin and other sins or trials that the Lord in his infinite wisdom imposes on those redeemed.…So much for the social principles of Christianity.[2]

Fortunately, there is another side to Christianity. Despite the impression one might get from Christian conservatives, God is not a right-wing Republican! The biblical Christ, for example, was almost inevitably aligned with the poor, the despised, and the disenfranchised. Established Christian doctrine is not inevitably on the side of entrenched power and opposed to social betterment. The Rev. Martin Luther King, Jr., developed the concept of social sin (notably segregation, economic oppression, and war-making). "Liberation theology," which originated in Latin America, also proclaims a vigorously *social* gospel, emphasizing the need for modern-day Christians to act on the social sensitivities of Christ. In 1979, for example, the General Conference of Latin-American Bishops issued a statement that includes the following:

> From the heart of Latin America, a cry rises to the heavens.…It is the cry of a people who suffer and who demand justice, freedom and respect for the fundamental rights of man.…In pain and anxiety, the Church discerns a situation of social sin, of a magnitude all the greater because it occurs in countries which call themselves Catholic and have the capacity to change.…We identify, as the most devastating and humiliating scourge, the situation of inhuman poverty in which millions of Latin Americans live, with starvation wages, unemployment and underemployment, malnutrition, infant mortality, lack of adequate housing, health problems, and labor unrest.

In *The City of God*, Augustine wrote that "it is the wrong-doing of the opposing party which compels the wise man to wage just wars" and that "war with the hope of peace everlasting" to follow was preferable to "captivity without any thought of deliverance." To Augustine

---

[2] Karl Marx, *On Religion* (New York: Schocken, 1964).

and those in the tradition of "Christian realism" that followed him, peace often requires violence against evildoers, and the soldier who goes to war in defense of right, and out of love for his neighbor, does not violate the commandment against killing. Still, if a Christian was expected to go to war, it was with a heavy heart and only after carefully examining his conscience, because the presumption was at all times supposed to be in favor of peace.

Samuel Johnson once wrote that the prospect of a hanging in the morning does wonders to clarify the mind. Similarly, the prospect of war in general and of nuclear annihilation in particular have done wonders to stimulate thought on religious obligation in the face of war. When it comes to nuclear war, for example, the many and detailed requirements of "just war" doctrine cannot be met. Some religious ethicists have even seriously doubted the legitimacy of nuclear deterrence (aside from actual nuclear war), arguing that if something is immoral to do, it is immoral to threaten, because the immorality resides first in the intent and only later in the act itself. Thus, the United Methodist Council of Bishops refused to condone deterrence:

> The moral case for nuclear deterrence, even as an interim ethic, has been undermined by unrelenting arms escalation. Deterrence no longer serves, if it ever did, as a strategy that facilitates disarmament....Deterrence must no longer receive the churches' blessing, even as a temporary warrant for the maintenance of nuclear weapons.

The United States Conference of Catholic Bishops spoke to this issue in 1983, issuing a "Pastoral Letter on War and Peace" after listening to three years of testimony from a wide range of experts. Although they decided that the possession of and threat to employ nuclear weapons (that is, deterrence) was provisionally acceptable, the Catholic bishops were unequivocal in rejecting the *use* of nuclear weapons under any circumstances.

There is a powerful and persistent tradition of explicit pacifism and antiwar activism within Christianity, as within most of the world's great religions. Many pacifists agree with G. K. Chesterton's sardonic observation that "the Christian ideal has not been tried and found wanting. It has been found difficult and left untried."

We turn now to religiously inspired teachers—not all of them Christian—who urge us toward this ideal, no matter how difficult it may be.

HINDUISM: THE BHAGAVAD GITA

The famed Hindu epic the *Mahabharata* contains as perhaps its most important treatise the *Bhagavad Gita*, which describes a great civil war in ancient India. During this war, one of the principal warriors, Arjuna, is reluctant to fight because many of his friends and relatives are on the opposing side. He is ultimately persuaded to fight by the God Krishna, who convinces Arjuna that he must act, not out of hatred or hope for personal gain, but from selfless duty. Although the *Gita* can and has been interpreted as calling for caste loyalty and a warrior spirit, it also inspired Gandhi and others as an allegory for the deemphasis of self in the pursuit of higher goals.

———————————————— ⊷ ————————————————

The wise grieve neither for the living nor for the dead. There has never been a time when you and I and the kings gathered here have not existed, nor will there be a time when we will cease to exist. As the same person inhabits the body through childhood, youth, and old age, so too at the time of death he attains another body. The wise are not deluded by these changes.

When the senses contact sense objects, a person experiences cold or heat, pleasure or pain. These experiences are fleeting; they come and go. Bear them patiently, Arjuna. Those who are not affected by these changes, who are the same in pleasure and pain, are truly wise and fit for immortality. Assert your strength and realize this!

The impermanent has no reality; reality lies in the eternal. Those who have seen the boundary between these two have attained the end of all knowledge. Realize that which pervades the universe and is indestructible; no power can affect this unchanging, imperishable reality. The body is mortal, but he who dwells in the body is immortal and immeasurable. Therefore, Arjuna, fight in this battle.

One man believes he is the slayer, another believes he is the slain. Both are ignorant; there is neither slayer nor slain. You were never born; you will never die. You have never changed; you can never change. Unborn, eternal, immutable, immemorial, you do not die when the body dies. Realizing that which is indestructible, eternal, unborn, and unchanging, how can you slay or cause another to slay?

As a man abandons worn-out clothes and acquires new ones, so when the body is worn out a new one is acquired by the Self, who lives within.

The Self cannot be pierced by weapons or burned by fire; water cannot wet it, nor can the wind dry it. The Self cannot be pierced or burned, made wet or dry. It is everlasting and infinite, standing on the motionless foundations of eternity. The Self is unmanifested, beyond all thought, beyond all change. Knowing this, you should not grieve.

O mighty Arjuna, even if you believe the Self to be subject to birth and death, you should not grieve. Death is inevitable for the living; birth is inevitable for the dead. Since these are unavoidable, you should not sorrow. Every creature is unmanifested at first and then attains manifestation. When its end has come, it once again becomes unmanifested. What is there to lament in this?

The glory of the Self is beheld by a few, and a few describe it: a few listen, but many without understanding. The Self of all beings, living within the body, is eternal and cannot be harmed. Therefore, do not grieve....

They live in wisdom who see themselves in all and all in them, who have renounced every selfish desire and sense craving tormenting the heart.

Neither agitated by grief nor hankering after pleasure, they live free from lust and fear and anger. Established in meditation, they are truly wise. Fettered no more by selfish attachments, they are neither elated by good fortune nor depressed by bad. Such are the seers.

Even as a tortoise draws in its limbs, the wise can draw in their senses at will. Aspirants abstain from sense pleasures, but they still crave for them. These cravings all disappear when they see the highest goal. Even of those who tread the path, the stormy senses can sweep off the mind. They live in wisdom who subdue their senses and keep their minds ever absorbed in me.

When you keep thinking about sense objects, attachment comes. Attachment breeds desire, the lust of possession that burns to anger. Anger clouds the judgment; you can no longer learn from past mistakes. Lost is the power to choose between what is wise and what is unwise, and your life is utter waste. But when you move amidst the world of sense, free from attachment and aversion alike, there comes the peace in which all sorrows end, and you live in the wisdom of the Self.

The disunited mind is far from wise; how can it mediate? How be at peace? When you know no peace, how can you know joy? When you let your mind follow the call of the senses, they carry away your better judgment as storms drive a boat off its charted course on the sea.

Use all your power to free the senses from attachment and aversion alike, and live in the full wisdom of the Self. Such a sage awakes to light in the night of all creatures. That which the world calls day is the night of ignorance to the wise.

As rivers flow into the ocean but cannot make the vast ocean overflow, so flow the streams of the sense-world into the sea of peace that is the sage. But this is not so with the desirer of desires.

They are forever free who renounce all selfish desires and break away from the ego-cage of "I," "me," and "mine" to be united with the Lord. This is the supreme state. Attain to this, and pass from death to immortality.

Thich Nhat Hanh

BUDDHISM: BEING PEACE

Buddhism, with its focus on compassion and the connectedness of all things, would seem to be a "natural" for a peace-loving, antiwar constituency. And so it is. On the other hand, "engaged Buddhism" does not represent a majority approach within the tradition, largely because the Buddha's teaching emphasizes personal enlightenment. However, Buddhism undeniably nurtures a nonviolent and socially responsible practice, as exemplified, for example, by organizations such as the Buddhist Peace Fellowship. Because Buddhist teachings are especially difficult for the uninitiated Western reader, we have chosen the following selection from a modern sage, Zen master Thich Nhat Hanh. He is a Vietnamese monk who led the Buddhist delegation to the Paris Peace Talks during the Vietnam War and is a leading interpreter of Buddhist practice in today's world.

Meditation is not to get out of society, to escape from society, but to prepare for a reentry into society. We call this "engaged Buddhism." When we go to a meditation center, we may have the impression that we leave everything behind—family, society, and all the complications involved in them—and come as an individual in order to practice and to search for peace. This is already an illusion, because in Buddhism there is no such thing as an individual.

Just as a piece of paper is the fruit, the combination of many elements that can be called non-paper elements, the individual is made of nonindividual elements. If you are a poet, you will see clearly that there is a cloud floating in this sheet of paper. Without a cloud there will be no water; without water, the trees cannot grow; and without trees, you cannot make paper. So the cloud is in here. The existence of this page is dependent on the existence of a cloud. Paper and cloud are so close. Let us think of other things, like sunshine. Sunshine is very important because the forest cannot grow without sunshine, and we humans cannot grow without sunshine. So the logger needs sunshine in order to cut the tree, and the tree needs sunshine in order to be a tree. Therefore you can see sunshine in this sheet of paper. And if you look more deeply, with the eyes of a bodhisattva, with the eyes of those who are awake, you see not only the cloud and the sunshine in it, but that everything is here: the wheat that became the bread for the logger to eat, the logger's father—everything is in this sheet of paper.

The Avatamsaka Sutra tells us that you cannot point to one thing that does not have a relationship with this sheet of paper. So we say, "A sheet of paper is made of non-paper elements." A cloud is a non-paper element. The forest is a non-paper element. Sunshine is a non-paper element. The paper is made of all the non-paper elements to the extent that if we return the non-paper elements to their sources, the cloud to the sky, the sunshine to the sun, the logger to his father, the paper is empty. Empty of what? Empty of a separate self. It has been made by all the non-self elements, non-paper elements, and if all these non-paper elements are taken out, it is truly empty, empty of an independent self. Empty, in this sense, means that the paper is full of everything, the entire cosmos. The presence of this tiny sheet of paper proves the presence of the whole cosmos. . . .

In Plum Village in France, we receive many letters from the refugee camps in Singapore, Malaysia, Indonesia, Thailand, and the Philippines, hundreds each week. It is very painful to read them, but we have to do it, we have to be in contact. We try our best to help, but the suffering is enormous, and sometimes we are discouraged. It is said that half the boat people die in the ocean; only half arrive at the shores in Southeast Asia.

There are many young girls, boat people, who are raped by sea pirates. Even though the United Nations and many countries try to help the government of Thailand prevent that kind of piracy, sea pirates continue to inflict much suffering on the refugees. One day we received a letter telling us about a young girl on a small boat who was raped by a Thai pirate. She was only twelve, and she jumped into the ocean and drowned herself.

When you first learn of something like that, you get angry at the pirate. You naturally take the side of the girl. As you look more deeply you will see it differently. If you take the side of the little girl, then it is easy. You only have to take a gun and shoot the pirate. But we cannot do that. In my meditation I saw that if I had been born in the village of the pirate and raised in the same conditions as he was, I am now the pirate. There is a great likelihood that I would become a pirate. I cannot condemn myself so easily. In my meditation, I saw that many babies are born along the Gulf of Siam, hundreds every day, and if we educators, social workers, politicians, and others do not do something about the situation, in twenty-five years a number of them will become sea pirates. That is certain. If you or I were born today in those fishing villages, we might become sea pirates in twenty-five years. If you take a gun and shoot the pirate, you shoot all of us, because all of us are to some extent responsible for this state of affairs. . . .

There is a Zen story about a man riding a horse which is galloping very quickly. Another man, standing alongside the road, yells at him, "Where are you going?" and the man on the horse yells back, "I don't know. Ask the horse." I think that is our situation. We are riding many horses that we cannot control. The proliferation of armaments, for instance, is a horse. We have tried our best, but we cannot control these horses. Our lives are so busy.

In Buddhism, the most important precept of all is to live in awareness, to know what is going on. To know what is going on, not only here, but there. For instance, when you eat a piece of bread, you may choose to be aware that our farmers, in growing the wheat, use chemical poisons a little too much. Eating the bread, we are somehow co-responsible for the destruction of our ecology. When we eat a piece of meat or drink alcohol, we can produce awareness that forty thousand children die *each day* in the third world from hunger and that in order to produce a piece of meat or a bottle of liquor, we have to use a lot of grain. Eating a bowl of cereal may be more reconciling with the suffering of the world than eating a piece of meat. An authority on economics who lives in France told me that if only the people in Western countries would reduce the eating of meat and the drinking of alcohol by 50 percent, that would be enough to change the situation of the world. Only 50 percent less.

Every day we do things, we are things, that have to do with peace. If we are aware of our lifestyle, our way of consuming, of looking at things, we will know how to make peace right in the moment we are alive, the present moment....

During the War in Vietnam we young Buddhists organized ourselves to help victims of the war rebuild villages that had been destroyed by the bombs. Many of us died during service, not only because of the bombs and the bullets, but because of the people who suspected us of being on the other side. We were able to understand the suffering of both sides, the Communists and the anti-Communists. We tried to be open to both, to understand this side and to understand that side, to be one with them. That is why we did not take a side, even though the whole world took sides. We tried to tell people our perception of the situation: that we wanted to stop the fighting, but the bombs were so loud. Sometimes we had to burn ourselves alive to get the message across, but even then the world could not hear us. They thought we were supporting a kind of political act. They didn't know that it was a purely human action to be heard, to be understood. We wanted reconciliation, we did not want a victory.

Working to help people in a circumstance like that is very dangerous, and many of us got killed. The Communists killed us because they suspected that we were working with the Americans, and the anti-Communists killed us because they thought that we were with the Communists. But we did not want to give up and take one side.

The situation of the world is still like this.... Reconciliation is to understand both sides, to go to one side and describe the suffering being endured by the other side, and then to go to the other side and describe the suffering being endured by the first side. Doing only that will be a great help for peace....

I would like to present to you a form of Buddhism that may be accepted here in the West. In the past twenty years we have been experimenting with this form of Buddhism, and it seems that it may be suitable for our modern society. It is called the Tiep Hien Order, the Order of "Interbeing."

The Tiep Hien Order was founded in Vietnam during the war. It derives from the Zen School of Lin Chi, and is the forty-second generation of this school. It is a form of engaged Buddhism, Buddhism in daily life, in society, and not just in a retreat center. *Tiep* and *hien* are Vietnamese words of Chinese origin. I would like to explain the meaning of these words, because understanding them helps in understanding the spirit of this order.

Tiep means "to be in touch." The notion of engaged Buddhism already appears in the word tiep. First of all, to be in touch with oneself. In modern society most of us don't want to be in touch with ourselves; we want to be in touch with other things like religion, sports, politics, a book—we want to forget ourselves. Any time we have leisure, we want to invite something else to enter us, opening ourselves to the television and telling the television to come and colonize us. So first of all, "in touch" means in touch with oneself in order to find out the source of wisdom, understanding, and compassion in each of us. Being in touch with oneself is the meaning of meditation, to be aware of what is going on in your body, in your feelings, in your mind. That is the first meaning of tiep.

Tiep also means to be in touch with Buddhas and bodhisattvas, the enlightened people in whom full understanding and compassion are tangible and effective. Being in touch with oneself means being in touch with this source of wisdom and compassion. You know that children understand that the Buddha is in themselves. One young boy claimed to be a Buddha on the first day of the retreat in Ojai, California. I told him that this is partly true, because sometimes he is Buddha, but sometimes he is not; it depends on his degree of being awake.

The second part of the meaning of tiep is "to continue," to make something more long-lasting. It means that the career of understanding and compassion started by Buddhas and bodhisattvas should be continued. This is possible only if we get in touch with our true self, which is like digging deep into the soil until we reach a hidden source of fresh water, and then the well is filled. When we are in touch with our true mind, the source of understanding and compassion will spring out. This is the basis of everything. Being in touch with our true mind is necessary for the continuation of the career started by the Buddhas and bodhisattvas.

Hien means "the present time." We have to be in the present time, because only the present is real, only in the present moment can we be alive. We do not practice for the sake of the future, to be reborn in a paradise, but to be peace, to be compassion, to be joy right now. Hien also means "to make real, to manifest, realization." Love and understanding are not only concepts and words. They must be real things, realized, in oneself and in society. That is the meaning of the word hien.

It is difficult to find English or French words which convey the same meaning as *Tiep Hien*. There is a term from *The Avatamsaka Sutra*, "interbeing," which conveys the spirit, so we have translated Tiep Hien as interbeing. In the sutra it is a compound term which means "mutual" and "to be." Interbeing is a new word in English, and I hope it will be accepted. We have talked about the many in the one, and the one containing the many. In one sheet of paper, we see everything else, the cloud, the forest, the logger. I am, therefore you are. You are, therefore I am. That is the meaning of the word "interbeing." We interare....

In Buddhism, the mind is the root of everything else. These then are the precepts of the Order of Interbeing:

First: Do not be idolatrous about or bound to any doctrine, theory, or ideology, even Buddhist ones. Buddhist systems of thought are guiding means; they are not absolute truth.

This precept is the roar of the lion. Its spirit is characteristic of Buddhism. It is often said that the Buddha's teaching is only a raft to help you cross the river, a finger pointing to the moon. Don't mistake the finger for the moon. The raft is not the shore. If we cling to the raft, if we cling to the finger, we miss everything. We cannot, in the name of the finger or the raft, kill each other. Human life is more precious than any ideology, any doctrine.... Peace can only be achieved when we are not attached to a view, when we are free from fanaticism....

Second: Do not think the knowledge you presently possess is changeless, absolute truth. Avoid being narrow-minded and bound to present views. Learn and practice nonattachment from views in order to be open to receive others' viewpoints. Truth is found in life and not merely in conceptual knowledge. Be ready to learn throughout your entire life and to observe reality in yourself and in the world at all times.

This precept springs from the first one. Remember the young father who refused to open the door to his own son, thinking the boy was already dead. The Buddha said, "If you cling to something as the absolute truth and you are caught in it, when the truth comes in person to knock on your door, you will refuse to let it in."...

Third: Do not force others, including children, by any means whatsoever, to adopt your views, whether by authority, threat, money, propaganda, or even education. However, through compassionate dialogue, help others renounce fanaticism and narrowness....

Fourth: Do not avoid contact with suffering or close your eyes before suffering. Do not lose awareness of the existence of suffering in the life of the world. Find ways to be with those who are suffering, including personal contact, visits, images, and sounds. By such means, awaken yourself and others to the reality of suffering in the world.

The first Dharma talk given by the Buddha was on the Four Noble Truths. The first truth is the existence of suffering. This kind of contact and awareness is needed. If we don't encounter pain, ills, we won't look for the causes of pain and ills to find a remedy, a way out of the situation.

America is somehow a closed society. Americans are not very aware of what is going on outside of America. Life here is so busy that even if you watch television and read the newspaper, and the images from outside flash by, there is no real contact. I hope you will find some way to nourish the awareness of the existence of suffering in the world. Of course, inside America there is also suffering, and it is important to stay in touch with that. But much of the suffering in the West is "useless" and can vanish when we see the real suffering of other people. Sometimes we suffer because of some psychological fact. We cannot get out…of our self, and so we suffer. If we get in touch with the suffering in the world, and are moved by that suffering, we may come forward to help the people who are suffering, and our own suffering may just vanish.

> Fifth: Do not accumulate wealth while millions are hungry. Do not take as the aim of your life fame, profit, wealth, or sensual pleasure. Live simply and share time, energy, and material resources with those who are in need.

The Eight Realizations of Great Beings Sutra says, "The human mind is always searching for possessions, and never feels fulfilled. Bodhisattvas move in the opposite direction and follow the principle of self-sufficiency. They live a simple life in order to practice the Way, and consider the realization of perfect understanding as their only career."…

> Sixth: Do not maintain anger or hatred. Learn to penetrate and transform them when they are still seeds in your consciousness. As soon as they arise, turn your attention to your breath in order to see and understand the nature of your anger and hatred and the nature of the persons who have caused your anger and hatred.

We have to be aware of irritation or anger as it arises, and try to understand it. Once we understand, we

are better able to forgive and love. Meditation on compassion means meditation on understanding. If we do not understand, we cannot love.

"Learn to look at other beings with the eyes of compassion" is quoted from *The Lotus Sutra*. …

…The original Chinese is only five words: "compassionate eyes looking living beings." The first time I recited *The Lotus Sutra*, when I came to these five words, I was silenced. I knew that these five words are enough to guide my whole life. …

> Eleventh: Do not live with a vocation that is harmful to humans and nature. Do not invest in companies that deprive others of their chance to live. Select a vocation that helps realize your ideal of compassion.

This is an extremely hard precept to observe. If you are lucky enough to have a vocation that helps you realize your ideal of compassion, you still have to understand more deeply. If I am a teacher, I am very glad to have this job helping children. I am glad that I am not a butcher who kills cows and pigs. Yet the son and the daughter of the butcher come to my class, and I teach them. They profit from my right livelihood. My son and daughter eat the meat that the butcher prepares. We are linked together. I cannot say that my livelihood is perfectly right. It cannot be. Observing this precept includes finding ways to realize a collective right livelihood.

You may try to follow a vegetarian diet, to lessen the killing of animals, but you cannot completely avoid the killing. When you drink a glass of water, you kill many tiny living beings. Even in your dish of vegetables, there are quite a lot of them, boiled or fried. I am aware that my vegetarian dish is not completely vegetarian, and I think that if my teacher, the Buddha, were here, he could not avoid that either. The problem is whether we are determined to go in the direction of compassion or not. If we are, then can we reduce the suffering to a minimum? If I lose my direction, I have to look for the North Star, and I go to the north. That does not mean I expect to arrive at the North Star. I just want to go in that direction.

> Twelfth: Do not kill. Do not let others kill. Find whatever means possible to protect life and prevent war.

The defense budgets in Western countries are enormous. Studies show that by stopping the arms race, we will have more than enough money to erase poverty, hunger, illiteracy, and many diseases from the world. This precept applies not only to humans, but to all living beings. As we have seen, no one can observe this precept to perfection; however, the essence is to respect and protect life, to do our best to protect life. This means not killing, and also not letting other people kill. It is difficult. Those who try to observe this precept have to be working for peace in order to have peace in themselves. Preventing war is much better than protesting against the war. Protesting the war is too late.

Thirteenth: Possess nothing that should belong to others. Respect the property of others, but prevent others from profiting from human suffering or the suffering of other species on Earth.

Bringing to our awareness the pain caused by social injustice, the thirteenth precept urges us to work for a more livable society. This precept is linked with the fourth precept (the awareness of suffering), the fifth precept (lifestyle), the eleventh precept (right livelihood), and the twelfth precept (the protection of life). In order to deeply comprehend this precept, we must also meditate on these four precepts.

To develop ways to prevent others from enriching themselves on human suffering...and the suffering of other beings is the duty of legislators and politicians. However, each of us can also act in this direction. To some degree, we can be close to oppressed people and help them protect their right to life and defend themselves against oppression and exploitation. Letting people enrich themselves from human suffering or the suffering of other beings is something we cannot do. As a community we must try to prevent this. How to work for justice in our own city is a problem that we have to consider. The bodhisattvas' vows—to help all sentient beings—are immense. Each of us can vow to sit in their rescue boats.

TAOISM: TAO DE CHING

The teachings of Confucius (circa 551–479 BCE) are often thought by Westerners to revolve exclusively around respect for tradition and authority, especially elders and ancestors. But Confucius did not hold to these ideas because he valued obedience and social order as such but, rather, because he felt that peace was the ultimate human goal and that it was attainable only through social harmony and equilibrium. Another renowned Chinese philosopher and religious leader, Mo-tzu (468–401 BCE), argued against offensive war under any circumstances, embracing instead an ethic of love as the universal human virtue, one that is within the grasp of everyone: "Those who love others will be loved in return. Do good to others and others will do good to you....What is hard about that?" (Confucius, in his Analects, had written, similarly: "Treat your subordinates as you would like to be treated by your superiors." It is hard not to notice the seeming ubiquity of this "Golden Rule.")

However, the most directly peace-relevant teachings of Chinese religious philisophy derives from Lao Tse (sixth century BCE), founder of Taoism and author of *Tao De Ching*.

Chan, Wing-Tsit, Way of Lao Tzu, The 1st Edition, © 1963, Pgs. 154–156, 212–213, 219–220, 236, 238–239. Reprinted by permission of Pearson Education, Inc., Upper Saddle River, NJ.

He emphasized that military force is not the "Tao" (pronounced "Dow") or "way" for human beings to follow. Taoists frequently refer to peaceful images of water or wind, both of them soft and yielding, yet ultimately triumphant over such "hard" substances as rock or iron. The following selections are from the *Tao De Ching*.

Fine weapons are instruments of evil.
They are hated by men.
Therefore those who possess Tao turn away from
    them.
The good ruler when at home honors
    the left.
When at war he honors the right.
Weapons are instruments of evil, not the
    instruments of a good ruler.
When he uses them unavoidably, he regards calm
    restraint as the best principle.
Even when he is victorious, he does not regard it as
    praiseworthy.
For to praise victory is to delight in the slaughter of
    men.

He who delights in the slaughter of men will not
    succeed in the empire.

In auspicious affairs, the left is honored.
In inauspicious affairs, the right is honored.
The lieutenant general stands on the left.
The senior general stands on the right.
This is to say that the arrangement follows that of
    funeral ceremonies.
For the slaughter of the multitude, let us weep with
    sorrow and grief.
For a victory, let us observe the occasion with
    funeral ceremonies....

Act without action.
Do without ado.
Taste without tasting.
Whether it is big or small, many or few, repay
    hatred with virtue.
Prepare for the difficult while it is still easy.

Deal with the big while it is still small.
Difficult undertakings have always started with
    what is easy.

And great undertakings have always started with
    what is small.
Therefore the sage never strives for the great,
And thereby the great is achieved.
He who makes rash promises surely
    lacks faith.
He who takes things too easily will surely
    encounter much difficulty.
For this reason even the sage regards things as
    difficult.
And therefore he encounters no difficulty....

All the world says that my Tao is great and does not
    seem to resemble (the ordinary).
It is precisely because it is great that it does not
    resemble (the ordinary).
If it did resemble, it would have been small for a
    long time.
I have three treasures. Guard and keep them:
The first is deep love,
The second is frugality,
And the third is not to dare to be ahead ... of the
    world.
Because of deep love, one is courageous.
Because of frugality, one is generous.
Because of not daring to be ahead of the world, one
    becomes the leader of the world.
Now, to be courageous by forsaking
    deep love,
To be generous by forsaking frugality,
And to be ahead of the world by forsaking
    following behind—
This is fatal.

For deep love helps one to win in the case of
    attack,
And to be firm in the case of defense.
When Heaven is to save a person,
Heaven will protect him through
    deep love....

There is nothing softer and weaker than water,
And yet there is nothing better for attacking hard
    and strong things.
For this reason there is no substitute for it.
All the world knows that the weak overcomes the
    strong and the soft overcomes the hard.
But none can practice it.
Therefore the sage says:
He who suffers disgrace for his country
Is called the lord of the land.
He who takes upon himself the country's
    misfortunes
Becomes the king of the empire.
Straight words seem to be their opposite....

To patch up great hatred is surely to leave some
    hatred behind.
How can this be regarded as good?
Therefore the sage keeps the left-hand...portion
    (obligation) of a contract
And does not blame the other party.

Virtuous people attend to their left-hand
    portions,
While those without virtue attend to other people's
    mistakes.

"The Way of Heaven has no favorites.
It is always with the good man."...
Let there be a small country with few...
    people.
Let there be ten times and a hundred...times as
    many utensils
But let them not be used.
Let the people value their lives highly and not
    migrate far.
Even if there are ships and carriages, none will ride
    in them.
Even if there are arrows and weapons, none will
    display them.
Let the people again knot cords and...use them
    (in place of writing).
Let them relish their food, beautify...their
    clothing, be content with their...homes, and
    delight in their customs.
Though neighboring communities overlook one
    another and the crowing of cocks and barking
    of dogs can be heard,
Yet the people there may grow old and die without
    ever visiting one another.

JUDAISM: THE OLD TESTAMENT

Peace as such is not prominent in the Old Testament. The God of Abraham, Moses,...and
David is in fact rather bellicose, even bloodthirsty, and the ancient Israelites were successful and merciless warriors. Exceptions exist, however, such as the prophets reprinted here,
most of whom nonetheless retain a kind of "peaceful ferocity." Despite the violence of the
Maccabees and the Zealots (early terrorist opponents of Roman rule in Palestine)—not
to mention the military prowess of modern Israel—Jewish practice has strongly endorsed
peacefulness as opposed to the warrior traditions of the Christian and Islamic societies
within which most Jews have lived. Perhaps it is more accurate, however, to say that Jewish,

Christian, and Islamic traditions all have bellicose components and periods in their history. A key question, then, is whether these warrior activities represent faithfulness to or deviation from their underlying religious values.

HOSEA 10:12–15

Sow for yourselves righteousness,
reap the fruit of steadfast love;
break up your fallow ground,
for it is the time to seek the LORD,
that he may come and rain
    salvation upon you.

You have plowed iniquity,
you have reaped injustice,
you have eaten the fruit of lies.
Because you have trusted in your chariots
and in the multitude of your warriors,
therefore the tumult of war shall arise
among your people,
and all your fortresses shall be destroyed,
as Shalman destroyed Betharbel on the day of
    battle;
mothers were dashed to pieces with their
    children.
Thus it shall be done to you, O house of Israel,
because of your great wickedness.
In the storm the king of Israel
shall be utterly cut off.

MICAH 3:9–12

Hear this, you heads of the house of Jacob
and rulers of the house of Israel,
who abhor justice
and pervert all equity,
who build Zion with blood
and Jerusalem with wrong.
Its heads give judgment for a bribe,
its priests teach for hire,
its prophets divine for money;
yet they lean upon the LORD and say,
"Is not the LORD in the midst of us?" . . .

Therefore because of you
Zion shall be plowed as a field;
Jerusalem shall become a heap of ruins,
and the mountain of the house a wooded
    height.

MICAH 4:1–4

It shall come to pass in the latter days
that the mountain of the house of the LORD
shall be established as the highest of the
    mountains,
and shall be raised up above the hills;
and peoples shall flow to it,
and many nations shall come, and say:
"Come, let us go up to the mountain . . .
    of the LORD,
to the house of the God of Jacob;
that he may teach us his ways
and we may walk in his paths."
For out of Zion shall go forth the law,
and the word of the LORD from Jerusalem.
He shall judge between many peoples,
and shall decide for strong nations afar off;
and they shall beat their swords into
    plowshares,
and their spears into pruning hooks;
nation shall not lift up sword against nation,
neither shall they learn war any more;
but they shall sit every man under
his vine and under his fig tree,
and none shall make them afraid;
for the mouth of the Lord of hosts
    has spoken.

AMOS 5:11–15

Therefore because you trample upon the poor
and take from him exactions of wheat,

you have built houses of hewn stone,
but you shall not dwell in them;
you have planted pleasant
vineyards,
but you shall not drink their wine.
For I know how many are your
transgressions,
and how great are your sins—
you who afflict the righteous, who take
a bribe,
and turn aside the needy in
the gate.

Therefore he who is prudent will keep silent in
such a time;
for it is an evil time.

Seek good, and not evil,
that you may live;
and so the LORD, the God of hosts, will be with you,
as you have said.
Hate evil, and love good,
and establish justice in the gate;
it may be that the LORD, the God of hosts,
will be gracious to the remnant of Joseph.

CHRISTIANITY: THE NEW TESTAMENT

It is in the doctrine of pacifism that Christianity makes its unique contribution to the religious ethics of war and peace. The First Commandment tells us not to kill, and the Second Commandment, to love our neighbor as ourselves. But the New Testament goes further, enjoining believers to love their *enemy*, and actively to return good for evil. Among modern Christian churches, the historic "peace churches," including the Society of Friends (Quakers), Mennonites, and the Church of the Brethren, are notable for their literal adherence to pacifist doctrines. The Mennonite theologian John Howard Yoder speaks for this pacifist tradition, based largely on the New Testament selections in this section.

Christians whose loyalty to the Prince of Peace puts them out of step with today's nationalistic world, because of a willingness to love their nation's friends but not to hate the nation's enemies, are not unrealistic dreamers who think that by their objections all wars will end. The unrealistic dreamers are rather the soldiers who think that they can put an end to wars by preparing for just one more... Christians love their enemies not because they think the enemies are wonderful people, nor because they believe that love is sure to conquer those enemies. They do not love their enemies because they fail to respect their native land or its rulers; nor because they are unconcerned for the safety of their neighbors; nor because another political or economic system may be favored...[but] because God does, and God commands His followers to do so; that is the only reason, and that is enough.[3]

LUKE 4:16–19

And he came to Nazareth, where he had been brought up; and he went to the synagogue, as his custom was, on the sabbath day. And he stood up to read; and there was given to him the book of the prophet Isaiah. He opened the book and found the place where it was written,

---

[3] John Howard Yoder, *Living the Disarmed Life: Christ's Strategy for Peace*, in J. Wallis, ed., *Waging Peace* (New York: Harper & Row, 1982).

"The Spirit of the Lord is upon me,
because he has anointed me to preach good news
 to the poor.
He has sent me to proclaim release to the
 captives
and recovering of sight to the blind,
to set at liberty those who are oppressed,
to proclaim the acceptable year of the Lord."

MATTHEW 4:23—5:10

And he went about all Galilee, teaching in their synagogues and preaching the gospel of the kingdom and healing every disease and every infirmity among the people. So his fame spread throughout all Syria, and they brought him all the sick, those afflicted with various diseases and pains, demoniacs, epileptics, and paralytics, and he healed them. And great crowds followed him from Galilee and the Decapolis and Jerusalem and Judea and from beyond the Jordan.

Seeing the crowds, he went up on the mountain, and when he sat down his disciples came to him. And he opened his mouth and taught them, saying:

"Blessed are the poor in spirit, for theirs is the kingdom of heaven.

"Blessed are those who mourn, for they shall be comforted.

"Blessed are the meek, for they shall inherit the earth.

"Blessed are those who hunger and thirst for righteousness, for they shall be satisfied.

"Blessed are the merciful, for they shall obtain mercy.

"Blessed are the pure in heart, for they shall see God.

"Blessed are the peacemakers, for they shall be called children of God.

"Blessed are those who are persecuted for righteousness' sake, for theirs is the kingdom of heaven."

MATTHEW 5:38–48

You have heard that it was said, "An eye for an eye and a tooth for a tooth." But I say to you, Do not resist one who is evil. But if any one strikes you on the right cheek, turn to him the other also; and if any one would sue you and take your coat, let him have your cloak as well; and if any one forces you to go one mile, go with him two miles. Give to him who begs from you, and do not refuse him who would borrow from you.

You have heard that it was said, "You shall love your neighbor and hate your enemy." But I say to you, Love your enemies and pray for those who persecute you, so that you may be sons of your Father who is in heaven; for he makes his sun rise on the evil and on the good, and sends rain on the just and on the unjust. For if you love those who love you, what reward have you? Do not even the tax collectors do the same? And if you salute only your brethren, what more are you doing than others? Do not even the Gentiles do the same? You, therefore, must be perfect, as your heavenly Father is perfect....

1 CORINTHIANS 13

If I speak in the tongues of men and of angels, but have not love, I am a noisy gong or a clanging cymbal. And if I have prophetic powers, and understand all mysteries and all knowledge, and if I have all faith, so as to remove mountains, but have not love, I am nothing. If I give away all I have, and if I deliver my body to be burned, but have not love, I gain nothing.

Love is patient and kind; love is not jealous or boastful; it is not arrogant or rude. Love does not insist on its own way; it is not irritable or resentful; it does not rejoice at wrong, but rejoices in the right. Love bears all things, believes all things, hopes all things, endures all things.

Love never ends; as for prophecies, they will pass away; as for tongues, they will cease; as for knowledge, it will pass away. For our knowledge is imperfect and our prophecy is imperfect; but when the perfect comes, the imperfect will pass away. When I was a child, I spoke like a child, I thought like a child, I reasoned like a child; when I became a man, I gave up childish ways. For now we see in a mirror dimly, but then face to face. Now I know in part; then I shall understand fully, even as I have been fully understood. So faith, hope, love abide, these three; but the greatest of these is love.

Ali Gomaa

ISLAM: THE MEANING OF JIHAD

Like all great religious traditions, Islam is complex and multifaceted when it comes to questions of peace and war, violence and nonviolence. Although many critics claim that violence is intrinsic to Islam, others argue that Islam is essentially a religion of peace. Indeed, similar arguments arise with respect to Judaism, Christianity, and Hinduism, leaving unsettled whether religious sanction of violence is essential to each religion in question or a departure from its primary message.

In any event, in the aftermath of the terrorist attacks of September 11, 2001, unusual attention has been directed to the teachings of Islam, especially the concept of "jihad," readily translated as holy war but, as argued in the following piece by an influential Muslim cleric, just as readily misunderstood.

Within Islam the term "jihad" refers to a large category of meanings. Today, however, there are attempts to isolate this term to only one form of jihad to the exclusion of all others. This includes a conception of jihad that at best refers only to armed struggle, and at worst to a barbaric form of warfare that seeks to destroy whatever peace may still remain in the world. This could not be further from the concept of jihad as understood by Muslims throughout history and the world over. For Muslims, jihad is much more than armed struggle against an enemy from the outside, for it includes constant struggles within both oneself and one's own society. When jihad actually does take the form of armed struggle, Muslims are aware that it can only be done for the sake of a just cause.

Once, upon returning from a battle, the Prophet Muhammad said to his companions, "We have returned from the lesser jihad to the greater jihad; the jihad of the soul." Here the term "jihad" refers to the spiritual exercise of opposing the lower self. This is referred to as the "greater" jihad, since people spend their entire lives struggling against the base desires within them that can harm both themselves and those around them.

Jihad is also used to refer to the pilgrimage to Mecca. When Aishah, the wife of the Prophet, was asked about the jihad of women, she said, "Your jihad is to make the pilgrimage." Here the pilgrimage is the lesser jihad of women and the elderly, who are not members of the armies that fight in defense of the country, so pilgrimage, which is a journey that is comprised of great difficulties due to the crowds and the physically demanding nature of its practices, is called jihad. The term "jihad" is also used to refer to speaking truth to those in power, so in Islam government oversight is a form of jihad.

In addition to these meanings, the term "jihad" refers to the defense of a nation or a just cause. This is what jihad was legislated for, and it must be differentiated from indiscriminate killing by the condition that it be "in the way of God," meaning to struggle in self-defense, to alleviate tyranny, or to prevent aggression. These are the characteristics that differentiate jihad from killing, which is a crime. These characteristics that amount to "in the way of God" are summed up in the Quran, "Fight in the way of God against those who wage war against you, but do not commit aggression—for, verily, God does not love aggressors" (Quran 2:190). This verse summarizes everything that has been agreed upon concerning guidelines of warfare, including the first and second Geneva Conventions.

As for suicide bombing, Islam forbids suicide; it forbids the taking of one's own life. In addition, Islam forbids aggression against others. Attacking civilians, women, children, and the elderly by blowing oneself up is absolutely forbidden in Islam. No excuse can be made for the crimes committed in New York, Spain, and London, and anyone who tries to make excuses for these acts is ignorant of Islamic law (shari'ah), and their excuses are a result of extremism and ignorance.

A. J. Muste

HOLY DISOBEDIENCE

Elders—whether parents or teachers, secular or religious—are often concerned with inculcating obedience. And yet, it may well be that more harm has come into the world by virtue of obedience than disobedience! At the same time, there is something self-contradictory about teaching disobedience! Protestant minister A. J. Muste was especially convinced of the value of personal disobedience when informed by individual conscience. He was one of the foremost advocates of religiously based pacifism in the United States, and the world. Muste's approach is reflected in this selection from his book, aptly titled *Holy Disobedience*.

It is pretty certainly an oversimplification to suggest...that the entire totalitarian, mechanized "system" under which men today live or into which they are increasingly drawn even in countries where a semblance of freedom and spontaneity remains, can be traced to its source in the military conscription which was instituted by the French Revolution in the eighteenth century. But what cannot, it seems to me, be successfully denied is that today totalitarianism, depersonalization, conscription, war, and the

conscripting, war-making power-state are inextricably linked together. They constitute a whole, a "system." It is a disease, a creeping paralysis, which affects all nations, on both sides of the global conflict. Revolution and counter-revolution, "peoples' democracies" and "Western democracies," the "peace-loving" nations on both sides in the war are cast in this mold of conformity, mechanization, and violence. This is the beast which, in the language of the Apocalypse, is seeking to usurp the place of the Lamb.

From *Holy Disobedience* by A. J. Muste, Copyright© 1952. New York: Harper. (First appeared in 1952 as a Pendle Hill pamphlet.)

We know that "war will stop at nothing," and we are clear that as pacifists we can have nothing to do with it. But I do not think that it is possible to distinguish between war and conscription, to say that the former is and the latter is not an instrument or mark of the Beast.

DISOBEDIENCE BECOMES IMPERATIVE

Nonconformity, holy disobedience, becomes a virtue and indeed a necessary and indispensable measure of spiritual self-preservation, in a day when the impulse to conform, to acquiesce, to go along, is the instrument which is used to subject men to totalitarian rule and involve them in permanent war. To create the impression at least of outward unanimity, the impression that there is no "real" opposition, is something for which all dictators and military leaders strive assiduously. The more it seems that there is no opposition, the less worthwhile it seems to an ever larger number of people to cherish even the thought of opposition. Surely, in such a situation it is important not to place the pinch of incense before Caesar's image, not to make the gesture of conformity which is involved, let us say, in registering under a military conscription law. When the object is so plainly to create a situation where the individual no longer has a choice except total conformity or else the concentration camp or death; when reliable people tell us seriously that experiments are being conducted with drugs which will paralyze the wills of opponents within a nation or in an enemy country, it is surely neither right nor wise to wait until the "system" has driven us into a corner where we cannot retain a vestige of self-respect unless we can say No. It does not seem wise or right to wait until this evil catches up with us, but rather to go out to meet it—to *resist*—before it has gone any further.

...Why should we hesitate to have ourselves branded on the cheek or on the buttock, with a hot iron, like cattle? The purges of "wrong-thinkers," so dear to the totalitarian regimes, would thus become infinitely easier.

To me it seems that submitting to conscription even for civilian service is permitting oneself thus to be branded by the State. It makes the work of the State in preparing for war and in securing the desired impression of unanimity much easier. It seems, therefore, that pacifists should refuse to be thus branded.

In the introductory chapter to Kay Boyle's volume of short stories about occupied Germany, *The Smoking Mountain*, there is an episode which seems to me to emphasize the need of Resistance and of not waiting until it is indeed too late. She tells about a woman, professor of philology in a Hessian university, who said of the German experience with Nazism, "It was a gradual process." When the first *Jews Not Wanted* signs went up, "there was never any protest made about them, and, after a few months, not only we, but even the Jews who lived in that town, walked past without noticing any more that they were there. Does it seem impossible to you that this should have happened to civilized people anywhere?"

The philology professor went on to say that after a while she put up a picture of Hitler in her classroom. After twice refusing to take the oath of allegiance to Hitler, she was persuaded by her students to take it. "They argued that in taking this oath, which so many anti-Nazis had taken before me, *I was committing myself to nothing, and that I could exert more influence as a professor than as an outcast in the town.*"

She concluded by saying that she now had a picture of a Jew, Spinoza, where Hitler's picture used to hang, and added, "Perhaps you will think that I did this ten years too late, and perhaps you are right in thinking this. *Perhaps there was something else we could all of us have done, but we never seemed to find a way to do it, either as individuals or as a group, we never seemed to find a way.*" A decision by the pacifist movement in this country to break completely with conscription, to give up the idea that we can "exert more influence" if we conform in some measure, do not resist to the uttermost—this might awaken our countrymen to a realization of the precipice on the edge of which we stand. It might be the making of our movement....

It is, of course, possible, perhaps even likely, that if we set ourselves apart as those who will have no dealings whatever with conscription, will not place the pinch of incense before Caesar's image, our fellow-citizens will stone us, as Stephen was stoned when he reminded his people that it was they who had "received the law as it was ordained by angels, and kept it not." So may we be stoned for reminding our people of a tradition of freedom and peace which was also, in a real sense, "ordained by angels" and which we no longer keep. But, it will thus become possible for them, as for Paul, even amidst the search for new victims to persecute, suddenly to see again the face of Christ and the vision of a new Jerusalem....

Our generation will not return to a condition under which every man may sit under his own vine and fig tree, with none to make him afraid, unless there are those who are willing to pay the high cost of redemption and deliverance from a regime of regimentation, terror, and war.

Finally, it is of crucial importance that we should understand that for the individual to pit himself in Holy Disobedience against the war-making and conscripting State, wherever it or he be located, is not an act of despair or defeatism. Rather, I think we may say that precisely this individual refusal to "go along" is now the beginning and the core of any realistic and practical movement against war and for a more peaceful and brotherly world. For it becomes daily clearer that political and military leaders pay virtually no attention to protests against current foreign policy and pleas for peace when they know perfectly well that when it comes to a showdown, all but a handful of the millions of protesters will "go along" with the war to which the policy leads. All but a handful will submit to conscription. Few of the protesters will so much as risk their jobs in the cause of "peace." The failure of the policymakers to change their course does not, save perhaps in very rare instances, mean that they are evil men who want war. They feel, as indeed they so often declare in crucial moments, that the issues are so complicated, the forces arrayed against them so strong, that they "have no choice" but to add another score of billions to the military budget, and so on and on. Why should they think there is any reality, hope or salvation in "peace advocates" who when the moment of decision comes also act on the assumption that they "have no choice" but to conform?

Precisely in a day when the individual appears to be utterly helpless, to "have no choice," when the aim of the "system" is to convince him that he is helpless as an individual and that the only way to meet regimentation is by regimentation, there is absolutely no hope save in going back to the beginning. The human being, the child of God, must assert his humanity and his sonship again. He must exercise the choice which he no longer has as something accorded him by society, which he "naked, weaponless, armourless, without shield or spear, but only with naked hands and open eyes" must create again. He must understand that this naked human being is the one *real* thing in the face of the mechanics and the mechanized institutions of our age. He, by the grace of God, is the seed of all the human life there will be on earth in the future, though he may have to die to make that harvest possible.

Thomas Merton

A DEVOUT MEDITATION IN MEMORY OF ADOLF EICHMANN

We conclude this chapter with the issue of nuclear weapons. Although with the end of the Cold War, the risk of all-out nuclear war is lower than at any time in the past several decades, the threat of accidental or terrorist use of nuclear weapons, or of small-scale nuclear "exchanges" between conflicting countries (e.g., India and Pakistan) may be at an all-time high. Moreover, the spiritual—no less than practical—aspects of nuclear weaponry remain as consequential as ever.

Thomas Merton was a Trappist monk, a writer and poet, and a powerful voice of Christian conscience. He stands in a tradition of dedicated Catholic clergy, including Dorothy Day, Philip and Daniel Berrigan, Raymond Hunthausen, and Jim Douglass. His critique of "sanity"—as defined by nuclear strategic planning—is valid for atheists too, although it may be especially relevant from faith-based perspectives. Adolf Eichmann, whose capture and trial provide the setting for the essay reprinted here, was an official directly responsible for the Nazi Holocaust, which killed 6 million innocent people.

One of the most disturbing facts that came out in the Eichmann trial was that a psychiatrist examined him and pronounced him *perfectly sane.* I do not doubt it at all, and that is precisely why I find it disturbing.

If all the Nazis had been psychotics, as some of their leaders probably were, their appalling cruelty would have been in some sense easier to understand. It is much worse to consider this calm, "well-balanced," unperturbed official conscientiously going about his desk work, his administrative job which happened to be the supervision of mass murder. He was thoughtful, orderly, unimaginative. He had a profound respect for system, for law and order. He was obedient, loyal, a faithful officer of a great state. He served his government very well.

He was not bothered much by guilt. I have not heard that he developed any psychosomatic illnesses.

Apparently he slept well. He had a good appetite, or so it seems. True, when he visited Auschwitz, the Camp Commandant, Hoss, in a spirit of sly deviltry, tried to tease...the big boss and scare him with some of the sights. Eichmann was disturbed, yes. He was disturbed. Even Himmler had been disturbed, and had gone weak at the knees. Perhaps, in the same way, the general manager of a big steel mill might be disturbed if an accident took place while he happened to be somewhere in the plant. But of course what happened at Auschwitz was not an accident: just the routine unpleasantness of the daily task. One must shoulder the burden of daily monotonous work for the Fatherland. Yes, one must suffer discomfort and even nausea from unpleasant sights and sounds. It all comes under the heading of duty, self-sacrifice, and obedience. Eichmann was devoted to duty, and proud of his job.

The sanity of Eichmann is disturbing. We equate sanity with a sense of justice, with humaneness, with prudence, with the capacity to love and understand other people. We rely on the sane people of the world to preserve it from barbarism, madness, destruction. And now it begins to dawn on us that it is precisely the *sane* ones who are the most dangerous.

It is the sane ones, the well-adapted ones, who can without qualms and without nausea aim the missiles and press the buttons that will initiate the great festival of destruction that they, *the sane ones,* have prepared. What makes us so sure, after all, that the danger comes from a psychotic getting into a position to fire the first shot in a nuclear war? Psychotics will be suspect. The sane ones will keep them far from the button. No one suspects the sane, and the sane ones will have *perfectly good reasons,* logical, well-adjusted reasons, for firing the shot. They will be obeying sane orders that have come sanely down the chain of command. And because of their sanity they will have no qualms at all. When the missiles take off, then, *it will be no mistake.*

We can no longer assume that because a man is "sane" he is therefore in his "right mind." The whole concept of sanity in a society where spiritual values have lost their meaning is itself meaningless. A man can be "sane" in the limited sense that he is not impeded by his disordered emotions from acting in a cool, orderly manner, according to the needs and dictates of the social situation in which he finds himself. He can be perfectly "adjusted." God knows, perhaps such people can be perfectly adjusted even in hell itself.

And so I ask myself, What is the meaning of a concept of sanity that excludes love, considers it irrelevant, and destroys our capacity to love other human beings, to respond to their needs and their sufferings, to recognize them also as persons, to apprehend their pain as one's own? Evidently this is not necessary for "sanity" at all. It is a religious notion, a spiritual notion, a Christian notion. What business have we to equate "sanity" with "Christianity"? None at all, obviously. The worst error is to imagine that a Christian must try to be "sane" like everybody else, that we *belong* in our kind of *society.* That we must be "realistic" about it. We must develop a *sane* Christianity: and there have been plenty of sane Christians in the past. Torture is nothing new, is it? We ought to be able to rationalize a little brainwashing, and genocide, and find a place for nuclear war, or at least for napalm bombs, in our moral theology. Certainly some of us are doing our best along those lines already. There are hopes! Even Christians can shake off their sentimental prejudices about charity, and become sane like Eichmann. They can even cling to a certain set of Christian formulas, and fit them into a Totalist Ideology. Let them talk about justice, charity, love, and the rest. These words have not stopped some sane men from acting very sanely and cleverly in the past....

No, Eichmann was sane. The generals and fighters on both sides, in World War II, the ones who carried out the total destruction of entire cities, these were the sane ones. Those who have invented and developed atomic bombs, thermonuclear bombs, missiles; who have planned the strategy of the next war; who have evaluated the various possibilities of using bacterial and chemical agents: these are not the crazy people, they are the *sane* people. The ones who coolly estimate how many millions of victims can be considered expendable in a nuclear war, I presume they do all right with the Rorschach ink blots too. On the other hand, you will probably find that the pacifists and the ban-the-bomb people are, quite seriously, just as we read in *Time,* a little crazy.

I am beginning to realize that "sanity" is no longer a value or an end in itself. The "sanity" of modern man is about as useful to him as the huge bulk and muscles of the dinosaur. If he were a little less sane, a little more doubtful, a little more aware of his absurdities and contradictions, perhaps there might be a possibility of his survival. But if he is sane, too sane...perhaps we must say that in a society like ours the worst insanity is to be totally without anxiety, totally "sane."

STUDY QUESTIONS

1. Given that most religions have had a checkered history when it comes to war and violence, how is it possible to be confident that a given tradition—pacifist or militarist—is more valid?

2. Look into historical trends concerning religious pacifism. Is there any reason to think that it is increasing or decreasing?

3. Describe and evaluate some religious writings that are especially relevant to positive peace.

4. Compare Christian "realism" with antiwar "idealism."

5. Can you begin to identify a truly encompassing, ecumenical, and nonsectarian religious peace tradition that is not limited to your own personal upbringing?

6. The famed military strategist Karl von Clausewitz argued that "to introduce into a philosophy of war a principle of moderation would be an absurdity. War is an act of violence pushed to its utmost bounds." Is there any way that a religious person could agree with this?

7. What about systems of animism, polytheism, paganism, and so on? Do they have any wisdom to offer on the question of war, violence, and peace?

8. Consider and compare systems of religious inspiration with regard to their underlying assumptions about human nature; for example, whether people are "inherently" good or evil.

9. Learn about "theodicy," the effort to make sense of how innocent human suffering can coexist with an all-powerful and benevolent God. What does this have to do with the topic of this chapter?

10. To what extent have famous peacemakers (of the past or the present) been inspired by religious teaching? What about war-makers?

SUGGESTIONS FOR FURTHER READING

Alt, Franz. 1985. *Peace Is Possible: The Politics of the Sermon on the Mount.* New York: Schocken Books.

Burns, J. Patout, ed. 1996. *War and Its Discontents: Pacifism and Quietism in the Abrahamic Traditions.* Washington, DC: Georgetown University Press.

Cecchini, Rose Marie. 1988. *Women's Action for Peace and Justice: Christian, Buddhist, and Muslim Women Tell Their Story.* Maryknoll, NY: Maryknoll Sisters.

Juergensmeyer, Mark. 2003. *Terror in the Mind of God: The Global Rise of Religious Violence.* Berkeley: University of California Press.

Kelsay, John, and James Turner Johnson, eds. 1991. *Just War and Jihad: Historical and Theoretical Perspectives on War and Peace in Western and Islamic Traditions.* New York: Greenwood Press.

Kimball, Charles. 2003. *When Religion Becomes Evil: Five Warning Signs.* New York: Harper One.

Klejment, Anne, and Nancy L. Roberts, eds. 1996. *American Catholic Pacifism: The Influence of Dorothy Day and the Catholic Worker Movement.* Westport, CT: Praeger.

Moen, Matthew C., and Lowell S. Gustafson, eds. 1992. *The Religious Challenge to the State*. Philadelphia: Temple University Press.

Polner, Murray, and Naomi Goodman, eds. 1994. *The Challenge of Shalom: The Jewish Tradition of Peace and Justice*. Philadelphia: New Society Publishers.

Wallis, Jim, ed. 1983. *Peacemakers: Christian Voices From the New Abolitionist Movement*. San Francisco: Harper & Row.

CHAPTER 7

Peace Movements, Transformation, and the Future

The Cold War generated much of the momentum for recent peace movements, in part because the simmering antagonism between the United States and the former Soviet Union gave rise to numerous "proxy wars," fueled by the U.S.–Soviet rivalry. (Of these, the Vietnam War is perhaps the most dramatic for Americans, although residents of the Korean peninsula, Cambodia, Angola, Mozambique, the Dominican Republic, Afghanistan, and others all have their own stories to tell.) In addition, Cold War fears contributed to a tendency for both sides to prop up dictatorial, unrepresentative governments, thereby foisting painful conditions of "structural violence" upon local populations. Notably, this applies to the role of the United States in supporting right-wing despotisms in Spain, Portugal, Cuba, most of Central and South America, Zaire, South Africa, Iran, Pakistan, South Korea, Indonesia, and so on, and to the actions of the Soviet Union throughout Communist Eastern Europe.

Most of all, perhaps, the Cold War threat of nuclear holocaust gave special energy and urgency to people deeply worried about personal survival as well as the prospect of global extinction. Along the way, numerous other concerns surfaced, for varying lengths of time and with varying intensity: for example, chemical and biological warfare, apartheid in South Africa, land reform in Central America, opposition to specific weapons, weapons testing, or the military draft generally.

A variety of other peace movements achieved successes, such as the independence of India and of other victims of colonialism, the progress of civil rights in the United States, treaties banning biological weapons and genocide, and so forth. The long-term effects of the Cold War's end remain to be seen, although one clear consequence has been a diminution in antinuclear activism. There has also been less opposition to specific weapons systems, even though new weapons are regularly developed and deployed, though the international arms trade continues in high gear, and within the United States at least, the military budget has declined only slightly.

244

Overall, there has been a decrease in warfare between states but no decrease in wars generally, as most wars currently take place within a given country. Ethnic and nationalist passions are as intense as ever, sometimes erupting into genocide. Proliferation of nuclear weapons has been less rampant than had been feared during the 1960s and 1970s, but an increase may be imminent. At the same time, the United States and Russia have signed a series of nuclear arms reduction treaties, and a worldwide Comprehensive Test Ban regime, although shaky, is currently in place.

There has been a welcome increase in democratization, notably in South and Central America, although Africa, the Middle East, and much of mainland Asia retain governments that are substantially less representative than most citizens would prefer. Human rights—especially religious freedom—are under attack in many places, although overall there seems to be progress. Women's rights and population policy are just beginning to receive their due. Economic fairness seems to be diminishing, as the gap between rich and poor continues to grow. Ecological issues are "all over the map." There have been improvements in air and water quality, for example, in certain parts of the "developed world," but if anything, air and water quality have generally gotten worse in most developing countries. Species extinction, global warming, and ozone depletion are, if anything, more severe than ever, while the earth's population continues to expand (albeit at a decreasing rate). On the positive side, there is more worldwide environmental awareness than ever before, an essential prerequisite for any significant and lasting progress.

In summary, movement toward a more peaceful world has been, at best, uneven and painfully slow. And yet, in some ways the world has changed remarkably: not just with the end of the Cold War but because of the breakup of the former Soviet Union itself, the transition to capitalism and at least a semblance of democracy in many countries where such change had been unimaginable, the end of apartheid in South Africa and the dramatic success of black African rule there, and the end of numerous insurrections and government repressions in Central and South America. There is still abundant room for peace movements in the future, and indeed, immense need for them. It seems likely, however, that in many cases they will focus on issues different from those of the past.

Nonetheless, certain things still have not changed. Militarism, violence, and the misdirection of national resources call for opposition. Denial of human rights, of economic fairness, and of ecological sustainability all demand redress. There is need for creative and empathic efforts to envision and promote a peaceful world. People must strive for both negative and positive peace.

It is a cliche for graduation speakers to announce that we have reached a crossroads and that the present time is uniquely consequential...not just for individuals making their personal life decisions but for society in general, even the world. But in fact, there truly may be unique opportunities as well as risks at this time in world history, when it often seems that we have been, as Matthew Arnold put it, "Wandering between two worlds, one dead, the other powerless to be born."[1]

---

[1] Matthew Arnold, "Stanzas from the Grande Chartreuse," *Essays and Poems of Matthew Arnold* (New York: Harcourt Brace Jovanovich, 1934).

The special hope of peace movements is that they might serve as midwives for that newer world, providing it with the impetus and power to be born at last. Just as birth may be difficult, often painful, even dangerous, the course of peace movements has not run altogether smoothly, nor have peace movements been unidimensional or universally welcomed. But just as birth is natural and necessary if life is to continue, it seems equally certain that peace is necessary (whether or not it is "natural") and that peace movements may contribute mightily toward success. Pope John Paul II once said that "it is only through a conscious choice and through a deliberate policy that humanity can survive." Peace movements and peace studies both strive to help establish such a policy and to represent such a choice.

Elise Boulding

BUILDING UTOPIAS IN HISTORY

When it comes to utopias—idealized images of a perfect world society—there is a tendency to extremism: to be carried away oneself on glorious flights of fantasy or to disparage others who are. Peace advocates can marginalize themselves as seemingly unrealistic dreamers, holding out for perfect solutions, which turn out to be unworkable and, thus, no solutions at all. The best, in short, can become the enemy of the good. On the other hand, it is also possible to be so jaded, pessimistic, even cynical, that all proposals for betterment appear unrealistic or unworkable, and self-proclaimed "hardheaded realists" find reasons to disparage any hope of amelioration. Or, giving up on the visionary approach altogether, one can become so willing to compromise that any measures ultimately adopted are inconsequential, or even counterproductive.

However there is a middle ground, one that recognizes the importance of goals and dreams, but without insisting that unless a specific reform directly equates with these dreams, it is not worth pursuing. To paraphrase Robert Browning: peace workers' reach must exceed their grasp, or what's a heaven for? Peace movements need substance, not just goals and images, and yet, as Isaiah put it, "Without vision, the people perish." In this next selection, Elise Boulding, one of the founding mothers of peace studies, reviews some peaceful visions and efforts.

From "Building Utopias in History" by Elise Boulding. In S. Mendlovitz and R. B. J. Walker, eds. *Towards a Just World Peace.* 1987. London: Butterworths.

HISTORICAL OVERVIEW

The human capacity to visualize *The Other* as different and better than the experienced present is found in archetypal form in all civilizational traditions through visions of the Elysian Fields, the Isles of the Blessed, Zion, Valhalla, Paradise. However, these visions are more ancient than civilizational. Anthropologists report that blessed isles are part of the dreamworld of tribal peoples. Nor are they confined to the West. Utopian elements are found in Taoism, Theravada Buddhism, medieval Islam, and in Chinese, Japanese, and Indian stories about imaginary havens of delight.

Under the pressure of social upheaval, the archetypal vision is transformed into concrete imagery that answers to specific social needs and dissatisfactions. Thus Plato's *Republic* was a response to the upheavals of the Peloponnesian Wars. The hundreds of desert communes established by Christian men and women in Egypt and Syria in the first few centuries of the Christian era were a response to the corruption of urban life in Imperial Rome, an affirmation of an alternative human potentiality that has continued as a viable monastic tradition for 2000 years. The millenialist crusades and utopian communities that erupted by the hundreds in the Middle Ages were a series of responses to plague, famine, and the gradual breakdown of the feudal order.

It is ironic then that utopia ("no place," as Thomas More named his pattern-setting *Utopia* in 1516) has come to be synonymous with a flight from reality. All the great utopians have been masterful critics of their own time. Utopians have many forms and functions, but one enduring function is to satirize society as it exists; another is to describe a more desirable way of organizing human affairs. One key problem of utopia-writing is that all utopias have implicit political goals, but few utopianists are able to devise political strategies to achieve their utopia which do not destroy these very goals. Historically, the theoreticians of utopia and the practitioners have not been the same people, and when they have, the results have been disastrous. On the other hand, the theoreticians have to be in touch with the currents of the times in very special ways....

The particular set of upheavals which ushered in modernism originated in Europe and provided the ingredients for the great utopias of the past three centuries, including: (1) the voyages of discovery, which brought news of many different lifestyles and cultures and produced a rash of literary island utopias; (2) a rapid rate of scientific discovery and technological invention, which gave a new sense of control over the environment to human beings; (3) urbanization and industrialization, which introduced the concept of class interests for new social groupings—industrial workers, and the bourgeoisie; and (4) the rise of the modern nation-state and the military expansion of the industrial order through colonization. All four of these factors contributed to the sense of social progress and control over the future. The four major ideologies of socialism, marxism, liberalism, and anarchism, which developed in different contexts within different social formations, all worked to realize their respective utopias....

Because utopia is always *The Other*—something totally different from existing society, a radical restructuring of the existing order—the changes implied by utopia are in effect revolutionary whether based on a commitment to gradual evolutionary change or sudden restructuring. This is why revolutionary violence keeps appearing in many utopian efforts, even when there is a commitment to peaceableness as with the Anabaptists. If the goal is a total restructuring of how humans live, whether on the micro- or macrolevel, then the destruction of existing arrangements, including the physical destruction of the human beings who maintain it, may come to be seen as a necessary wiping clean of the slate....

Violence has been particularly important in certain third world settings. Frantz Fanon, speaking of the process of liberation in Algeria, writes that "for the native, life can only spring up again out of the rotting corpse of the settler." And again, "...violence is a cleansing force. It frees the native from his inferiority complex and from his despair and inaction; it makes him fearless and restores his self-respect." In the West, the very size of the challenge posed by the abstract globalism of a revolutionary commitment to free all humans everywhere would seem to necessitate violence to prepare the ground for change. During the crisis, when the time is ripe, anything goes....

It is an oversimplification to say that the resort to violence has been the operative cause of utopian failures, since nonviolent utopias also fail. The same problems of human learning beset both types of utopia. It is true however that the visibility of revolutionary violence, and the pride and fear it engenders, affects deeply our assessment of radical change, and indeed the assessment of utopias in general. With rising tides of violence in industrial countries (to say nothing of the third world), there is a loss of faith today in the capacity for peaceful change....

Buber takes the position that no revolution can succeed unless it has already happened, that the taking of power by a new group can only be the formal legitimation of a process that has already taken place. He focuses on the pre-existing traditional structures in every case, and shows how the richness of those associational structures determines the capacity of a society to engage in participatory change that is responsive to local situations and local needs while fitting into a larger societal picture....We will see how differently various experimental groups have dealt with the tension between the rage for order and the longing for the spontaneity of organic processes; between the desire for central control, and the recognition that locality has its own competence; between the desire to destroy all traces of oppressive structures and wipe the slate clean before beginning anew, and the impulse to nurture the seeds of the new within the shell of the old, trusting that gentleness, not violence, will free the goodness in humans; and finally the tension between structural redesign and trying to produce new kinds of human beings to achieve the new society....

While the United States cannot be technically regarded as a utopian experiment, for many, historically, the United States *was* utopia. As indicated earlier, it was seen as the new Garden of Eden. It became the home of many utopian experiments that could not take place in Europe because there was not enough room, both physically and socially. If the United States is the home of many utopian experiments at the microlevel, it could be said that Europe has been a prime exporter of such experiments. The United States has always rejected socialism, but its values of individualism have enabled

it to give space to socialist, anarchist, and religious experiments of every kind. Europe has gone much further with socialism, but few states would conceive of themselves as utopian experiments. Sweden is an exception. The Swedish experiment is comprehensive in terms of providing a welfare state without parallel in Europe. At the state level it has been possible because Sweden has the richest associative structures of any country on the continent. Early in the nineteenth century, it had a country-wide adult education program at the village level, and village debating forums, which would be the envy of any Western country today. It was those structures which enabled Sweden to develop the first effective, country-wide participatory population control policy of any country in the world. These local structures continue alive and well as Sweden moves into the twenty-first century.

Microlevel Utopian Experiments

Microlevel utopian experiments are much easier to initiate than macrolevel ones, since the responsibility of the experimenters is only to a limited group of people operating on a small scale. Microlevel utopias are thought of as a Western phenomenon, but in fact there are many village-level utopian experiments in the third world. They have a special characteristic of reaching into the past to find traditional local structures which can be redeveloped to make a better life at the village level under contemporary conditions.

Microlevel Utopias in the First World

When Charles Nordhoff did his survey of *Communistic Societies in the United States* in the early 1870s, he found there were eight societies for the promotion of communes and 72 communes which had developed between 1794 and 1852....The culture was very limited, and no one had higher education. But they were all good farmers! Nordhoff pointed out that the commune members seemed to enjoy life, and find pleasure in amusements which looked tame to him.

What do such communes achieve? A demonstration of a more serene and humane way of life, with a higher level of altruism than in the outside world.

These utopias do not set out to change the world, only to show that it is possible to live differently in it. Economic forces should not be ignored in considering the founding of this type of commune. Its members are working class people who frequently have a hard time making it alone. More new communes are founded during times of economic depression than at any other time. Many single women who could not find a place in the economy joined these communities and prospered. These religious communities were primarily agrarian. During this same period there were 47 socialist experiments, studied by John Humphrey Noyes, all of which failed in rather short order. Unlike the religious communities, the socialist utopians tried to develop a model which could change the world. Their founders were, as Noyes says, "high-minded, highly cultivated men and women, with sufficient means, one would think, to achieve success." Unlike their religious counterparts, the socialist utopians were rarely skilled farmers. Equally unlike their counterparts, they were highly individualistic....

The last round of utopian experiments came with the so-called hippie communes in the 60s and 70s. Lacking the social disciplines which the religious and social communitarians were able to establish, most of them disintegrated rapidly. However a few have survived, usually through the persistence of an articulate leader.... Secular communes which survive have achieved some minimal degree of work discipline, and a critical mass of altruistic members with some vision of a society for which they are willing to keep working. This vision includes the abolition not only of militarism, but also war itself, and (frequently) the end of the nation-state system as we now know it. It includes a sense of social justice, a strong environmental ethic, and (usually) a discerning attitude toward science and technology. Most communes are rural because it is easier to live simply and cheaply in such a setting, and not just because of a desire to escape the city. The longer-lived ones all have active urban-rural networks. The misuse of power is a major issue with communitarians. Most of them find that leadership is important, but insist on a highly participatory process, with strong checks against authoritarianism.

None of these communities, whether long or short-lived, act as powerful social forces in contemporary society. Very few of them do overtly political work, and there seems to be a huge gulf between their very small-scale efforts at human betterment and state-level utopian designs. Are they therefore insignificant failures? Or are they laboratories functioning as laboratories do: providing a more or less controlled environment for discovery?...

CONNECTING THE MICRO AND THE MACRO: THE FUTURE OF UTOPIANISM

One context in which the micro–macro linkage of utopian experiments should be seen is the rapid development of transnational nongovernmental organizations (NGOs) in this century. Over four thousand transnational nongovernmental networks bring diverse peoples together through common interests and concerns, and are today a major new set of actors in the international system. Compared to nation-states they have few resources and little power. Yet most of the world's intellectual resources and many of its craft and social skill resources are concentrated in these organizations, particularly in the scientific, cultural, and social welfare associations. Research on major world problems, such as the threat of nuclear war, environmental deterioration, malnutrition, disease, and climatic change, is done by scientific NGOs with support from the United Nations and largely nongovernmental sources. Governments would be helpless without the policy recommendations NGOs are able to make, based on their research and experience, although the advisory process is nearly invisible to the general public. Most major policy initiatives at the international level of the UN and governments in recent decades have been based on the work of transnational nongovernmental organizations. Many of the most innovative community development projects at the local level are also NGO projects.

... If, as Kenneth Boulding says, our most significant learnings are from failure, not success, then each utopian experiment is successful to the extent that learning from its failures takes place.... Even very short-lived utopias represent thoughtfully chosen responses to upheaval and change, and presumably have enabled the experimenter to move on to other more sustained responses.

The message about the importance of associative richness as the basis for utopia-building on anything beyond the local scale has gotten across to the extent that "networking" is a word almost as common as Coca-Cola. The message about the importance of a focus on learning has not had equal promotion. There is still a tendency to believe that designing the situation will produce the desired behaviors. People may denounce Skinnerian philosophy, but they prefer manipulation by design to venturing out on the uncharted seas of human learning. How does anyone learn a really new thing? Since utopias are by definition "new," "not-yet," "other," how will human beings be able to function in them in ways that do not throw us back to the old order if we do not pay more attention to learning? Wishful thinking about the desired transformation of consciousness as an inevitable historical process distracts us from studying the difficult disciplines that will make transformation possible.

The real test of whether we have learned from the failures of past utopias is whether we can develop a theory of utopia-building that solves the problem of scale in human organization in a new way. Weber's theory of bureaucracy carried us from feudalism to industrialism, but it cannot carry us to the post-industrial society. We are paralyzed by the centralist-decentralist dilemma, since efficiency appears to require lines of hierarchical authority, yet the need to match policy to local terrain requires local participation. Buber's theory of associative richness as the basis for effective responses to social change beyond the local level, and the phenomenon of an increasingly dense network of transnational nongovernmental associations on a global scale, suggest new solutions to the old dilemmas. The overall theory has, however, yet to be formulated.

Most writers on utopia focus on only one type. An examination of the whole range of utopian experiments in their highly diverse settings, going beyond the very broad generalizations I have made here in the interest of length, may lead to a more sophisticated theory of utopia-building. Such a theory will have to deal with the problematic fact that utopia is at once a vision, a way of life, and a tool.

Richard Falk

ON HUMANE GOVERNANCE

Long before President George H. W. Bush spoke of a "new world order" in 1990, peace advocates were concerned with remaking the world political system to be responsive to social justice, environmental protection, human rights, democratization, and the demilitarization of international relations. One of the leaders in this effort has been Richard Falk, an active participant in the decades-long World Order Models Project, affectionately known as WOMP. The following selection is from the last chapter of Falk's book *On Humane Governance: Toward a New Global Politics*, a superb overall introduction to socially responsible, hardheaded, yet visionary futurism, informed by a deep commitment to all dimensions of peace.

What is most revealing in this world is not where we are, but where we are going.

—Anonymous saying

Every child is born with the message that God is not yet discouraged with humanity.

—Rabindranath Tagore

The contemporary quest for humane governance builds on kindred efforts in the past, while being rooted in an unfolding present, and above all aspiring to achieve an imagined future. The idea of humane governance is itself a way of expressing this process that is sensitive to the shortcomings, achievements, and gropings toward human betterment on this planet. What shapes the orientation and gives it substantive content in diverse settings is this normative underpinning, a blend of legal, moral, and spiritual perspectives.

To endow this underpinning with greater concreteness and sense of direction, this chapter briefly depicts ten dimensions of this world-encompassing normative project, acknowledging its historical depth yet also identifying its inspirational and prophetic assumptions about the future. Such a depiction should not be regarded as a listing of attributes or an inventory, and far less as a program. Each aspect that is rendered as distinct touches and influences the others in countless ways....

The normative project posits an imagined community for the whole of humanity which overcomes the most problematic aspects of the present world scene: the part (whether as individual, group, nation, religion, civilization) and the whole (species, world, universe) are connected; difference and uniformities across space and through time are subsumed beneath an overall commitment to world order values in the provisional shape of peace, economic well-being, social and political justice, and environmental sustainability. As such, the normative project partakes of shared values and aspirations, trends, fears and expectations about the future, rooted hopes, visions of the possible. The framing of this project acknowledges primarily the efforts of movements and peoples at the grass roots, but also takes note of the participation of prominent leaders, governments, and other institutions, as well as the specificity of opportunities and challenges arising in the aftermath of the Cold War. The normative project has ten dimensions.

Taming war The contemporary normative project has its roots in the reaction to the barbarity of warfare. It was Grotius's horrified response to the Thirty Years War in Europe that gave birth to international law in the seventeenth century and to the specific regulatory urge to put limits on what states could do in the midst of war. This impulse ripened through time, leading to the Hague Conferences of 1899 and 1907 which brought together the leaders of the dominant states of the day, purporting to be the managers of the global order. For the first time a series of international law treaties were drafted and adopted to regulate the tactics and weaponry of warfare to some degree, incorporating some customary principles of behavior embodied at high levels of abstraction in religion and morality: the requirement that tactics and weaponry distinguish between civilian and military targets, sparing the former; that force be used in a proportionate manner; that cruelty be avoided, including unnecessary suffering for those wounded or captured, even if part of the opposing military forces.

This endeavor to tame the conduct of war has persisted to the present. After World War II the Geneva Conventions of 1949 placed great stress on specific duties to protect the victims of war, including civilians and those military personnel wounded or captured in battle. These protections were later extended to the circumstances of intervention and civil war by the Geneva Protocols of 1977. Much current attention at the grassroots and governmental levels is being devoted to regimes of prohibition associated with weaponry of mass destruction: nuclear, chemical, and biological. At present, with respect to nuclear weaponry, the governmental emphasis has been on maintaining a partial regime (nonproliferation) as opposed to the efforts of transnational democratic initiatives to achieve a comprehensive regime of prohibition (delegitimizing nuclear weapons as such and arranging for their phased elimination from arsenals, thereby treating these weapons as chemical and biological weapons have been treated).

Whether this enterprise has been successful, on balance, remains controversial. Advocates claim that the suffering of war has been mitigated for millions of participants. Skeptics believe that the law of war is a hypocritical and deceptive misnomer which deflects reformist energy from war itself. At the root of the difficulty is the subordination of the principle of restraint to the achievement of victory in war by whatever means it takes. The supremacy of "military necessity" has tended to overwhelm the normative pressures of law, morality, and religion. This supremacy has been abetted by continuous innovation in the weaponry of war, the search by states for military superiority, and the development, reliance, and use of ultimate weapons and tactics in the course of winning World War II. Evidence of civilian devastation rarely inhibits tactics or weaponry. The current movement to prohibit land mines is illustrative. Despite the evidence of overwhelming civilian injury, much of it long after hostilities have ceased, governments seem reluctant to ban land mines, partly because of their cost–benefit advantages compared to other weapons. The debate itself confirms that nothing significant will happen until civil initiatives mount strong pressures.

Although the results are disappointing, the struggle to tame war continues alongside the wider, more dramatic series of efforts to abolish war itself as a hideous and outmoded social institution.

Abolishing war The more fundamental struggle, at the very center of the normative project, is to challenge war itself, the social and political process of mass, intentional killing in the name of the state, for the sake of wealth and power, in defense of ideology and a way of life, allegedly on behalf of security in self-defense, but also to satisfy expansionist ambitions. This challenge directed against war is often analogized to the struggle against slavery, the divine right of kings, colonialism, each a social institution that like war was once generally accepted, at least by elites, as necessary and inevitable. Arguably, all advances in the human condition have involved challenging institutions and practices treated as necessary and inevitable.

The real and imagined carnage of war has been the principal impetus to abolitionist efforts, as have certain pacifist traditions of religious and secular thought. After World War I, in particular, antiwar sentiments flourished, taking aim at the legality of so-called "aggressive war" and at "the merchants of death" (those who made profits from arms sales). Public pressures were so great that leading countries subscribed to the Kellogg-Briand Pact of 1928 (also known as the Pact of Paris) that renounced war as an instrument of national policy, authorizing war only as a response to aggression, in a posture of self-defense. This new ground rule was invoked after World War II as a principal basis for convicting German and Japanese leaders of crimes against the peace for their role in planning and waging aggressive warfare. This prohibition is reproduced in the UN Charter in the form of Article 2(4), which prohibits altogether the use of force, although it is qualified by Article 51 which preserves the "inherent right of self-defense." The Charter seeks to restrict the scope of self-defense by requiring that only in situations of "prior armed attack" is self-defense permitted, and even then the claimant state is required to seek immediate approval from the Security Council.

As with the efforts to tame war, those to abolish war remain controversial and are not implemented to any great extent. States interpret for themselves what self-defense means, and have ignored the requirement of armed attack. The mobilization of response against aggression has been inconsistent and often halfhearted. Preparation for war, the tactics, secrecy, and weaponry have made war an integral part of the global landscape, especially in the South where more than 125 wars have been fought in the last 50 years. In the North, fear of catastrophic war, reinforced by deterrence and containment, avoided direct war during the Cold War, but added to the frequency and intensity of warfare in the South.

With the Cold War over, there is at present no strategic rivalry of the sort likely to produce warfare, but the war system seems as rooted as ever in the operational code of statecraft, expressed by way of large military establishments, expensive weapons innovations, huge arms sales, and interventionary diplomacy. What is also discouraging, especially during this period of geopolitical moderation, is the absence of moves from above or below that challenge seriously the war system, or even move toward large reductions of spending and embark upon ambitious types of disarmament. Yet the abolition of war remains a centerpiece of the normative project, and its political relevance is embedded in each and every dimension.

The intractability of war as a social institution suggests that unlike slavery and the other analogies relied upon by the new abolitionists, war is different: it presupposes shifts in the structures of power and authority, or at least in their normative foundations. Those who argue on the basis of structure generally regard world government as the precondition for disarmament; those who emphasize normative foundations tend either to insist upon democratizing the world (on the presumption that democracies don't go to war against one another and hence that if the foundations of authority in all states become democratic, there will be no political will to engage in war and the war system will wither away) or to disseminate the ethos of nonviolence throughout the whole gamut of social relations so widely that it undermines support for military approaches to conflict, displacing the war system in time by pacifism.

Making individuals accountable . . . One dimension of the normative project has been to make those in authority accountable for their transgressions, especially with respect to war and in relation to severe abuses of human rights. The essence of this approach has been to criminalize *aggressive* war, while not challenging rights of self-defense or military preparations. The Nuremberg and Tokyo War Crimes Tribunals at the end of World War II were the foundation of this struggle to impose individual accountability, and the decisions reached rejected defenses based on reason of state or superior orders. It was also notable that secondary trials were held to assess the individual responsibility of doctors, judges, business leaders, local military commanders, and local officials, expanding the reach of accountability to encompass those who variously implemented the policies of the regime or carried out independent atrocities of their own.

This Nuremberg experience, now being widely reassessed during the fiftieth anniversary year of the main judgment, has been criticized as "victors' justice." The crimes of the victorious powers, most notably the use of atomic bombs and the excesses of strategic bombing, were exempted from any scrutiny. The prosecutors at Nuremberg did pledge that the principles being laid down to judge the defendants would become binding international law that would henceforth be made applicable to the whole world and its leaders. Indeed, the UN General Assembly by unanimous vote endorsed the Nuremberg principles, seeking their authoritative formulation by the International Law Commission, the expert body at the UN, which in 1950 provided the text of these principles that is relied upon to this day to identify the nature of individual accountability.

Governments have not implemented the Nuremberg principles. Indeed, the victorious powers in World War II, the countries which provided the judges, have each engaged subsequently in aggressive war. Further, these leading states have opposed efforts to institutionalize Nuremberg through the creation of procedures and some sort of international criminal court. The Nuremberg idea has been kept alive by two major developments: first, by activists who relied on the Nuremberg idea to challenge the supremacy of the state in the war/peace area, validating the emergence of civil resistance as a step beyond what Thoreau and others had in mind by "civil disobedience"; secondly, after the Cold War, by moves toward convening war crimes tribunals to address allegations of genocidal behavior in Bosnia and Rwanda (even prior to this, issues of accountability emerged in various countries in South America as the transitions were made from the authoritarian rule of the 1960s to some sort of constitutional governance).

The importance of individual accountability to the establishment of global governance is evident. Crimes of states need to be deterred and, once committed, dealt with effectively if confidence in the emergence of wider regional communities of participation is to arise and if the formation of an eventual global community is to be encouraged. At this point, all the contradictions of world order are present: powerful states enjoy the full prerogatives of territorial supremacy and sovereignty, exempting leaders from accountability, especially if an authoritarian political order prevails; further, the diplomacy of reconciliation and peace often sharply conflicts with the impulse to impose individual responsibility—without surrender or defeat, the accused leadership is elusive and may well prolong its period of rule, fearing what the Argentinean human rights activist Jacopo Timmermann referred to in the 1970s as "the ghosts of Nuremberg."

Collective security ... One important strand of the normative project for a reformed world was to replace balance-of-power geopolitics with a rule-governed global security system that protected states threatened by aggressive war. Woodrow Wilson championed such an approach and advocated the creation of the League of Nations to achieve collective security. These efforts have persisted in various forms. The League was created but the United States refused to join, and when aggressive war occurred in Asia and Europe the response was ineffectual. Yet the idea of collective security persisted, and was embodied in a more detailed form in Chapter VII of the UN Charter. Again the experience of the Cold War confirmed the inadequacy of existing mechanisms of collective security, highlighted by the bipolarity of the period and the inability of the opposed blocs of states to agree upon the identity of an aggressor in most situations involving the outbreak of war. The defense of South Korea in 1950 was nominally a UN operation, but was substantively controlled by the United States, receiving a UN mandate only because the Soviet Union deprived itself of its veto by temporarily boycotting the Security Council in protest against the unrelated failure to seat representatives from the People's Republic of China.

The Gulf crisis of 1990 presented a renewed, neo-Wilsonian opportunity to establish collective security. The conditions were finally right: clear aggression against a UN member; a political consensus of the permanent members of the Security Council; a threat to the strategic interests of leading countries; and the political will to provide the capabilities to perform effectively. The Gulf War that resulted in 1991 has had an ambiguous impact. It certainly established the possibility of UN effectiveness since Kuwait's sovereignty was restored and aggression was reversed. Yet the undertaking was again essentially geopolitical in motivation and character, the decisions being made in Washington, not at the Security Council in New York. When the challenge of Serbian aggression and ethnic cleansing in Bosnia arose a year later, the old circumstance of ineffectuality was again evident. Without both political consensus and a strategic stake of magnitude, leading states are not willing to pay the price for maintaining collective security. It was clear that countries without strategic relevance were on their own; the case of East Timor is exemplary, with Indonesia's aggression and crimes against humanity being neglected almost totally in the setting of collective security.

Not only is geopolitical practice discouraging, but leading states oppose the creation of independent UN capabilities by way of a peace force of volunteers and a reliable means to finance collective security. Perhaps collective security will take hold on a regional level during the decade ahead. In any event, the time has come to rethink collective security within the UN setting, associating UN uses of force with ideas of policing and reconciliation, not as a species of war-making. Such a reorientation would also greatly constrain uses of force that could not be focused on the elite responsible for aggression or genocide. The Wilsonian impulse survives. Without collective security as an interim mechanism to deter and resist aggression, the prospects of abolishing war in the near future seem severely diminished.

Rule of law The legal mind-set has exerted considerable influence on shaping the priorities of the normative project for a reformed world order. In particular, U.S. reformist energies since the Wilsonian era have stressed the importance of judicial procedures for the settlement of disputes. The establishment of a World Court in The Hague, initially in 1920, has epitomized this logic of world peace through law, although isolationist tendencies within the United States have polarized opinion on the desirability of enhancing the role and prestige of the judicial arm of the UN.

This manifested itself strongly during the controversy with the Sandinista government in Nicaragua in the 1980s. The Court decided in favor of Nicaragua with respect to the basic contention as to whether the U.S. was illegally sponsoring Contra violence against an established state. This outcome so angered the White House that it withdrew the U.S. from full participation, limiting its role to ad hoc arrangements to appear before the Court if it specifically agreed to do so. Additionally, the U.S. government refused to abide by the 1986 decision, and the Security Council did not fulfill its Charter responsibility to implement World Court decisions. Surprisingly perhaps, the Non-Aligned Movement picked up the dropped baton, impressed by the objectivity of the World Court and its willingness to decide in favor of Nicaragua. It is highlighting the importance of obliging all countries to resolve their disputes by recourse to the World Court if diplomacy fails, and setting as a goal the year 1999, the hundredth anniversary of the initial Hague peace conference.

So far the reliance on judicial solutions has not been very successful in relation to fundamental conflicts involving core interests of states. The World Court has effectively resolved potentially troubling, long-festering, marginal disputes, especially involving disputed frontiers and maritime boundaries, as well as other technical matters. The regional role of judicial institutions in Europe is suggestive of how far the rule of law can be carried in crucial matters of economic policy and the protection of human rights, according precedence to supranational authority and subordinating in the event of conflict the highest expressions of judicial and legislative authority at the level of the sovereign state. The structuring of global governance on the basis of enhanced judicial roles within the various regional settings and for the world as a whole would be a major step in averting both civil and international warfare, being expressive of the disposition of well-governed political communities to entrust even the most serious disputes to third party procedures.

Nonviolent revolutionary politics …The thrust of Mahatma Gandhi's courageous and brilliantly managed nonviolent anticolonial struggle against British rule in India introduced a radical new dimension into many subsequent political struggles for freedom, dignity, independence, and well-being that have been at the center of numerous historical narratives of the last half century. Martin Luther King, Jr., imaginatively and powerfully carried a nonviolent orientation into the domain of race relations, specifically on behalf of civil rights for black Americans. Such victories were until recently viewed as special cases, and nonviolence was not widely regarded as capable of challenging major structures of oppression around the world. Then came a series of developments in the 1980s that gave a great potency to nonviolent political strategies, although with outcomes that were sometimes disappointing in various ways: the Khomeini-led revolutionary movement against the Shah in Iran; the People Power movement of Corazon Aquino in the Philippines; the various emancipatory struggles in East Europe against Communist rule; the *intifada* in occupied Palestine; the prodemocracy movement in China and other Asian countries, including Burma, Nepal, and South Korea; the negotiated settlements of longlasting and seemingly perpetual armed struggles in South Africa, El Salvador, possibly Cambodia—and most recently even the struggle in Northern Ireland appears to be moving on to a political plane. (It has to be realized that these and other manifestations of nonviolence were never pure, and that recourse to nonviolent tactics often seemed to be for opportunistic and temporary reasons, and sometimes merely done as a clever adjustment to the lack of weaponry.)

This sense that nonviolence can challenge formidable power systems is indispensable in relation to the central struggles against war, militarism, and civic abuse of all types. It represents the countertradition to the persisting dominance of violence at all levels of social organization, and underpins the various approaches to the construction of a global civil society that both constitutes and is constituted by cosmopolitan democracy. Yet to achieve enduring results in relation to governance the commitment to nonviolence must be constantly deepened and extended to the most private spheres of human existence, including the socializing of the young, the reconceiving of "manhood," the aims of education, and the "pleasures" nurtured in the marketplace. The theory and practice of nonviolence involves the reconstruction of society, culture, and even consciousness, challenging many current practices, beliefs, and worldviews in various civilizational spaces. Yet without the substantial displacement of violence in all its forms, humane governance is not attainable, especially given the global character of interaction that is becoming standard. Rwanda and Bosnia are neighborhood events for the entire world, and as such are not capable of being cordoned off even in a physical sense: refugees and disease flow across borders and reach distant shores by boat and plane.

Human rights …Sovereignty and democracy are profoundly affected by the realization of human rights. The European idea of past centuries that the governing authority of a territorial state is supreme and unaccountable is challenged to the extent that the standards of human rights are effectively superimposed by either citizen initiative or external intervention. Sovereignty is subverted from without and diluted from within, giving rise to interventionary and resistance claims and prerogatives on behalf of the victims of abuse. In particular, the citizenry is morally and legally empowered to the extent it appreciates that its leaders can be challenged when they transgress the restraints on power as contained in the international law of human rights. In these regards, the protection of human rights represents a radical tendency in our historical period, but the potency of this effort depends on education (human rights need to be far better understood as empowering by those most victimized if they are to function even more widely as a political instrument of

resistance and transformation) and a focus of conviction (human rights must appear consistent with cultural values, or at least these values must themselves be reassessed from within).

Recourse to genocidal practice by any government is increasingly regarded as a forfeiture of its claim to sovereign authority within territory. Other breakdowns of authority in terms of minimal provision of food, shelter, and medicine are being perceived as calling for a response by the wider regional and global communities. The extension of human rights from their civil and political character in liberal democracies to the economic and social concerns of the poor is a crucial transition in thought. The socialist challenge to capitalism and the individualist ethic were responsible for the broad, earlier acceptance that every person has the material entitlement to the necessities of life, a ground rule for humane governance already present in the seminal document, the Universal Declaration of Human Rights in 1948. With the market ascendant since the late 1980s, international competitiveness has been elevated as a criterion for policy choice and socialist concerns have been discredited. As matters now stand, the unmet challenge of economic and social rights is greater than ever. Ground has been lost in recent years. The only hope now is that globalization from below, with the many initiatives of transnational democracy and the emergence of global civil society, will rearticulate human solidarity in a manner that gives political weight to a renewed movement to achieve social and economic rights.

In the end, the struggle for human rights is the struggle against all forms of abuse, neglect, humiliation, and vulnerability. As Upendra Baxi has so eloquently argued in the setting of India, human rights in the end is a matter of taking suffering seriously. Looking back on this century of world wars and weaponry of mass destruction, it may well be that the gradual development of a human rights framework will be the centerpiece of a more hopeful narration of the experience of the period. Of course, the evolution of human rights is itself a source of suspicion, emanating from the West, reeking of hypocrisy, selective application, and contradictory implications. A wider process of creation and application is unfolding, and is essential, bringing into the domain of human rights the interplay of diverse tendencies within and between cultures, combining the educative imperative to know with the religious imperative to listen, to be humble in the face of the claims of the other, and above all, to refrain from linking the right of self-determination to claims of ethnic exclusivity.

Stewardship of nature A recent addition to the normative agenda has been the rediscovery of human dependence on natural surroundings. Ancient peoples, of course, were acutely sensitive to their vulnerability to the severities of nature, especially cycles of drought and flooding. The modern scientific illusion supposed that technological ingenuity could enable human society to master nature, ignore limitations on resource availability, and expand indefinitely both resource-consuming lifestyles and the population of the planet. An emergent environmental consciousness over the last several decades, while still subordinate to market pressures and an ideology of growth, is emphasizing anew ideas of sustainability and limits. What these limits should be is a matter of fundamental political controversy, raising issues of conditions of survival at one end of the debate and matters of the conditions of human happiness and relations to the animal kingdom at the other end.

The distinctive challenge in the establishment of humane governance is to connect development with the stewardship of nature in a manner that realizes economic and social rights for all peoples, adjusting for unevenness of circumstance....At the same time, the enjoyment of the beauty of nature is the foundation of spirituality and creativity, and thus stewardship cannot be conceived of merely in materialist terms.

Positive citizenship The foundations of community reflect the contours of individual and group identity, and more specifically in relation to governance, the quality of participation. In the West, positive participation has been associated with the shift from the status of "subject" (slave, vassal, serf) to "citizen." The modern media-shaped political life threatens individuals with a new type of postmodern serfdom, in which elections, political campaigns, and political parties provide rituals without substance, a politics of sound bytes and manipulative images, reducing the citizen to a mechanical object to be controlled, rather than being the legitimating source of legitimate authority.

What forms of political participation can combine rootedness in the circumstances of a given place (the grassroots test of integrity and relevance) with the connections and aspirations of an emergent global civil society is an essential, variable challenge. Empowerment from below as an alternative to the ritualization of politics at the level of the state and to subordination to those types of globalization that express market priorities is at the core of the evolving normative project. The projection of a global identity, without the conditions of community, and the claim now to be "world citizens" express striving for humane governance, but they also arouse serious suspicions that the necessary struggles associated with transformation are being evaded by the sentimental, New Age pretense that a reorientation of personal energy will suffice.

Positive citizenship, stressing this interplay between the concreteness of situation and the imagined community that represents humane governance, will mean various things in different societies. The idea of citizenship is being promoted, also, as extending beyond state/society relations and involving all relationships of a participatory nature, that is, institutions and practices that invoke authority. Positive citizenship also draws on nonviolence and human rights as inspirational sources. The greatest challenge, at present, is to reconcile the territorial dimensions of citizenship with the temporal dimensions: acting in the present for the sake of the future, establishing zones of humane governance as building blocks.

Cosmopolitan democracy This is the binding idea of democracy encompassing all relationships, providing the grounds of institutional legitimacy, and establishing the basis for procedures and practices linking individuals and groups with institutions. It is becoming the pervasive underpinning that has been evolving along several tracks for several centuries, and now, in tandem with technology and high finance, is necessarily operative across statist boundaries as well as within them. Of course, leadership styles based on hierarchy and soft authoritarianism remain potent realities, especially in the Asian/Pacific region and in Islamic countries; elsewhere, a democratic facade is fashioned to hide the persistence of authoritarian institutional controls. But what gives promise to the vision of cosmopolitan democracy is the legitimation of democratic ideas of governance on a universal basis, the embodiment of these ideas in human rights as specified in global instruments, the democratic implications of nonviolent approaches to resistance and reform, and most of all, the deeply democratic convictions of transnational initiatives that have begun to construct the alternative paradigm of a global civil society.

We can expect many ebbs and flows, many relapses and pitfalls, endless discussion about the failure and character of democracy, and yet the cumulative drift of the normative project has been and remains dedicated to the deepening and the expansion of democracy in relation to all fields of human endeavor. It is virtually impossible to imagine humane governance as a global phenomenon without presupposing the increasing influence and acceptance of participatory politics, whether or not called "democracy," resting on the dignity and worth of the individual, but also of the group. Democracy, in these senses, provides the indispensable organizing principle, with the aim that it can be eventually presupposed, possibly to such an extent that the label can and will be dropped.

These ten dimensions of the normative project, some of recent origin, but all with many antecedents throughout the world, suggest the contours of humane governance. Their emergence remains...generally subordinate to globalization from above, acutely uneven, provisional, precarious, at the margins, but yet undeniable. Whether the dynamics of emergence will create a toppling of "the Berlin wall" of militarist, market-driven, materialist globalism is far from assured. At the same time, such a shift in fundamental prospects for governance is a sufficiently plausible outcome as to make the struggle to achieve it the only responsible basis for positive citizenship at this stage of history. Whether ours is an axial moment of normative restructuring of collective and individual life cannot yet be determined, but such possibilities inherent in the present situation provide us with the best and most realistic basis of hope about how to work toward human betterment, as understood and applied in many separate ways around the world.

Betty Reardon

SEXISM AND THE WAR SYSTEM

Making peace, in the deepest sense, requires us to acknowledge that the personal is political, and vice versa. Among the most personal human traits is gender, which has numerous implications—just beginning to be recognized—for social behavior, including but not limited to violence and oppression. In the following selection, longtime peace educator, feminist, and activist Betty Reardon examines some of the connections between sexism and the war system as well as some alternatives, including the importance of personal transformation.

The problems and issues to be explored in this examination of sexism and the war system are viewed through four major conceptual lenses: the war system, sexism, feminism, and world order. Each concept comprises a set of subconcepts and the underlying assumptions that determine the connotations carried by the conceptual terms. I offer the following definitions not as an assertion of the essential meaning of the concepts but rather to clarify the terms as they are used in this work. They are offered as well to expose my own underlying assumptions and to support the thesis that the two phenomena, sexism and the war system, arise from the same set of authoritarian constructs....

THE WAR SYSTEM: ENFORCEMENT OF PATRIARCHY

My use of the term "war system" refers to our competitive social order, which is based on authoritarian principles, assumes unequal value among and between human beings, and is held in place by coercive force. The institutions through which this force is currently controlled and applied are dominated by a small minority, elites who run the global economy and conduct the affairs of state. These

elites are men from industrial countries, primarily Western, and for the most part educated to think in Western, analytic terms. Although their relationship is competitive within the elite structures, there is a common objective that holds the elites together: the maintenance of their own control and dominance. This purpose accounts for the degree of accommodation and cooperation that can be found among all elites. Their primary competition is therefore with the nonelites, the majority of the world's people. Control is maintained by force in the form of threat, intimidation, and, when necessary, violent coercion. The control system requires that only intimidation and threat of force be used whenever possible, in part to save the cost of violent coercion but mainly to keep the majority at a sufficient level of well-being to maintain their productive capacity.

This latter, fundamental purpose of maintaining productive capacity necessitates a level of subelites within the general hierarchical structure. These subelites, for example, heads of client states, military officers, or favorite wives, carry out the day-to-day management of the productive functions of the majority of the population. Their lot is sufficiently better than the majority, from whose ranks they are usually drawn, to convince them that service to the elites and maintenance of the system is in their own best interest. They help keep the basic conflict between the elites and the majority submerged in cultural norms, traditional myths, and political ideologies. Their effectiveness depends on their remaining as removed as possible from the actual application of force, which is executed by more replaceable individuals. With the exception of those states so militarized that state violence need not be obscured, a general characteristic of the system is that the higher the level of command, the farther away it is from the actual application of violent force or the conduct of warfare....

Militarism—the belief system that upholds the legitimacy of military control of the state—is based on the assumption that military values and policies are conducive to a secure and orderly society. It has served to legitimate both warfare and civil use of coercive force (i.e., national guards and militia) in the interest of "national security." It is not surprising, given the relationship between patriarchy and the war system, that the more militarist a society tends to be the more sexist are its institutions and values. Feminists have noted this relationship in such cases as Nazi Germany and, more recently, Chile.

Militarization—the process of emphasizing military values, policies, and preparedness, often transferring civil functions to military authority—assumes that when a society is in crisis or threatened, the crisis or threat can best be weathered by strengthening the military. Two significant indicators of militarization are public expenditures, particularly the percentage of total expenditures allocated to military purposes, and the discussion or application of military measures as solutions to problems and conflicts that are basically political or economic. It should be noted that women take virtually no part in the decision making regarding such policies and that increasing military spending at the cost of social expenditures impacts most negatively on women. It contributes significantly to the feminization of poverty. Sivard indicates that the majority of the world's poor will soon be women.

The militarization of post–World War II Euro-American society has paralleled the women's movement. Given the chronological relationship of the two phenomena and some of the working assumptions shared by feminists and the peace movement, this relationship is likely to be more than coincidental. It was to be expected that Phyllis Schlafly, heroine of the New Right, would take on the nuclear freeze movement in the wake of the defeat of the Equal Rights Amendment. Much of contemporary feminism that is anathema to the New Right springs from conceptual roots totally antithetical to the concepts of war, warfare, militarism, and militarization, which derive from negative masculine values. Militarism manifests the excesses of those characteristics generally referred to as *machismo*, a term that originally connoted the strength, bravery, and responsibility necessary to fulfill male social functions. Militarist concepts and values are upheld by patriarchy, the structures and practices of which have been embodied in the state, forming the basic paradigm for the nation-state system. Thus there is in all aspects of that system an inevitable sexist bias that is especially acute in matters related to security, the term all political units apply to self-preservation. Security is the impulse that produces the *military*— "structures of organized violence controlled by the state."...

The military, then, is the distilled embodiment of patriarchy; the militarization of society is the unchecked manifestation of patriarchy as the *overt* and *explicit* mode of governance....

WORLD ORDER VALUES: INDICATORS OF MILITARISM AND SEXISM

World order studies inquire into the possibilities for abolishing war and developing a peaceful and human global order. This inquiry offers the greatest potential for the integration of feminism and feminist perspectives into both peace research and the political struggle for peace. The concept of world order studies... provides a normative approach to global problems. It projects and evaluates alternatives to the present system that could achieve world order values and open possibilities for the evolution of a more peaceful and just social order. Those who adopt a world order perspective view such evolution as progress toward the universal enjoyment of values that they see as fundamental criteria for the assessment of peace and justice and that they assert should be the basic norms upheld by the structures of a transformed global system. As I will explicate in a later section, these values are somewhat wanting from a feminist perspective in minimal standards for humane norms and global transformation. They do, however, provide us with some basic guidelines for assessing the degree of those antitheses of peace and justice, *violence* (that is, the unnecessary and avoidable harm to life and well-being) and *oppression* (the humanly devised barriers to the exercise of choice and self-determination), which characterize and bind together sexism and the war system. A brief review of world order values is offered here to illustrate this point and to support the case that substantive progress toward either peace or justice cannot be achieved without the elimination of sexism.

Each of the five world order values—economic equity, social justice, ecological balance, political participation, and peace—can be used to demonstrate that the present global order, the war system, is maintained by violence and oppression, and that women are more victimized by the system than are men. The current severe frustration of these values also suggests the possibility that both increased militarization and the male-chauvinist backlash are symptoms of an authoritarian system responding to a threat to its continuation.

The degree to which economic equity is frustrated by the war machine has been clearly documented each year by *World Military and Social Expenditures,* edited annually by Ruth Sivard.... It provides data that demonstrate that global poverty is greatly exacerbated as a result of military spending. It also documents an alarming increase in militarization, which is revealed by the number of governments that have fallen under military control, thereby verifying the assertion that public expenditures are an indicator of militarism.

Structural design certainly figures into my notion of transformation, but its role in the total change process is secondary to that of significant changes in human relations. The fundamental values of equity and mutuality, which I advocate as the norms to guide the changes, would of necessity also influence social and political structures. The structural changes, however, should emerge from the changing relations rather than coming prior to them. In other words, structures should facilitate human relations and give institutional form to the fundamental values rather than dictate and control relations and values as they have in male-dominated society. Thus a blueprint is not part of these reflections on the question of transformation. The emphasis here is more on the need for personal and relational change. If we cannot change ourselves, I doubt we can change the world.

In this context transition strategies are means by which personal and relational changes are translated into social movement and political action. The personal and the political are thoroughly intertwined in the present reality and therefore cannot be divided neatly into two distinct separate arenas for change in any transition plan that purports to be headed toward genuine transformation. This intertwining of the personal and the political makes education, viewed as the process by which we learn new ways of thinking and behaving, a very significant component of the transition-transformation processes. Education is that process through which we glimpse what might be and what we ourselves can become. It is also the process through which we articulate what might be and through which we strive to become what we choose to be. Through it we learn to choose and to pursue choices. Education is transformative when it produces visions to be pursued (that is, the goal of the *transformation*) and when it develops the capacities to achieve the goal (that is, *transition* skills, the strategies for struggle)....

It has long been my belief that authentic transformation of the global order is as much a matter of emotional maturity as of structural change. The crux of the argument set forth in this book, that neither sexism nor the war system can be overcome independently from the other, lies in the assumption that structural, even revolutionary, changes in the public order without significant inner psychic changes in human beings will be ineffective, old wine in new bottles....

This indeed is the lesson we learn from a long history of revolutions. Authentic transformations have occurred only when people themselves have changed their worldviews, their values, and their behaviors as a basis for change in the social and political structures. Such changes usually involve the society coming to perceive itself as a manifestation of a new set of human, sometimes cosmic, relationships. This assumption about the interrelationship of personal and political change, which has been a major influence on my approach to peace education, began as an intuition but has evolved into a fundamental hypothesis, one that is shared by other feminists.

This hypothesis is what lies at the base of feminist insistence that the personal circumstances of women have political roots and political significance. It is central to what some have perceived as an inordinate feminist emphasis on specific details of personal relationships between men and women and preoccupation with domestic social and economic policies that affect the everyday quality of life for women. Child care, abortion rights, and payment for housework, although conceptualized and expressed in terms of improving women's lot, are at base as structural as the concerns with such issues as peacekeeping forces and adjudication procedures that world order models have emphasized.

Such feminist proposals integrated into our concepts of transformation and transition could introduce into world order studies notions of the human and quotidian, the everyday lived experience of ordinary people, to which most people can relate more readily. It is at least one approach to overcoming the commonly held perception that world order models and peace research proposals lack relevance to the real world. It is, in fact, this lack of human detail that gives the pejorative connotation to the criticism that such academic visions of a peaceful and just world system are utopian. Feminist utopias provide flesh and bone, human and quotidian dimensions that enable us to catch a glimpse of what human life might be like in a preferred future. As the phrase "think global, act local" has characterized futurist efforts to involve people where "they're at" (that is, geographically and socially), feminists might include the human element in the phrase "think futuristically, act daily," giving the movement a different kind of

time dimension, making it more relevant to the present and the personal.

Feminists also see the task of future building as preserving and nurturing the positive elements and small-scale changes we all perceive and participate in. A positive future most likely will be made up of these elements of the preferred present that reflect the requisite values, behaviors, and worldview changes that will constitute the larger transformation. Because of their more intimate physical connection to the life cycle, women understand that the future is not an abstract condition in a remote time. It is the process of becoming. Women know in their bones that the achievement of a preferred future requires us to act in the present on the basis of the norms and values we enshrine in our visions of transformation....

As individual human development is cyclical, and often regresses at stages rather than progresses, so too a feminist view of transition is not a step-by-step linear progression but rather an organic, flowing and eddying notion of change. It is, I believe, this very notion of organic change with its expectation and understanding of recurrent regression that keeps women from despairing of their failures and infuses their continued struggle for a better life and for peace. I am, in fact, convinced that linear, step-by-step concepts of transition not only are bound to lead to severe disappointments, but are more likely to result in the despair that engulfs so many as the militarist negative trends increase in volume and speed....

MASCULINE MODE, FEMININE MODE: SEPARATION AND CONNECTION

Gilligan points out how a masculine bias in the study of the different development emphases between men and women—men striving for separation and independence and women for connection and interdependence—has given us an unbalanced and inadequate notion of maturity. And, I would add, it has led to an overemphasis on individualism and the power to control, which so characterize the present dangerous stage of the war system, the arms race. These observations help us to see how the masculine bias actually has limited the conceptual repertoire and styles of problem resolution we bring to the arenas of politics and conflict. Individuation and separation have so determined our concepts of national interests that we are blinded to the many realities of interdependence that are the major determinants of our present world situation. That we are willing to risk our very survival to defend the national interest is not so surprising in a masculine-biased system when we understand that "the morality of rights differs from the morality of responsibility in its emphasis on separation rather than connection, in its consideration of the individual rather than the relationship as primary."...

This significant difference in the types of morality that are developed by men and women provides us with an important insight into the causes of our present crises. It also suggests that transformation, the realization of global change, and transition, the process of achieving it, may well depend on the integration of masculine and feminine perspectives and modes in the processes of designing new structures and the political and educational programs to achieve them.

Finally, it seems to me, Gilligan's work lends further support to the hypothesis of reciprocal causation and provides grounds for the assertion that the structures of violence that constitute the war system are as much imbedded in the human psyche as in social structure. They are undoubtedly influenced by the attributes we use to guide the development of masculine identity and by masculine modes of public decision making. These factors are revealed only when the whole truth about the human experience is no longer filtered through an exclusive masculine bias, for "in the different voice of women lies the truth of an ethic of care, the tie between relationships and responsibility and the origins of aggression in the failure of connection."...

The masculine mode approaches transformation and transition of the global order in the same analytic abstract fashion as it approaches other intellectual issues. The two concepts are perceived as a discrete set of end circumstances and a specific sequence of strategies to achieve them. The transformation, the end circumstances, generally are described in terms of *specific* structures and processes. These very often take the form of models that

frequently appear to feminist and third world eyes to be a rearrangement of traditional forms of power rather than a full and authentic transformation of the present reality.

Masculine models of transformation, frequently referred to as "system change," tend to be abstracted from everyday human conditions, to display a central concern with power arrangements, and to be preoccupied with the concept of sovereignty, an essentially patriarchal notion. Some focus much attention on determining which component of the revised structures will be endowed with the power and the right legitimately to use force, whether that force be armed or "nonviolent." Such models can be depicted by charts, diagrams, computer games, and institutional descriptions, but almost never do they have any explicit element of human relations or affective, emotional content, and few have displayed any cultural dimension.

The strategies set forth in the masculine mode for the transition process tend to be primarily political and economic. They are at their best in proposals for staged disarmament and plans for industrial conversion. They are conceived as steps to be taken in the public arena in a particular, incremental style (though of varying degrees of rapidity) and impacting primarily on public life. The value changes included in transition scenarios tend to be norms for social and public policies such as protection for human rights and procedures for conflict resolution. They are corporate rather than personal and conceived so as to have a direct impact on the public domain. The consequent effects of value changes on the private and personal spheres are given little if any more attention in world order transition strategies than in present public policy formation. This blindness to "secondary" consequences gives feminists, who do assess policy impact on women, cause for concern that the proposals are indeed more rearrangement than transformation. Indeed, it is this masculine preoccupation with the public and structural that has aborted the transformative potential of most twentieth-century revolutions. It kept them as just that: a revolution, a turning of the major power wheels that failed to produce changes in the fundamental global order. Such changes remove a particular group from political power but do not make connections to changes in the interpersonal realm nor to the nonmaterial sources of personal empowerment that feminism emphasizes. (It must be noted that some women researchers and futurists, myself included, have produced these same kinds of masculine scenarios.) The transition scenarios in the masculine mode have always been far weaker, less convincing, and less relevant either to the goal or the present reality than are their visions of transformed structures. In general there is a significant disjuncture between the transformative visions and the plans for the process to achieve them. Masculine models of transformation exhibit little or no consideration of the personal and individual changes that will be required. It is my opinion that this weakness in world order modeling results from the lack of the human, explicit, behavioral elements that are characteristic of the feminine mode....

Most feminist visions or models of the future world order are found not in academic essays, computerized games, graphs, or charts but in novels, poetry, works of art, and specific behavioral changes that women are currently making in themselves and seeking to help others to make. Women are significantly active in initiating political movements, particularly movements related to peace and justice, but they have yet to be as concerned with political strategy design and the devising of structural changes for the institutionalization of the kind of human interrelationships they seek. Yet their current efforts and their visions of healing and wholeness are in some ways far more transformative than the precise structural designs and abstract political processes that male researchers have offered to date.

TRANSCENDING POLARIZATION: RECONCILIATION AS A WORLD ORDER VALUE

To move toward a broader comprehension of the meaning of healing and wholeness in our fragmented world and to comprehend the full dimensions of the transformational task, we need to take note of the many damaging divisions and separations that are in large part a consequence of the masculine

bias in science, politics, and social structures in general. We need to focus on the major separations and dichotomies in thought and social functions and the consequent inequity, conflict, and violence that this bias has produced. Among the deepest of these divisions that the feminine flow toward healing and wholeness call us to transcend are those between science and philosophy, fact and value, the individual and the community, the family and the state, the public and the private spheres, citizens and nurturers, and male and female social roles. For example, citizenship in a feminist future order would carry responsibility to nurture and enhance life as well as participate in politics and public affairs....

What I am advocating here is a new world order value, reconciliation, and perhaps even forgiveness, not only of those who trespass against us, but primarily of ourselves. By understanding that no human being is totally incapable of the most reprehensible of human acts, or of the most selfless and noble, we open up the possibilities for change of cosmic dimensions. Essentially this realization is what lies at the base of the philosophy of nonviolence. If we are to move through a disarmed world to a truly nonviolent one, to authentic peace and justice, we must come to terms with and accept the other in ourselves, be it our masculine or our feminine attributes or any of those traits and characteristics we have projected on enemies and criminals, or heroes and saints.

If we advocate the equal value and dignity of all persons, we need also accept their shortcomings as well as their gifts and talents, and understand that all (even ourselves) are capable of changing. The question is whether we will be motivated to do so. My own belief is that this motivation is primarily a task for education, particularly for peace education. Indeed, we have seen little evidence of motivation to change either in the bastions of male chauvinism or in the entrenched militaristic social system. But without the possibility of such change there is little hope of escaping from the war system trap. Education is an enterprise based on hope and the possibility of change.

At its best, education, like the struggle for peace, is motivated by love. The facts that men and women continue to love each other, and that some even struggle to understand each other despite the overwhelming dimensions of the system that separates and alienates us from each other, are a tremendous source of hope. So, too, is the growing bonding among women transcending a socialization that separated and alienated them from each other, setting them into competition to win the favor of men. As men have bonded in the hunt and on the battlefields and playing fields, women now bond in the feminist movement and in the peace movement, offering each other some of the love and support they have been socialized to lavish on husbands and children. They are supporting and nurturing each other through personal change and political challenge. Such sources of hope make it possible to believe we can change. It is this belief that feminists find empowering and from which we take a new definition of *power:* the capacity to change, to change ourselves and our environment.

Indeed, the empowerment of the powerless is the fundamental change required to transcend sexism and the war system. It would be the very antithesis of the present coercive use of power. It is one of the major motivations behind the feminist demand that women have control over their own bodies, the prime requisite of empowerment, and it clearly makes these women's issues world order issues. It means as well that world order must at last fully embrace that elusive fifth value, *participation,* as it moves toward the stronger, more transformative value of universal human empowerment. Only through this kind of process can we be liberated from the continued global dominance of the industrial male elites. Women's movements, anticolonial movements, and all forms of human rights movements are evidence that such a process is under way. All such movements begin with the refusal of the oppressed to continue to accept their inferior status as inevitable or deserved. Value of self, a primary value of feminism, is essential to the process of liberation and to the development of mature responsibility....The most significant aspect of the process is recognizing the costs. Empowerment, self-respect, and authentic responsibility are not easily come by, not by individuals or societies. Nor do we have the specific strategies of empowerment at hand.

However, given the commitment and the visions, feminist strategies are born out of specific contexts and conditions.

These examples hold forth the possibility of relating to others, and to the other, as full persons, not as enemies or objects. The focus was on both political objective, or social model, and on human relations. They seemed to combine the masculine abstract intellectual approach with the feminine concrete, practical approach. This, it seems to me, is what we need in transition strategies—a convergence of masculine and feminine styles of change.

There is a significant similarity between feminist peace strategists and male practitioners of nonviolence in their refusal to accede to the seemingly unchangeable, and their challenge to the authority of raw, coercive power. They have taken responsibility to ask the fundamental questions about the necessity of human suffering. Questioning, taking responsibility, empowerment, and value of self are attributes of maturity and transformation. They are evidence, too, of the convergence of positive masculine and feminine values, modes of thought, and styles of action. These developments are cited as signs of the hoped-for convergence of feminism and the peace movement, and to indicate that the possibilities for truly transformatory movements can be greatly enhanced by encouraging and widening this convergence. The possibility of a cultural transformation of unprecedented proportions is, indeed, emerging. The chances of making that possibility become a probability, of achieving a truly human future, will be enhanced by deeper study of the connections between sexism and the war system. The potential for transformation that I see in the knowledge such study would yield gives me hope at a time when ordinary politics and traditional scholarship offer none.

CONCLUSION: REPRODUCING THE FUTURE

Because one major purpose of this monograph has been to reflect on the life-enhancing possibilities of feminism and women's movements, the language of human reproduction provides an appropriate frame for the conclusion. The conception of a transformed society will be found in the actualizing of the central ideas that will give birth to that society. As male and female genetic material converge in the conception of an individual human life, so must masculine and feminine perceptions, modes, and participation merge into a conception of a truly human society. This conception can be politically symbolized by taking on as one goal the two major transformative tasks of our generation: achieving equality for women and complete disarmament. Achieving the first task would give social value to positive feminine human traits, and the accomplishment of the second would require denial of social value to the most negative masculine traits.

The gestation of the transformed society would be in the processes we devise to develop the basic conception into a living social order, capable of maturing into an entity no longer dependent on specific structures or controlled by the circumstances that led to its conception. Such processes are likely to be simultaneous and complementary behavioral and structural changes guided by the masculine values of justice and equality and the feminine values of care and equity. Transition strategies equal to this task can be designed only by men and women together working in a style of true mutuality.

The "cry of life" of the transformation might be the public articulation and institutionalization of the fundamental values derived from the parents. The birth would be symbolized, as have been the births of societies for centuries, by the inauguration of new governing structures. Such an inauguration might be the formal recognition of the institutional framework of a global peace system, derived as the result of the equal political participation of men and women in the maintenance and development of a disarmed and demilitarized world.

The maturity of such a peace system would be indicated by continuous reflection on and challenge to its rules and structures and by its capacity to change in response to new conditions leading to new stages of human maturation. Maturity is, in the last analysis, the capacity to transform, and to bring forth new life. Transformation is the continuous process by which human beings exercise choice, change reality, and find meaning. Transformation is life. Feminism chooses life.

Dalai Lama

A HUMAN APPROACH TO WORLD PEACE

Certain individuals, by virtue of their moral authority, are especially well positioned to prick the global human conscience. Among these, the Dalai Lama is especially prominent, with impact not limited to his Buddhist followers. Thus, he has long stood for firm but nonviolent resistance to Chinese encroachment into Tibet, but beyond this, for the prospect that all human beings might liberate themselves from pain and suffering—not simply via an afterlife or longed-for future nirvana but through genuine love and compassion in this life.

When we rise in the morning and listen to the radio or read the newspaper, we are confronted with the same sad news: violence, crime, wars, and disasters. I cannot recall a single day without a report of something terrible happening somewhere. Even in these modern times it is clear that one's precious life is not safe. No former generation has had to experience so much bad news as we face today; this constant awareness of fear and tension should make any sensitive and compassionate person question seriously the progress of our modern world.

It is ironic that the more serious problems emanate from the more industrially advanced societies. Science and technology have worked wonders in many fields, but the basic human problems remain. There is unprecedented literacy, yet this universal education does not seem to have fostered goodness but only mental restlessness and discontent instead. There is no doubt about the increase in our material progress and technology, but somehow this is not sufficient as we have not yet succeeded in bringing about peace and happiness or in overcoming suffering.

We can only conclude that there must be something seriously wrong with our progress and development, and if we do not check it in time there could be disastrous consequences for the future of humanity. I am not at all against science and technology—they have contributed immensely to the overall experience of humankind; to our material comfort and well-being and to our greater understanding of the world we live in. But if we give too much emphasis to science and technology, we are in danger of losing touch with those aspects of human knowledge and understanding that aspire toward honesty and altruism.

Science and technology, though capable of creating immeasurable material comfort, cannot replace the age-old spiritual and humanitarian values that have largely shaped world civilization, in all its national forms, as we know it today. No one can deny the unprecedented material benefit of science and technology, but our basic human problems remain; we are still faced with the same, if not more, suffering, fear, and tension. Thus it is only logical to try to strike a balance between material developments on the one hand and the development of spiritual, human values on the other. In order to bring about this great adjustment, we need to revive our humanitarian values....

SOLVING HUMAN PROBLEMS THROUGH TRANSFORMING HUMAN ATTITUDES

Of the many problems we face today, some are natural calamities and must be accepted and faced with equanimity. Others, however, are of our own making, created by misunderstanding, and can be corrected. One such type arises from the conflict of ideologies, political or religious, when people fight each other for petty ends, losing sight of the basic humanity that binds us all together as a single human family. We must remember that the different religions, ideologies, and political systems of the world are meant for human beings to achieve happiness. We must not lose sight of this fundamental goal and at no time should we place means above ends; the supremacy of humanity over matter and ideology must always be maintained.

By far the greatest single danger facing humankind—in fact, all living beings on our planet—is the threat of nuclear destruction. I need not elaborate on this danger, but I would like to appeal to all the leaders of the nuclear powers who literally hold the future of the world in their hands, to the scientists and technicians who continue to create these awesome weapons of destruction, and to all the people at large who are in a position to influence their leaders: I appeal to them to exercise their sanity and begin to work at dismantling and destroying all nuclear weapons. We know that in the event of a nuclear war there will be no victors, because there will be no survivors! Is it not frightening just to contemplate such inhuman and heartless destruction? And, is it not logical that we should remove the cause of our own destruction when we know the cause and have both the time and the means to do so? Often we cannot overcome our problems because we either do not know the cause or, if we understand it, do not have the means to remove it. This is not the case with the nuclear threat.

Whether they belong to more evolved species like humans or to simpler ones such as animals, all beings primarily seek peace, comfort, and security. Life is as dear to the mute animal as it is to any human being; even the simplest insect strives for protection from dangers that threaten its life. Just as each one of us wants to live and does not wish to die, so it is with all other creatures in the universe, though their power to effect this is a different matter.

Broadly speaking there are two types of happiness and suffering, mental and physical, and of the two, I believe that mental suffering and happiness are the more acute. Hence, I stress the training of the mind to endure suffering and attain a more lasting state of happiness. However, I also have a more general and concrete idea of happiness: a combination of inner peace, economic development, and, above all, world peace. To achieve such goals, I feel it is necessary to develop a sense of universal responsibility, a deep concern for all irrespective of creed, color, sex, or nationality.

The premise behind this idea of universal responsibility is the simple fact that, in general terms, all others' desires are the same as mine. Every being wants happiness and does not want suffering. If we, as intelligent human beings, do not accept this fact, there will be more and more suffering on this planet. If we adopt a self-centred approach to life and constantly try to use others for our own self-interest, we may gain temporary benefits, but in the long run we will not succeed in achieving even personal happiness, and world peace will be completely out of the question.

In their quest for happiness, humans have used different methods, which all too often have been cruel and repellent. Behaving in ways utterly unbecoming to their status as humans, they inflict suffering upon fellow humans and other living beings for their own selfish gains. In the end, such shortsighted actions bring suffering to oneself as well as to others. To be born a human being is a rare event in itself, and it is wise to use this opportunity as effectively and skillfully as possible. We must have the proper perspective, that of the universal life process, so that the happiness or glory of one person or group is not sought at the expense of others.

All this calls for a new approach to global problems. The world is becoming smaller and smaller—and more and more interdependent—as a result of rapid technological advances and international trade as well as increasing transnational relations. We now depend very much on each other. In ancient times problems were mostly family-size, and they were naturally tackled at the family level, but the situation has changed. Today we are so interdependent, so closely interconnected with each other, that without a sense of universal responsibility, a feeling of universal brotherhood and sisterhood, and an understanding and belief that we really are part of one big human family, we cannot hope to overcome the dangers to our very existence—let alone bring about peace and happiness.

One nation's problems can no longer be satisfactorily solved by itself alone; too much depends on the interest, attitude, and cooperation of other nations. A universal humanitarian approach to world problems seems the only sound basis for world peace. What does this mean? We begin from the recognition mentioned previously that all beings cherish happiness and do not want suffering. It then becomes both morally wrong and pragmatically unwise to pursue only one's own happiness oblivious to the feelings and aspirations of all others who surround us as members of the same human family. The wiser course is to think of others also when pursuing our own happiness. This will lead to what I call "wise self-interest," which hopefully will transform itself into "compromised self-interest," or better still, "mutual interest."

Although the increasing interdependence among nations might be expected to generate more sympathetic cooperation, it is difficult to achieve a spirit of genuine cooperation as long as people remain indifferent to the feelings and happiness of others. When people are motivated mostly by greed and jealousy, it is not possible for them to live in harmony. A spiritual approach may not solve all the political problems that have been caused by the existing self-centered approach, but in the long run it will overcome the very basis of the problems that we face today.

On the other hand, if humankind continues to approach its problems considering only temporary expediency, future generations will have to face tremendous difficulties. The global population is increasing, and our resources are being rapidly depleted. Look at the trees, for example. No one knows exactly what adverse effects massive deforestation will have on the climate, the soil, and global ecology as a whole. We are facing problems because people are concentrating only on their short-term, selfish interests, not thinking of the entire human family. They are not thinking of the earth and the long-term effects on universal life as a whole. If we of the present generation do not think about these now, future generations may not be able to cope with them.

COMPASSION AS THE PILLAR OF WORLD PEACE

According to Buddhist psychology, most of our troubles are due to our passionate desire for and attachment to things that we misapprehend as enduring entities. The pursuit of the objects of our desire and attachment involves the use of aggression and competitiveness as supposedly efficacious instruments. These mental processes easily translate into actions, breeding belligerence as an obvious effect. Such processes have been going on in the human mind since time immemorial, but their execution has become more effective under modern conditions. What can we do to control and regulate these "poisons"—delusion, greed, and aggression? For it is these poisons that are behind almost every trouble in the world.

As one brought up in the Mahayana Buddhist tradition, I feel that love and compassion are the moral fabric of world peace. Let me first define what I mean by compassion. When you have pity or compassion for a very poor person, you are showing sympathy because he or she is poor; your compassion is based on altruistic considerations. On the other hand, love toward your wife, your husband, your children, or a close friend is usually based on attachment. When your attachment changes, your kindness also changes; it may disappear. This is not true love. Real love is not based on attachment, but on altruism. In this case your compassion will remain as a humane response to suffering as long as beings continue to suffer.

This type of compassion is what we must strive to cultivate in ourselves, and we must develop it from a limited amount to the limitless. Undiscriminating, spontaneous, and unlimited compassion for all sentient beings is obviously not the usual love that one has for friends or family, which is alloyed with ignorance, desire, and attachment. The kind of love we should advocate is this wider love that you can have even for someone who has done harm to you: your enemy.

The rationale for compassion is that every one of us wants to avoid suffering and gain happiness. This, in turn, is based on the valid feeling of "I," which determines the universal desire for happiness. Indeed, all beings are born with similar desires and should have an equal right to fulfill them. If I compare myself with others, who are countless, I feel that others are more important because I am just one person whereas others are many. Further, the Tibetan Buddhist tradition teaches us to view all sentient beings as our dear mothers and to show our gratitude by loving them all. For, according to Buddhist theory, we are born and reborn countless numbers of times, and it is conceivable that each being has been our parent at one time or another. In this way all beings in the universe share a family relationship.

Whether one believes in religion or not, there is no one who does not appreciate love and compassion. Right from the moment of our birth, we are under the care and kindness of our parents; later in life, when facing the sufferings of disease and old age, we are again dependent on the kindness of others. If at the beginning and end of our lives we depend upon others' kindness, why then in the middle should we not act kindly toward others? The development of a kind heart (a feeling of closeness for all human beings) does not involve the religiosity we normally associate with conventional religious practice. It is not only for people who believe in religion, but is for everyone regardless of race, religion, or political affiliation. It is for anyone who considers himself or herself, above all, a member of the human family and who sees things from this larger and longer perspective. This is a powerful feeling that we should develop and apply; instead, we often neglect it, particularly in our prime years, when we experience a false sense of security.

When we take into account a longer perspective, the fact that all wish to gain happiness and avoid suffering, and keep in mind our relative unimportance in relation to countless others, we can conclude that it is worthwhile to share our possessions with others. When you train in this sort of outlook, a true sense of compassion—a true sense of love and respect for others—becomes possible. Individual happiness ceases to be a conscious self-seeking effort; it becomes an automatic and far superior by-product of the whole process of loving and serving others.

Another result of spiritual development, most useful in day-to-day life, is that it gives a calmness and presence of mind. Our lives are in constant flux, bringing many difficulties. When faced with a calm and clear mind, problems can be successfully resolved. When, instead, we lose control over our minds through hatred, selfishness, jealousy, and anger, we lose our sense of judgement. Our minds are blinded, and at those wild moments anything can happen, including war. Thus, the practice of compassion and wisdom is useful to all, especially to those responsible for running national affairs, in whose hands lie the power and opportunity to create the structure of world peace....

INDIVIDUAL POWER TO SHAPE INSTITUTIONS

Anger plays no small role in current conflicts such as those in the Middle East, Southeast Asia, the North–South problem, and so forth. These conflicts arise from a failure to understand one another's humanness. The answer is not the development and use of greater military force, nor an arms race. Nor is it purely political or purely technological. Basically it is spiritual, in the sense that what is required is a sensitive understanding of our common human situation. Hatred and fighting cannot bring happiness to anyone, even to the winners of battles. Violence always produces misery and thus is essentially counter-productive. It is, therefore, time for world leaders to learn to transcend the differences of race, culture, and ideology and to regard one another through

eyes that see the common human situation. To do so would benefit individuals, communities, nations, and the world at large....

As all nations are economically dependent upon one another more than ever before, human understanding must go beyond national boundaries and embrace the international community at large. Indeed, unless we can create an atmosphere of genuine cooperation, gained not by threatened or actual use of force but by heartfelt understanding, world problems will only increase. If people in poorer countries are denied the happiness they desire and deserve, they will naturally be dissatisfied and pose problems for the rich. If unwanted social, political, and cultural forms continue to be imposed upon unwilling people, the attainment of world peace is doubtful. However, if we satisfy people at a heart-to-heart level, peace will surely come.

Within each nation, the individual ought to be given the right to happiness, and among nations, there must be equal concern for the welfare of even the smallest nations. I am not suggesting that one system is better than another and all should adopt it. On the contrary, a variety of political systems and ideologies is desirable and accords with the variety of dispositions within the human community. This variety enhances the ceaseless human quest for happiness. Thus each community should be free to evolve its own political and socioeconomic system, based on the principle of self-determination.

The achievement of justice, harmony, and peace depends on many factors. We should think about them in terms of human benefit in the long run rather than the short term. I realize the enormity of the task before us, but I see no other alternative than the one I am proposing—which is based on our common humanity. Nations have no choice but to be concerned about the welfare of others, not so much because of their belief in humanity, but because it is in the mutual and long-term interest of all concerned. An appreciation of this new reality is indicated by the emergence of regional or continental economic organizations such as the European Economic Community, the Association of South East Asian Nations, and so forth. I hope more such transnational organizations will be formed, particularly in regions where economic development and regional stability seem in short supply.

Under present conditions, there is definitely a growing need for human understanding and a sense of universal responsibility. In order to achieve such ideas, we must generate a good and kind heart, for without this, we can achieve neither universal happiness nor lasting world peace. We cannot create peace on paper. While advocating universal responsibility and universal brotherhood and sisterhood, the facts are that humanity is organized in separate entities in the form of national societies. Thus, in a realistic sense, I feel it is these societies that must act as the building blocks for world peace. Attempts have been made in the past to create societies more just and equal. Institutions have been established with noble charters to combat antisocial forces. Unfortunately, such ideas have been cheated by selfishness. More than ever before, we witness today how ethics and noble principles are obscured by the shadow of self-interest, particularly in the political sphere....

Such human qualities as morality, compassion, decency, wisdom, and so forth have been the foundations of all civilizations. These qualities must be cultivated and sustained through systematic moral education in a conducive social environment so that a more humane world may emerge. The qualities required to create such a world must be inculcated right from the beginning, from childhood. We cannot wait for the next generation to make this change; the present generation must attempt a renewal of basic human values. If there is any hope, it is in the future generations, but not unless we institute major change on a worldwide scale in our present educational system. We need a revolution in our commitment to and practice of universal humanitarian values.

It is not enough to make noisy calls to halt moral degeneration; we must do something about it. Since present-day governments do not shoulder such "religious" responsibilities, humanitarian and religious leaders must strengthen the existing civic, social, cultural, educational, and religious organizations to revive human and spiritual values. Where necessary, we must create new organizations to achieve these goals. Only in so doing can we hope to create a more stable basis for world peace....

Finally, a few words about material progress. I have heard a great deal of complaint against material progress from Westerners, and yet, paradoxically, it has been the very pride of the Western world. I see nothing wrong with material progress per se, provided people are always given precedence. It is my firm belief that in order to solve human problems in all their dimensions, we must combine and harmonize economic development with spiritual growth.

However, we must know its limitations. Although materialistic knowledge in the form of science and technology has contributed enormously to human welfare, it is not capable of creating lasting happiness. In America, for example, where technological development is perhaps more advanced than in any other country, there is still a great deal of mental suffering. This is because materialistic knowledge can only provide a type of happiness that is dependent upon physical conditions. It cannot provide happiness that springs from inner development independent of external factors.

For renewal of human values and attainment of lasting happiness, we need to look to the common humanitarian heritage of all nations the world over. May this essay serve as an urgent reminder lest we forget the human values that unite us all as a single family on this planet....

Chalmers Johnson

EMPIRE V. DEMOCRACY: WHY NEMESIS IS AT OUR DOOR

Democracy is a bit like Mom and apple pie: everyone claims to be in favor of it. At its heart, however, the notion that countries should be governed according to the will of their people is radical indeed. Some of the most astounding and hope-giving events of the late twentieth century involved democratization: in South Africa, South Korea, the Philippines, Haiti, much of Latin America, even, haltingly, in Russia and the former "Soviet bloc" states of Eastern Europe.

On the negative side, democracy is nearly always under siege. In 1941, sociologist Harold Lasswell warned in a now-classic paper about the possible rise of "garrison states—a world in which the specialists on violence are the most powerful group in society." Lasswell predicted that there would likely be "transitional forms, such as the party propaganda state, where the dominant figure is the propagandist, and the party bureaucratic state, in which the organization men of the party make the vital decisions."[2] It can be debated whether the United States has risen—or sunk—to any of these levels and whether or to what extent other countries are in transition.

On the other hand, with the end of the Cold War and the apparent spread of democracy, peace researchers have been actively debating another of the more optimistic generalizations: that democracies do not go to war against other democracies. This gives added cogency to the question of "garrison states," incipient or hidden garrison states, and the relationship between militarism and democracy.

Another important—and sometimes troubling—aspect of democracy is that it invokes serious questions about responsibility: the responsibility of each citizen for his or her immediate social unit, larger community, and world. These questions are increasingly cogent in a world of globalization and thus of cultural, political, economic, and social homogenization. And yet, certain countries—because of their greater power and influence—bear not only unusual responsibility for circumstances as they are; they also have the opportunity to exert a disproportionately positive influence, should they choose to do so. More than any other country, this is true of the United States, although given how difficult it is for individuals—or countries—to account for their wrongdoing or to acknowledge difficult work ahead, it remains to be seen whether the United States will acknowledge either of these factors.

---

[2] Harold Lasswell, "The Garrison State," *The American Journal of Sociology* 46 (1941): 455–468.

I ... set out to explain how exactly our government came to be so hated around the world. As a CIA term of tradecraft, "blowback" does not just mean retaliation for things our government has done to, and in, foreign countries. It refers specifically to retaliation for illegal operations carried out abroad *that were kept totally secret from the American public.* These operations have included the clandestine overthrow of governments various administrations did not like, the training of foreign militaries in the techniques of state terrorism, the rigging of elections in foreign countries, interference with the economic viability of countries that seemed to threaten the interests of influential American corporations, as well as the torture or assassination of selected foreigners. The fact that these actions were, at least originally, secret meant that when retaliation does come—as it did so spectacularly on September 11, 2001—the American public is incapable of putting the events in context. Not surprisingly, then, Americans tend to support speedy acts of revenge intended to punish the actual, or alleged, perpetrators. These moments of lashing out, of course, only prepare the ground for yet another cycle of blowback.

A WORLD OF BASES

As a continuation of my own analytical odyssey, I then began doing research on the network of 737 American military bases we maintained around the world (according to the Pentagon's own 2005 official inventory). Not including the Iraq and Afghanistan conflicts, we now station over half a million U.S. troops, spies, contractors, dependents, and others on military bases located in more than 130 countries, many of them presided over by dictatorial regimes that have given their citizens no say in the decision to let us in.

As but one striking example of imperial basing policy, for the past 61 years, the U.S. military has garrisoned the small Japanese island of Okinawa with 37 bases. Smaller than Kauai in the Hawaiian Islands, Okinawa is home to 1.3 million people who live cheek-by-jowl with 17,000 Marines of the 3rd Marine Division and the largest U.S. installation in East Asia—Kadena Air Force Base. There have been many Okinawan protests against the rapes, crimes,

accidents, and pollution caused by this sort of concentration of American troops and weaponry, but so far the U.S. military—in collusion with the Japanese government—has ignored them....

As our occupations of Afghanistan and Iraq turned into major fiascoes, discrediting our military leadership, ruining our public finances, and bringing death and destruction to hundreds of thousands of civilians in those countries, I continued to ponder the issue of empire. In these years, it became ever clearer that George W. Bush, Dick Cheney, and their supporters were claiming, and actively assuming, powers specifically denied to a president by our Constitution. It became no less clear that Congress had almost completely abdicated its responsibilities to balance the power of the executive branch. Despite the Democratic sweep in the 2006 election, it remains to be seen whether these tendencies can, in the long run, be controlled, let alone reversed.

Until the 2004 presidential election, ordinary citizens of the United States could at least claim that our foreign policy, including our illegal invasion of Iraq, was the work of George Bush's administration and that we had not put him in office. After all, in 2000, Bush lost the popular vote and was appointed president thanks to the intervention of the Supreme Court in a 5–4 decision. But in November 2004, regardless of claims about voter fraud, Bush actually won the popular vote by over 3.5 million ballots, making his regime and his wars ours.

Whether Americans intended it or not, we are now seen around the world as approving the torture of captives at Abu Ghraib prison in Iraq, at Bagram Air Base in Kabul, at Guantánamo Bay, Cuba, and at a global network of secret CIA prisons, as well as having endorsed Bush's claim that, as commander-in-chief in "wartime," he is beyond all constraints of the Constitution or international law. We are now saddled with a rigged economy based on record-setting trade and fiscal deficits, the most secretive and intrusive government in our country's memory, and the pursuit of "preventive" war as a basis for foreign policy. Don't forget as well the potential epidemic of nuclear proliferation as other nations attempt to adjust to and defend themselves against Bush's preventive wars, while our own already staggering nuclear arsenal expands toward first-strike primacy and we expend unimaginable billions on futuristic ideas for warfare in outer space.

THE CHOICE AHEAD

…The combination of huge standing armies, almost continuous wars, an ever growing economic dependence on the military-industrial complex and the making of weaponry, and ruinous military expenses as well as a vast, bloated "defense" budget, not to speak of the creation of a whole second Defense Department (known as the Department of Homeland Security) has been destroying our republican structure of governing in favor of an imperial presidency. By republican structure, of course, I mean the separation of powers and the elaborate checks and balances that the founders of our country wrote into the Constitution as the main bulwarks against dictatorship and tyranny, which they greatly feared.

We are on the brink of losing our democracy for the sake of keeping our empire. Once a nation starts down that path, the dynamics that apply to all empires come into play—isolation, overstretch, the uniting of local and global forces opposed to imperialism, and in the end, bankruptcy.

History is instructive on this dilemma. If we choose to keep our empire, as the Roman republic did, we will certainly lose our democracy and grimly await the eventual blowback that imperialism generates. There is an alternative, however. We could, like the British Empire after World War II, keep our democracy by giving up our empire. The British did not do a particularly brilliant job of liquidating their empire, and there were several clear cases where British imperialists defied their nation's commitment to democracy in order to hang on to foreign privileges. The war against the Kikuyu in Kenya in the 1950s and the Anglo-French-Israeli invasion of Egypt in 1956 are particularly savage examples of that. But the overall thrust of postwar British history is clear: the people of the British Isles chose democracy over imperialism.

In her book *The Origins of Totalitarianism*, the political philosopher Hannah Arendt offered the following summary of British imperialism and its fate:

On the whole it was a failure because of the dichotomy between the nation-state's legal principles and the methods needed to oppress other people permanently. This failure was neither necessary nor due to ignorance or incompetence. British imperialists knew very well that "administrative massacres" could keep India in bondage, but they also knew that public opinion at home would not stand for such measures. Imperialism could have been a success if the nation-state had been willing to pay the price, to commit suicide and transform itself into a tyranny. It is one of the glories of Europe, and especially of Great Britain, that she preferred to liquidate the empire.

…As a form of government, imperialism does not seek or require the consent of the governed. It is a pure form of tyranny. The American attempt to combine domestic democracy with such tyrannical control over foreigners is hopelessly contradictory and hypocritical. A country can be democratic or it can be imperialistic, but it cannot be both.

THE ROAD TO IMPERIAL BANKRUPTCY

The American political system failed to prevent this combination from developing—and may now be incapable of correcting it. The evidence strongly suggests that the legislative and judicial branches of our government have become so servile in the presence of the "imperial presidency" that they have largely lost the ability to respond in a principled and independent manner. Even in the present moment of congressional stirring, there seems to be a deep sense of helplessness. Various members of Congress have already attempted to explain how the one clear power they retain—to cut off funds for a disastrous program—is not one they are currently prepared to use.

So the question becomes, If not Congress, could the people themselves restore constitutional government? A grassroots movement to abolish secret government, to bring the CIA and other illegal spying operations and private armies out of the closet of imperial power and into the light, to break the hold of the military-industrial complex, and to establish genuine public financing of elections may be at least theoretically conceivable. But given the conglomerate control of our mass media and the difficulties of mobilizing our large and diverse population, such an opting for popular democracy, as we remember it from our past, seems unlikely.

It is possible that, at some future moment, the U.S. military could actually take over the government and declare a dictatorship (though its commanders would undoubtedly find a gentler, more user-friendly name for it). That is, after all, how the Roman republic ended—by being turned over to a populist general, Julius Caesar, who had just been declared dictator for life. After his assassination and a short interregnum, it was his grandnephew Octavian who succeeded him and became the first Roman emperor, Augustus Caesar. The American military is unlikely to go that route. But one cannot ignore the fact that professional military officers seem to have played a considerable role in getting rid of their civilian overlord, secretary of defense Donald Rumsfeld. The new directors of the CIA, its main internal branches, the National Security Agency, and many other key organs of the "defense establishment" are now military (or ex-military) officers, strongly suggesting that the military does not need to take over the government in order to control it. Meanwhile, the all-volunteer army has emerged as an ever more separate institution in our society, its profile less and less like that of the general populace.

Nonetheless, military coups, however decorous, are not part of the American tradition, nor that of the officer corps, which might well worry about how the citizenry would react to a move toward open military dictatorship. Moreover, prosecutions of low-level military torturers from Abu Ghraib prison and killers of civilians in Iraq have demonstrated to enlisted troops that obedience to illegal orders can result in dire punishment in a situation where those of higher rank go free. No one knows whether ordinary soldiers, even from what is no longer in any normal sense a citizen army, would obey clearly illegal orders to oust an elected government or whether the officer corps would ever have sufficient confidence to issue such orders. In addition, the present system already offers the military high command so much—in funds, prestige, and future employment via the famed "revolving door" of the military-industrial complex—that a perilous transition to anything like direct military rule would make little sense under reasonably normal conditions.

Whatever future developments may prove to be, my best guess is that the U.S. will continue to maintain a façade of constitutional government and drift along until financial bankruptcy overtakes it. Of course, bankruptcy will not mean the literal end of the U.S. any more than it did for Germany in 1923, China in 1948, or Argentina in 2001–2002. It might, in fact, open the way for an unexpected restoration of the American system—or for military rule, revolution, or simply some new development we cannot yet imagine.

Certainly, such a bankruptcy would mean a drastic lowering of our standard of living, a further loss of control over international affairs, a sudden need to adjust to the rise of other powers, including China and India, and a further discrediting of the notion that the United States is somehow exceptional compared to other nations. We will have to learn what it means to be a far poorer country—and the attitudes and manners that go with it. As Anatol Lieven, author of *America Right or Wrong: An Anatomy of American Nationalism*, observes,

> U.S. global power, as presently conceived by the overwhelming majority of the U.S. establishment, is unsustainable....The empire can no longer raise enough taxes or soldiers, it is increasingly indebted, and key vassal states are no longer reliable....The result is that the empire can no longer pay for enough of the professional troops it needs to fulfill its self-assumed imperial tasks.

In February 2006, the Bush administration submitted to Congress a $439 billion defense appropriation budget for fiscal year 2007. As the country enters 2007, the administration is about to present a nearly $100 billion supplementary request to Congress just for the Iraq and Afghan wars. At the same time, the deficit in the country's current account—the imbalance in the trading of goods and services as well as the shortfall in all other cross-border payments from interest income and rents to dividends and profits on direct investments—underwent its fastest ever quarterly deterioration. For 2005, the current account deficit was $805 billion, 6.4 percent of national income. In 2005, the U.S. trade deficit, the largest component of the current account deficit, soared to an all-time high of $725.8 billion, the fourth consecutive year that America's trade debts set records. The trade deficit with China alone rose to $201.6 billion, the highest imbalance ever recorded with any country. Meanwhile, since mid-2000, the country has lost nearly 3 million manufacturing jobs.

To try to cope with these imbalances, on March 16, 2006, Congress raised the national debt limit from $8.2 trillion to $8.96 trillion. This was the fourth time since George W. Bush took office that it had to be raised. The national debt is the total amount owed by the government and should not be confused with the federal budget deficit, the annual amount by which federal spending exceeds revenue. Had Congress not raised the debt limit, the U.S. government would not have been able to borrow more money and would have had to default on its massive debts.

Among the creditors that finance these unprecedented sums, the two largest are the central banks of China (with $853.7 billion in reserves) and Japan (with $831.58 billion in reserves), both of which are the managers of the huge trade surpluses these countries enjoy with the United States. This helps explain why our debt burden has not yet triggered what standard economic theory would dictate: a steep decline in the value of the U.S. dollar followed by a severe contraction of the American economy

when we found we could no longer afford the foreign goods we like so much. So far, both the Chinese and Japanese governments continue to be willing to be paid in dollars in order to sustain American purchases of their exports.

For the sake of their own domestic employment, both countries lend huge amounts to the American treasury, but there is no guarantee of how long they will want to, or be able to do so. Marshall Auerback, an international financial strategist, says we have become a "Blanche Dubois economy" (so named after the leading character in the Tennessee Williams play *A Streetcar Named Desire*), heavily dependent on "the kindness of strangers." Unfortunately, in our case, as in Blanche's, there are ever fewer strangers willing to support our illusions.

So my own hope is that—if the American people do not find a way to choose democracy over empire—at least our imperial venture will end not with a nuclear bang but a financial whimper. From the present vantage point, it certainly seems a daunting challenge for any president (or Congress) from either party even to begin the task of dismantling the military-industrial complex, ending the pall of "national security" secrecy and the "black budgets" that make public oversight of what our government does impossible, and bringing the president's secret army, the CIA, under democratic control. It's evident that Nemesis—in Greek mythology the goddess of vengeance, the punisher of hubris and arrogance—is already a visitor in our country, simply biding her time before she makes her presence known.

Desmond Tutu

NO FUTURE WITHOUT FORGIVENESS

Although there is no shortage of bad news in the world (readers are encouraged to suggest, e.g., their "top ten"), there is good news as well. Thus, peace workers are fond of pointing out that many characteristics of human society that were long considered "natural" and therefore "inevitable" have given way and become so discredited as to appear peculiar social fossils: dueling, chattel slavery, the "divine right of kings." Modern times have also witnessed dramatic changes in circumstances that had appeared permanent features of the political landscape...until they disappeared, in some cases virtually overnight. Consider the end of the Cold War; the dissolution of the U.S.S.R. and with it, the end of Soviet hegemony over Eastern Europe; the end of long-standing dictatorships in Haiti, the Philippines, Indonesia, Korea, and elsewhere; as well as the (mostly) nonviolent demise of apartheid in South Africa.

Following that remarkable success, South African President Nelson Mandela empowered a nationwide Truth and Reconciliation Commission, headed by Bishop Desmond Tutu, whose goal—largely successful—was to help that traumatized country face the future without being dragged down by the pain, resentment, and angers of the past. The process, based on the African concept of *ubuntu*—social cohesion and shared goals and responsibility—was extraordinary, involving public testimony about abuses, intimidation, and murder, in the hope of achieving national reconciliation. The prospect beckons that one way to approach peace is to acknowledge the evils of the past, accept responsibility, and then move on. As Bishop Tutu shows, it is a terribly difficult but immensely rewarding process and one that might well be appropriate for every country.

In relations between individuals, if you ask another person for forgiveness you may be spurned; the one you have injured may refuse to forgive you. The risk is even greater if you are the injured party, wanting to offer forgiveness. The culprit may be arrogant, obdurate, or blind; not ready or willing to apologize or to ask for forgiveness. He or she thus cannot appropriate the forgiveness that is offered. Such rejection can jeopardize the whole enterprise. Our leaders were ready in South Africa to say they were willing to walk the path of confession, forgiveness, and reconciliation with all the hazards that lay along the way. And it seems their gamble might be paying off, since our land has not been overwhelmed by the catastrophe that had seemed so inevitable.

It is crucial, when a relationship has been damaged or when a potential relationship has been made impossible, that the perpetrator should acknowledge the truth and be ready and willing to apologize. It helps the process of forgiveness and reconciliation immensely. It is never easy. We all know just how difficult it is for most of us to admit that we have been wrong. It is perhaps the most difficult thing in the world—in almost every language the most difficult words are, "I am sorry." Thus it is not at all surprising that those accused of horrendous deeds and the communities they come from, for whom they believed they were committing these atrocities, almost always try to find ways out of even admitting that they were indeed capable of such deeds. They adopt the denial mode, asserting that such-and-such has not happened. When the evidence is incontrovertible, they take refuge in feigned ignorance. The Germans claimed they had not known what the Nazis were up to. White South Africans have also tried to find refuge in claims of ignorance. The former apartheid cabinet member Leon Wessels was closer to the mark when he said that they had not wanted to know, for there were those who tried to alert them. For those with eyes to see, there were accounts of people dying mysteriously in detention. For those with ears to hear, there was much that was disquieting and even chilling. But, like the three monkeys, they chose neither to hear, nor see, nor speak of evil. When some did own up, they passed the blame to others, "We were carrying out orders," refusing to acknowledge that as morally responsible individuals each person has to take responsibility for carrying out unconscionable orders.

We do not usually rush to expose our vulnerability and our sinfulness. But if the process of forgiveness and healing is to succeed, ultimately acknowledgment by the culprit is indispensable—not completely so but nearly so. Acknowledgment of the truth and of having wronged someone is important in getting to the root of the breach. If a husband and wife have quarreled without the wrongdoer acknowledging his or her fault by confessing, so exposing the cause of the rift; if a husband in this situation comes home with a bunch of flowers and the couple pretend all is in order, then they will be in for a rude shock. They have not dealt with their immediate past adequately. They have glossed over their differences, for they have failed to stare truth in the face for fear of a possible bruising confrontation. They will have done what the prophet calls healing the hurt lightly by crying, "'Peace, peace,' where there is no peace."[3] They will have only papered over the

cracks and not worked out why they fell out in the first place. All that will happen is that, despite the beautiful flowers, the hurt will fester. One day there will be an awful eruption and they will realize that they had tried to obtain reconciliation on the cheap. True reconciliation is not cheap. It cost God the death of his only begotten Son.

Forgiving and being reconciled are not about pretending that things are other than they are. It is not patting one another on the back and turning a blind eye to the wrong. True reconciliation exposes the awfulness, the abuse, the pain, the degradation, the truth. It could even sometimes make things worse. It is a risky undertaking but in the end it is worthwhile, because in the end dealing with the real situation helps to bring real healing. Spurious reconciliation can bring only spurious healing.

If the wrongdoer has come to the point of realizing his wrong, then one hopes there will be remorse, or at least some contrition or sorrow. This should lead him to confess the wrong he has done and ask for forgiveness. It obviously requires a fair measure of humility, especially when the victim is someone in a group that one's community had despised, as was often the case in South Africa when the perpetrators were government agents.

The victim, we hope, would be moved to respond to an apology by forgiving the culprit. As I have already tried to show, we were constantly amazed in the commission at the extraordinary magnanimity that so many of the victims exhibited. Of course there were those who said they would not forgive. That demonstrated for me the important point that forgiveness could not be taken for granted; it was neither cheap nor easy. As it happens, these were the exceptions. Far more frequently what we encountered was deeply moving and humbling.

In forgiving, people are not being asked to forget. On the contrary, it is important to remember, so that we should not let such atrocities happen again. Forgiveness does not mean condoning what has been done. It means taking what happened seriously and not minimizing it; drawing out the sting in the memory that threatens to poison our entire

---

[3] Jeremiah 6:14 and 8:11.

existence. It involves trying to understand the perpetrators and so have empathy, to try to stand in their shoes and appreciate the sort of pressures and influences that might have conditioned them.

Forgiveness is not being sentimental. The study of forgiveness has become a growth industry. Whereas previously it was something often dismissed pejoratively as spiritual and religious, now because of developments such as the Truth and Reconciliation Commission in South Africa it is gaining attention as an academic discipline studied by psychologists, philosophers, physicians, and theologians. In the United States there is an International Forgiveness Institute attached to the University of Wisconsin, and the John Templeton Foundation, with others, has started a multimillion-dollar Campaign for Forgiveness Research. Forgiving has even been found to be good for your health.

Forgiving means abandoning your right to pay back the perpetrator in his own coin, but it is a loss that liberates the victim. In the commission we heard people speak of a sense of relief after forgiving. A recent issue of the journal *Spirituality and Health* had on its front cover a picture of three U.S. ex-servicemen standing in front of the Vietnam Memorial in Washington, DC. One asks, "Have you forgiven those who held you prisoner of war?" "I will never forgive them," replies the other. His mate says, "Then it seems they still have you in prison, don't they?"[4]

Does the victim depend on the culprit's contrition and confession as the precondition for being able to forgive? There is no question that, of course, such a confession is a very great help to the one who wants to forgive, but it is not absolutely indispensable. Jesus did not wait until those who were nailing him to the cross had asked for forgiveness. He was ready, as they drove in the nails, to pray to his Father to forgive them, and he even provided an excuse for what they were doing. If the victim could forgive only when the culprit confessed, then the victim would be locked into the culprit's whim, locked into victimhood, whatever her own attitude or intention. That would be palpably unjust.

I have used the following analogy to try to explain the need for a perpetrator to confess. Imagine you are sitting in a dank, stuffy, dark room. This is because the curtains are drawn and the windows have been shut. Outside the light is shining and a fresh breeze is blowing. If you want the light to stream into that room and the fresh air to flow in, you will have to open the window and draw the curtains apart; then that light which has always been available will come in, and air will enter the room to freshen it up. So it is with forgiveness.

The victim may be ready to forgive and make the gift of her forgiveness available, but it is up to the wrongdoer to appropriate the gift—to open the window and draw the curtains aside. He does this by acknowledging the wrong he has done, so letting the light and fresh air of forgiveness enter his being.

In the act of forgiveness we are declaring our faith in the future of a relationship and in the capacity of the wrongdoer to make a new beginning on a course that will be different from the one that caused us the wrong. We are saying here is a chance to make a new beginning. It is an act of faith that the wrongdoer can change. According to Jesus,[5] we should be ready to do this not just once, not just seven times, but seventy times seven, without limit—provided, it seems Jesus says, your brother or sister who has wronged you is ready to come and confess the wrong they have committed yet again.

That is difficult, but because we are not infallible, because we will hurt especially the ones we love by some wrong, we will always need a process of forgiveness and reconciliation to deal with those unfortunate yet all too human breaches in relationships. They are an inescapable characteristic of the human condition.

Once the wrongdoer has confessed and the victim has forgiven, it does not mean that is the end of the process. Most frequently, the wrong has affected the victim in tangible, material ways. Apartheid provided the whites with enormous benefits and privileges, leaving its victims deprived and exploited. If someone steals my pen and then asks me to forgive him, unless he returns my pen the sincerity of his contrition and confession will be considered to be

---

[4] Vol. 2, No. 1 (New York, Trinity Church: Spirituality & Health Publishing).

[5] Matthew 18:22.

nil. Confession, forgiveness, and reparation, wherever feasible, form part of a continuum.

In South Africa the whole process of reconciliation has been placed in very considerable jeopardy by the enormous disparities between the rich, mainly the whites, and the poor, mainly the blacks. The huge gap between the haves and the have-nots, which was largely created and maintained by racism and apartheid, poses the greatest threat to reconciliarion and stability in our country. The rich provided the class from which the perpetrators and the beneficiaries of apartheid came, and the poor produced the bulk of the victims. That is why I have exhorted whites to support transformation taking place in the lot of blacks.

For unless houses replace the hovels and shacks in which most blacks live, unless blacks gain access to clean water, electricity, affordable health care, decent education, good jobs, and a safe environment—things which the vast majority of whites have taken for granted for so long—we can just as well kiss reconciliation good-bye.

Reconciliation is liable to be a long-drawn-out process with ups and downs, not something accomplished overnight and certainly not by a commission, however effective. The Truth and Reconciliation Commission has only been able to make a contribution. Reconciliation is going to have to be the concern of every South African. It has to be a national project to which all earnestly strive to make their particular contribution—by learning the language and culture of others; by being willing to make amends; by refusing to deal in stereotypes by making racial or other jokes that ridicule a particular group; by contributing to a culture of respect for human rights, and seeking to enhance tolerance—with zero tolerance for intolerance; by working for a more inclusive society where most, if not all, can feel they belong—that they are insiders and not aliens and strangers on the outside, relegated to the edges of society.

To work for reconciliation is to want to realize God's dream for humanity—when we will know that we are indeed members of one family, bound together in a delicate network of interdependence. . . .

If we are going to move on and build a new kind of world community, there must be a way in which we can deal with a sordid past. The most effective way would be for the perpetrators or their descendants to acknowledge the awfulness of what happened, and the descendants of the victims to respond by granting forgiveness, providing something can be done, even symbolically, to compensate for the anguish experienced, whose consequences are still being lived through today. It may be, for instance, that race relations in the United States will not improve significantly until Native Americans and African Americans get the opportunity to tell their stories and reveal the pain that sits in the pit of their stomachs as a baneful legacy of dispossession and slavery. We saw in the Truth and Reconciliation Commission how the act of telling one's story has a cathartic, healing effect.

If the present generation could not legitimately speak on behalf of those who are no more, then we could not offer forgiveness for the sins of South Africa's racist past, which predates the advent of apartheid in 1948. The process of healing our land would be subverted, because there would always be the risk that some awful atrocity of the past would come to light that would undermine what had been accomplished thus far; or that people would say, "It is all right so far as it goes in dealing with the contemporary situation, but it is all utterly ineffectual because it has failed to deal with the burden of the past."

True forgiveness deals with the past, all of the past, to make the future possible. We cannot go on nursing grudges even vicariously for those who cannot speak for themselves any longer. We have to accept that what we do we do for generations past, present, and yet to come. That is what makes a community a community or a people a people—for better or for worse.

I have wished desperately that those involved in seeking solutions for what have seemed intractable problems in places such as Northern Ireland and the Middle East would not despise the value of seemingly small symbolic acts that have a potency and significance beyond what is apparent. I have been distressed to learn that some of those most intimately connected to the peace process in Northern Ireland have not been seen shaking hands in public, that some have gone to odd lengths not to be photographed together with those on the other side, their current adversaries. It was wonderful that, at the funeral of King Hussein of Jordan, President Ezer Weizman of Israel had the courage to shake hands with the leader of a radical Palestinian group. It was a gesture that helped to humanize his adversary, where before much had conspired to demonize him. A small handshake can make the unthinkable, the improbable—peace, friendship, harmony, and tolerance—not quite so remote.

I also hope that those who are at this moment enemies around the world might consider using more temperate language when describing those with whom they disagree. Today's "terrorist" could very well be tomorrow's president. That has happened in South Africa. Most of those who were vilified as terrorists are today our cabinet ministers and others sitting in the government benches of our National Assembly. If those we disagree with today are possibly going to be our colleagues tomorrow, we might begin by trying to describe them in language that won't be an embarrassment when that time of change does come.

It is crucial too that we keep remembering that negotiations, peace talks, forgiveness, and reconciliation happen most frequently not between friends, not between those who like one another. They happen precisely because people are at loggerheads and detest one another as only enemies can. But enemies are potential allies, friends, colleagues, and collaborators. This is not just utopian idealism. The first democratically elected government of South Africa was a government of National Unity made up of members of political parties that were engaged in a life-and-death struggle. The man who headed it had been incarcerated for twenty-seven years as a dangerous terrorist. If it could happen there, surely it can happen in other places. Perhaps God chose such an unlikely place deliberately to show the world that it can be done anywhere.

If the protagonists in the world's conflicts began to make symbolic gestures for peace, changed the way they described their enemies, and began talking to them, their actions might change too. For instance, what is it doing for future relations in the Middle East to go on constructing Jewish settlements in what is accepted to be Palestinian territory, when this causes so much bitterness

and resentment among the Palestinians, who feel belittled and abused? What legacy does it leave for the children of those who are destined to be neighbors? I have asked similar questions when Arab nations have seemed so completely unrealistic in thinking they could destroy Israel. What a wonderful gift to the world, especially as we enter a new millennium, if true peace would come in the land of those who say *salama*, or *shalom*, in the land of the Prince of Peace.

Peace is possible, especially if today's adversaries were to imagine themselves becoming friends and begin acting in ways that would promote such a friendship developing in reality. It would be wonderful if, as they negotiated, they tried to find ways of accommodating each other's needs. A readiness to make concessions is a sign of strength, not weakness. And it can be worthwhile sometimes to lose a battle in order in the end to win the war. Those who are engaged in negotiations for peace and prosperity are striving after such a splendid, such a priceless goal that it should be easier to find ways for all to be winners than to fight; for negotiators to make it a point that no one loses face, that no one emerges empty-handed, with nothing to place before his or her constituency. How one wishes that negotiators would avoid having bottom lines and too many preconditions. In negotiations we are, as in the process of forgiveness, seeking to give all the chance to begin again. The rigid will have a tough time. The flexible, those who are ready to make principled compromises, end up being the victors.

I have said ours was a flawed commission. Despite that, I do want to assert as eloquently and as passionately as I can that it was, in an imperfect world, the best possible instrument so far devised to deal with the kind of situation that confronted us after democracy was established in our motherland. With all its imperfections, what we have tried to do in South Africa has attracted the attention of the world. This tired, disillusioned, cynical world, hurting so frequently and so grievously, has marveled at a process that holds out considerable hope in the midst of much that negates hope. People in the different places that I have visited and where I have spoken about the truth and reconciliation process see in this flawed attempt a beacon of hope, a possible paradigm for dealing with situations where violence, conflict, turmoil, and sectional strife have seemed endemic, conflicts that mostly take place not between warring nations but within the same nation. At the end of their conflicts, the warring groups in Northern Ireland, the Balkans, the Middle East, Sri Lanka, Burma, Afghanistan, Angola, the Sudan, the two Congos, and elsewhere are going to have to sit down together to determine just how they will be able to live together amicably, how they might have a shared future devoid of strife, given the bloody past that they have recently lived through. They see more than just a glimmer of hope in what we have attempted in South Africa.

God does have a sense of humor. Who in their right minds could ever have imagined South Africa to be an example of anything but the most ghastly awfulness, of how *not* to order a nation's race relations and its governance? We South Africans were the unlikeliest lot, and that is precisely why God has chosen us. We cannot really claim much credit ourselves for what we have achieved. We were destined for perdition and were plucked out of total annihilation. We were a hopeless case if ever there was one. God intends that others might look at us and take courage. God wants to point to us as a possible beacon of hope, a possible paradigm, and to say, "Look at South Africa. They had a nightmare called apartheid. It has ended. Northern Ireland (or wherever), your nightmare will end too. They had a problem regarded as intractable. They are resolving it. No problem anywhere can ever again be considered to be intractable. There is hope for you too."...

Victoria Bonney

ANTIWAR ACTIVISTS, WHERE ARE YOU?

Democracy is based on citizen participation, in return for which, governance is supposed to reflect the popular will. And yet, a paradoxical consequence of democracy is that it often leads citizens to *avoid* personal involvement, assuming that others—especially the "experts"—will do what is right and necessary. Moreover, despite the fact that young people are widely assumed to be most involved in political activism in general and antiwar activism in particular, the reality is that voting participation is typically lowest among people ages eighteen to twenty-five, and that ever since the Vietnam War (in large part, perhaps, because of the absence of a military draft), young people have been notably *under*represented in antiwar activism. The following selection, written by a college student, appeared as an op-ed article in the *Boston Globe* newspaper. It is a question—and a plea—that readers of this book might well take to heart.

My fellow young Americans, the evidence is mounting that this war we are fighting in Iraq is not a "just" war. No, this is a dirty fight, and we're in it for the long haul. But I guess that's the problem— "we" are not in it at all.

"We" are here in our land of iPods and cell phones, luxuriating in our apathetic comas while our soldiers are over there.

I know what you're thinking. You have that magnetic yellow ribbon on your SUV, and, boy, if that is not uber-effective I do not know what is. But let me ask you, if you'd just put your podcast on pause and cell phone on silence for a moment, is this all enough?

Two wars ago, during the Vietnam disaster, there was Generation Activist. The youth of America rallied against "the man." How did they do it? They didn't have e-boards or e-mail, for that matter.

Yet somehow, this archaic mob of longhairs and peaceniks managed to mobilize. They marched on the National Mall. They protested everywhere, even in bed (refer to your hippie handbook, under John Lennon and Yoko Ono's "bed-in"). Their methods were not always nonviolent, but they were creative and incorrigible.

Why is Generation Apathetic unable to have the same resounding roar?

For starters we have a woman from Generation Activist doing our dirty work. Former flower child Cindy Sheehan[1] is out on the front lines with a pack of her patchouli-wearing alliances. What is the youth of America doing in the meantime?

We are watching it on our car television sets thinking about the jerk in front of us who is not driving fast enough.

It's not our fault that we all have Attention Deficit Disorder. We are conditioned like Pavlov's dogs to jump at the sound of "You've got mail!" But we are in dereliction of our duty as a thorn in the side of authority. Our parents shouldn't have to bail us out of everything. So while we appreciate the help of Cindy and her comrades, this is our fight.

It's not only apathy that is killing the spirit of our generation, it's the execution of our dissidence. For some reason the youth of America think that violence is the most effective method of rebellion (albeit something we learned from our PlayStations).

That brings us to another nifty way that the young inactivists of America are making life easier for our elected warmongers—E-Marches.

Yes, E-Marches are the newest way to protest your government. All it takes is a double click, and you will be part of a simulated march on Washington.

Oh, dear, sweet, well-intentioned youth, don't you see? Just as easily as you signed up to electronically protest your senators, they can delete you from their in-box. The Internet is a resource for sports scores, CliffsNotes, and porn—not a venue for modern dissent.

We are a generation with potential coming out of our ears. We could move mountains if only we'd turn off our televisions. They only tell us we are powerless and to just give up.

So this is what you have to do. Tomorrow when you stop into Starbucks for your venti latte and the person behind the counter gives you your change, look at it. Look closely. There, written on your bills is our American mantra in a defunct language.

It says, *E Pluribus Unum*, which means, "out of many, one." Let this be your daily reminder. Generation Apathetic, we are in this boat together.

It's up to us to chart a course. We cannot live our lives on cruise control.

---

[1] Editor's note: Ms. Sheehan's son was killed in the Iraq War, after which she became an influential anti-war activist. Prior to this, she had simply been an "ordinary citizen."

A FEW POETIC VISIONS

We end with some poetic visions: tragic, ironic, idyllic, pessimistic, optimistic, corny, and profound…sometimes all of these at the same time. If such ambiguity is occasionally frustrating, it is at least consistent with the world situation, as we approach what might eventually be peace.

WAR IS KIND: STEPHEN CRANE

Do not weep, maiden, for war is kind.
Because your lover threw wild hands toward the
    sky
And the affrighted steed ran on alone.
Do not weep
War is kind.

Hoarse, booming drums of the regiment,
Little souls who thirst for fight,
These men were born to drill and die.
The unexplained glory flies above them,
Great is the Battle-God, great, and his Kingdom—
A field where a thousand corpses lie.

Do not weep, babe, for war is kind.
Because your father tumbled in the yellow
    trenches,
Raged at his breast, gulped and died,
Do not weep.
War is kind.

Swift blazing flag of the regiment,
Eagle with crest and red and gold,
These men were born to drill and die.
Point for them the virtue of slaughter,
Make plain to them the excellence of killing
And a field where a thousand corpses lie.

Mother, whose heart hung humble as a button
On the bright splendid shroud of your son,
Do not weep.
War is kind.

ANTHEM FOR DOOMED YOUTH: WILFRED OWEN

What passing-bells for these who die as cattle?
—Only the monstrous anger of the guns.
Only the stuttering rifles' rapid rattle
Can patter out their hasty orisons.
No mockeries now for them: no prayers nor bells;
Nor any voice of mourning save the choirs,—
The shrill, demented choirs of wailing shells;
And bugles calling for them from sad shires.

What candles may be held to speed them all?
Not in the hands of boys, but in their eyes
Shall shine the holy glimmers of good-byes.
The pallor of girls' brows shall be their pall;
Their flowers the tenderness of patient minds,
And each slow dusk a drawing-down of blinds.

DULCE ET DECORUM EST: WILFRED OWEN

Bent double, like old beggars under
    sacks,
Knock-kneed, coughing like hags, we cursed
    through sludge,

Till on the haunting flares we turned our backs
And towards our distant rest began to trudge.
Men marched asleep. Many had lost their boots
But limped on, blood-shod. All went lame; all
    blind;
Drunk with fatigue; deaf even to the hoots
Of tired, outstripped Five-Nines that dropped
    behind.

Gas! Gas! Quick, boys!—An ecstasy of fumbling,
Fitting the clumsy helmets just in time;
But someone still was yelling out and stumbling,
And flound'ring like a man in fire or lime...
Dim, through the misty panes and thick green light,
As under a green sea, I saw him drowning.

In all my dreams, before my helpless sight,
He plunges at me, guttering, choking, drowning.

If in some smothering dreams you too could pace
Behind the wagon that we flung him in,
And watch the white eyes writhing in his face,
His hanging face, like a devil's sick of sin;
If you could hear, at every jolt, the blood
Come gargling from the froth-corrupted lungs,
Obscene as cancer, bitter as the cud
Of vile, incurable sores on innocent tongues,—
My friend, you would not tell with such high zest
To children ardent for some desperate glory,
The old Lie: Dulce et decorum est
Pro patria mori.

THE SECOND COMING: W. B. YEATS

Turning and turning in the widening gyre
The falcon cannot hear the falconer;
Things fall apart; the centre cannot hold;
Mere anarchy is loosed upon the world,
The blood-dimmed tide is loosed, and
        everywhere
The ceremony of innocence is drowned;
The best lack all conviction, while the worst
Are full of passionate intensity.

Surely some revelation is at hand;
Surely the Second Coming is at hand.
The Second Coming! Hardly are those words out
When a vast image out of *Spiritus Mundi*
Troubles my sight somewhere in sands of the desert
A shape with lion body and the head of a man,
A gaze blank and pitiless as the sun,
Is moving its slow thighs, while all about it
Reel shadows of the indignant desert birds.
The darkness drops again; but now I know

That twenty centuries of stony sleep
Were vexed to nightmare by a rocking cradle,
And what rough beast, its hour come round at
        last,
Slouches towards Bethlehem to be born?

THE LAKE ISLE OF INNISFREE: W. B. YEATS

I will arise and go now, and go to Innisfree,
And a small cabin build there, of clay and wattles
        made:
Nine bean-rows will I have there, a hive for the
        honey-bee,
And live alone in the bee-loud glade.

And I shall have some peace there, for peace comes
        dropping slow,
Dropping from the veils of the morning to where
        the cricket sings;
There midnight's all a glimmer, and noon a purple
        glow,
And evening full of the linnet's wings.

I will arise and go now, for always night
        and day
I hear lake water lapping with low sounds by the
        shore;
While I stand on the roadway, or on the pavements
        grey,
I hear it in the deep heart's core.

ABOU BEN ADHEM: LEIGH HUNT

Abou Ben Adhem (may his tribe increase!)
Awoke one night from a deep dream of peace,
And saw, within the moonlight in his room,
Making it rich, and like a lily in bloom,
An Angel writing in a book of gold:
Exceeding peace had made Ben Adhem bold,
And to the Presence in the room he said,
"What writest thou?" The Vision raised its head,
And with a look made of all sweet accord
Answered, "The names of those who love
        the Lord."
"And is mine one?" said Abou. "Nay, not so,"
Replied the Angel. Abou spoke more low,

But cheerily still; and said, "I pray thee, then,
Write me as one that loves his fellow men."

The Angel wrote, and vanished.
        The next night
It came again with a great wakening light,
And showed the names whom love
        of God had blessed,
And, lo! Ben Adhem's name led all the rest!

A MAN WHO HAD FALLEN AMONG THIEVES: E. E. CUMMINGS

a man who had fallen among thieves
lay by the roadside on his back
dressed in fifteenthrate ideas
wearing a round jeer for a hat

fate per a somewhat more than less
emancipated evening
had in return for consciousness

endowed him with a changeless grin

whereon a dozen staunch and leal
citizens did graze at pause
then fired by hypercivic zeal
sought newer pastures or because

swaddled with a frozen brook
of pinkest vomit out of eyes
which noticed nobody he looked
as if he did not care to rise

one hand did nothing on the vest
its wideflung friend clenched weakly dirt
while the mute trouserfly confessed
a button solemnly inert.

Brushing from whom the stiffened puke
i put him all into my arms
and staggered banged with terror through
a million billion trillion stars

STUDY QUESTIONS

1. What are some important lessons to be learned from peace movements of the past, and how might they inform peace movements of the future?
2. What do you see as one or more likely scenarios for the world in the near future? The distant future?
3. What would you *like* to see as one or more likely scenarios for the world in the near future? The distant future?
4. Many people claim that "peace begins with me." Discuss some pros and cons of this attitude.
5. Suggest a classification of peace movements other than those presented in this chapter.
6. Describe differences between the anti–Iraq War peace movement and its earlier, anti–Vietnam War counterpart. Try to explain these differences and discuss what lessons, if any, might be learned as a result.
7. Insofar as the twenty-first century has been lacking in peace, to what extent is it appropriate to blame the United States? Where else might blame be fairly be placed?

8. If peace studies did not exist, perhaps it would be necessary to invent it. Try your hand at inventing peace studies, as though it did not exist; consider education, practical action, connections to other traditions, and so on.
9. Look deeply into one or more of the poems included in this chapter, and/or suggest some others; to what extent does their imagery add to your intellectual grasp of the issue? What are some "futuristic" novels that might also fit into this chapter?
10. Have you been treating the material in this book as anything other than just one more text to be studied, learned from, tested and graded on, and then filed away somewhere? If so, why? If not, why not?

SUGGESTIONS FOR FURTHER READING

Boyte, Harry C. 2008. *The Citizen Solution: How You Can Make a Difference.* St. Paul: Minnesota Historical Society Press.

Brock, Peter. 1991. *Studies in Peace History.* Syracuse, NY: Syracuse University Press.

Carter, April. 1992. *Peace Movements: International Protest and World Politics Since 1945.* New York: Longman.

Cortright, David. 2008. *Peace: A History of Movements and Ideas.* New York: Cambridge University Press.

Downton, James V. 1997. *The Persistent Activist: How Peace Commitment Develops and Survives.* Boulder, CO: Westview Press.

Fry, Douglas P. 2007. *Beyond War: The Human Potential for Peace.* New York: Oxford University Press.

Guigni, Marco. 2004. *Social Protest and Policy Change: Ecology, Antinuclear, and Peace Movements in Comparative Perspective.* Lanham, MD: Rowman & Littlefield.

Reardon, Betty. 1993. *Women and Peace: Feminist Visions of Global Security.* Albany: State University of New York Press.

Rochon, Thomas R., and David S. Meyer, eds. 1997. *Coalitions and Political Movements: The Lessons of the Nuclear Freeze.* Boulder, CO: Lynne Rienner.

Zisk, Betty H. 1992. *The Politics of Transformation: Local Activism in the Peace and Environmental Movements.* Westport, CT: Praeger.

Index